LONDON FILM
LOCATION GUIDE

Simon R H James

BATSFORD

First published in the United Kingdom in 2007 by
Batsford
10 Southcombe Street
London W14 0RA

An imprint of Anova Books Company Ltd

ISBN: 9780713490626

A CIP catalogue record for this book is available from the British Library.

15 14 13 12 11 10 09 08 07
10 9 8 7 6 5 4 3 2 1

Reproduction by Mission Productions Ltd, Hong Kong
Printed by SNP Leefung Printers Ltd, China
Design by Lee-May Lim

This book can be ordered direct from the publisher at the website:
www.anovabooks.com, or try your local bookshop.

Distributed in the United States and Canada by Sterling Publishing Co.,
387 Park Avenue South, New York, NY 10016, USA.

Contents

Introduction 6

Map of London 8

West End Central London 10

West London 28

South-west London 82

South-east London 146

East Central London 186

East London 210

North-west London 234

North London 256

Film Index 266

Street Index 271

introduction

London continues to occupy the minds of writers, producers, directors, stars, cinematographers and location scouts, who plan to further immortalize this great city for celluloid posterity. They have been busy for over 100 years and a rich historical record has been captured as views and buildings come and go. These images are beamed around the world and tourists come eagerly flocking to boost the capital's economy. And London can offer so much to the filmmaker. Rain? No problem. Sun? Use lights. Atmosphere? Absolutely. Dark and dingy, dank and dangerous, misty and menacing, colourful and cosmopolitan, the capital is full of woods, parks, squares, streets, avenues, cul-de-sacs, churches, palaces, towers, prisons, warehouses, wharves, docks and, of course, the river. A myriad of locations beckon, all within reasonable travelling distance to and from a wide variety of studios where highly regarded world-class technicians practise their art. From Hollywood to Bollywood, filmmakers keep visiting and continually augment London's exposure in the cinema.

Location spotting has gathered pace since 1982, when American Leon Smith first brought this genre of cinematic appreciation to the fore with a guide to Los Angeles. However, it was Dave Holland's personal tour of central California's scenic Lone Pine and it's film locations that initially inspired me to write this book. By the mid-1990s the British caught on to the location-spotting trend – local film commissions began keeping careful records of films shot in London, tourist boards published movie maps and discussion forums on websites escalated. DVD, with its slow motion, still facilities and helpful directors' commentaries, is a vast improvement on videotape, and the art of location identification is now set to run and run.

In tackling London, I have gone back to basics. Too many times, like Chinese whispers, false or misleading information on locations is given. Wandsworth, for example, tends to be cited as Thamesmead in *A Clockwork Orange* (1971), while Waterloo Bridge is often muddled with Vauxhall in *Alfie* (1966). The end of a film's credits often lists the director's appreciation for hotels, shops and other vague 'filmed-in-London' clues. But these clues are just that, and there is a lot of checking to be done. Was a scene shot indoors or outdoors? Did the scene make the final cut? Is that scene really outdoors or is it a clever studio mock-up? How much has a location changed? Filmmakers have a nasty, albeit practical, habit of hiring condemned buildings so one has to be quick off the mark. And it's not much help being told that a film was shot at a site without knowing which scene to jog the memory. With all this in mind, I have watched all the films discussed in this book, utilising slow motion and freeze frame. I have taken notes, used screen grabs, consulted telephone directories, maps and aerial photographs and, most importantly, got out there to see for myself.

I have generally ignored second-unit work – where scenes are shot that don't involve the actors of the film – unless the view is tantalisingly familiar but not particularly obvious to the uninitiated. In most cases a star, or at least an impressive double, has to be there. For the same reason, over-familiar establishment shots such as Trafalgar Square, back projections, car chases, tours and montages have not been included in this guide. Generally indoor scenes have suffered the same fate, unless they appear time and time again or are in buildings that are free to enter. Interiors are often cited as bona fide locations but cannot be verified because they are inaccessible, restricted to the public or are simply sets. TV shows, music videos and documentaries have also been excluded, although these are well served on the internet.

Despite a 25-year familiarity with London, it wasn't until I started this project that I began to realise how little I actually knew this ever-changing city. As I pounded the pavements in the quest for locations, I discovered undreamt-of nooks and crannies. My appreciation of local history accelerated as I researched locations in unlikely scholarly study. Unusual angles forced me to use my eyes properly. So much has disappeared or been replaced. Often I had to go back to the film to re-check, and doubtless there are times I have been fooled by the clever trickery that is at filmmaker's fingertips. I apologize for any mistakes now – they are entirely of my own doing. I also apologize if your favourite film does not appear herein. The IMDb (Internet Movie Database) website, by no means complete, lists well over 1000 films made in London, several of which are now discontinued on video or await DVD release, and are rarely, if ever, shown on television. Rightly or wrongly the more mainstream titles have had a better chance of mention, though eBay has provided an entertaining chase for more obscure titles. Many of these, due to story, performances and even locations, deserve a second lease of life that – who knows – these pages may provide. Businesses come and go with alarming rapidity; the ones I describe were in place between 1999 and 2007.

Chapters are arranged by postal codes, which have been in operation since 1917. This year felicitously coincides with roughly the time feature-length cinema found its feet in the UK. When one is walking around, these codes are the one reliable attachment to London's street signs. Favourite films and real streets can be looked up in the two indices at the back of the book and journeys of nostalgic pilgrimage planned accordingly.

Simon James, London 2007

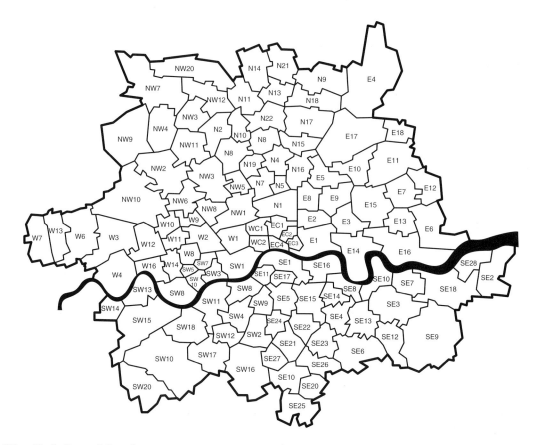

West End Central London

WC1 (Bloomsbury, St Pancras) • **WC2** (Charing Cross, Trafalgar Square, Leicester Square, Covent Garden, Holborn, Aldwych, Strand, Embankment)

West London

W1 (Marylebone, Fitzrovia, Park Lane, Mayfair, Regent Street, Soho, Piccadilly) • **W2** (Kensington Gardens, Bayswater, Maida Vale, Paddington, Hyde Park) • **W3** (Acton) • **W4** (Strand on the Green, Acton Green, Turnham Green, Chiswick) • **W5** (Ealing) • **W6** (Hammersmith) • **W7** (Hanwell) • **W8** (Holland Park) • **W9** (West Kilburn, Maida Vale) • **W10** (Notting Hill, North Kensington) • **W11** (Notting Hill) • **W12** (Shepherd's Bush) • **W13** (West Ealing) • **W14** (West Kensington)

South-west London

SW1 (St James's, Westminster, Westminster, Millbank, Pimlico, Chelsea, Knightsbridge, Belgravia, Victoria) • **SW2** (Streatham

Hill, south Brixton, west Tulse Hill) • **SW3** (Chelsea, Brompton) • **SW4** (Clapham Park) • **SW5** (Earl's Court) • **SW6** (Fulham, Sands End) • **SW7** (Brompton, South Kensington, Knightsbridge) • **SW8** (Clapham, Battersea, Nine Elms, Vauxhall) • **SW9** (Stockwell, north Brixton) • **SW10** (West Brompton) • **SW11** (Battersea) • **SW12** (Balham) • **SW13** (Barnes) • **SW14** (East Sheen, Mortlake) • **SW15** (Putney Heath, Putney Vale, Roehampton) • **SW16** (Furzedown, Streatham Park, Streatham Vale) • **SW17** (Summerstown, Upper Tooting, Tooting Graveney, Colliers Wood) • **SW18** (West Hill, Southfields, Wandsworth) • **SW19** (Wimbledon, Merton Park)

South-east London

SE1 (Lambeth, South Bank, Waterloo, Bankside, Borough) • **SE2** (Abbey Wood, South Thamesmead) • **SE3** (Kidbrooke, Blackheath Vale) • **SE4** (Brockley) • **SE5** (Camberwell) • **SE6** (Catford, Bell Green, Bellingham) • **SE7** (Charlton) • **SE8** (Deptford, St John's) • **SE9** (Eltham) • **SE10** (Greenwich) • **SE11** (Kennington, Lambeth) • **SE12** (Lee) • **SE13** (Lewisham, Ladywell, Hither Green) • **SE14** (New Cross, New Cross Gate) • **SE15** (Peckham, Nunhead) • **SE16** (Bermondsey, Rotherhithe, Surrey Quays) • **SE17** (Walworth) • **SE18** (Woolwich, Plumstead) • **SE19** (Norwood New Town, Upper Norwood, Crystal Palace) • **SE20** (Anerley) • **SE21** (Dulwich Village) • **SE22** (East Dulwich, west Honor Oak) • **SE23** (Forest Hill) • **SE24** (Herne Hill) • **SE25** (South Norwood) • **SE26** (Sydenham) • **SE27** (West Norwood) • **SE28** (Thamesmead)

East Central London

EC1 (Clerkenwell, Finsbury, St Luke's, Farringdon) • **EC2** (City, Barbican, Liverpool Street) • **EC3** (Monument, Bank, Leadenhall, **Tower** Hill) • EC4 (Blackfriars, St Paul's)

East London

E1 (Tower Bridge, Whitechapel, Spitalfields, Bethnal Green, Stepney, Shadwell, Wapping) • **E2** (Shoreditch, Bethnal Green) •

E3 (Old Ford, Bromley-by-Bow) • **E4** (Chingford Green, Friday Hill, Chingford Heath, Highams Park) • **E5** (Clapton Park, Lower Clapton, Lea Bridge) • **E6** (Upton Park, Wallend, Beckton) • **E7** (Forest Gate, Upton) • **E8** (Dalston) • **E9** (Homerton, Hackney Wick, South Hackney) • **E10** (Lea Bridge) • **E11** (Leytonstone, Wanstead, Snaresbrook) • **E12** (Manor Park) • **E13** (Plaistow, West Ham) • **E14** (Limehouse, Canary Wharf, Millwall, Blackwall) • **E15** (Stratford Marsh, Mill Meads, Temple Mills, Stratford New Town) • **E16** (Canning Town, Silvertown) • **E17** (Higham Hill, Upper Walthamstow)

North-west London

NW1 (Marylebone, Regent's Park, Camden, Euston, St Pancras, King's Cross) • **NW2** (Dollis Hill, Cricklewood) • **NW3** (Primrose Hill, Swiss Cottage, Hampstead, Belsize Park, Chalk Farm) • **NW4** (Hendon) • **NW5** (Kentish Town, Maitland Park, Dartmouth Park) • **NW6** (Kensal Rise, Kilburn, southwest Hampstead) • **NW7** (Mill Hill) • **NW8** (St John's Wood) • **NW9** (Colindale) • **NW10** (Neasden, Church End, Stonebridge, North Acton, Park Royal, Harlesden, College Park, Willesden Green, Kensal Green) • **NW11** (Golders Green, Hampstead Garden Suburb)

North London

N1 (King's Cross, Islington, Old Street) • **N2** (East Finchley) • **N3** (Finchley) • **N4** (Finsbury Park, Harringay) • **N5** (Highbury) • **N6** (Highgate) • **N7** (Barnsbury, Lower Holloway, Tufnell Park) • **N8** (Hornsey Vale, Crouch End) • **N9** (Lower Edmonton) • **N10** (Muswell Hill, Cranley Gardens) • **N11** (Brunswick Park, New Southgate) • **N12** (North Finchley, Colney Hatch, Woodside Park) • **N13** (Palmers Green, Bowes Park) • **N14** (Osidge, Oakwood) • **N15** (West Green, South Tottenham) • **N16** (Stamford Hill, Shacklewell) • **N17** (Tottenham) • **N18** (Upper Edmonton) • **N19** (Upper Holloway) • **N20** (Totteridge, Whetstone, Oakleigh Place) • **N21** (Grange Park, Bush Hill, Winchmore Hill) • **N22** (Noel Park)

west end central london

The busy heart of London, graced with a number of well-known locations such as Trafalgar Square, WC2 is particularly well exploited by filmmakers. WC1 is less frenetic with quiet residential streets, squares and offices.

WC1: Bloomsbury, St Pancras

Bloomsbury

Brenda Blethyn and Marianne Jean-Baptiste meet at Holborn tube on Kingsway in *Secrets & Lies* (1996). Underground, Craig Kelly fiddles with his police wire in *The Young Americans* (1993). Rudi Davies uses the tube in *The Object of Beauty* (1991) after stealing a Henry Moore bronze. John Mills evades his police stalker here in *The Long Memory* (1952).

Ray Winstone and Ian McShane conspire to rob James Fox's bank, actually a branch of Lloyds in Victoria House on Vernon Place, in *Sexy Beast* (2000).

James Cossins enters Russell Square tube on Bernard Street in *Death Line* (1972). Albert Finney loses Fulton Mackay on the platform in *Gumshoe* (1971). Andy Garcia tries to evade his tail in *American Roulette* (1988).

The *Morons from Outer Space* (1985) stay at the Russell Hotel, on Russell Square, outside which Dinsdale Landen serenades Joanne Pearce. In *Lifeforce* (1985) riotous zombies cause chaos outside Chancery Lane tube, since redeveloped. Alistair Sim sets off home after seeing Avril Angers at her office by tube in *The Green Man* (1956).

Jude Law walks under Barter Street's arch to visit Clive Owen's office at 18 Southampton Place in *Closer* (2004).

Rhys Ifans interrupts Daniel Craig's browse in the London Review Bookshop, 14 Bury Place, opposite Gilbert Place, in *Enduring Love* (2004).

In *Gumshoe* (1971) Albert Finney questions proprietor George Innes at Atlantis, occult book sellers, 49a Museum Street.

Mark Rylance works at the AKA bar on West Central Street in **Intimacy** (2000). This location is also the 'Raven' nightclub in **The Last Minute** (2001), outside which Max Beesley is mugged.

Police chase the blackmailer to his doom at the British Museum on Great Russell Street in **Blackmail** (1929). In **Night of the Demon** (1957) Dana Andrews, researching witchery, meets Niall MacGinnis in the museum's famous round reading room. Hywel Bennett as **Percy** (1971) obtains a list of possible donors there from nurse Pauline Delaney. Edward Fox researches Charles de Gaulle in **The Day of the Jackal** (1973). In **Maurice** (1987) James Wilby and Rupert Graves bump into Simon Callow, Wilby's old schoolmaster, in the museum's Assyrian Saloon. Vanessa Redgrave in **Isadora** (1968), Derek Jacobi in **Love Is the Devil** (1998) and David Morrissey and Jane Horrocks in **Born Romantic** (2000) all admire the Elgin Marbles. Richard Widmark climbs into his car in front of the museum in **To the Devil, a Daughter** (1975). Brendan Fraser and John Hannah, after freeing Rachel Weisz, flee in a double-decker bus outside the museum in **The Mummy Returns** (2001). Mariel Hemingway and Mike Binder loiter outside, while Colin Firth and Irène Jacob share a fascination with the exhibits inside in **Londinium** (2001).

At the corner of Bloomsbury Street and Great Russell Street, Pauline Collins as **Shirley Valentine** (1989) is splashed by old friend Joanna Lumley's Rolls as it parks outside the Bloomsbury Hotel.

Cillian Murphy sets off a car alarm in deserted St Giles' Circus in **28 Days Later** (2002). Richard Seifert's prominent Centrepoint, by the circus, plays host to two separate offices in

Above:
Museum Street
(above left). Albert
Finney visits Atlantis
Books (above
centre and right) in
Gumshoe (1971).

The Naked Runner (1967). Frank Sinatra's firm of architects in the bridge overlooks St Giles High Street. Sinatra enters from Charing Cross Road to see Peter Vaughan in the main tower. It is also seen briefly in ***Give My Regards to Broad Street*** (1984).

Edward Furlong leaves Tottenham Court Road tube in ***Three Blind Mice*** (1999). At the Dominion Theatre just by the exit Michael Caine and Janet Suzman meet up in ***The Black Windmill*** (1974).

Delphine Seyrig lives at 40 Bedford Square in ***Accident*** (1967). Ben Kingsley's office is in the same corner at Montague Place in ***Betrayal*** (1983). Michael Kitchen crosses here into Bedford Square Gardens in ***Mrs Dalloway*** (1997) and later Katie Carr catches a bus from the square. Sigourney Weaver visits 47 Bedford Square to sign onto 'Jasmine's', an escort agency run by Niall O'Brien in ***Half Moon Street*** (1986). In ***Piccadilly Jim*** (2004) Sam Rockwell, reading a newspaper outside 19 Bedford Square, rescues Frances O'Connor from the traffic at the north-east corner. Outside 13 Bedford Square James Wilby and Rupert Graves discuss their plans for the evening in ***Maurice*** (1987).

Catherine Deneuve and then David Bowie visit the 'Park West Clinic', in the foyer of Senate House on Malet Street, where Susan Sarandon and Cliff De Young work in ***The Hunger*** (1983). In ***1984*** (1984) John Hurt visits Richard Burton at the building, which is draped with a Big Brother awning. Maggie Smith curses son Ian McKellen in his headquarters, the foyer again, in ***Richard III*** (1995). The foyer is Katie Holmes' courthouse in ***Batman Begins*** (2005).

In ***The Most Dangerous Man in the World*** (1968) Gregory Peck and Anne Heywood walk around the corner just before Malet Street.

In ***Stage Fright*** (1950) the police follow Richard Todd to RADA, 62–64 Gower Street, where Todd meets up with Jane Wyman studying there. University College on Gower Street is 'St Swithin's Hospital' in ***Doctor in the House*** (1954) and ***Doctor at Large*** (1957), relegated to an establishing shot in ***Doctor in Love*** (1960). It is the 'London Academy of Music and the Arts' in ***Raising the Wind*** (1961), outside which Jennifer Jayne backs into David Lodge's cab. Clifton Webb visits the college, now a mortuary, to prepare the body of ***The Man Who Never Was*** (1956). Paul McCartney dreams that Ian Hastings dies on the steps in ***Give My Regards to Broad Street*** (1984). It is the 'Bank of England' in ***Thunderbirds*** (2004), seen as Ben Kingsley is led away. Andy Garcia descends the steps for a champagne reception on the green in ***American Roulette*** (1988), where he survives an assassination attempt by a sniper on the fire escape of the University College Hospital buildings opposite, while Robert Stephens and Kitty Aldridge look on, horrified. The college stands in for the British Museum in **The Awakening** (1980), with Charlton Heston's office just to the north of the entrance, and in **The Mummy Returns** (2001).

In **Tom & Viv** (1994) Miranda Richardson posts a chocolate bar through the letterbox of 36 Endsleigh Place, supposedly the offices of publishers Faber & Faber where Willem Dafoe works. When it is rejected, Richardson responds by pouring in warm liquid chocolate.

Taxi driver Timothy Spall drops off Kathryn Hunter at The Ambassadors, Upper Woburn Place, in **All or Nothing** (2002).

St Pancras

In **Death Line** (1972) David Ladd lives in the Grafton Mansions on Duke's Road. Shell-shocked Rupert Graves throws himself out of a window in **Mrs Dalloway** (1997). Close by, Michael Kitchen checks into the Jenkins Hotel on the corner of Burton Place and Cartwright Gardens. Richard E Grant cashes his US cheque in a 'bank' just north of Grafton Mansions in **Keep the Aspidistra Flying** (1997). The bookshop he works at, supposedly in Hampstead, is 12 Woburn Walk – a well-preserved alley between Upper Woburn Place and Duke's Road.

Anthony Hopkins and Debra Winger emerge from a Hastings Street door opposite Thanet Street after their marriage of convenience in **Shadowlands** (1993). While witness Norman Bird and Hopkins hurry off, Winger and Edward Hardwicke cross towards Judd Street to find a drink. Barbara Murray exits the Judd Street side of Camden Town Hall in **A Cry from the Streets** (1958).

The approach to Katie Johnson's cottage at the end of Frederica Street (N7) in **The Ladykillers** (1955) is in fact Argyle Street. When panicky Cecil Parker slips over the cottage's wall at the sight of the police he pops up in Argyle Street, meeting Peter Sellers in Argyle Square. Under the credits of **Bad Behaviour** (1993) planning officer Stephen Rea goes to work at Camden Town Hall on the corner of Argyle Street and Euston Road. After arriving at King's Cross from Newcastle, Jack Watson walks past McDonald's Hotel, 44–46 Argyle

Below:
Woburn Walk (top). Richard E Grant and Helena Bonham Carter stroll past his workplace (bottom) in **Keep the Aspidistra Flying** (1997).

Square, on his way to a hostel in *Schizo* (1976). Steve Jones walks to the 'Cambridge Rapist Hotel', Montana Hotel, 14–16 Argyle Square, in *The Great Rock 'n' Roll Swindle* (1979).

Stephen Rea and Jaye Davidson hide out at the Northumberland Hotel, Crestfield Street, in *The Crying Game* (1992). At Vernon Square *The Ladykillers* (1955) wait by the phone while Katie Johnson collects their loot, hidden in a trunk, from King's Cross.

In *A Cry from the Streets* (1958) Max Bygraves and Barbara Murray find a suicide at Percy Circus.

In *Mona Lisa* (1986) Bob Hoskins chauffeurs Cathy Tyson from her flat in Trinity Court on Gray's Inn Road, south of the Eastman Dental Hospital. The drunk confusedly enters the ladies lavatories on Guildford Street opposite Coram's Fields in *The Sandwich Man* (1966).

Ben Kingsley works in a bookshop on Lamb's Conduit Street on a now-rebuilt block just south of Emerald Street in *Turtle Diary* (1985). Here Glenda Jackson obtains his address from Harriet Walter. In *I'll Sleep When I'm Dead* (2003) Charlotte Rampling's restaurant, visited first by Jamie Foreman and then by Clive Owen, is Cigala, 54 Lamb's Conduit Street, on the corner of Rugby Street.

Catherine McCormack is stood up outside the Renoir Cinema on Hunter Street in *Born Romantic* (2000) while just to the north-east Jane Horrocks is bored by Mel Raido going on about his ex-girlfriend in St George's Gardens. Aidan Gillen and Kate Ashfield visit the Renoir in *The Low Down* (2001).

The north end of the Brunswick Shopping Centre on Bernard Street appears in *The Passenger* (1975) when Jack Nicholson descends steps, now residents-only lifts, passing Maria Schneider reading on a bench on the ground level. In the residential upper level Heather Graham interviews a rape victim in *Killing Me Softly* (2002) and Amanda Redman lives here in *For Queen and Country* (1988).

WC2: Charing Cross, Trafalgar Square, Leicester Square, Covent Garden, Holborn, Aldwych, Strand, Embankment

Charing Cross

On the pre-2002 pedestrian Hungerford Bridge, Gabriel Byrne and Greta Scacchi chat about governmental intrigue in *Defence of the Realm* (1985). Here Hardy Kruger enjoys the view in **Blind Date** (1959). In **Subterfuge** (1969) Gene Barry chases Suzanne Leigh from SE1 along the bridge but is delayed by heavies while Leigh makes her escape on Victoria Embankment. **Sliding Doors** (1998) opens with Gwyneth Paltrow exiting Embankment tube.

At Charing Cross Pier Peter Finch and Mary Peach take a boat trip in **No Love for Johnnie** (1961). Nigel Patrick joins his informers John Cowley and Colin Blakely on a boat to Westminster in **The Informers** (1964).

As **Callan** (1974) Edward Woodward walks from Embankment tube, then known as Charing Cross, up Villiers Street, onto John Adam Street and up George Court, evading his shadowers by bicycle on the Strand. In **Damage** (1992) Jeremy Irons's office, the Department of the Environment – which he enters on Villiers Street – is PricewaterhouseCoopers, 1 Embankment Place, above Charing Cross station.

In **The Leading Man** (1996) Lambert Wilson and Thandie Newton rehearse at the Playhouse Theatre on Northumberland Avenue. Watched by Clinton Greyn, diamond thieves posing as ambulancemen complete their **Robbery** (1967) from a car crash on Northumberland Avenue. Richard Burton as **The Spy Who Came in From the Cold** (1965) gets out of a car to meet his boss at what is now a side entrance of Books Etc. on Northumberland Avenue.

In **The Ipcress File** (1965), **Funeral in Berlin** (1966) and **Billion Dollar Brain** (1967), Guy Doleman's office is situated between Whitehall and Northumberland Avenue, overlooking Trafalgar Square.

Virginia McKenna and later Peter Finch visit Geoffrey Keen's office above Drummonds, between Whitehall and Spring Gardens, in **A Town Like Alice** (1956). Paul Newman walks from Charles I's statue (at the top of Whitehall) to a side door of Drummonds to see Harry Andrews in **The Mackintosh Man** (1973). George Peppard as **The Executioner** (1970) tries to interest Charles Gray

Below:
The entrance to
1 Embankment
Place in Villiers
Street, where
Jeremy Irons works
in **Damage** (1992).

with his investigation while standing by this statue. In front of Admiralty Arch, Rhys Ifans holds up traffic in **Notting Hill** (1999).

Trafalgar Square

At Trafalgar Square John Loder engineers a chance meeting with Sylvia Sydney and son by the lions guarding Nelson's Column in **Sabotage** (1936). Richard Widmark meets Francis L Sullivan at one of the two fountains in **Night and the City** (1950). Joan Dowling and Lawrence Payne discuss an escape to Canada in **Train of Events** (1954) before diving into the Strand tube (now Charing Cross tube). Ingrid Bergman admires the lions in **The Inn of the Sixth Happiness** (1958). Kenneth More strides across the square in **Sink the Bismarck** (1960). Sophia Loren picks up Gregory Peck hiding behind the lions in **Arabesque** (1966). Michael Bentine walks past the statue of Henry Havelock in **The Sandwich Man** (1966). A UFO abducts Joanna Pettet here in **Casino Royale** (1967). As **Joanna** (1968) Genevieve Waite runs past the lions. In **Subterfuge** (1969) photographer Ron Pember passes on secret information to Gene Barry. Mark Lester and Jack Wild play in **Melody** (1971). Donald Pleasence and Dana Andrews pass through the square in **Innocent Bystanders** (1973). George Segal crosses in **A Touch of Class** (1973). Norman Beaton crosses Cockspur Street to the square in **Black Joy** (1977). In **Carry On Emmannuelle** (1978) Kenneth Connor chauffeurs Suzanne Danielle around the square.

In **An American Werewolf in London** (1981) David Naughton tries to get himself arrested by insulting things British and swearing. In **Who Dares Wins** (1982) Lewis Collins catches a no. 73 bus on the west side. He jumps off the bus almost immediately outside the National Gallery, runs back to the original stop and takes a no. 24 in an attempt to lose his shadow. He fails to notice, however, that a second shadow, Ingrid Pitt, has hopped on after him. **Wayne's World 2** (1993) sends up the body-double idea with a back view of Wayne and Garth among the pigeons. **A Business Affair** (1994) ends with Jonathan Pryce and Carole Bouquet in the square. Martin Clunes and Anna Chancellor catch a cab in front of General Napier's statue in **Staggered** (1994). Jon Bon Jovi strolls through the square in **The Leading Man** (1995). Joely Richardson cycles, with Perdita trotting alongside, by the east fountain in **101 Dalmatians** (1996). Ralph Fiennes rescues Uma Thurman from the weather here in **The Avengers** (1998). Noah Taylor sleeps off a heavy night in the paws of a lion in **Shine** (1996), as does Aidan Gillen in **Mojo** (1997). Joanna Lumley trots through in **Mad Cows** (1999).

In *Honest* (2000) Nicole Appleton and Peter Farinelli frolic in the west fountain. Carmine Canuso and Celia Meiras play next to the fountain in *Day of the Sirens* (2001). Christina Ricci waits for John Simm by the lions in *Miranda* (2002). In *The Core* (2003) pigeons start dropping out of the sky and cause chaos in the square. In *Reign of Fire* (2003) Ben Thornton is amidst more benign birds. V-masked protestors push their way past soldiers here in *V For Vendetta* (2005). *Enigma* (2002) opens with Saffron Burrows walking through the square. Dougray Scott meets Kate Winslett on the steps of St Martin-in-the-Fields. Dirk Bogarde passes by the church, followed by the police in *Victim* (1961). From the steps Joan Collins and Glyn Houston admire the square in *Turn the Key Softly* (1953). Daniel Auteuil meets Marianne Denicourt in *The Lost Son* (1999) under the portico.

In the National Portrait Gallery restaurant Julia Roberts and Clive Owen discuss their love life in *Closer* (2004).

Michael Caine photographs a spy delivering secret papers to the South African Embassy's side entrance on Duncannon Street in *The Fourth Protocol* (1987). Opposite, Anthony Hopkins catches his bus home in *84 Charing Cross Road* (1986).

From the post office on the corner of William IV Street and St Martin's Place Keir Dullea makes a call to sister Carol Lynley in *Bunny Lake Is Missing* (1965). In *Brannigan* (1975) John Wayne and Judy Geeson watch dispatch rider Tony Robinson collecting packages of ransom money from the post office, now partly converted to a Prêt-à-Manger.

James Fox chases a girl mistaken for his daughter down Brydges Place into St Martin's Lane in *Runners* (1983).

In *The Human Factor* (1979) Nicol Williamson's contact is 'Halliday and Son, Antiquarian Books' at 24 Cecil Court, which he visits three times in the film. Anthony Hopkins browses outside 14 Cecil Court, Mark Sullivan Antiques, in *84 Charing Cross Road* (1986). John Hurt browses along no.s 21, 23 and 25 in *Love and Death on Long Island* (1997). In *The Lost Son* (1999) Daniel Auteuil lives at Burleigh Mansions on Charing Cross Road, overlooking Cecil Court.

In *Gumshoe* (1971), just after Albert Finney leaves Atlantis bookshop (WC1) in a hurry, he appears again in Hunt's Court, off Charing Cross Road.

Leicester Square

Joan Collins visits the Leicester Square Theatre in *Turn the Key Softly* (1953). Jon Finch meets Anna Massey's taxi outside the Odeon, Leicester Square, in *Frenzy* (1972). Malcolm

McDowell wanders around the square in **O Lucky Man!** (1973). Peter Sellers busks in front of the Swiss Centre there in **The Optimists** (1973). Anna Nygh hails a taxi in **Sweeney 2** (1978). Escorting Marilu Tolo from the Odeon, Anthony Quinn as **The Greek Tycoon** (1978) is served with a writ for divorce. In **Secrets & Lies** (1996) Brenda Blethyn and Marianne Jean-Baptiste also exit the cinema. In **101 Dalmatians** (1996) Natasha Richardson cycles along the north side of the square heading for Cranbourn Street pursued by Jeff Daniels, who is propelled round the corner of the Swiss Centre through Leicester Fields. Hugh Grant and Julia Roberts attend the Empire Cinema in **Notting Hill** (1999). Paul Nicholls mistakes a passer-by for his girlfriend in **If Only** (2004).

In **Séance on a Wet Afternoon** (1964) Richard Attenborough enters Leicester Square tube on Charing Cross Road next to Wyndham's Theatre, grabs Mark Eden's ransom bag inside a Piccadilly line tube, and returns to Leicester Square to catch a no. 24 bus back home. The interior of Wyndham's stands in for that of the Royal Opera House in **Murder By Decree** (1978). Paul McCartney busks outside Leicester Square tube in **Give My Regards to Broad Street** (1984). Reece Dinsdale chants football slogans with his new friends as they emerge from the tube exit next to the Hippodrome in **I.D.** (1994).

In **Victim** (1961) Peter McEnery visits Norman Bird's bookshop in St Martin's Court, where Dirk Bogarde makes a blackmail payment later. The pub on the corner by St Martin's Lane is The Salisbury Arms.

Queues line up to see Annette Bening at the Albery Theatre, formerly the New Theatre and now the Noel Coward Theatre, in **Being Julia** (2004), and on the same corner Lucy Punch hugs Shaun Evans when she wins a part in Jeremy Irons's next production.

Richard Widmark crosses St Martin's Lane to Goodwin Court, The Silver Fox's location, in **Night and the City** (1950).

Maggie Smith brings Alec McCowen to the flat she is sharing with Lou Gossett above The Salisbury in **Travels With My Aunt** (1972). Later John Hamill collects Smith from St Martin's Court and takes her to a car in front of The Lamb and Flag on Rose Street to collect money from Robert Flemyng. Robin Phillips as **David Copperfield** (1970) bumps into Michael Redgrave outside the pub. Judy Geeson chauffeurs John Wayne as **Brannigan** (1975) down Rose Street to the Garrick Club in Garrick Street to meet Richard Attenborough.

'Mack Travel Agency' is established on the corner of New Row and Covent Garden in **Where the Spies Are** (1965).

Stepmum Noelle Adams goes to St Martin's College, 107–111 Charing Cross Road, to meet moody Gillian Hills and (vainly) try to befriend her in **Beat Girl** (1960).

Charles Lloyd-Pack and Frank Thornton are barbers at 'Henry's of Harborn Street', actually on Earlham Street, where Derren Nesbitt induces Lloyd-Pack's heart attack in **Victim** (1961). It has since been rebuilt, but The Marquis of Granby is still next door.

Joan Collins and Harry Fowler swim at Oasis outdoor pool on the corner of High Holborn and Endell Street in **I Believe in You** (1952). The Oasis Leisure Centre has replaced the open-air site.

Above:
Charing Cross Road (above left). **Beat Girl** (1960) Noelle Adams visits St Martin's College (above right).

Covent Garden

In **Agent Cody Banks 2** (2004) Frankie Muniz is kidnapped from a rickshaw when Hannah Spearritt buys a drink from Caffè Nero between Monmouth Street and Earlham Street at Seven Dials.

Charlotte Gainsbourg stays at the Covent Garden Hotel, 8 Monmouth Street in **Ma Femme est une Actrice** (2001).

In Neal's Yard Richard E Grant first meets Samantha Mathis before she is fired in **Jack & Sarah** (1995). In **Sorted** (2000) Fay Masterson visits Tim Curry's laboratory, 'The Apothecary', at 19 Shorts Gardens on the corner of Neal's Yard.

In **The Red Shoes** (1948) Marius Goring and Moira Shearer report for work at the Royal Opera House, Bow Street. Here Shearer first meets Anton Walbrook. In **Frenzy** (1972) Bernard Cribbins fires barman Jon Finch at The Globe, 37 Bow Street. Finch spends the last of his money in Nell of Old Drury, 29 Catherine Street, while Gerald Sim and Noel

Johnson discuss the necktie murders. Friend Barry Foster works in Covent Garden Market (which moved south of the river Thames in 1974) and lives on the second floor of 3 Henrietta Street.

In *Blue Ice* (1992) Michael Caine treats Sean Young to the opera. In *The Fifth Element* (1997) Chris Rock escorts Bruce Willis into a show there before aliens shoot up the interior. In the lobby a cheery trio of Robin Phillips as *David Copperfield* (1970), Corin Redgrave and Nicholas Pennell bump into Ron Moody and Susan Hampshire. Redgrave climbs up the nearest lamppost in Broad Court, across Bow Street. Emily Mortimer takes a shine to Jonathan Rhys Meyers at the opera in *Match Point* (2005). Rob Lowe and Jennifer Baxter enjoy a night at the opera in *Perfect Strangers* (2004). Later he and Anna Friel leave a restaurant for her car parked alongside Broad Court.

At Bow Street Law Court Katherine Woodville bails out Nigel Patrick in *The Informers* (1964).

At The Dôme, now Café Rouge, 34 Wellington Street, Andie MacDowell counts her 33 lovers to bemused Hugh Grant in *Four Weddings and a Funeral* (1994).

Emma Thompson rushes to the premiere of 'Elephant' at the Theatre Royal, Drury Lane on the corner of Catherine Street and Russell Street in *The Tall Guy* (1989). In *Londinium* (2001) Mike Binder and Mariel Hemingway find themselves growing closer together on Russell Street.

On the corner of Great Queen Street and Drury Lane at 'Stone & Co.' a robbery takes place in *The Long Arm* (1956). This building, and The Sugar Loaf next door (now called O'Neills), are unchanged since the filming in the 1950s. The Freemason's Hall, on the corner of Great Queen Street and Wild Street, is 'MI7', the base of Rowan Atkinson as *Johnny English* (2003). It is the court where David Morrissey testifies in *Basic Instinct 2* (2005), and faces Hugh Dancy's questions outside.

David Hemmings and Daniel Massey leave the New Connaught Rooms on Great Queen Street and chat under the covered way on Newton Street in *Fragment of Fear* (1972).

Holborn

The Collector (1965) Terence Stamp spies on Samantha Eggar, a student, at 'Blake's School of Art' on Remnant Street off Kingsway. The disused tramline tunnel under the Kingsway is, along with some computer trickery altering the background, the entrance to 'The Ministry' in *The Avengers* (1998).

In *The Day of the Triffids* (1962) Howard Keel watches a blind man climbing over the steps of a water fountain at the corner of Serle Street. Later Howard Keel and Janina Faye find a dog mysteriously killed by a Triffid on the east side of Lincoln's Inn Fields.

On the south-east corner The Land Registry is the wartime headquarters of the Dutch Government in exile in *Soldier of Orange* (1977). As Guus Hermus leaves, he notices Rutger Hauer following and leads him into New Square. Hauer prepares to shoot from under the steps of 1 New Square but is frustrated when Hermus disappears into New Square Passage. In *A Pair of Briefs* (1961) James Robertson Justice manages to avoid a banana peel outside Michael Craig's chambers at 12 New Square. In *A Fish Called Wanda* (1988) Jamie Lee Curtis visits John Cleese's chambers in 2 New Square. As *David Copperfield* (1970) Robin Phillips visits 'Wickfield and Heep', a supposedly Canterbury-based firm of solicitors, at 3 New Square.

On the west side of New Square Albert Finney as *Tom Jones* (1963) chats with Jack MacGowran about extrication from an affair. Then he visits Rosalind Knight at 23 New Square, actually on Old Buildings, and is forced into a swordfight with husband George A Cooper in the vaulted undercroft below Lincoln's Inn Chapel. David Warner pays off a couple of 'witnesses' prepared to lie about the fight under the steps at the basement level of New Square. The undercroft, with added glazing, is Annette Bening's conservatory where she breakfasts with Robert Downey Jnr in *Richard III* (1995).

In *Wilde* (1997) Stephen Fry lives in Stone Buildings, though this shot is cut in with several of Somerset House. David Thewlis twice stops to question David Morrissey on the

Below:
Stone Buildings (below left).
Stephen Fry leaves his house (below right) in *Wilde* (1997).

west side of Old Buildings in **Basic Instinct 2** (2005). In **The Importance of Being Earnest** (2002) Colin Firth and Rupert Everett walk across Old Square to the undercroft of Lincoln's Inn Chapel, where Everett is forced to make a hasty escape. Rupert Everett lives in New Square. Dustin Hoffman and Johnny Depp share the same walk in **Finding Neverland** (2004).

Billy Connolly frustrates an assassination attempt on Judi Dench as **Mrs Brown** (1997) as her entourage descends the steps of the library of Lincoln's Inn Hall. Tom Bell and Christian Anholt discuss their case on a bench on the grass to the east of the hall in **Preaching to the Perverted** (1997). Here in **Basil** (1998) Jared Leto and Rachel Pickup meet Christian Slater.

In **A Fish Called Wanda** (1988) John Cleese exits the rear of the Royal Courts on Carey Street and joins Jamie Lee Curtis to make their escape in his car towards Chancery Lane and on to Heathrow. Wilfred Brambell and Harry H Corbett as **Steptoe And Son** (1972) leave court after obtaining Corbett's divorce to find a parking ticket stuck on their horse Delilah's forehead. On Chancery Lane the old Public Record Office, now King's College's Maugham Library, is used as the Tower of London, where Rowan Atkinson as **Johnny English** (2003) attempts to guard the Crown Jewels.

Barrister John Gregson, gleefully leaving the the Royal Courts of Justice on Strand, joins his beloved vintage Darracq called **Genevieve** (1953), casually parked by St Clement Danes. A match-seller passes a secret message to Diana Rigg, approaching the courts in **The Assassination Bureau** (1968). Ian Carmichael pesters Miles Malleson to be taken on as a pupil in **Brothers-in-Law** (1957) in front of The George. Next to the George at BK News, 212 Strand, Renée Zellweger misses an important interview for her TV station because she is buying some cigarettes, but meets Colin Firth again, in **Bridget Jones's Diary** (2001). The courts are an establishing shot in **Incognito** (1997) as Ian Richardson attempts to prosecute Jason Patric. Richard Jordan escapes from court after sentencing, goes across Strand and down Arundel Street in **A Nightingale Sang in Berkeley Square** (1979) to join Oliver Tobias in his ice cream van on Victoria Embankment.

At Temple tube on Temple Place Michael Caine sees off Millicent Martin in **Alfie** (1966). Here an ambulance picks up drunk Stacy Keach in **The Squeeze** (1977).

In **A Pair of Briefs** (1961) Michael Craig argues with Mary Peach at the gates of Clement's Inn. In **Star!** (1968) the same gates establish Julie Andrews's arrival in a bankruptcy court.

Aldwych

Christopher Plummer works at Australia House in **Nobody Runs Forever** (1968). Hopeful immigrants Jack Hawkins and family visit in **Touch and Go** (1955). Barry Crocker visits in **Barry McKenzie Holds His Own** (1975) and finds a full-blown Aussie party inside. In **Castaway** (1987) Amanda Donohoe fumes outside with the fact that she has to be married to Oliver Reed to appease Australian immigration law before moving to their Pacific island. In **Harry Potter and the Philosopher's Stone** (2002) the interior is Gringott's bank, best seen from the back on Melbourne Place.

On Surrey Street, Aldwych tube (closed since 1994), recognizable by its cream and green tiles, is a convenient film location. In **Gideon's Day** (1958) Cyril Cusack is involved in an exchange there. The stairway appears in **Postman's Knock** (1962), **Subterfuge** (1969) and in **Honest** (2000). It is used as a shelter in **Battle of Britain** (1969). In **The Black Windmill** (1974) Michael Caine approaches the station on Surrey Street, travels one stop, runs up the stairs (which are Aldwych again), and emerges at Shepherd's Bush. In **Prick Up Your Ears** (1987) Gary Oldman picks up some custom on the stairway. In **The Krays** (1990) it stands in as Bethnal Green tube when the family shelters from the Blitz. In **Patriot Games** (1992) the Burlington Arcade bookseller, an IRA contact, runs to the station – quite a distance. Playing Down Street, a disused station near Green Park closed in 1932, it is the bedroom of **Creep** (2005).

Marianne Jean-Baptiste goes to St Catherine's House, 10 Kingsway, on Kingsway and Aldwych, to find her mother on her birth certificate in **Secrets & Lies** (1996). Opposite, waiting for a bus, Cecil Parker exchanges banter with newly probationed Harry Fowler in **I Believe in You** (1952). In **Shining Through** (1992) as he is about to enter Bush House,

Above:
Surrey Street (above left), location for **The Black Windmill** (1974). Michael Caine enters Aldwych tube (above right).

Michael Douglas silences a protestor while Melanie Griffith looks on. Simone Signoret, trailed by Harry Andrews, picks up some theatre tickets for the Royal Shakespeare Company next to the Waldorf Hotel on Aldwych and posts them in *The Deadly Affair* (1967). Here Matthew Rhys and Jason Donovan are forced to leap onto a bus to escape their pursuers after Donovan's shoplifting escapade in *Sorted* (2000). Outside the Waldorf Michael Caine hijacks Martin Landau in his limousine in *Shiner* (2000).

Strand

Somerset House, bordering Lancaster Place, Strand and Victoria Embankment, is currently home to the Inland Revenue and the Courtauld Institute Galleries, and former home to the registration of marriages, births and deaths, since moved to St Catherine's House. Edward

Left:
Somerset House is a popular location for numerous films, including *The Private Life of Sherlock Holmes* (1790), shown opposite.

Above left and right:
Robert Stephens
and Colin Blakely
visit The Diogenes
Club in *The Private
Life of Sherlock
Holmes* (1970).

Fox researches a birth certificate here to procure a false identity in **The Day of the Jackal** (1973). Opposite the Courtauld Institute is 'The Diogenes Club', where Robert Stephens and Colin Blakely visit Christopher Lee in **The Private Life of Sherlock Holmes** (1970).

Jack Hawkins on his investigations pays a visit through the arched colonnaded entrance to Somerset House in **The Long Arm** (1956). Outside, Minnie Driver's family bid her farewell as she leaves for Skye in **The Governess** (1998). When she returns during a cholera outbreak, the deep basement level, which runs along the length of the buildings enclosing the open courtyard, stands in for London streets. In **King Ralph** (1991) the courtyard is supposed to be Buckingham Palace's. Peter O'Toole meets a panicky Leslie Phillips and Richard Griffith, who report that John Goodman has gone to Soho. Later, forbidden to leave, Goodman drives Camille Coduri around the courtyard on a date.

The western façade of King's College is the 'German Embassy,' dressed in Nazi flags, in **Lassiter** (1986). The east archway within Somerset House frames the embassy's gates. Tom Selleck, Joe Regalbuto, Ed Lauter and Jane Seymour conspire to steal Lauren Hutton's diamonds outside the gates on the north side of Somerset House. Selleck escapes along the passageway of the basement level.

Bob Hoskins visits the 'Russian Embassy', now the Courtauld Institute, to see Eddie Izzard in **The Secret Agent** (1996). Jim Broadbent confronts Robin Williams at the basement level. An appearance of period London streets are again the aim in the David Thewlis scenes in **Black Beauty** (1994). In **Portrait of a Lady** (1996) Viggo Mortensen visits Nicole Kidman, staying at 'Pratt's Club' on the basement level on the east side.

In **Golden Eye** (1995) Joe Don Baker meets Pierce Brosnan in the west corner of the courtyard, supposedly in St Petersburg, and encourages his temperamental Moskvich to start with a hammer. Brosnan reports for duty here in **Tomorrow Never Dies** (1997) in an establishing shot. In **Wilde** (1998) Stephen Fry's carriage comes from the archway leading to King's College heading west. Later Jennifer Ehle exits a carriage here. The scene stands in for New York when Johnny Depp and Christina Ricci leave a carriage here in **Sleepy Hollow** (1999). In **The Importance of Being Earnest** (2002) Rupert Everett is chased through the basement level. Later Colin Firth is supposedly in a busy London street – the space between Somerset House and King's College – with St Paul's imposed onto the background. Stephen Campbell Moore and Emily Mortimer as **Bright Young Things** (2003) attend Harriet Walker's ball through the courtyard. In **Shanghai Knights** (2003) Jackie Chan and Fann Wong look on as Thomas Fisher requests the use of Owen Wilson's name. Despite an establishing shot of Buckingham Palace, the orchestra arrives at Somerset House in **Agent Cody Banks 2** (2004).

In **London Voodoo** (2004) Doug Cockle celebrates with his office mates in Sitar, situated at 149 Strand.

In **23 Paces to Baker Street** (1956) Van Johnson's balcony overlooks the Thames from what could be a suite in the Savoy Hotel, given the view. His flat entrance is in W1. Dana Andrews is dropped off at Savoy Place by Peggy Cummins in **Night of the Demon** (1957). In **The Big Sleep** (1978), as Sarah Miles descends the Savoy steps, often gated off, from Savoy Court to the back of The Coal Hole, an attempted mugging by Dudley Sutton is thwarted by Robert Mitchum, who sends him on his way down Carting Lane. Judy Garland stays at the Savoy Hotel for her tour in **I Could Go On Singing** (1963). Laurence Harvey arrives at Savoy Court to lunch with Robert Morley and Nigel Davenport in **Life at the Top** (1965). In **The Long Good Friday** (1980) Bob Hoskins is bundled into the wrong car by the IRA. Meryl Streep has a room in the hotel with a view towards Hungerford Bridge in **The French Lieutenant's Woman** (1981). Michael Caine is called to a meeting at the hotel bar in **Bullet to Beijing** (1995). As he walks through the entrance, Jason Connery is delivered by taxi. Sean Connery gets into a taxi, watched by Catherine Zeta-Jones from a car, in **Entrapment** (1999). Hugh Grant dives into the Savoy to interrupt Julia Roberts's press conference in **Notting Hill** (1999).

Sidney Poitier first meets Esther Anderson in **A Warm December** (1973) in the Victoria Embankment Gardens. Sam Rockwell meets Frances O'Connor by the statue of Robert

Raikes in the gardens – which are playing the zoo in New York's Central Park – in *Piccadilly Jim* (2004). In a flashback in *The Criminal* (1999) Natasha Little appears in the gardens. The climax takes place in Ivybridge Lane off Savoy Place, an alleyway running alongside the Shell-Mex building. In *Richard III* (1995) Ian McKellen turns down Jim Broadbent's request for an earldom in front of Shell-Mex's clock.

Windsor policeman James Booth, investigating the philatelic pedigree of the *Penny Gold* (1974), visits the Stanley Gibbons shop at 391 Strand, since rebuilt, while the shop itself has now moved to 399 Strand.

As Heather Graham turns from Adam Street into John Adam Street, she is mugged. Joseph Fiennes chases the perpetrator to Adelphi Terrace and beats him up in *Killing Me Softly* (2002). Adelphi Terrace provides the entrance to *The Daily Excess*, the tabloid paper owned by Dan Aykroyd in *Bright Young Things* (2003). This is also the New York building housing Austin Pendleton and Brenda Blethyn's apartment in *Piccadilly Jim* (2004), while the steps to the east lead to a 'subway station'.

Embankment

Iman meets Robert Morley on a floating restaurant moored just west of Waterloo Bridge in *The Human Factor* (1979) to discuss husband Nicol Williamson's defection. *Mona Lisa* (1986) opens with Bob Hoskins walking south on Waterloo Bridge. *Alfie* (1966) opens with a dog on the north-west side and ends with Caine meeting the dog and asking, 'What's it all about?' Together they head south. In *The Young Americans* (1993) Harvey Keitel surveys the Thames from here, looking east.

On Victoria Embankment to the east, bus conductor Graham Stark considerately allows Julia Foster onto his full bus in *Alfie* (1966).

In *Indiscreet* (1958) Cary Grant and Ingrid Bergman walk along Victoria Embankment between the northern Sphinx and Cleopatra's Needle to view the Thames, where Bergman signs autographs. Susan Maugham sings 'Please Give Me A Chance' here in *What a Crazy World* (1963). Daniel Auteuil exercises in *The Lost Son* (1999). A little further to the west, William Hurt's umbrella blows inside out in *The Accidental Tourist* (1988).

John Mills meets Lionel Jeffries in *The Vicious Circle* (1957) just west of Cleopatra's Needle. Jeffries boards a pleasure boat from Charing Cross Pier and Mills follows. Unaware that they are under police surveillance, they discuss a blackmail proposition as the boat passes under Waterloo Bridge.

west london

Versatile west London cuts a swathe west, from Oxford Street shops and Soho bars, through the enormous green spaces of Hyde Park and Kensington Gardens and grand housing of Notting Hill to more modest Ealing streets.

W1: Marylebone, Fitzrovia

Marylebone

North of Marble Arch, Hywel Bennett leaves a taxi at Cumberland Place in *Percy* (1971).

After her release from prison Yvonne Mitchell stays at 16 Wyndham Place in *Turn the Key Softly* (1953). At St Mary's Church on the same street Anthony Hopkins and Vanessa Redgrave attend a rain-swept wedding in *Howards End* (1992). John Standing buys flowers outside the curved portico in *Mrs Dalloway* (1997).

Mary Peach catches a taxi at Knox Street after attending Fenella Fielding's party in *No Love for Johnnie* (1961).

Phil Daniels enters 'Overlord Records', 66 Chiltern Street on the corner of Paddington Street, with an armful of the same single record he has hyped into the chart in *Breaking Glass* (1980). Gwyneth Paltrow delivers sandwiches to Jeanne Tripplehorn's office here in *Sliding Doors* (1998).

Elaine Cassidy is a gardener at Paddington Street Gardens in *Felicia's Journey* (1999).

In *If Only* (1998) Douglas Henshall enters Daunt Books, 83 Marylebone High Street, for a chat with fiancée Penelope Cruz who is working there. Lena Headey spies on Henshall from across the road.

In *Help!* (1965) the Beatles walk west to 6–8 Blandford Street, the site of the Rajahama Restaurant, and now the Giraffe Restaurant with an added alfresco seating area.

Hertford House, located in Manchester Square, provides the exterior of 'The Majestic Hotel' where Oliver Reed shoots Brian Poycer in front of wife Sheila Steafel in *Parting Shots* (1998).

At Selfridges, between Baker Street, Duke Street and Oxford Street, Shabani Azmi and son Navin Chowdhry are summoned to explain a hair found in their food supplied to the store in **Madame Sousatzka** (1988). Susannah York and Colin Dale evade Peter Eyre and Nicholas Grace here in **Just Ask for Diamond** (1988). In **Just Like a Woman** (1992) Julie Walters and Adrian Pasdar (dressed in drag) encounters his boss Paul Freeman in a lift. After Alan Rickman meets Emma Thompson outside Carluccio's on the corner of Barrett Street and St Christopher's Place, they enter Selfridges, where Rickman tries to prevent Rowan Atkinson elaborately gift-wrapping a necklace before she catches him with his purchase in **Love Actually** (2003).

Derek Thompson and Bryan Marshall sit outside the Boulevard Café, now Its, on the corner of Easley Mews and 60 Wigmore Street in **The Long Good Friday** (1980). Here Patti Love spits at Thompson, whom she astutely blames for her husband's murder by the IRA.

After proudly touching the Harley Street sign outside 1 Harley Street, Dirk Bogarde buys a stethoscope at Bell and Croyden, 50 Wigmore Street on the junction with Welbeck Street, in **Doctor in the House** (1954).

Lynne Frederick visits her psychiatrist at 82 Wimpole Street, near Welbeck Mews, while Jack Watson observes outside in **Schizo** (1976). Julie Christie parks her mini at a meter while visiting Laurence Harvey at 40–41 Wimpole Street in **Darling** (1965). Round the corner on Weymouth Street, though it's addressed as 35 Harley Street, is Harvey's fencing gym. Lino Ventura investigates Lee Remick at 44 Wimpole Street, on the corner of Weymouth Street, in **The Medusa Touch** (1978).

Tony Beckley is taxied to 115 Harley Street, on the corner of Devonshire Street, to plan **The Italian Job** (1969) with Noel Coward, who is granted leave from prison so that he can visit his dentist. John Mills works at 'The Mayfair Clinic', 117–19 Harley Street, in **The Vicious Circle** (1957).

Fitzrovia

The Olsen twins' American delegation stays at the Langham Hotel on Portland Place in **Winning London** (2001). Jonathan Pryce exits Oxford Circus tube and arrives for work at BBC Broadcasting House, on the corner of Langham Place and Langham Road, in **The Ploughman's Lunch** (1983). Paul McCartney and Bryan Brown arrive at the BBC in **Give My Regards to Broad Street** (1984).

In **Blue Ice** (1992) Michael Caine stops at the red light at the intersection of New Cavendish Street and Great Portland Street. Sean Young, distracted on the phone, shunts him from behind.

In **The Life and Death of Peter Sellers** (2004) Geoffrey Rush visits agent Henry Goodman, and meets his fourth wife at 33 Portland Place (a scene cut from the theatrical release but available in the bonus section of the DVD). As **Vera Drake** (2004) Imelda Staunton descends the steps to the basement of 33 Portland Place despite a shot establishing Fitzroy Square (see below). Another establishing shot places Gregory Peck's house in **The Paradine Case** (1947) at 60 Portland Place on the corner of Weymouth Street. 74 Portland Place contains Van Johnson's flat, seen as Patricia Laffare visits, in **23 Paces to Baker Street** (1956), despite his view overlooking the Thames (WC2). In **Ring of Spies** (1963) William Sylvester finds Great Portland Street tube locked, and resorts to his car parked in NW1.

Vanessa Redgrave as **Mrs Dalloway** (1997) lives at 3 Fitzroy Square. In **The Heart of Me** (2002) Paul Bettany and Olivia Williams live at 2 Fitzroy Square. Bettany has a clandestine encounter with sister-in-law Helena Bonham Carter in the square's gardens. A shot of no.s 5 and 6 Fitzroy Square establishes Lesley Manville's house, where Imelda Staunton works, in **Vera Drake** (2004).

Andy Garcia, after leaving Warren Street tube, runs down Fitzroy Court to meet Alfred Michelson parked in Whitfield Place in **American Roulette** (1988). The pursuers presumably

Left:
Vanessa Redgrave as **Mrs Dalloway** (1997) leaves 3 Fitzroy Square.

eluded, they drive across Grafton Way down Whitfield Street. To stock up on food the refugees raid the Budgens food store, now a Sainsbury's Local, at 145 Tottenham Court Road in *28 Days Later* (2002). Derek Jacobi and Daniel Craig pause at Heal's and Son, 196 Tottenham Court Road, in *Love Is the Devil* (1998), where Jacobi hallucinates in the shop window. In *Three Blind Mice* (1999) Edward Furlong, looking at surveillance camera shops, realizes he is being tailed at 26 Tottenham Court Road. In *An American Werewolf* in London (1981) a city worker becomes the werewolf's sixth victim on a Northern Line platform of Tottenham Court Road tube.

In *Elephant Juice* (2000) Lennie James exits Goodge Street tube and Daniel Lapaine visits the Lloyd's cashpoint before taking Sean Gallagher to his usual sex arrangement in SE1.

In *Bedazzled* (1967) Peter Cook demonstrates his devilry to Dudley Moore by releasing pigeons that relieve themselves on passers-by from near the top of the Post Office Tower (now the BT Tower) on the corner of Cleveland Street and Howland Street. Susannah York and Dirk Bogarde enjoy tea in the rotating restaurant at the top of the tower in *Sebastian* (1968). The tower also serves as rather too obvious a phallic symbol when Hywel Bennett drives up Conway Street in penis-transplant comedy *Percy* (1971).

David Thewlis shelters in the doorway of Ariel House, 74a Charlotte Street close to Chitty Street, in *Naked* (1993). Kindly security guard Peter Wight lets him in to share mints and biblical thoughts. The Beatles run from Charlotte Mews to the Scala Theatre, now demolished, on Tottenham Street in *A Hard Day's Night* (1964).

In *Sliding Doors* (1998) Gwyneth Paltrow gets drunk – with John Lynch or Zara Turner depending on which of the two characters she is – at Bertorelli's, 19 Charlotte Street. John Hannah gives Paltrow and Turner a lift home in his taxi. In *Sapphire* (1959) the police pick up Paul Massie for questioning at Foscari's, 14 Charlotte Street on the corner of Windmill Street. The Thai Metro, Fin and currently Siam Central have all occupied this corner. Rita Tushingham and Lynn Redgrave walk down Charlotte Street after Redgrave's party at the Post Office Tower in *Smashing Time* (1967).

Peeping Tom (1960) opens with a prostitute guiding her killer through a doorway, 10 Newman Passage, above The Newman Arms, 23 Rathbone Street. Karl Boehm returns to the scene to film the discovery of the body. Then he goes to work on his scooter above 29 Rathbone Place, now Caffè V.

The mysteriously clad figure of Jonathan Rhys-Meyers walks west along Hanway Place, under the titles of *Velvet Goldmine* (1998).

At Legends, 119 Oxford Street, an ornate wrought-iron grill above one of the doorways gives away the fact that this was once a passageway, down which in *Frenzy* (1972) was Barbara Leigh-Hunt's 'Blaney Bureau'. Julia McKenzie helps Pauline Collins buy panties for her Greek holiday at Littlewoods, Oxford Circus, in *Shirley Valentine* (1989). Samantha Eggar exits Oxford Street tube to catch a bus near the start of *The Walking Stick* (1970). At Skechers, 291a Oxford Street, Hugh Grant buys some cool trainers, albeit short-lived, for Nicholas Hoult in *About a Boy* (2002). Debenham's at 334–338 Oxford Street refuses entry to Stacy Keach while Freddie Starr goes in to nick some clothes in *The Squeeze* (1977).

W1: Park Lane, Mayfair, Regent Street, Soho, Piccadilly

Park Lane

On Apsley Way, dominated by the Wellington Arch (also known as Constitution Arch), Stanley Baker meets Ursula Andress in *Perfect Friday* (1970). Michael Bentine as *The Sandwich Man* (1966) walks by the arch after witnessing a runaway lawnmower receiving a parking ticket on the west side of Green Park. Gregory Peck and Ingrid Bergman take a stroll around the arch in *Indiscreet* (1958). Donald Pleasence and Dana Andrews walk through the arch in *Innocent Bystanders* (1973). George Segal wanders by in *A Touch of Class* (1973). Christopher Lawford convinces Mariel Hemingway to return to LA here in *Londinium* (2001).

At the Inter-Continental Hotel, 1 Hamilton Place, Roger Moore steals luggage in *Bullseye!* (1990). Later he pops into Le Soufflé bar, on the corner of Park Lane, with Michael Caine. At Achilles Way on Park Lane, chauffeur Bob Hoskins persuades Cathy Tyson to get back into their car in *Mona Lisa* (1986).

On Old Park Lane at the former Londonderry Hotel, now the Metropolitan, Gregg Henry and Elizabeth Daily are up to their tricks in *Funny Money* (1983).

Between Achilles Way and Curzon Gate, on a little stretch of grass, some of which used to be paved, Jon Finch pours out his woes to Anna Massey in *Frenzy* (1972), after which old friend Clive Swift spots them, while Swift's wife Billie Whitelaw watches them from a first floor balcony of the enormously tall London Hilton Hotel, 22 Park Lane. Adam Faith enjoys a Hilton balcony view in *Stardust* (1974), and Kenneth Haigh as the *Man at the Top* (1973) celebrates his elevated position in his room. Outside the Hilton Michael Callan attempts to pull a Silver Lady off the bonnet of a Rolls Royce in **You Must Be Joking** (1965) before being picked up by Gabriella Licudi. Sam Waterston and Ned Beatty catch a taxi from the hotel in **Hopscotch** (1980). In **The Theory of Flight** (1998) Kenneth Branagh and Helena Bonham Carter watch a gigolo enter the hotel and, taking a room there, decide to hire his services.

Also on this stretch of Park Lane Samantha Eggar ponders her loyalty to David Hemmings to the tune of 'Cavatina' in **The Walking Stick** (1970). Michael Bentine as **The Sandwich Man** (1966) takes off his sandwich boards and falls into conversation with Fred Emney and Wilfrid Hyde-White. Ann Lynn and stepdaughter Linda Hayden pass here in **Baby Love** (1968), and Kirk Douglas is followed by two of Marlene Jobert's pupils here in **To Catch a Spy** (1971). Summer Phoenix as **Suzie Gold** (2004) runs past the car salesrooms of Park Lane after her sister's wedding. Deborah Kerr drops off Roger Livesey at the Home Guard Headquarters, 139 Park Lane, actually on North Row, in **The Life and Death of Colonel Blimp** (1943). It is now part of a Marriott hotel.

Mayfair

Tom Courtenay as **Otley** (1969) is taxied to the Playboy Club, ostentatiously tips the cabbie and is recognized by James Bolam and Fiona Lewis outside the entrance at 18a Curzon Street, now a branch of HSBC.

In **The Bitch** (1979) Michael Coby, leaving the club, is chased and beaten up next to 10 Curzon Place. The west side was bulldozed in 2001 to form Curzon Square. In **Stage Fright** (1950) Jane Wyman turns from Curzon Place, passing Alfred Hitchcock on her way to Marlene Dietrich's house at 78 South Audley Street. A cut suggests that Wyman can see the house from Curzon Place, but actually it's around the corner opposite Audley Square. Vanessa Redgrave leaves 2 South Audley Place, 'The Cadogan Hotel', in **Wilde** (1998).

Redgrave also dances in Robert Stephens's sports car as they drive north up South Audley Street in **Morgan** (1966). James Spader takes Dexter Fletcher and Ione Skye to Richoux, 41a South Audley Street, in **The Rachel Papers** (1989). Christian Anholt visits the Counter Spy Shop, 60 South Audley Street, before his mission in **Preaching to the Perverted** (1997). Opposite at the Grosvenor Chapel, Colin Firth marries Irène Jacob in **Londinium** (2001). Chiwetel Ejiofor and Keira Knightley's wedding here is jazzed up with a rendition of 'All You Need Is Love' in **Love Actually** (2003). Roger Moore and Michael Caine raid their doubles' safety deposit boxes at 'Lacey's', actually T. Gunn & Co., 17–20 South Audley Street, in **Bullseye!** (1990). Opposite, Robert Mitchum meets Deborah Kerr as she exits no. 67 in **The Grass Is Greener** (1960).

The 'Royal Park Hotel' in **The Divorce of Lady X** (1937) is the Dorchester, on the corner of Deanery Street, and the view from Laurence Olivier's window shows Stanhope Gate flanked by lodges that used to stand opposite Stanhope Street in Park Lane. Robert Newton and Celia Johnson sit on a bench in Hyde Park opposite the gate and lodges in **This Happy Breed** (1944), and they are seen again in **The Astonished Heart** (1949). The current view is seen in **Crossplot** (1969), when Roger Moore breaks off his romancing for the office.

Edward Rigby stays at the Dorchester when he wins the football pools in **Easy Money** (1947). Cliff Richard signs autographs, while Yolande Donlan realizes his star appeal is outshining hers in **Expresso Bongo** (1959). David Warner as **Morgan** (1966), dressed as a gorilla, disrupts the wedding reception of Vanessa Redgrave and Robert Stephens on the Dorchester's windy terrace. Here Peter Vaughan instructs Frank Sinatra on his 'Leipzig mission' in **The Naked Runner** (1967). Peter Sellers and his two young assistants pass the hotel in **The Optimists** (1973). John Vernon and Mel Ferrer make it their base in **Brannigan** (1975). Jeremy Irons drops off Leslie Caron here in **Damage** (1992), and returns later to find Juliette Binoche. Tennis stars of **Wimbledon** (2004) Paul Bettany and Kirsten Dunst stay here.

David Warner steals a motorbike on Aldford Street and drives off down Park Lane in **Morgan** (1966). George Peppard drops off Judy Geeson at her flat in 14 Park Street, though the entrance is round the corner in Aldford Street, in **The Executioner** (1970).

In **Players** (1979) Dean-Paul Martin and Ali MacGraw run into The Guinea, 30 Bruton Place, pursued by photographers. Matthew Rhys visits Sienna Guillory working at the 'Peter Gwyther Gallery', actually the Halcyon Gallery, 29 Bruton Street in **Sorted** (2000). In **Londinium** (2001) a taxi nearly knocks over Mariel Hemingway here.

The interior of the English Speaking Union, 37 Dartmouth House, Charles Street, is Tim Curry's house in **Sorted** (2000). Roger Moore and Michael Caine exit here while Sally Kirkland watches them from across the street in **Bullseye!** (1990). She bumps into their car deliberately at Hay's Mews and Chesterfield Hill.

On the corner of Waverton Street, outside 38 Hill Street, 'The Candelabra' in **Gangster No. 1** (1999), David Thewlis is shot while Jamie Foreman slashes Saffron Burrows's neck, all observed dispassionately by Paul Bettany.

Hugh Laurie loses his beard and hair at the renowned barbers G F Trumper, 9 Curzon Street, in **Maybe Baby** (2000).

In **Match Point** (2005) at the Curzon Mayfair cinema Matthew Goode joins Emily Mortimer and Jonathan Rhys Meyers, who's disappointed that he's turned up without Scarlett Johansson.

Jane Wyman follows police detective Michael Wilding to the Shepherd's Tavern on the corner of Shepherd Street and Hertford Street in **Stage Fright** (1950). Towards The King's Arms, there's an alleyway leading to Shepherd Market, where Jack May searches for his next victim in **Night, After Night, After Night** (1969).

Julie Christie seeks comfort at the Church of the Immaculate Conception in Mount Street Gardens in **Darling** (1965). Robin Phillips as **David Copperfield** (1970) warns Pamela Franklin there about their impending poverty. Here too Jonathan Rhys-Meyers confesses his affair to Rupert Penry-Jones in **Match Point** (2005). Lindsay Lohan calls her twin from the phone box at the entrance to the gardens before walking through the park in **The Parent Trap** (1998). At 115 Mount Street is Johnny Shannon's office in **Performance** (1970).

On the corner of Park Lane and Mount Street, James Nesbitt and Lennie James attempt to rob a bank, actually Grosvenor House Hotel, in **Lucky Break** (2001). There ensues a chase through the Aldford Street underpass to Hyde Park. Roger Moore and Claudia Lange evade the police in this underpass in **Crossplot** (1969).

Ian McShane visits Ray Winstone dining in the Bollinger Room of the Grosvenor House Hotel in **Sexy Beast** (2000). Jason Flemyng and Mark Benton pick up a magazine award at the hotel and walk down Park Lane after the ceremony in **Lighthouse Hill** (2001).

Below:
Park Lane (below left). Jason Flemyng and Mark Benton leave Grosvenor House Hotel (below right) in **Lighthouse Hill** (2001).

Gregory Peck, as US ambassador to the Court of St James's, enters the American Embassy in Grosvenor Square in *The Omen* (1976) pursued by cameramen, including David Warner, who photographs ejected Patrick Troughton. In *The Final Conflict* (1981) Sam O'Neill and Don Gordon face a similar press greeting to Peck's. Gene Barry visits in *Subterfuge* (1969). The group of alien *Children of the Damned* (1964) takes the pedestrian crossing to the square. Richard Roundtree uses the same crossing in *A Game for Vultures* (1979). In *Obsession* (1949) superintendent Naunton Wayne overhears 'Thanks, pal' – a vital clue – from US Navy personnel gathered around the Roosevelt Memorial in the square.

Charlotte Gainsbourg sneaks out of the Connaught Hotel, Carlos Place, after a night with Terence Stamp in *Ma Femme est une Actrice* (2001).

Nicol Williamson and Derek Jacobi escort Robert Morley to 34 Grosvenor Mansions, Grosvenor Street, in *The Human Factor* (1979). Williamson and Jacobi continue east, crossing just before Davies Street.

Alan Bates, professing true love, chases Lynn Redgrave as *Georgy Girl* (1966) through an underpass leading from Cumberland Gate to the island with the three fountains west of Marble Arch. Donald Pleasence and Dana Andrews pass the fountains in *Innocent Bystanders* (1973). These fountains are now silent.

Bond Street features, unsurprisingly, in *Bond Street* (1948). Alan Bates visits the newsvendor's in front of Sotheby's, 35 New Bond Street, in *Nothing but the Best* (1964). Peter Sellers and Ringo Starr buy the nose (only) from a painting from John Cleese in *The Magic Christian* (1969). In *Octopussy* (1983) Roger Moore watches Louis Jourdan and Kristina Wayborn being picked up by Kabir Bedi in a limousine from the newsvendor's stall.

Ralph Bates works at 179 New Bond Street above Davidson, now Mikimoto, in *I Don't Want to Be Born* (1975). In *Match Point* (2005) Jonathan Rhys Meyers exits Cartier, 175 New Bond Street, hands his purchases to chauffeur John Fortune and bumps into old friend Rupert Penry-Jones. At no. 172, Bulgari (now Mousaieff) opposite Bentley and Skinner, is a victim of a Jeremy Irons scam in *And Now ... Ladies and Gentlemen* (2003). Later he dreams that he returns some money to its new location, a few doors north at no. 168.

In *The Parent Trap* (1998) Natasha Richardson and Lindsay Lohan walk through Royal Arcade from Old Bond Street and catch a cab in Albemarle Street. At Asprey and Garrard, on the corner of Old Bond Street and Grafton Street, the Beatles try to have Ringo Starr's ring removed in *Help!* (1965). Charles Dance and Jenny Seagrove buy a ring here in *Don't Go Breaking My Heart* (1998). On the corner Scarlett Johansson spots Jonathan Rhys Meyers, thus discovering he's not in Greece as he said in **Match Point** (2005).

In **The Titfield Thunderbolt** (1953) a civil servant rides a foldaway scooter from Berkeley Street along the east side of Berkeley Square to the Ministry of Transport, 14 Berkeley Square House. This building is also the 'Atlantic and City Bank' in **A Nightingale Sang in Berkeley Square** (1979), which David Niven and Richard Jordan rob via the fire exit on Bruton Lane. Since then a perspex frontage has been added.

David Hemmings and Samantha Eggar pass through the square with his artwork in **The Walking Stick** (1970). At the hut in the middle of the square Charles Grodin grills James Mason about security at **11 Harrowhouse** (1974), the diamond exchange that is actually 46 Berkeley Square. Oliver Reed and axe appear on the south-east side under the credits of **I'll Never Forget What's'isname** (1967). Charles Dance and Jenny Seagrove buy a car from Jack Barclay's, 18 Berkeley Square on the corner of Bruton Street, in **Don't Go Breaking My Heart** (1998). Robin Askwith fails to get a job in this showroom in **Cool it Carol!** (1970).

Juliette Binoche, leaving work from the rear of Sotheby's at 6–7 St George Street, crosses the street, dominated by St George's Church, to two phone boxes, now not there, outside the Royal Sandwich Bar, now Il Pan d'Oro, to phone Jeremy Irons in **Damage** (1992). At this café Ann Lynn and Linda Hayden meet Derek Landon in **Baby Love** (1968). In **The Knack** (1965) Michael Crawford, Donal Donnelly and Rita Tushingham park the bedstead at a meter to eat their picnic north of the church.

The Alphabet Murders (1965) opens with Tony Randall in front of Clifford Baths on the corner of Clifford Street and Savile Row. While following Tony Randall, Robert Morley and James Villiers pause by the Museum of Mankind in Burlington Gardens. Randall visits his tailor Richard Watts at 14 Savile Row.

From the roof of 3 Savile Row the Beatles give passers-by a free concert in ***Let It Be*** (1970). In ***Blow Up*** (1966) David Hemmings, catching sight of Vanessa Redgrave on Regent Street, parks his Rolls next to Heddon Street and heads into New Burlington Mews. At the end of the mews, iron fire escape steps lead him into a Yardbirds concert.

Regent Street

In ***A Touch of Class*** (1973) George Segal and Glenda Jackson as 'his mother' pick up tickets for Spain at 188–96 Regent Street, now Regents Clothes, on the corner of New Burlington Street. Tom Cruise and Nicole Kidman do Christmas shopping at Hamley's, Regent Street, in ***Eyes Wide Shut*** (1999). Alex Pettyfer collects his gadgets from Stephen Fry here in ***Stormbreaker*** (2006).

Leslie Phillips tries to buy some 'with it' clothes in Carnaby Street in ***Doctor In Clover*** (1966). Photographer Michael York spots Lynn Redgrave in the trendy street in ***Smashing Time*** (1967).

Keira Knightley helps Parminder Nagra buy football boots at Soccer Scene, at the corner of Beak Street and Carnaby Street, in ***Bend It Like Beckham*** (2002). The green-tiled building on the corner of Beak Street and Great Pulteney Street establishes Anna Friel and Rob Lowe's London office in ***Perfect Strangers*** (2004).

At the London Palladium on Argyll Street Judy Garland appears in ***I Could Go On Singing*** (1963). The front is seen in an establishing shot in ***Follow A Star*** (1959).

Soho

In ***101 Dalmatians*** (1996) Pongo catches sight of Joely Richardson cycling through the east entrance of Soho Square with Perdita by her side and sets off in pursuit as Jeff Daniels attaches him to his bicycle. Anthony Hopkins watches the 1960s go by from a bench south of the Soho Square folly in ***84 Charing Cross Road*** (1986). Jon Finch makes a call outside Twentieth Century House, 31–32 Soho Square, in ***Frenzy*** (1972). Matthew Rhys and Sienna Guillory share a walk in the square in ***Sorted*** (2000) while on their way to the record shops. Leigh Zimmerman advises Ed Byrne to lose his jacket here in ***Are You Ready for Love?***

(2006). He dates rather too chubby a girl at Bar Italia on Frith Street. In *Melody* (1971) Mark Lester and Jack Wild mock-fight with their satchels in the square and then catch a taxi home on the west corner of Greek Street and Old Compton Street.

Parked on the east corner of Greek Street, Jason Donovan and Matthew Rhys snort cocaine in *Sorted* (2000). Keira Knightley takes Parminder Nagra to The Three Horseshoes pub opposite in *Bend It Like Beckham* (2002).

In *Sid And Nancy* (1986) Gary Oldman and Andrew Schofield swagger outside The Spice of Life, 6 Moor Street, before attacking a limo in Berwick Street.

The Palace Theatre, Cambridge Circus, is St James's Theatre for the première of 'Lady Windermere's Fan' in *Wilde* (1988). Here Aria Argento and Jonathan Rhys-Meyers pick up Vincent Regan for a robbery in *B. Monkey* (1996). Emily Mortimer arrives at the theatre for 'Woman In White' in *Match Point* (2005).

Aidan Gillen passes by the Caffè Nero on the corner of Frith Street and Old Compton Street in *The Low Down* (2001).

John Wayne as *Brannigan* (1975) shares an evening with Judy Geeson at Terrazzo, now Lupo, on the corner of Dean Street and Romilly Street.

Wonderland (1999) opens with Gina McKee on a blind date at a Pitcher and Piano bar on the corner of Meard Street and Dean Street. She works at Duke's Bar, 27 Old Compton Street, where all three sisters – McKee, Debbie Henderson and the pregnant Molly Parker – meet. Parker's water breaks outside the Bank of East Asia at 75 Shaftesbury Avenue on the corner with Dean Street.

Old Compton Street is a particular favourite for numerous films of the 1950s and early 1960s set in Soho's coffee bar scene, such as *Expresso Bongo* (1959) and *The Boys* (1962). Ewan McGregor and Steven Mackintosh's recording studio is above Gerry's, 74 Old Compton Street, in *Blue Juice* (1995).

Jonathan Pryce and Carole Bouquet live at 79 Wardour Street, quoted as being above an Ann Summers shop, in *A Business Affair* (1994). This corner of Wardour Street at the west end of Old Compton Street is seen briefly as the *Hard Men* (1996) go to raid a club.

George Segal and Glenda Jackson set up a pied-à-terre for their affair at 3 Macclesfield Street (though quoted as no. 8) just south of Dawsey Place in *A Touch of Class* (1973). When Jackson returns from Dean Street to buy oregano, she sees Segal and wife Hildegard Neil leaving the Queen's Theatre on the corner of Shaftesbury Avenue and Wardour Street. She declines to share a taxi with Stuart Damon on Gerrard Street.

Harrison Liu introduces Chen Hsiao Hsuan to Hong Xiang who runs a restaurant called Yee Tung at 26 Gerrard Street in *Foreign Moon* (1995). Frankie Muniz and Hannah Spearritt hire a cycle rickshaw outside The Dragon Inn, 12 Gerrard Street, in *Agent Cody Banks 2* (2004).

Rob Lowe buys fish in Newport Street near the pagoda in *Perfect Strangers* (2004).

In *Mona Lisa* (1986) Bob Hoskins cruises the area as Genesis's 'In Too Deep' plays. Turning south from Gerrard Street into Wardour Street, he drops into a peep show opposite Pizza Express. He then visits a porn shop across Shaftesbury Avenue at 1 Brewer Street. He also visits Michael Caine at Paul Raymond's Revuebar in Walker's Court. Later he buys a Cathy Tyson video on Little Crown Court off Rupert Street. Here Mark Addy and Charlie Creed-Miles are enticed into a peepshow in *The Last Yellow* (1999). Peter O'Toole collects John Goodman as *King Ralph* (1991) from a Soho burlesque in Winnett Street, just off Rupert Street.

Andy Serkis picks up Max Beesley in his car on the intersection of Brewer Street and Rupert Street in *Five Seconds to Spare* (1999). Karim Belkhadra walks up Rupert Street to Madame Jo Jo's on Brewer Street, where Lewis works in *Room to Rent* (2002).

David Morrissey follows Sharon Stone through Walker's Court in *Basic Instinct 2* (2005). Gary Oldman visits Robert Carlyle's 'Parrot Club', next door to the Revuebar, in *Dead Fish* (2004).

Below:
Charlie Creed-Miles and Mark Addy (below left) are lured into a peepshow (below right) in *The Last Yellow* (1999).

Left:
Little Crown Court,
seen in **Mona Lisa**
(1986) and **The
Last Yellow** (1999).

Richard Attenborough buys fruit in Berwick Street Market in **Séance on a Wet Afternoon** (1964). Opposite, Matthew Rhys and Sienna Guillory scour the record shops in **Sorted** (2000).

In **Naked** (1993) David Thewlis sits down in the doorway of Lina's Stores Ltd., 18 Brewer Street, on the corner with Green's Court. Here he meets head-twitching Ewen Bremner looking for his girlfriend Susan Vidler. In **Are You Ready for Love?** (2006) love gurus Michael Brandon and Leigh Zimmerman host a get-together with their pupils at Zilli's Fish Restaurant, 36 Brewer Street. Outside the Vintage Magazine Shop, 39 Brewer Street (incidentally an excellent store for movie paraphernalia) Andy Nyman dumps them. Further north on the corner of Broadwick Street and Poland Street Lucy Punch prematurely tells Brandon she's found her true love.

In **The Great Rock 'n' Roll Swindle** (1979) Steve Jones investigates the Moulin cinema, Great Windmill Street, where in the lobby Tenpole Tudor sings 'Who Killed Bambi'. Yul Brynner following Charles Gray in **File of the Golden Goose** (1969), Peter Sellers in **The Optimists** (1973) and Stacy Keach in **The Squeeze** (1977) all pass by the Windmill Theatre.

Piccadilly

In **An American Werewolf in London** (1981) David Naughton calls home from Piccadilly Circus, goes to the Eros cinema, turns into a werewolf and causes chaos and carnage in the circus. In **Passport to Pimlico** (1949) three local Pimlico lads watch a newsreel called 'Siege of Burgundy' at the cinema, now a fast-food outlet. Peter Cook strides through Piccadilly

Circus towards Shaftesbury Avenue in **Bedazzled** (1967). In **Brannigan** (1975) Mel Ferrer makes a ransom payment at a fake postbox there. Richard Attenborough and John Stride watch from Lower Regent Street, John Wayne and Judy Geeson from Air Street and the kidnappers themselves from a gap in the neon advertising signs on the north side between the Coca Cola and Skol displays. Dirk Bogarde appears in **The Blue Lamp** (1950) in front of the neon, followed by Ronald Lacey in **The Boys** (1962). In **Bridget Jones's Diary** (2001) Renée Zellweger passes the neon signs with her daily consumption statistics displayed on the Nescafé advert, formerly the Fosters space, above the TDK one. In **Bridget Jones: The Edge of Reason** (2004) the space, now devoted to Coca Cola, proclaims Mark and Bridget to be the real thing. In **You Must Be Joking!** (1965) fans besiege the Rolls of pop group The Cavemen, enabling Michael Callan and Gabriella Licudi to escape with the group's Silver Lady. Yul Brynner's search of saunas starts here in **File of the Golden Goose** (1969).

Donald Sumpter sits at the Angel of Charity fountain in the Circus, known as Eros, in **Night, After Night, After Night** (1969). In **Percy** (1971) Hywel Bennett meets Julia Foster here. In **This Year's Love** (1999) Dougray Scott spray-paints the pavement as Kathy Burke looks on admiringly. Eros was moved south in the 1990s, and the traffic islands redesigned. Cillian Murphy surveys a boarded-up Eros with messages attached in an eerily deserted Circus in **28 Days Later** (2002). Carmine Canuso picks up Celia Meiras here in **Day of the Sirens** (2002). As **The Mother** (2003) Anne Reid sits by the fountain until Oliver Ford Davies finds her.

In **Staggered** (1994) Martin Clunes exits Piccadilly tube. In **Darling** (1965) Julie Christie buys several copies of *The Evening News* (now long defunct) from the newsstand next to Swan and Edgar. Inside Swan and Edgar, Alistair Sim tries to get himself arrested for shoplifting in **Laughter in Paradise** (1951). After a spell as Tower Records, during which Ivan Attal and Charlotte Gainsbourg shop there in **Ma Femme est une Actrice** (2001), the store is now a Virgin. In **Croupier** (1998) Clive Owen visits girlfriend Gina McKee, the store detective. John Goodman as **King Ralph** (1991) meets Camille Coduri at the underground to go for burgers. Parminder Nagra and Keira Knightley travel by tube in **Bend It Like Beckham** (2002).

Deliberately ridiculous doubles of Wayne and Garth appear in the Circus ('What a shitty circus.' 'Good call, there's no animals or clowns, what a rip off.') in **Wayne's World 2** (1993). In **Bring Me the Head of Mavis Davis** (1998) Rik Mayall runs along the south side of Piccadilly while hurriedly dressing for lunch. In **If Only** (1998) Douglas Henshall crosses the

Circus. Alex Norton listens by telephone to *Little Voice* (1998) from an office on the corner of Piccadilly and Lower Regent Street. Harry Eden and Keira Knightley enjoy an evening at the Trocadero in *Pure* (2002), outside which Frankie Muniz and Hannah Spearritt enjoy a rickshaw ride to Coventry Street in *Agent Cody Banks 2* (2004). Millwall fans chase Danny Dyer and Roland Manookian here in *The Football Factory* (2004). The Circus is first port of call for Fiona Allen and Sophie Thompson as *Fat Slags* (2004).

At Fortnum and Mason, on the corner of Duke Street and Piccadilly, Julie Christie and Roland Curram try their hand at shoplifting in *Darling* (1965). In *Howards End* (1992) Vanessa Redgrave and Emma Thompson shop there.

Daniel Auteuil checks into Le Meridien, Piccadilly, in *The Lost Son* (1999). He wanders in the Burlington Arcade between Piccadilly and Burlington Gardens. While Charles Gray is kitted out in the arcade, Edward Woodward is recognized by his wife's friend, thus sealing his doom in *File of the Golden Goose* (1969). In *The Stud* (1978) Oliver Tobias walks through the arcade. James Fox meets daughter Kate Hardie here in *Runners* (1983). In *Patriot Games* (1992) IRA contact Alex Norton poses as an antique books seller in the arcade. Jeff Daniels is dragged into the arcade from Burlington Gardens in *101 Dalmatians* (1996). John Standing and Oliver Ford Davies chat near this end in *Mrs Dalloway* (1997), and Jason Patric catches up with Irène Jacob in *Incognito* (1997).

In *To the Devil, a Daughter* (1976) Denholm Elliott crashes Richard Widmark's booksigning at 'The Piccadilly Gallery', 6 Clarebell House, Cork Street. Roger Moore as *The Man Who Haunted Himself* (1970) goes to a jeweller's on the east corner – since rebuilt – of Burlington Gardens and Cork Street to check on a necklace he bought.

Alan Bates avoids a taxi fare by using different exits of Green Park tube on Piccadilly in *Nothing but the Best* (1964). In *Sorted* (2000) Matthew Rhys arrives in central London at the tube here.

Stephen Boyd tries to check a hotel receipt found on the body of *The Man Who Never Was* (1956) at the old Naval and Military Club, 94 Piccadilly. Gene Barry and Joan Collins survey artwork pinned up on the railings of Green Park opposite Half Moon Street in *Subterfuge* (1969). The ballroom of the Park Lane Hotel, Piccadilly, appears in *Dance with a Stranger* (1985) and *Lassiter* (1986). Daniel Auteuil meets one of a gang of child pederasts at El Pirata on Down Street in *The Lost Son* (1999).

The Wellington Arch underpass is where Martin Landau turns the tables on Michael Caine in *Shiner* (2000).

W2: Kensington Gardens, Bayswater, Maida Vale, Paddington, Hyde Park

Kensington Gardens

At Kensington Gardens' Round Pond in **The Final Conflict** (1981), Sam Neill charms Lisa Harrow by spoiling her son, who is toy-boating. Joan Collins and Michael Coby walk round the south side of the pond near the bandstand in **The Bitch** (1979). In **Basil** (1998) Jared Leto complains to Rachel Pickup of his drab life. At the end Leto and Pickup return to the pond for a reconciliation of sorts with father Derek Jacobi. In **Ring of Spies** (1963) Bernard Lee and Margaret Tyzack meet their contact at the Round Pond and pass George Watts's statue Physical Energy, which is commented upon by Stephen Fry, Zoë Wanamaker, Jennifer Ehle and Michael Sheen in **Wilde** (1998). George Frampton's Peter Pan statue is a special place for Jesse Spencer and Mary-Kate Olsen in **Winning London** (2001), while Ashley Olsen and Brandon Tyler play with the boats on the Round Pond, and Eric Jungmann and Rachel Roth feed the geese. Sam Neill, Lisa Harrow and son look out over the Long Water opposite the Peter Pan statue after boating on the Round Pond in **The Final Conflict** (1981). A pram – without its baby – is found at the statue in **Lost** (1955). Returning here, mother Julia Arnall is led through The Fountains, also known as The Italian Gardens, near Marlborough Gate, by a girl who claims she can help.

As **Joanna** (1968) Genevieve Waite walks through The Fountains and asks the statue, 'Why don't you grow up?' Noel Coward and Margaret Leighton discuss their affair at The Fountains overlooking The Long Water in **The Astonished Heart** (1949). Later in the film Coward returns to reminisce. James Donald escorts Jean Kent here in **Trottie True** (1948). June Thorburn and John Fraser share a romantic walk in **Touch and Go** (1955). In **Yield to the Night** (1956) Diana Dors and Michael Craig canoodle here, and Dors returns here in sadder times. Virginia McKenna picks up French soldier and future husband Alain Saury here in **Carve Her Name With Pride** (1958). Gene Barry and Joan Collins walk here in **Subterfuge** (1969). In **The Big Sleep** (1978) Joan Collins meets Robert Mitchum in the folly by The Fountains. In **Bridget Jones: The Edge of Reason** (2004) Colin Firth challenges Hugh Grant to a fight that ends up in the small pool between the fountains. The pavilion to the north is extended with brick walls to match the interior of the Serpentine Gallery, where Grant is presenting an art show. Paul Bettany and Kirsten Dunst chat next to the pool in **Wimbledon** (2004).

Opposite:
The fountains at Kensington Gardens (top), seen in numerous films including **Yield to the Night** (1956), where Diana Dors and Michael Craig share happier times at the Italian Gardens (bottom left and right).

Bayswater

First port of call for Michael Caine after release is the Royal Lancaster Hotel on Westbourne Street in *The Italian Job* (1969). Hywel Bennett follows Hayley Mills's Mini on his motorbike to outside 24 Lancaster Gate in *Endless Night* (1972) after meeting her in the countryside. At the same spot in *Scandal* (1989) Joanne Whalley-Kilmer encourages Leslie Phillips to pay Bridget Fonda's owed rent. Here Chiwetel Ejiofor drops off Emilia Fox in *Three Blind Mice* (2002). At the former headquarters of the Football Association at 16 Lancaster Gate, Ricky Tomlinson as *Mike Bassett England Manager* (2001) starts his new job.

The wedding reception in *Notting Hill* (1999) is in the Zen garden across the road from the Hempel Hotel at Craven Hill Gardens.

Nigel Patrick investigates an ex-guest at the 'King's Court Hotel' in Leinster Gardens in *Forbidden Cargo* (1954). It is now the side of Caesar's Hotel dominating the north side of Queen's Gardens.

At the Inverness Hotel, on the west side of Inverness Terrace close to Bayswater Road, Donald Sutherland and Elliott Gould on the trail of Kenneth Griffith cause chaos in the dining room to avoid paying their bill in *S*P*Y*S* (1974). John Thaw meets Barry Foster inside the hotel, as 'The Dorchester Club', in *Sweeney!* (1976). Gary Oldman and Chloe Webb as *Sid & Nancy* (1986) play with cap guns outside before entering to meet 'Rockhead'. Amanda Donohoe meets Oliver Reed here in *Castaway* (1987). Earlier at Bayswater tube Donohoe, flicking through an abandoned *Time Out* on her way to Notting Hill Gate, had seen Reed's advert for a wife to join him on a tropical island.

At Whiteley's on Queensway, Michael Caine checks a suspicious thermos flask by using a pedoscope in *Billion Dollar Brain* (1967). Rupert Graves and Nisha K. Nayer shop here in *Different for Girls* (1997). Lennie James and Emmanuelle Béart meet their respective partners here in *Elephant Juice* (2000). Julia Roberts holds an exhibition in *Closer* (2004). Outside the central entrance on Queensway Jude Law sees off Natalie Portman. Jon Finch takes Anna Massey for an afternoon of passion at the Coburg, now the Hilton Hyde Park, 129 Bayswater Road in *Frenzy* (1972). A taxi drops off Telly Savalas at the St Petersburgh Place entrance to the London Embassy Hotel, 150 Bayswater Road, to meet James Mason in *Inside Out* (1975).

Richard Chamberlain marries Glenda Jackson in St Sophia's Greek Cathedral on Moscow Road in *The Music Lovers* (1971). In *Golden Eye* (1995) Izabella Scorupco arranges to meet treacherous Alan Cumming there.

Glenda Jackson lives in a flat at 17 Pembridge Square in **Turtle Diary** (1988), from where Ben Kingsley picks her up in a van to transport turtles from London Zoo.

In **Sliding Doors** (1998) Gwyneth Paltrow and John Lynch live in Hazel Court, 38–40 Leinster Square. A taxi drops her off opposite by Calpe House, 47 Prince's Square.

In **Runners** (1983) Edward Fox follows daughter Kate Hardie from Paddington (see below) to 31 Monmouth Road, a dead end leading south off Westbourne Grove. Here Fox abducts her in his desperation to convince her to return home.

In **Damage** (1992) Jeremy Irons stops his chauffeured car to make a call from one of the two phone boxes on Chepstow Place. In **If Only** (1998) Penélope Cruz works in and is fired from a bar, no longer there, in Rede Place. Douglas Henshall meets her at the nearer of the two phone boxes in Chepstow Place. Only one box now remains.

In **Martha, Meet Frank, Daniel and Laurence** (1998) the men in the title (Rufus Sewell, Tom Hollander and Joseph Fiennes) meet at trendy restaurant '236' in Chepstow Place (now gone), directly opposite the '99' dry cleaners and the antique shop Sean Arnold.

Ben Keyworth and mother Fanny Ardant walk along 'Lancaster Road W14' – in fact Artesian Road – towards St Mary's Roman Catholic Church, along with its hall, 26 Artesian Road, in **Afraid of the Dark** (1991). Keyworth imagines that the hall is the 'Reach Out Clinic for the Blind' and that his mother and sister Clare Holman are indeed blind. In fact the hall, which is the 'Lancaster Avenue [sic] Kindergarten' is the venue for Holman's wedding reception.

Round the corner is Moorhouse Road, which old maps show was originally called Westmoreland Road and used to run across Talbot Road to Westbourne Park Road. North of Talbot Road, now a housing estate, was the site of the boarding house shared by Leslie Caron, Tom Bell, Brock Peters and Cicely Courtneidge in **The L-Shaped Room** (1962). The house was on the corner just north of Burlington Mews East.

Michael Caine as **Alfie** (1966) and neighbour Melvin Murray live in 29 St Stephen's Gardens, on the corner of Chepstow Road. On the corner of Chepstow Road and St Stephen's Mews was the antiques shop, run by Peggy Ashcroft and Pamela Brown, that Elizabeth Taylor visits in **Secret Ceremony** (1968).

Hugh Grant asks Nicholas Hoult to be his son when they call round to Rachel Weisz's flat at 1 St Stephen's Crescent, opposite St Stephen's Church in **About a Boy** (2002).

Barry Jones takes a room at '70 Glisby Road', actually 70 Westbourne Park Villas, in **Seven Days to Noon** (1950). When he walks up Westbourne Park Passage, a narrow alley from

Westbourne Park Road, he stops by no. 74 to see a police car outside no. 70, and so crosses the road to a footbridge over the Metropolitan Line. In the middle of the bridge he dumps his raincoat onto the tracks. A protective barrier prevents this nowadays. In **Children of the Damned** (1964) Ian Hendry follows Barbara Ferris's trail down the passage. The next shot cuts to SE1, a not inconsiderable walk.

The Mr Creosote episode of **Monty Python's the Meaning of Life** (1983) was filmed at Porchester Hall, apparent only when waiter Eric Idle leads the camera out through the back into Porchester Road, across the zebra crossing and down Gloucester Terrace.

Maida Vale (see also page 70)

Daniel Craig's new place on Torquay Street overlooks the Westway in **Some Voices** (2001).

The Grand Union Canal and St Mary Magdalene Church on Rowington Close are the only survivors of **The Blue Lamp** (1950), which shows a different system of terraced streets, now replaced by high-rise housing. Bernard Lee orders the search of Regent's Canal for Dirk Bogarde's gun. Bruce Seton follows Bogarde from Blomfield Road (W9) over the footbridge, now redesigned, to a flat on the corner of Delamere Terrace and Lord Hills Road. Bogarde makes a dash for it in his car, nearly running down Jimmy Hanley as he speeds down Clarendon Street.

Also now lost forever is the array of streets housing Peter Sellers's garage, the café, pub and Adam Faith's flat in **Never Let Go** (1960). These were in Chichester Place. Demolition has started by the time of **The Boys** (1962). Indeed Tony Garnett is seen working on Delamere Terrace while the area between the old Cirencester Street and Senior Street has been levelled. He, along with Dudley Sutton, Ronald Lacey and Jess Conrad all appear to live in an enclosed tenement block where in fact the canal is. The area has changed further by the time Elizabeth Taylor, followed by Mia Farrow, gets off a bus to visit St Mary Magdalene Church in **Secret Ceremony** (1968). Here Julianne Moore makes her confession in **The End of the Affair** (1999).

Dick Emery visits a tattooist on a barge tied up alongside Delamere Terrace in **Ooh, You Are Awful** (1972).

At Westbourne Terrace Bridge Road Jack Warner and Jimmy Hanley chat on the beat before Hanley answers a distress call at 38 Warwick Crescent in **The Blue Lamp** (1950). In **The End of the Affair** (1955) John Mills and Van Johnson spy on Deborah Kerr visiting Michael Goodliffe at '12 Cedar Road, NW8'. It's actually Warwick Crescent. This handsome terrace has now been replaced with modern housing. Rupert Graves lives in Beauchamp House, 2 Warwick Crescent, on the corner of Harrow Road in *Different for Girls* (1997).

In front of Maida Avenue's church by the canal James Mason asks Lynn Redgrave to marry him in *Georgy Girl* (1966). Thomas Georgeson is arrested at 7 Maida Avenue (Aubrey House) in *A Fish Called Wanda* (1988). Next door, 6 Maida Avenue (Douglas House) contains Judy Geeson's flat in *Brannigan* (1975). Geeson takes John Wayne here after his own flat in Battersea (SW11) is blown up. Outside, hitman Daniel Pilon nearly kills Geeson, mistaking her in the rain for Wayne.

In *Georgy Girl* (1966) Lynn Redgrave and Charlotte Rampling share a flat, which is at the rear of a block facing Edgware Road, up the second set of stairs from Maida Avenue. Heather Graham meets reporter Yasmin Bannerman at the Café Laville overlooking the canal in *Killing Me Softly* (2002).

362 Edgware Road was the Regent's Milk Bar, now Chicken Cottage, seen in *B. Monkey* (1996) when Jonathan Rhys Meyers picks up Aria Argento for a robbery.

In *The Blue Lamp* (1950) the police station itself was on the north side of Harrow Road opposite Bishop's Bridge Road, so the view south is just recognizable despite Westway now running over the station's site. Close by, to the east, is Paddington Green, also changed, but the hospital at no. 19 – now Mary Adelaide House and converted into flats – is recognizable. In *Withnail & I* (1986) the police stop Richard E Grant's dilapidated Jaguar on Harrow Road at the south end of Warwick Avenue and instruct him to 'get in the back of the van'.

In *Naked* (1993) David Thewlis abandons his stolen car on Hermitage Street, a turning off Harrow Road.

In *Twenty One* (1991) Patsy Kensit meets Rufus Sewell in her office overlooking the easternmost part of the elevated Westway. Sewell gets his drugs from underneath Westway. Phil Bailey takes Brenda Blethyn and Diana Quick for a similar deal in *Saving Grace* (2000).

In *If Only* (1998) two mysterious Spaniards encounter Douglas Henshall on Bishop's Bridge Road and grant him a chance to change his life.

Paddington

Derren Nesbitt lives on his ill-gotten gains at 88 Gloucester Terrace on the corner of Chilworth Street in *The Informers* (1964). The main action however occurs to the side in Gloucester Mews, where Nigel Patrick snoops around Nesbitt's Bentley, and at the climax Colin Blakely and Michael Coles launch an attack on his house, with the two gangs clashing in the mews. In **The London Connection** (1979) Dudley Sutton kidnaps David Kossoff from Roy Kinnear in the mews.

Michael Caine lives at 101 Eastbourne Mews in **The Fourth Protocol** (1987).

In **The October Man** (1947) John Mills searches through Paddington Station's left luggage office to clear his name. Alec Guinness fails to meet Donald Houston and Meredith Edwards, who are arriving here from Wales in **A Run for Your Money** (1949). In **The Man Who Never Was** (1956) Stephen Boyd catches a taxi from the rank that then separated platforms 1–8 from 10–14. In **Performance** (1970) James Fox also catches a taxi here. In **Murder, She Said** (1961) Margaret Rutherford catches a train for 'Milchester'. Ingrid Bergman arrives at Paddington in **The Inn of the Sixth Happiness** (1958). Ian Carmichael leaves for his election constituency in **Left, Right and Centre** (1959). Alan Bates helps Denholm Elliott collect his luggage in **Nothing but the Best** (1964). Peter Ustinov takes a train for Wales in **Hot Millions** (1968). Genevieve Waite as **Joanna** (1968) arrives and leaves again, during which time the cast sing and dance on the platform. In **Subterfuge** (1969) Tom Adams departs after quarrelsome words with Joan Collins. In **Perfect Friday** (1970) Stanley Baker greets Ursula Andress after seeing off her husband David Warner. Patti Love collects her husband's coffin at the station in **The Long Good Friday** (1980). Searching for

Left and opposite: Gloucester Terrace (left) where Nigel Patrick is on the case in **The Informers** (1964) (opposite).

American cooking, William Hurt samples a hot dog in ***The Accidental Tourist*** (1988). James Fox meets wife Eileen O'Brien and daughter Ruti Simm here in ***Runners*** (1983). Later, Fox parks outside the Great Western Hotel, now a Hilton, on Praed Street to spy on Kate Hardie and her friends distributing leaflets outside the tube. The station, now revamped, is seen in ***Dead Fish*** (2004) when Gary Oldman prevents the theft of Elena Anaya's mobile phone on the crosswalk. The confusion caused by the subsequent exchange of their phones leads to Andrew Lee Potts and Jimi Mistry going to the lockers while being spied upon by Billy Zane. Paul Nicholls and Jennifer Love Hewitt catch a train from Paddington in ***If Only*** (2004).

Clive Owen visits Alex Kingston at the 'Journey's End Hotel', 4 Norfolk Square in ***Croupier*** (1997). The entrance is now blocked up and absorbed by the Tudor Court Hotel. Kerry Fox holds acting classes with students, including Marianne Faithfull, in Talbot Square in ***Intimacy*** (2000).

At The Gyngleboy, 27 Spring Street, Steve Coogan fails, due to Helena Bonham Carter's sabotage, at reconciliation with wife Sandra Reiton in ***The Revengers' Comedies*** (1998).

In ***Percy*** (1971) Elke Sommer lives at Castleacre, a tall block of flats on the corner of Southwick Street and Hyde Park Crescent. Outside, Hywel Bennett is hit by a man falling from her flat and has to be rushed to hospital for an emergency operation. Later, Bennett

Left:
Bathurst Mews,
seen in *Scandal*
(1989).

returns to visit Sommer himself, but ends up outside the flat's window clinging on for dear life. James Coburn sends Michael Jayston to kill Ian Hendry at flat no. 716 Castleacre in **The Internecine Project** (1974).

In **Trainspotting** (1996) Ewan McGregor, Robert Carlyle, Ewen Bremner and Jonny Lee Miller enter the Royal Eagle Hotel, Craven Road, from Smallbrook Mews to do a drug deal. McGregor passes under the arch, absconding with the money later.

Just inside the entrance of Bathurst Mews, off Sussex Place, is no. 42, which was John Hurt's flat in **Scandal** (1989). Here Joanne Whalley-Kilmer has affairs with Ian McKellen and Jeroen Krabbé.

When John Mills visits Herbert Lom in Sussex Mews, he parks in Sussex Place opposite Sussex Lodge in **Mr Denning Drives North** (1951). The arch is still the same, but Herbert Lom's flat has now been replaced by parking spaces. David Farrar investigates a lead outside 31 Hyde Park Gardens Mews, at the corner of Sussex Place, in **Lost** (1955). In **No Love for Johnnie** (1961) Peter Finch contrives a chance meeting with Mary Peach at the same corner.

Impecunious Telly Savalas is forced to hand over his car in front of his house, 38 Connaught Square, in **Inside Out** (1975).

Hyde Park

By Victoria Gate is Hyde Park's pet cemetery, now closed, which Peter Sellers, Donna Mullane and John Chaffey visit in **The Optimists** (1973).

At Speakers' Corner, in the north-east corner of Hyde Park, Robert Newton and Celia Johnson opt for a cup of tea rather than listen to a fascist speaker in **This Happy Breed** (1944). Eric Portman loses police tail Bill Shine in **Wanted for Murder** (1946). In **The End of the Affair** (1955) Michael Goodliffe's denouncement of supreme beings impresses Deborah Kerr. When Sam Neill and Lisa Harrow pass by the corner in **The Final Conflict** (1981), Neill feels disconcerted by a speaker who is one of the seven assigned to kill him. In **The Executioner** (1970) George Peppard takes a breather at the Joy of Life fountain from the inquiry he's instigated.

In **Ring of Spies** (1963) copied top-secret papers are handed back to Bernard Lee and Margaret Tyzack during a recital from the bandstand close to Serpentine Road. Here Anita Ekberg steals Tony Randall's hat in **The Alphabet Murders** (1965). Genevieve Waite as **Joanna** (1968) dances within the bandstand alone to the strains of Scott Walker's 'When Joanna Loved Me'. Paul Williamson commits suicide here in **Man at the Top** (1973). Jeff

Above:
Hyde Park Gardens Mews (above left), where David Farrar investigates a lead (above right) in **Lost** (1955).

Daniels and Joely Richardson circle the bandstand on their bicycles as a band plays 'Daisy, Daisy' in *101 Dalmatians* (1996).

Close to the Dell restaurant Colin Firth, Mariel Hemingway, Mike Binder and Irène Jacob picnic in *Londinium* (2001). Later they watch a rock band playing in the bandstand. In *The Deadly Affair* (1967) James Mason and Maximilian Schell dine in the Dell. Eric Portman meets Dulcie Gray by the Achilles statue, they go to the bandstand and he takes her boating to the island in the middle of the Serpentine in *Wanted for Murder* (1946).

Gregory Peck takes Jane Griffiths boating on the Serpentine in *The Million Pound Note* (1954). Peter Finch and Mary Peach also go boating there in *No Love for Johnnie* (1961). Roger Moore trades industrial secrets on the Serpentine in *The Man Who Haunted Himself* (1970).

On a dark Serpentine Road, Michael Caine meets Nigel Green at 'bench T108' in *The Ipcress File* (1965). In the same area Stanley Baxter joins Julie Christie on a bench and kicks a child's ball into the Serpentine in *Crooks Anonymous* (1963). Michael Caine as *Alfie* (1966) chats up a 'bird' while taking 'his sister's baby' out in a pram. Jack May feeds the ducks here in *Night, After Night, After Night* (1969).

The Dell restaurant, seen in *The Deadly Affair* (1967), above, is similar to the one that used to stand on the south-east side of the Serpentine Bridge alongside West Carriage Drive, where, in *Theatre of Blood* (1973), duplicitous Diana Rigg picks up critic Harry Andrews just before a police car arrives to protect him. In *Robbery* (1967) policeman James Booth chats with his snitch. In *Subterfuge* (1969) Gene Barry and Joan Collins dine, watched by husband Tom Adams. In *Madame Sousatzka* (1988) Leigh Lawson takes Navin Chowdhry for lunch before visiting the Royal Albert Hall (SW7). The restaurant is recognizable, with its views of the bridge and its concrete pillars fanning out to the top of a glass roof. All that remains now is the car park to the south.

Doomed US ambassador Robert Arden walks under the Serpentine Bridge and meets a drooling hound of Satan who puts it into his mind that he no longer wants his life in *The Final Conflict* (1981). Alison Elliott takes refuge from the rain in the Serpentine Gallery in *The Wings of the Dove* (1997) and finds Linus Roache and Helena Bonham Carter inside. Hugh Grant presents an art show here in *Bridget Jones: The Edge Of Reason* (2004).

On the south side of the Serpentine, Mariel Hemingway and Mike Binder discuss his play in *Londinium* (2001). Later in the same place Colin Firth bids farewell to Binder, who then meets Kate Magowan, a potential future love. John Malkovich and Andie MacDowell ponder

their future here in ***The Object of Beauty*** (1991). George Segal first meets Glenda Jackson while playing baseball in ***A Touch Of Class*** (1973). Michael York enjoys a muddy football game in ***Success Is the Best Revenge*** (1984).

Michael Coby and John Ratzenberger walk along Rotten Row in ***The Bitch*** (1979). Riding scenes along Rotten Row include Tony Randall's confrontation with James Villiers in ***The Alphabet Murders*** (1965) and Rod Taylor's pay-off to Eric Sykes in ***The Liquidator*** (1965). The chase in ***Stormbreaker*** (2006) begins as Alex Pettyfer joins Sarah Bolger on her grey before galloping through Wellington Arch, Piccadilly and Bank.

W8: Holland Park

The top flat of 48 Lexham Gardens, on the corner of Lexham Walk, is the base for ***The Pleasure Girls*** (1965).

In ***The Squeeze*** (1977) Stacy Keach leaves St Mary Abbots Hospital on the east side of Marloes Road and promptly enters The Devonshire Arms on the corner of Marloes Road and Stratford Road for a sherry with Freddie Starr. The hospital is now flats.

In ***Sunday Bloody Sunday*** (1971) doctor Peter Finch lives and works at 38 Pembroke Square, renumbered 68 for the film.

Michael Caine as ***Alfie*** (1966) visits one of his 'birds' at the dry cleaner's where she works at 32–34 Earl's Court Road.

Linley Sambourne House, 18 Stafford Terrace, favoured by the Merchant-Ivory team for its period interiors, is Hugh Grant's London home in ***Maurice*** (1987) and Daniel Day-Lewis's in ***A Room With a View*** (1986).

Watched by Michael Caine parked outside the library on Phillimore Walk, Anton Rodgers makes a drop at Palms, 3 Campden Hill Road, in ***The Fourth Protocol*** (1987).

East of the Orangery in Holland Park, now the Belvedere Restaurant, is an arcaded causeway with a fountain in front. In ***Every Home Should Have One*** (1970) Marty Feldman considers how to make porridge sexy, and in a fantasy sequence becomes the god Pan dancing with nymphs through the colonnade and in the garden west of the remaining wing of Holland House. In ***Sweeney!*** (1975) John Thaw comes here to meet his grass Joe Melia, who wants him to investigate his girlfriend's death. In ***The Big Sleep*** (1978) Robert Mitchum embraces Sarah Miles in front of the colonnade. In ***Who Dares Wins*** (1982) Lewis Collins bikes to the colonnade to meet wife Rosalind Lloyd, witnessed by Ingrid Pitt.

The Kyoto Garden, opened in 1991, is where Jeremy Irons meets Juliette Binoche in ***Damage*** (1992) just to the north of the Koi pond. Chris Rea and Peter Davison walk over the bridge in front of the garden's waterfall in ***Parting Shots*** (1998) in their third park scene. Their first is to the west of Holland House, which is now a youth hostel.

Michael Crawford teaches at Holland Park School in ***The Knack*** (1965). Crawford, Donal Donnelly and Rita Tushingham steer a bedstead down Aubrey Road to cross Holland Park Avenue towards The Mitre. Gene Barry visits gym mistress Joan Collins at the school in ***Subterfuge*** (1969).

In ***Bullseye!*** (1990) Michael Caine cycles up the western side of Campden Hill Square before losing control of his vehicle. In ***Morgan*** (1966) Vanessa Redgrave lives at 13 Campden Hill Square, on the north-east corner, while divorced husband David Warner camps out in her car outside to the bemusement of local bobby on the beat Bernard Bresslaw. The entrance is just off the square towards Hillsleigh Road.

Christopher Neame lives at 75 Hillgate Place, distinctive for its drive-in alley at the end of the road, close to Farm Place in ***Dracula A.D. 1972*** (1972).

Above:
*Michael Crawford, Donal Donnelly and Rita Tushingham steer the bedstead down Aubrey Road, towards Holland Park Avenue in **The Knack** (1965).*

Jason Flemyng and Anthony Sher leave Il Carretto restaurant, 20 Hillgate Street, in ***Alive And Kicking*** (1996).

Stood up by Ione Skye, Dexter Fletcher waits at the Kensington Place Restaurant, 205 Kensington Church Street, in ***The Rachel Papers*** (1989).

Ioan Gruffud and Alice Lewis walk by 40 Brunswick Gardens, oblivious to Dalmatian thief Tim McInnerny clinging to the first-floor window ledge in ***102 Dalmations*** (2000).

In ***Georgy Girl*** (1966) Lynn Redgrave window-shops on the north side of Kensington High Street. She commits herself to a misguided hairdo opposite 135 Kensington High Street. Later Alan Bates chases her by the Royal Garden Hotel, 2 Kensington High Street. Treacherous Bernard Lee and Margaret Tyzack hand over secrets to William Sylvester at the roof gardens on top of the former Derry & Tom's, 99 Kensington High Street, in ***Ring of Spies*** (1964). In ***23 Paces to Baker Street*** (1956) Cecil Parker follows Patricia Laffan to Barker's, 63 Kensington High Street, opposite Kensington Church Street.

Billie Whitelaw enters Durward House at the corner of Kensington Court Place in ***Make Mine Mink*** (1960).

Laurence Harvey escorts Mia Farrow to her Albert Mews flat in ***A Dandy in Aspic*** (1968).

In ***Lost*** (1955) a nanny crosses from Kensington Gardens to the corner of Palace Gate and enters a chemist, outside which her pram with baby Simon is snatched.

In ***The Big Sleep*** (1978) Robert Mitchum investigates a bookshop run by Joan Collins at 15 Victoria Place, now Parfums De Nicolai. He follows suspicious Derek Deadman along Canning Place to Canning Passage. The chase then cuts to Kynance Mews (SW7). Mitchum returns and later follows a suspicious van by taxi from DeVere Gardens to SW15.

Jeremy Irons and fellow Polish workers move into '5 Onslow Gardens', actually 44 DeVere Gardens, to spruce it up for their boss in ***Moonlighting*** (1982). Irons steals, and eventually returns, a bicycle from outside no. 45. He makes calls to Poland from a phone box next to Canning Passage, and is forced to spend a night in a skip in Canning Place. Director Jerzy Skolinowski returned to the same location for ***Success Is the Best Revenge*** (1984) where it is now home to Michael York and Joanna Szczerbic, with the courtyard at the back featuring as son Michael Lyndon's favoured mode of entry.

In ***The Black Windmill*** (1974) Janet Suzman extracts a lift from her surveillance team to 29 Eldon Road, on the corner of Stanford Road, and evades them by the back garden.

James Purefoy and Kevin McKidd join Simon Callow's self-discovery group in ***Bedrooms and Hallways*** (1998) at the architecturally eye-catching 51–52 Kelso Place.

W14: West Kensington

Trottie True (1948) opens with Jean Kent, followed by James Donald, arriving at 8 Addison Road, known as Peacock (for its green and blue tiling) or Debenham House. Here Mia Farrow takes in Elizabeth Taylor in *Secret Ceremony* (1968). It is also the 'Arabian Embassy' in *Carry on Emmannuelle* (1978), opposite Kenneth Williams's 'French Embassy' at 78 Addison Road. In *The Chain* (1984) Judy Parfitt and John Rowe move out of 78 Addison Road and Billie Whitelaw moves in.

At the corner of Oakwood Court, Gary Oldman and Andrew Schofield vandalize a Rolls Royce and tease a dog in *Sid and Nancy* (1986).

In *Peeping Tom* (1960) Karl Boehm lives at 5 Melbury Road, where Farley Court now stands.

At 12 Holland Park Road, Leighton House Museum houses the Arab Hall where Jonathan Pryce watches Jim Broadbent giving Katharine Helmond a facelift in *Brazil* (1988). Here Nicholas Rowe disappoints Edward Fox and Christopher Plummer by withdrawing his investment in *Nicholas Nickleby* (2003).

Opposite the junction of Russell Road and Kensington High Street is the huge Charles House, offices for the Inland Revenue, where Amanda Donohoe works before becoming a *Castaway* (1987). The offices are also seen in *The Constant Husband* (1955). Despite an aerial establishing shot of Paddington Station (W2), James Fox overhears talk of an available room in the waiting room of Kensington Olympia station in *Performance* (1970). New building has altered the view looking east to the houses on Russell Road.

At the Kensington Olympia exhibition centre on Olympia Way Michael Barrett reports on a 'dog' eating fellow entrants to Crufts Dog Show in *The Magic Christian* (1969). Bryan Forbes introduces Nanette Newman, who parades her horse at Olympia in *International Velvet* (1978).

Jeremy Irons parks his bicycle in Southcombe Street in *Moonlighting* (1982) and operates his shopping scam at Lyons Master Butcher on the corner, since demolished, of Hammersmith Road and Lyons Walk.

At Mornington Avenue Griff Rhys-Jones takes the *Morons from Outer Space* (1985) to a flat overlooking West Cromwell Road, where they are besieged by police and fans.

Estate agent Ewan McGregor moves Robert Carlyle and Jonny Lee Miller into 78a North End Road, on the corner of Talgarth Road, in *Trainspotting* (1996).

Opposite:
The Knack (1965). Michael Crawford and Donal Donnelly push Rita Tushingham on a bedstead (bottom) to the junction of Queensdale Road and Addison Avenue (top).

John Thaw and Dennis Waterman hurry for work to Baron's Court tube on Gliddon Road in **Sweeney!** (1976).

At the south end of Palliser Road is the Queen's Club, where tennis pro Jonathan Rhys Meyers meets Matthew Goode and enters high society in **Match Point** (2005).

Bruce Cook as **Thunderpants** (2002) and Rupert Grint attend Addison Gardens School, with its playground best seen from Bolingbroke Road.

W11: Notting Hill

On the corner of Queensdale Road and Norland Road is the Central Gurdwara, venue for Archie Panjabi's marriage in **Bend It Like Beckham** (2002).

12 Royal Crescent is the musical quintet's lodgings, run by dotty Esma Cannon, in **Raising The Wind** (1961).

Val Kilmer as **The Saint** (1997) plans his next job at the Halcyon Hotel on the west corner of Holland Park Avenue and Holland Park.

Oskar Werner follows Barbara Ferris to her flat in Holland Park in **Interlude** (1968). Meryl Streep moves in to join Charles Dance on the same road in **Plenty** (1985).

In **Corruption** (1967) Peter Cushing and Sue Lloyd attend a party in Holland Park Mews during which a quarrel leads to Lloyd's facial disfigurement. In **Crossplot** (1969) Roger Moore attends an alternative wake there, led by Alexis Kanner.

On the intersection of Addison Avenue and Queensdale Road, Michael Crawford and Donal Donnelly with Rita Tushingham on a bedstead get up to 1960s tomfoolery in **The Knack** (1965). In **National Lampoon's European Vacation** (1985) Chevy Chase drives into a parked car, then Ballard Berkeley's car before

finally cheerful cyclist Eric Idle slides over his bonnet on Addison Avenue in front of St James's Church in St James's Gardens.

To the west is 2 St James's Gardens, Jeremy Irons's house in *The French Lieutenant's Woman* (1981). To the east is no. 54, Phyllida Law's house, where Tom Courtenay as *Otley* (1969) has half a shave after a rough night at Gatwick Airport. Richard E Grant and Imogen Stubbs live at no. 22 in *Jack & Sarah* (1995). Ian McKellen lives outside in the skip they've hired while doing up the house, until Grant invites him in. Pauline Murray accompanies her employer to the Prince of Wales in *It Happened Here* (1964). He promptly gets into a fight, which turns into a near riot out at the back on Pottery Lane.

The exterior of David Hemmings' photography studio in *Blow Up* (1966) is 77 Pottery Lane, next door to the now-closed Earl of Zetland. Opposite, Andy Garcia leaves a christening at St Francis of Assisi Catholic Church in *American Roulette* (1988).

In *The Knack* (1965) Michael Crawford and Rita Tushingham wheel the bedstead around The Portland Arms, once Orsino's and now Cowshed, while Donal Donnelly enters via the Portland Road door and out of the Penzance Place door to join the bedstead with an armful of sandwiches.

Above:
St. James's Gardens, seen in *Jack & Sarah* (1995).

Left:
Donal Donnelly takes a short cut through the Portland Arms (far left) on the junction of Portland Road and Penzance Place (left) in *The Knack* (1965).

Rod Steiger as **Hennessy** (1975) seeks refuge with Lee Remick, visiting her dress shop, now Elanbach, at 96 Portland Road.

Opposite is Julie's Bar, which with Julie's Restaurant is 135–37 Portland Road, seen twice in **American Roulette** (1988), most notably when Al Matthews makes Andy Garcia and Kitty Aldridge an offer. Jonathan Rhys Meyers and Scarlett Johansson go on a secret date to Julie's in **Match Point** (2005).

The brief view from the eponymous pair's flat window in **Withnail & I** (1987) show Markland House and Frimstead House, suggesting that they live where the modern housing of Ansleigh Drive now is.

In **Leo the Last** (1970) Marcello Mastroianni's mansion was at the west end of Testerton Street, intersected by Barandon Street just south of Latimer Road tube. The road was completely redeveloped in the 1970s. On the corner of Silchester Road and Lancaster Road were the Kensington Public Baths, where Mastroianni and Billie Whitelaw enjoy a communal nude therapy session.

During his driving test with James Cossins, Tom Courtenay as **Otley** (1969) reverses onto Grenfell Road from Treadgold Street. He then speeds off down Sirdar Road to avoid villains, but jeopardizes passing his exam.

In **10 Rillington Place** (1971) Richard Attenborough lives in the very street, then a terraced cul-de-sac of ten houses on either side, overlooked by Bartlett's Iron Foundry. The street has been completely redeveloped, was briefly renamed Rustin Close and is now called Bartle Close.

The rear of Lee Remick's shop in Portland Road (see above) appears to lead to Elgin Mews when Rod Steiger as **Hennessy** (1975) leaves by the back, followed by Eric Portman, who suddenly finds himself in Ladbroke Grove.

Richard E Grant is clamped while visiting Barclays Bank at the corner of Lancaster Road and Ladbroke Grove in **Jack & Sarah** (1995). He clings to the clamper's van as it travels south down Ladbroke Grove, turning around at Lansdowne House. Before moving to **Half Moon Street** (1986), Sigourney Weaver makes her way home from the old Ladbroke Grove tube exit between the railway and Westway.

On the corner of Portobello Road and Lancaster Road, near Ladbroke Grove tube station, fans of actors Stephen Baldwin and Sadie Frost turn ugly as they confuse Baldwin with his killer character in **Crimetime** (1996). Brenda Blethyn goes to the Market Bar here to sell her weed in **Saving Grace** (2000).

The Mas Café, now called Manor, at 6–8 All Saints Road, plays 'Clive's Restaurant', for which Gwyneth Paltrow handles the PR in *Sliding Doors* (1998). Under the credits of *The L-Shaped Room* (1962) Leslie Caron passes by All Saints Road and down Clydesdale Road in her search for lodgings. On the corner of All Saints Road and St Luke's Mews, Douglas Henshall quickly loses his cigarette in *If Only* (1998) on the approach of girlfriend Lena Headey. Outside 26 St Luke's Mews, he tries to dissuade her from going to the gym, where he's afraid she'll meet some hunk. Henshall lives close by at 29 Lancaster Road.

Sienna Guillory lives at 16 St Luke's Mews in *Sorted* (2000), where Matthew Rhys and Stephen Marcus slug it out both inside and outside the flat. Opposite is no. 27, the pink mews house of Chiwetel Ejiofor and Keira Knightley in *Love Actually* (2003). On the street Andrew Lincoln, pretending to be a group of carollers, declares his love for Knightley using signs while 'Silent Night' plays on his tape machine. Peter Gallagher drops off Bill Murray to play a rôle in the 'Theatre of Life' at '6 Bishop's Mews W4', actually St Luke's Road in *The Man Who Knew Too Little* (1997). Muggers challenge naïve Murray in St Luke's Mews, but his insouciance scares them off.

Outside 4 St Luke's Road, her temporary home before eviction, Joanna Lumley posts Anna Friel's letter in **Mad Cows** (1999).

In **A Hard Day's Night** (1964) Ringo Starr photographs a milk bottle in a crate outside 4 Lancaster Road. Recognized by fans, he is chased down Lancaster Road and hides in the shop at the corner with All Saints Road. On the corner of St Luke's Road and Tavistock Crescent is the 'Old Mother Black Cap', from where Richard E Grant and Paul McGann have to flee in **Withnail & I** (1987). The pub has been called The Tavistock Arms, Fudrucker's, Baboushka, and is now named after its appearance in the film, the Old Mother Black Cap – an excellent example of capitalizing on cinematic fame. As The Tavistock Arms it appeared in **The L-Shaped Room** (1962), when Tom Bell sees Leslie Caron chat to Mark Eden on the opposite corner outside Fred's Café, 38 Tavistock Crescent, on a corner now rebuilt. In **Virtual Sexuality** (1999) Laura Fraser is on a date at the pub during its time as Baboushka. It is also seen as Chiwetel Ejiofor leaves on his bike after visiting Emilia Fox in **Three Blind Mice** (2002).

Between the railway lines under Westway, captured by a shot from Trellick Tower, is the squatters' camp where Roland Gift takes Frances Barber in *Sammy and Rosie Get Laid* (1987). Shashi Kapoor also visits Gift there, followed by Claire Bloom, to witness the camp's destruction by developers.

Freddie Starr waits for Stacy Keach to buy some booze at an off-licence, 223 Westbourne Park Road, on the corner of Powis Terrace, in *The Squeeze* (1977). Here too after wife Imogen Stubbs's death in *Jack & Sarah* (1995) Richard E Grant consoles himself by stopping at the same shop.

25 Powis Square is the exterior of Mick Jagger's house in *Performance* (1970). At the end, James Fox is escorted to a Rolls parked in Colville Terrace and driven off towards Ledbury Road. Fox returns to Powis Square in *Runners* (1983), playing on the slide in a new playground in the square. Seeing his runaway daughter, he chases her past the corner of Ledbury Road and Talbot Road.

Jennifer Ehle with James Purefoy run Coin's Café, 105–107 Talbot Road, in *Bedrooms and Hallways* (1998). The café was later called Cashbar, and is now Raoul's.

Scarlett Johansson leaves her work at Paul and Joe's, 39–41 Ledbury Road, and catches a taxi on the corner of Westbourne Grove in *Match Point* (2005). Hugh Grant has his hair cut at Guy Parsons, 243 Westbourne Grove, in *About a Boy* (2002). It was then called Parsons Skott. Yul Brynner follows Charles Gray to the Portobello Antique Supermarket, 282 Westbourne Grove, now B Lipka & Son Antique Gallery, in *File of the Golden Goose* (1969). Jennifer Love Hewitt and Paul Nicholls live in Westbourne House, 122 Kensington Park Road, on the corner of Westbourne Grove in *If Only* (2004). Hewitt is splashed by a coke outside the Wine Factory on Westbourne Grove.

Yul Brynner follows Charles Gray to his house at 47 Kensington Park Road at the west end of Chepstow Villas in *File of the Golden Goose* (1969). St Peter's Church on Kensington Park Road, framed by Stanley Gardens, is seen in *Notting Hill* (1999) during the rush to the press conference; in *Spice World* (1997); to establish Tom Hollander's flat in *Martha, Meet Frank, Daniel and Laurence* (1998); and to show Steven Mackintosh's house in *The Mother* (2003).

In *Afraid of the Dark* (1991) 'Eyesight Opticians', run by Robert Stephens, is 13 Needham Road, next to the Cork and Bottle.

Dick Emery and Pat Coombs live at 9 Stanley Crescent in *Ooh…You Are Awful* (1972). At 11 Stanley Crescent Navin Chowdhry attends piano lessons with Shirley MacLaine as

Madame Sousatzka (1988). MacLaine's neighbour Geoffrey Bayldon is beaten up in the alleyway just to the north of St Peter's Church.

Michael Caine lives off Portobello Market at 18 Denbigh Close, next to the colourful junkshop Alice's, in **The Italian Job** (1969). Under the titles of **Otley** (1969) Tom Courtenay walks past Denbigh Close, then Denbigh Terrace, passing the old Heneky's, now The Earl of Lonsdale, at the junction of Portobello Road and Westbourne Grove. He is evicted from his digs at 'Trad', 67 Portobello Road, now Cheshire Galleries. Phyllida Law's shop is at no. 83. Justin Chadwick and Steven Mackintosh squat at 50 Chepstow Villas near the corner of Portobello Road in **London Kills Me** (1991). Round the corner, as he passes 85–93 Portobello Road, Mackintosh spreads the word to cyclist Naveen Andrews, and the gang move in for a short-lived stay. Gong, 142 Portobello Road, formerly Nicholls Antique Arcade on the corner of an entrance to Colville Primary School, is Hugh Grant's travel bookshop visited by Julia Roberts in **Notting Hill** (1999). The area between Elgin Crescent and Blenheim Crescent is seen in the opening titles and during the Four Seasons sequence. Rhys Ifans and Joseph Fiennes walk down Portobello Road in **Rancid Aluminium** (2000) turning to their car parked on Colville Terrace.

Stephen Baldwin and Sadie Frost exit the Ground Floor Bar on the corner of Talbot Road and Portobello Road with Philip Davis in **Crimetime** (1996), and enjoy some vigorous sex in the doorway next to the Electric Cinema. In **Virtual Sexuality** (1999) Luke de Lacey tries to talk Laura Fraser out of fancying Rupert Penry-Jones as they pass the cinema. He is left alone outside the Salvation Army. After an evening at the Electric, Lee Gregory and Summer Phoenix as **Suzie Gold** (2004) return to their car parked in Elgin Crescent. The Ground Floor Bar is where the squatters meet in **London Kills Me** (1991). Here Marianne Jean-Baptiste collects Justin Chadwick, and they pass the Electric. On Talbot Road German tourist Sean Pertwee, to whom Chadwick 'rents' a room in his squat, utters the film's title.

Rufus Sewell and Joseph Fiennes walk into Mike's café, now simply M's, at 12 Blenheim Crescent, in **Martha, Meet Frank, Daniel and Laurence** (1998).

Jean-Pierre Leaud lives in a flat at 227 Portobello Road, overlooking the intersection of Portobello Road and Westbourne Park Road, in **I Hired a Contract Killer** (1990). Opposite is The Warwick Castle, now called The Castle, where he meets flower seller Margi Clarke. Killer Kenneth Colley watches Clarke entering Leaud's flat through the door on Westbourne Park Road right next to the famous 'blue door'.

In **Notting Hill** (1999) Hugh Grant lives at 280 Westbourne Park Road, famed for its blue door and columns, outside which Rhys Ifans poses in his underpants. Across Portobello, Grant spills orange juice over Julia Roberts in front of Coffee Republic after collecting it from Café Lavazza, round the east corner on Westbourne Park Road.

Grant and Roberts go to Tim McInnerny and Gina McKee's dinner party at 91 Lansdowne Road. They climb the gate ('Whoops-a-daisies') leading into Rosmead Gardens from Rosmead Road.

In **The Final Conflict** (1981), after a rather long walk from the canal in Maida Vale (W2), a mother lets slip her pram at the corner of St John's Gardens, renamed St John's Hill, and it trundles west down the hill to be knocked over by a taxi in Lansdowne Road. Tom Courtenay has to perform a hill-start for his driving test here in **Otley** (1969). Hugh Moxey lives at 2 St John's Gardens in **Hennessy** (1975). Rod Steiger enters to take his place, and outside Richard Johnson and Peter Egan ambush Eric Portman, leading to Egan clinging to Portman's car, which shakes him off at the bottom of the hill. St John's Church is the exterior of 'St Stephen's, Westminster' in **Seven Days to Noon** (1950). Barry Jones runs out of the south door and gets shot by a nervous Victor Maddern. Harry H Corbett, somewhat odoriferous after searching for the wedding ring in a pile of rotting hay, enters the north door to marry Carolyn Seymour in **Steptoe and Son** (1972).

Above:
Victor Maddern guns down Barry Jones (above left) at St John's Church, St John's Gardens (above right), in **Seven Days to Noon** (1950).

Jack Nicholson hovers at 4 Lansdowne Crescent before deciding to adopt another identity in **The Passenger** (1975).

The police station in **A Hard Day's Night** (1964) stood at 83 Clarendon Road, but has now been replaced by housing.

At Notting Hill Gate tube James Villiers passes a briefcase across an escalator to Tom Courtenay as **Otley** (1969), who then hands it over to Leonard Rossiter on the platform. In **Morgan** (1966) David Warner makes gorilla noises to the ticket collector at the barrier.

As **Alfie** (1966) Michael Caine addresses the camera on Notting Hill Gate in front of Ivy House and Campton Hill Towers, where Shelley Winters lives.

W10: Notting Hill, North Kensington

Notting Hill

The car chase in **The Blue Lamp** (1950) passes The Bramley Arms at the junction of Freston Road – then known as Latimer Road – and Bramley Road. In **The Lavender Hill Mob** (1951) two police cars tear round the crescent and crash outside the pub, narrowly missing the water trough in front.

Marcello Mastroianni as **Leo the Last** (1970) picks up Glenna Forster-Jones inside The Bramley Arms and decides to 'save' her. In **The Squeeze** (1977) Stephen Boyd and David Hemmings, brandishing shotguns, order Edward Fox out of a security van under the railway bridge in Freston Road. Their getaway van heads down Freston Road but stops in front of The Bramley Arms because Stacy Keach is holding a gun to Boyd's daughter in the middle of the road.

In **Quadrophenia** (1979) mod Gary Shail's bike breaks down outside a junkyard opposite the pub, and he receives a kicking from some passing rockers while his girlfriend watches helplessly. Later Phil Daniels asks Garry Cooper for some pills at the junkyard, which offices have only recently replaced. In **Betrayal** (1983) Jeremy Irons crosses Freston Road to The Bramley Arms to meet Patricia Hodge within. **Withnail & I** (1987) leave for the country in their Jaguar parked on Bard Road, as it is being demolished, and turn up Freston Road, actually a dead end.

In **Sid And Nancy** (1986) the Sex Pistols are having a drink and throwing darts at each other inside The Bramley Arms, here renamed 'The Old Mason'. Chloe Webb, upset over an unreturned loan, storms out followed by Gary Oldman, as she turns up Freston Road towards the railway bridge. Further up Freston Road opposite the Harrow Club, James Purefoy and Kevin McKidd exchange phone numbers in **Bedrooms and Hallways** (1998).

Chris Rea eludes his police shadow at Latimer Road tube on Bramley Road in **Parting Shots** (1998). Andy Garcia paces up and down the platform awaiting Kitty Aldridge in **American Roulette** (1988). The car chase in **Otley** (1969) passes under the bridge just outside the station.

Under the Westway roundabout a rock concert with **Breaking Glass** (1980) performing turns into a riot; Hazel O'Connor witnesses a stabbing, which leads to her breakdown.

Police Milo O'Shea and Eric Sykes chase a taxi-driving wino in the same area close to Darfield Way in **Theatre of Blood** (1973). Christina World as **The Golden Lady** (1978) and June Chadwick, chased by car to this spot, overcome their aggressors. Freddie Starr rescues Stacey Keach from fellow drinking dossers here in **The Squeeze** (1977).

North Kensington

The Westway Sports Centre has now filled in the clear area. Daniel Auteuil plays football on the Crowthorne Road pitch in **The Lost Son** (1999). Laura Fraser and her chums admire the sporty Kieran O'Brian and write off anorak Luke de Lacey in **Virtual Sexuality** (1999).

Jane Asher looks over the railway lines and the buildings on Barlby Road from the bridge on Ladbroke Grove in **Runners** (1983), wondering where her runaway son might be.

Charlotte Rampling gives birth at St Charles' Hospital, between St Mark's Road and Exmoor Street, in **Georgy Girl** (1966). After his visit, Alan Bates finds Lynn Redgrave waiting for him at the Exmoor Street entrance to the hospital.

Harry H Corbett and Wilfrid Brambell live at '26a Oil Drum Lane' in a junkyard, now gone, on the east side of tiny Adela Street, off Kensal Road, in **Steptoe and Son** (1972) and **Steptoe and Son Ride Again** (1973).

In **Intimacy** (2000) Mark Rylance follows Kerry Fox to The Earl of Derby, 50 Bosworth Road, on the corner with Southern Row, where he befriends her husband Timothy Spall at the pool table while she acts in a downstairs theatre.

The Ernö Goldfinger-designed Trellick Tower, a key landmark in this area on the corner of Golborne Road and Statham Road, features in **For Queen and Country** (1988), providing the graffiti-scrawled football pitch on which policeman Brian McDermott joins a game while Denzel Washington spectates.

Under the credits of **London Kills Me** (1991) Justin Chadwick walks over Portobello Bridge and is joined by Emer McCourt, Steven Mackintosh and Tony Haygarth at the corner of Golborne Road and Bevington Road. The card shop Portfolio on this corner is Brad Dourif's restaurant where Chadwick aspires to work. This shop is Richard McCabe's restaurant in **Notting Hill** (1999). Outside, Hugh Grant, Emma Chambers, Hugh Bonneville, Tim McInnerny, Rhys Ifans and Gina McKee pile into a car to stop Julia Roberts flying home. Opposite here Brenda Blethyn's taxi drops her off in **Saving Grace** (2000). In **Love Actually** (2003) Kris Marshall bids pal Abdul Sario goodbye in the flat above Lisboa Delicatessen, 54 Golborne Road.

Laura Fraser, Marcelle Duprey and Natasha Bell pass Kieran O'Brian and Luke de Lacey on the bridge in **Virtual Sexuality** (1999). Rupert Penry-Jones receives intructions on windscreen washing on Golborne Road and he is knocked over by a van outside The Carnavon Castle. Off Wornington Road is the basketball court where Bell notices Penry-Jones's attractions.

In **The Squeeze** (1977) Stacy Keach finds refuge in The Bevington Arms, no longer a pub, down Bevington Road near Blagrove Road, while Freddie Starr investigates a car they've been following. The gang they seek is – though they don't realize it – just round the corner in Acklam Road, now redeveloped, where Stephen Boyd and David Hemmings hold Carol White and daughter captive, overlooking Westway.

In **The Man Who Knew Too Little** (1997) Bill Murray receives the wrong set of instructions from a phone box opposite 307 Portobello Road, near Golborne Road, while Peter Gallagher looks on.

W9: West Kilburn, Maida Vale

West Kilburn

On Bravington Road near the corner of Mozart Street a police shooting starts a riot in **Sammy and Rosie Get Laid** (1987). Shashi Kapoor arrives from India somewhat bemused by the scenes. This corner has since been rebuilt.

Diana Quick bails Brenda Blethyn from the police station at 325 Harrow Road in **Saving Grace** (2000). In **The Blue Lamp** (1950) Dirk Bogarde shoots Jack Warner at the Coliseum cinema, 324 Harrow Road, now rebuilt as the Paddington Churches Housing Association.

Daniel Craig and Kelly MacDonald walk along the towpath by the Grand Union Canal, overshadowed by the northern curve of the Westway, in **Some Voices** (2001).

Maida Vale (see also page 48)

Peter Coyote searches for old pal Mel Smith at 22 Formosa Street in **Slayground** (1983), filmed mostly in New York State and Blackpool. After a darts match at the Prince Alfred on the corner of Formosa Street and Castellain Road, John Goodman as **King Ralph** (1991) and Rudolph Walker throw spears in an empty lot across the road while Peter O'Toole and Richard Griffith look on. The empty lot is now 1 Warrington Gardens, a block of flats. Jared Harris first sights Aria Argento as **B. Monkey** (1996) inside the same pub. Outside, Jonathan Rhys Meyers damages Rupert Everett's car. In **The End of the Affair** (1999) Ralph Fiennes chats inside with Ian Hart and later with Stephen Rea. Paul Nichols drinks and plays snooker with his buddies here in **If Only** (2004).

In **The Final Conflict** (1981) Rossano Brazzi, followed by Lisa Harrow's son, ascends the stairs out of Warwick Avenue tube on his way to see Don Gordon's wife. Rita Tushingham tries to negotiate the pedestrian crossing on the corner of Warwick Avenue and Clifton Villas in **The Knack** (1965). Christopher Walken lives at Clifton House, 12 Clifton Villas, in **A Business Affair** (1994). When Jonathan Pryce loses his wife Carole Bouquet to Walken, he tries to climb over the gate until the police stop him.

In **Bunny Lake Is Missing** (1965) Clive Revill meets Laurence Olivier and Carol Lynley for a drink at the Warrington Hotel, 93 Warrington Crescent, at the corner of Randolph Avenue, before Keir Dullea intercedes.

The basement of 221 Elgin Avenue near Maida Vale tube is Michael Caine's flat in **The Black Windmill** (1974). Here John Vernon and Delphine Seyrig plant evidence to incriminate Caine.

James Fox chases after daughter Kate Hardie all the way from Powis Square (W11) to Maida Vale tube in **Runners** (1983). They have an awkward conversation on the stairs just inside the station. Julianne Moore descends the same staircase in **The End of the Affair** (1999). In **If Only** (1998) at the tube Lena Headey reads a copy of the *Evening Standard* announcing her ex-boyfriend's nuptials. In **Man About the House** (1974) Richard O'Sullivan and Doug Fisher drop off Paula Wilcox at the station.

Hugh Grant takes his girlfriends to Otto's Dining Lounge – and dumps them there – on the corner of Sutherland Avenue and Maida Vale in **About a Boy** (2002).

Further south, Rachel Weisz invites Ralph Fiennes into her house at 22 Clarendon Gardens in *The Constant Gardener* (2005).

In *Blue Ice* (1992) Ian Holm lives at 41 Blomfield Road. When Jack Shepherd goes there for help they walk to the footbridge alongside Westbourne Terrace Road bridge, where Holm stabs him and allows his body to fall into the canal. In *Interlude* (1968) Virginia Maskell and her children enjoy a canal cruise underneath this bridge. Lena Headey and Douglas Henshall, the latter in a fitness drive to impress the former, go jogging over the Warwick Avenue Bridge in *If Only* (1998).

Little Venice, with a well-placed canal boat renamed in Dutch, stands in for Amsterdam in *11 Harrowhouse* (1974) when Charles Grodin and Candice Bergen visit diamond cutter Cyril Shaps at 31 Blomfield Road. Paul McCartney parks in Blomfield Road near Maida Vale in *Give My Regards to Broad Street* (1984). Jamie Lee Curtis and Kevin Kline watch from their car in Blomfield Road Thomas Georgeson's arrest in Maida Avenue (W2) in *A Fish Called Wanda* (1989). Here in *Georgy Girl* (1966) Charlotte Rampling asks Lynn Redgrave to stay after she marries Alan Bates.

Below:
Blomfield Road (below left). Charles Grodin and Candice Bergen leave a diamond cutter's house, supposedly in 'Amsterdam' (below right) in ***11 Harrowhouse*** (1974).

W12: Shepherd's Bush

In *Moonlighting* (1982) Jeremy Irons and his crew attend St Andrew Bobola's Roman Catholic Polish Church on Leysfield Road, near the junction of Askew Road and Goldhawk Road.

In *Quadrophenia* (1979) Phil Daniels drives his moped, with Leslie Ash riding pillion, past Goldhawk Road tube. Rocker Ray Winstone is beaten up at Shepherd's Bush Market by a gang of Mods driving up from Wells Road and across Goldhawk Road. Anne Reid as *The Mother* (2003) and Peter Vaughan stand outside the tube on Wells Road, a little lost.

In *Some Voices* (2001) Kelly MacDonald throws Peter McDonald out of her flat above Toni's Textiles at 51 Goldhawk Road. After Daniel Craig moves in, he constructs a spiral made out of rubbish outside The Bushranger pub, on the corner of Wells Road and Goldhawk Road.

In *Sid and Nancy* (1986) Gary Oldman and Andrew Schofield approach from Rockwood Place – passing a gang of girls with hockey sticks merrily vandalizing cars – to visit a friend living in Pennard Road.

Michael Caine emerges from Shepherd's Bush tube (the Central Line exit) and takes the now demolished footbridge leading over Uxbridge Road to the Concord Centre, now called simply W12, to evade his tail in *The Black Windmill* (1974). In *The Mother* (2003) Peter Vaughan feels the pace of London life on the north side of Shepherd's Bush Common outside C J Jones, 124 Uxbridge Road, as he walks with Anne Reid and Steven Mackintosh. Later Reid finds herself lost a little further west. 307 Uxbridge Road is Pete's, David Morrissey's restaurant, in *Some Voices* (2001). A deliberate shot of a photograph inside betrays its real name, the Harp Café. Amanda Redman works at The Princess Victoria, 217 Uxbridge Road, the second pub Tony Slattery, Adrian Dunbar, James Purefoy and Neil Stuke visit in their stag night in *The Wedding Tackle* (1999).

Michael Caine lives at 9 Stanlake Villas on the corner of Stanlake Road in *The Ipcress File* (1965).

Rex Harrison is released from Her Majesty's Prison Wormwood Scrubs to a crowd of his admiring wives in *The Constant Husband* (1955). To avoid them the warden lets him out the side entrance between the prison and Hammersmith Workhouse, no longer there, where Margaret Leighton picks him up. Claire Bloom meets Richard Burton on his release in *The Spy Who Came in From the Cold* (1965) while Michael Hordern watches from across Du

Cane Road. Charlotte Rampling collects Dudley Sutton, Kenneth Griffith and James Beckett in **Rotten to the Core** (1965). James Robertson Justice picks up Leslie Phillips doing his rounds at the prison in **Doctor in Clover** (1966). David Warner as **Morgan** (1966) spends a brief spell inside. Peter Ustinov is released in **Hot Millions** (1968). Michael Caine is picked up in Du Cane Road in a stolen car in **The Italian Job** (1969). Caine is released again in **Bullseye!** (1990), unsuccessfully boarding a bus. A shot in **Frenzy** (1972) establishes Jon Finch's place of internment. In **Sweeney 2** (1978) John Thaw, driven by Michael J Jackson, visits the prison to interview his old guv'nor, Denholm Elliott. Oliver Tobias picks up Richard Jordan in **A Nightingale Sang in Berkeley Square** (1979). Newlyweds Chris Rea and Felicity Kendal visit Oliver Reed in **Parting Shots** (1998). Bill Nighy is imprisoned here in **I Capture the Castle** (2002).

Above:
Stanlake Villas (above left). In **The Ipcress File** (1965), Michael Caine approaches Stanlake Villas on Stanlake Road (top right) and enters no.9 (bottom right).

Left:
Digby Mansions
overlooks
Hammersmith
Bridge in *The Man
Who Never Was*
(1956), *Repulsion*
(1965) and *Theatre
of Blood* (1973).

Denzel Washington is dropped off at the approach to Wood Lane from Westway in *For Queen and Country* (1988).

Bernard Lee and Jimmy Hanley chase Dirk Bogarde into White City Stadium in *The Blue Lamp* (1950). In *Crooks in Cloisters* (1963) Bernard Cribbins bets on the dogs. Peter Noone's greyhound wins in *Mrs Brown, You've Got a Lovely Daughter* (1967). In *The Games* (1969) Charles Aznavour just beats Michael Crawford in a pre-Olympic warm-up race. In *Steptoe and Son Ride Again* (1973) Wilfred Brambell and Harry H Corbett watch their greyhound Hercules II fail to chase the hare in practice. The stadium has now been converted into BBC offices.

W6: Hammersmith

Bill Travers and Virginia McKenna mistake 'Slouborough's Grand Cinema', actually London's Hammersmith Apollo between Queen Caroline Street and Fulham Palace Road, as the one they've inherited in *The Smallest Show On Earth* (1957).

Anthony Hopkins as *The Good Father* (1985) lives in College Court on Sussex Place, immediately south of, and with a view of, the roaring traffic of the Hammersmith Flyover.

Chelsea supporters catch a coach for an away game in Liverpool in *The Football Factory* (2003). Ray Winstone hitches a ride to Torbay on the corner of Hammersmith Bridge Road and Great West Way in *That Summer* (1979).

Cosh Boy (1952) opens with a mugging by James Kenney and Ian Whittaker close to the river near Queen Caroline Street.

Gloria Grahame and Josephine Griffin share a flat, '44 River Court', in Digby Mansions in ***The Man Who Never Was*** (1956). William Russell embraces Grahame outside the entrance to 39–48. Clifton Webb and Robert Flemyng follow spy Stephen Boyd from here over Hammersmith Bridge. Catherine Deneuve walks over the bridge in ***Repulsion*** (1965), heading north and going mad. Later she passes Digby Mansions, oblivious of a car crash's aftermath. Michael Hordern's flat in Digby Mansions overlooks the bridge in ***Theatre of Blood*** (1973).

Glenda Jackson drives south across Hammersmith Bridge to drop off her pets in ***A Touch of Class*** (1973). To buy a Dior dress, Angela Lansbury saves bus money by walking across the bridge in ***Mrs 'Arris Goes to Paris*** (1992). In ***Night and the City*** (1950) Mike Mazurki dumps Richard Widmark into the Thames while Herbert Lom looks on from the bridge. In ***Martha, Meet Frank, Daniel and Laurence*** (1998) Joseph Fiennes and Monica Potter quarrel as they cross the west side of the bridge before sitting down to admire the sunset. Daniel Craig has a brief funny turn on the bridge in ***Some Voices*** (2001).

In ***Sliding Doors*** (1998) the dark-haired Gwyneth Paltrow, with Zara Turner, passes by The Blue Anchor on Lower Mall, where the blonde Paltrow is inside. When Jeanne Tripplehorn and John Lynch pass by, he notices Paltrow inside and Tripplehorn storms off.

Opposite Mall Road Peter Bowles and Dinsdale Landen emerge soaking wet from the Thames after plunging into the river in a van in SE16 in ***The Steal*** (1994). Here Heathcote Williams collects them. Laurence Harvey ponders his future in ***Life at the Top*** (1965).

In ***Emergency Call*** (1952) Jack Warner and Anthony Steel chase Geoffrey Hibbert along Lower Mall and under Hammersmith Bridge. On her way home (in SW7) from the pub (in NW3) Beryl Reid walks along Lower Mall in ***The Killing of Sister George*** (1968).

Richard Widmark seeks refuge at Maureen Delaney's houseboat in ***Night and the City*** (1950). When Gene Tierney visits, Widmark pushes her against The Blue Anchor before his capture outside Digby Mansions.

Dirk Bogarde and Sylvia Syms discuss his blackmail in ***Victim*** (1961) by the pier of Furnival Gardens. Near the end of ***The Steal*** (1994) Helen Slater and Alfred Molina in a rubber dinghy enter a storm outlet that runs underneath Furnival Gardens to steal money from offices. Quite a row, since the offices are in EC3! They check that their money transfer has gone through on the Thames by Upper Mall just east of Rivercourt Road.

Daniel Craig and Anne Reid enjoy a lunchtime drink on the promontory close to The Old Ship, 25 Upper Mall, in **The Mother** (2003). They return later with Cathryn Bradshaw and Oliver Ford Davies to the same spot.

In **Nobody Runs Forever** (1968) Lilli Palmer takes a lethal clock to Daliah Lavi at 28 St Peter's Square, on the west side. Christopher Plummer, Rod Taylor and Camilla Sparv arrive too late to save them. His search for his donor leads Hywel Bennett to Cyd Hayman at 35 St Peter's Square in **Percy** (1971). He moves in, but she temporarily dumps him next to the statue in the middle of the square. In **The Naked Truth** (1957) a long line of scouts crosses a zebra crossing on the south side of the square, holding up a police car.

The Pumpkin Eater (1964) opens with Anne Bancroft forlornly looking out of the window at 7 St Peter's Square, on the east side, where she lives with her husband Peter Finch and her large brood of children. James Bolam tries to persuade Melissa Stribling to invest in art at no. 6 in **Crucible of Terror** (1971). **Betrayal** (1983) opens with Patricia Hodge and Ben

Kingsley seeing off dinner guests from their home at 10 St Peter's Square.

In *Percy* (1971) the school where Hywel Bennett chases up a false alarm early in his search for his donor is St Peter's, on St Peter's Road between Black Prince Lane and St Peter's Grove.

Bruce Cook lives on an upper floor and Rupert Grint at 124 Flora Gardens on the ground floor, just off Dalling Road, in *Thunderpants* (2002).

James Kenney lives in the basement of 40 Leamore Street in *Cosh Boy* (1952). The eastern side of the street has since been demolished and the bridge rebuilt.

Jeremy Irons takes fellow Polish workers to buy watches at Terry's Jewellers next to Dixon's in King's Mall off King Street in *Moonlighting* (1982). At the end they wheel their luggage trolleys on the way to Heathrow.

In *The Knack* (1965) Michael Crawford and Ray Brooks welcome Donal Donnelly as a new lodger at 1 Melrose Terrace, and Rita Tushingham helps Crawford and Donnelly push a bedstead down Melrose Gardens towards the house, renumbered 37.

When St Paul's Junior School, known as Colet Court, moved across the river from 100 Hammersmith Road, filming moved in to the vacated premises. The galleried hall in *Melody* (1971) is the school's assembly hall. Malcolm McDowell attends an audition here before Lindsay Anderson in *O Lucky Man!* (1973) and Colin Welland's office here is bombed in *Sweeney!* (1976).

W4: Strand on the Green, Acton Green, Turnham Green, Chiswick

Strand on the Green

Peter O'Toole visits Petula Clark at 59 Strand on the Green, quoted as '223 River Walk, Chiswick', in *Goodbye Mr Chips* (1969). He meets Siân Phillips on the steps and takes Clark for a walk along the Strand. The Beatles visit the City Barge, 27 Strand on the Green, in *Help!* (1965).

Underneath the bridge is the Strand on the Green boating club, where Michael Caine knocks out a couple of policemen in *The Jigsaw Man* (1984). Caine and Laurence Olivier chat as they pass the Bull's Head. Further to the east is the alleyway where Caine is shot from a van parked on Thames Road. Olivier lives at 1 Strand on the Green.

On the east side of the bridge, Dirk Bogarde and Julie Christie frolic by the river while the tide is out in *Darling* (1965). They then peer into cottages dreaming of doing them up. The Chef & Brewer chain beat them to it by buying up and extending the Bull's Head. Denise van Outen appears here briefly in *Are You Ready for Love?* (2006).

Acton Green

Richard Burton emerges on the railway footpath from Acton (W3) onto Kingswood Road in *Villain* (1970).

Turnham Green

At Turnham Green, bisected by Town Hall Avenue alongside Christ Church, Rod Steiger as *Hennessy* (1975) dumps his car containing Patrick Stewart's body, bins his gun on the corner of Heathfield Terrace and crosses the road to catch a taxi outside Chiswick Town Hall. Alan Shearman as *Bullshot* (1983) arrives at the Town Hall, which is the 'Institute of Scientific Discoveries'. Michael Caine visits Sigourney Weaver, who works here – though this time it is the 'Arab-Anglo Institute' – in *Half Moon Street* (1986).

In *Nuns on the Run* (1990) Eric Idle and Robbie Coltrane steal from the Triads in Woodstock Road, where a car blows up. After the robbery they duck behind a car on Priory Avenue and then escape into St Michael and All Angels, which is playing a convent. Camille Coduri is shot in the arm on the corner of Woodstock Road and Priory Avenue before being seized by the Triads.

Chiswick

Anne Reid as *The Mother* (2003) and Daniel Craig visit the tranquil grounds of St Nicholas's Church on Church Street close to the river to admire the William Hogarth memorial there.

Emma Thompson and Helena Bonham Carter attend a party at Strawberry House, Chiswick Mall, opposite the east end of Eyot Green, in *Howards End* (1992). They meet Anthony Hopkins outside, who gives them some bad advice about the firm Porphyrion to pass on. In *The Golden Bowl* (2000) Jeremy Northam visits James Fox and Anjelica Houston, who live there. Dirk Bogarde and Sylvia Syms live next door at Morton House in *Victim* (1961). For a scene overlooking the Thames, which appears to be just across the road from the front door, a view further east in W6 is used to capture Hammersmith Bridge.

James Fox and Wendy Craig visit his parents Richard Vernon and Catherine Lacey at Chiswick House in *The Servant* (1963). Eddie Izzard oversees a photo session of Jonathan Rhys Meyers in front of the northern façade of Chiswick House in *Velvet Goldmine* (1998).

Above:
Chiswick park provides the background for Jonathan Rhys Meyers' photo session in *Velvet Goldmine* (1998).

W3: Acton

In *Hue and Cry* (1946) near Acton Town tube the gang pile off the bus travelling along Gunnersbury Lane.

Richard Burton parks a stolen Zodiac at the end of Ramsay Road in *Villain* (1970) and crosses a footbridge over the railway towards Fletcher Road (W4).

Above and opposite:
Jonathan Rhys
Meyers poses for a
photo session
(above) among the
statues in Chiswick
park (opposite) in
Velvet Goldmine
(1998).

W5: Ealing

Raw police recruits Kenneth Williams, Leslie Phillips and Kenneth O'Connor stroll along St Mary's Road to their new posting in *Carry On Constable* (1960).

Heather Graham is crossing the small area of grass between Mattock Lane and Ealing Green in *Killing Me Softly* (2002) when she receives a mobile call from John Hughes. She ponders her guilt on a bench facing Pitshanger House in Walpole Park. This is Colin Firth's manor house in *The Importance of Being Earnest* (2002).

When Lionel Jeffries tries to arrest the Australian gang in *The Wrong Arm of the Law* (1962), he goes through an entrance signposted 32–50 Haven Green Court, opposite Ealing Broadway tube. However, the gang – Bill Kerr, Ed Devereux and Reg Lye – makes good its escape. In *Doctor in Distress* (1963) Dirk Bogarde drives Samantha Eggar back home to flat 23b Haven Green Court after her hospital treatment.

John Goodman applies for permission to demolish the house of *The Borrowers* (1997) at Ealing Town Hall on the corner of New Broadway and Longfield Avenue.

Longfield House, 18–20 Uxbridge Road, contains the flats of both Joseph Fiennes and Ray Winstone, to whom the former confides in *Martha, Meet Frank, Daniel and Laurence* (1998).

W13: West Ealing

Jason Statham's wrecked amusement arcade in *Snatch* (2000) is Jesters, since renamed Reels, at 127 Broadway just east of Coldershaw Road.

In *Carry On Constable* (1960) Leslie Philips's beat takes him down The Avenue to Drayton Green Road next to West Ealing station, while Kenneth Williams's is along Manor Road just to the west.

south-west london

Stretching from Chelsea and Fulham and across the Thames to Wimbledon, filmmakers have been using this area for 100 years for St James's clubland, government buildings at Whitehall and smart Knightsbridge mews.

SW1 (north of Victoria Street): St James's, Westminster

St James's

At 170 Victoria Street is the American Steak House, next to the Scotch Steak House at 168, in turn next to the Angus Steak House, which is next to the American Pancake House. In *The Accidental Tourist* (1988) William Hurt parades from west to east in pursuit of Baltimore home cooking, settling for pancakes. The steak houses remain but the pancake house has gone.

In *Howards End* (1992) Victoria Square, now surrounded by railings, is 'Wickham Place'. Emma Thompson and Helena Bonham Carter live at no. 6. Samuel West follows his umbrella there in the rain and much later his wife Nicola Duffett seeks him there. Vanessa Redgrave, Anthony Hopkins and James Wilby supposedly live opposite the back of Victoria Square, so in an establishing shot taken from Lower Grosvenor Place a matte effect produces a vast block of flats. The real flat however is not far away in St James's Court (see below). At the corner of Victoria Square and Lower Grosvenor Place, Cantinflas parks his penny farthing bicycle by an old-fashioned postbox to look for a job at an employment agency in *Around the World in Eighty Days* (1956) after circling a nanny in Victoria Square.

On the corner of Allington Street opposite The Stag Tavern is the café, now called Moca, where Julie Walters works in *Personal Services* (1986), sharing scenes with Shirley Stelfox and Danny Schiller. Walters studies the double-meaning advertisements in the newsagent's window next door.

The Victoria Palace is the venue for 'The Dixie Collins Show' in *Expresso Bongo* (1959). At the stage door on Allington Street Cliff Richard sees off Laurence Harvey in a taxi and waits for Yolande Danlon.

Ooh…You Are Awful (1972) opens with Dick Emery as 'Miss' exiting the Queen's Gallery at Buckingham Gate and then being accosted on Spur Road. Ronald Fraser and Emery later leave the gallery in haste after a scam, running from Buckingham Gate to Stafford Place.

In *The Long Good Friday* (1980) Bob Hoskins finds a bomb at his 'Mayfair' club, actually at 15 Catherine Place.

The gatehouse of Westminster City School in Palace Street is the China Missionary Society, where Ingrid Bergman applies for a posting in *The Inn of the Sixth Happiness* (1958). In *Victim* (1961) Peter McEnery flees from his construction work opposite the school. Much of this block only lasted some forty years before being rebuilt in 2004.

The exterior of Anthony Hopkins's flat in *Howards End* (1992) is 51 St James's Court off Buckingham Gate, opposite Vandon Street. St James's Hotel on Buckingham Gate establishes John Malkovich and Andie MacDowell's hotel in *The Object of Beauty* (1991). At the

Above:
Lower Grosvenor Place (above left), where Cantinflas seeks employment (above right) in *Around the World in Eighty Days* (1956).

corner of Buckingham Gate David Hemmings pauses for a moment in his Rolls outside The Albert in **Blow Up** (1966), before turning up Victoria Street where a protester mounts a placard in his car.

Bob Hoskins chauffeurs for Cathy Tyson at the Jolly St Ermin's Hotel, Caxton Street in **Mona Lisa** (1986). In **The London Connection** (1979) a motorist drops off Jeffrey Byron and Larry Cedar at the then Caxton Hotel. The interior is seen in **Reds** (1981) when George Plimpton attempts to seduce Diane Keaton. In **Sid and Nancy** (1986) Gary Oldman and Chloe Webb enjoy a rooftop toy gun battle there.

Across Broadway is New Scotland Yard, the current Metropolitan Police headquarters (since 1967), with its oft-photographed rotating triangular sign. Usually this is just an establishing shot to let the audience know that the police are on the case, as in **Inspector Clouseau** (1968), **Dracula A.D. 1972** (1972), **The Saint** (1997) and (with a kitten on top) **Preaching to the Perverted** (1997). In **File of the Golden Goose** (1969) Edward Woodward enters Scotland Yard. Jeremy Kemp arrives here in **The Strange Affair** (1969). In **Sweeney!** (1975) John Thaw and Dennis Waterman run from St James's Park tube towards the offices.

Michael Caine parks with the sign reflecting cinematically in his window in **Blue Ice** (1993). Alec McCowen's office in **Frenzy** (1972) has genuine-looking views to the east, while in **Hennessy** (1975) interior scenes with Trevor Howard and Richard Johnson look north.

In **The Big Sleep** (1978) Robert Mitchum drives away from New Scotland Yard, followed by Colin Blakely. He drives down Buckingham Gate into Castle Lane, right into Palace Street, then right again down Wilfred Street. Blakely gives up on Palace Street.

Left:
Cockpit Steps feature in **Mrs Dalloway** (1997).

Left:
The Two Chairmen
on Dartmouth
Street, seen in *The
Big Sleep* (1978)
and *Keep the
Aspidistra Flying*
(1997).

The Women's Institute conference in **Calendar Girls** (2003) is held in the Methodist Central Hall at Storey's Gate, seen very briefly.

Bryan Brown ushers Paul McCartney into their office at 34a Queen Anne's Gate in **Give My Regards to Broad Street** (1984). Trevor Howard goes to 24 Queen Anne's Gate to see Wilfrid Hyde-White in **The Liquidator** (1965). Rod Taylor tries to pick up Jill St John outside, where later Howard instructs Derek Nimmo. Michael Caine visits John Gielgud at no. 26 opposite, near the end of **The Whistle Blower** (1986).

Edward Fox spies on Richard Boone as Boone steps from Lewisham Street, a passageway next to The Two Chairmen on Dartmouth Street, in **The Big Sleep** (1978). He watches Boone picking up blackmail money from Sarah Miles on a bench in St James's Park. In the pub itself Richard E Grant, well oiled and temporarily well heeled, buys drinks for all in **Keep the Aspidistra Flying** (1997). Vanessa Redgrave as **Mrs Dalloway** (1997) passes through Cockpit Steps – dressed for 1923 – between Dartmouth Street and Birdcage Walk, and meets Oliver Ford Davies 'on the way to the palace' in the park.

Rita Tushingham's search for the YWCA takes her to Buckingham Palace in **The Knack** (1965). Michael Crawford and Oliver Reed escort Lotte Tarp to the Queen Victoria Memorial in front of the palace in **The Jokers** (1966), as they discuss plans for a headline-grabbing robbery. Ringo Starr cleans his teeth at the memorial after a night's camping in the park in **The Magic Christian** (1969), and Donald Pleasence and Dana Andrews walk past the memorial in **Innocent Bystanders** (1973).

Tom Courtenay and Romy Schneider congratulate Alan Badel on receiving his knighthood by the gates to Green Park in **Otley** (1969). There is a quick shot of the palace as 'the biggest recording studio in the world' in **Jubilee** (1977). The Olsen twins try to make a guard laugh outside the gates of Buckingham Palace in **Winning London** (2001). Toby Stephens lands by parachute for the benefit of the press and is interviewed just inside Green Park in **Die Another Day** (2002), with Pierce Brosnan looking on sceptically. John Goodman is driven down The Mall to become **King Ralph** (1991).

Gregory Peck and Sophia Loren escape from Alan Badel's house, 2 Carlton Gardens (now The Privy Council), in **Arabesque** (1966) running down the steps onto The Mall. In the next shot they take refuge in distant London Zoo (NW1), still on foot! Yul Brynner follows Charles Gray to his gambling house on Carlton Gardens, the 'Branbury Club' in **File of the Golden Goose** (1969). Donald Sutherland leads David Hemmings to this house in **Murder By Decree** (1978). Photo-rat Simon McBurnley gatecrashes a party, again at 2 Carlton Gardens, at the start of **Bright Young Things** (2003) before being chased out onto The Mall.

On the bridge over St James's Park's lake Nigel Green meets Guy Doleman to discuss Aubrey Richards's amnesia in **The Ipcress File** (1965). They head south to Birdcage Walk and turn east for a spot of lunch at Doleman's club ('the Dover sole's rather good'). In **The Deadly Affair** (1967) James Mason and Robert Flemyng meet on the bridge to discuss the latter's Communist sympathies. In **Joanna** (1968) Genevieve Waite weeps here, and Peter Sellers meets down-and-out Ringo Starr in **The Magic Christian** (1969). Together they walk north to The Mall gates. At the end, both doss in sleeping bags in the park.

In **101 Dalmatians** (1996) Jeff Daniels first meets Joely Richardson – and Pongo finally catches up with Perdita – south of the lake. Both humans are soaking wet, Daniels taking a dip in the lake next to the fountain north of Duck Island and Richardson suffering a similar watery fate on the western side of the lake. Aidan Gillen and Kate Ashfield cross The Mall for a stroll in the park in **The Low Down** (2001). Terence Alexander and Tony Britton walk west, away from Horse Guards Parade, discussing the Jackal in **The Day of the Jackal** (1973). At Horse Guards Parade a guardsman seizes Joanna Pettet in **Casino Royale** (1967). Alan Bates walks through here in **Nothing but the Best** (1964).

Rufus Sewell chases after Monica Potter in **Martha, Meet Frank, Daniel and Laurence** (1998) just after they leave the Park Café (SW11). Jonathan Rhys Meyers and Emily Mortimer stroll here in **Match Point** (2005). In **Hanover Street** (1979) Christopher Plummer and Alec McCowen walk south of the artificial rock formation – so favoured by the pelicans – towards Duck Island and the period World War II cars on Horse Guards Road as they discuss Plummer's mission behind enemy lines. Arthur Lowe leads David Hemmings the other way to a man on a bench in *Fragment of Fear* (1970).

Under the opening credits *The Yellow Rolls Royce* (1964) is shipped to its showroom from Great George Street along Horse Guards Road, down The Mall and then Marlborough Road past St James's Palace.

The white and gold interior of Lancaster House on Stable Yard Road is seen as a 'winter palace' in *Reds* (1981), in *What a Girl Wants* (2003) and in *The Importance of Being Earnest* (2002) when Colin Firth visits Judi Dench.

Kenneth Connor parks outside St James's Palace on Cleveland Row in *Carry On Emmannuelle* (1978) for a studio shot of Suzanne Danielle trying to distract one of the guards. The Royal Automobile Club, 89 Pall Mall, is the 'Athletic Club' from which John Vernon is kidnapped in *Brannigan* (1975).

Bruce Willis visits 'Jennings & Company Bank', 16 St James's Street, to organize his financial affairs with Leslie Philips and order a gun from the bank's computer in *The Jackal* (1997). The students ragging in a jeep at the beginning of *Blow Up* (1966) drive around the pedestrian Economist Plaza before running down St James's Street. Susannah York in her jeep follows Dirk Bogarde's taxi to Bury Street in *Sebastian* (1968). Bogarde crosses the plaza to Brook's on St James's Street. In *I'll Never Forget What's'isname* (1967) Oliver Reed with an axe turns at the Brod Gallery into 25 Economist Plaza, 'The Lute Corporation', to hand in his notice. Chauffeur Hywel Bennett gazes into the gallery at 24 Economist Plaza while waiting for his shopping client in *Endless Night* (1971).

At the Ritz Hotel on the corner of Arlington Street and Piccadilly Hugh Grant visits Julia Roberts in *Notting Hill* (1999). In the chase finale to stop her leaving London the Ritz is the first port of call. It's seen in *Modesty Blaise* (1966) when Harry Andrews and Monica Vitti are driven there. Bob Hoskins and Cathy Tyson enter in *Mona Lisa* (1986). Christopher Walken meets Jonathan Pryce and Carole Bouquet on separate occasions inside the Ritz in *A Business Affair* (1994). Daniel Auteuil meets Ciaran Hinds to take on the case of searching for *The Lost Son* (1999). He meets the family of Cyril Shaps, Billie Whitelaw and Nastassja Kinski in a room overlooking Piccadilly.

In *Parting Shots* (1998), on Arlington Street opposite The Blue Posts (6 Bennett Street), Felicity Kendal hails a cab for Chris Rea after escaping from 'St Crispian's General Hospital' while Oliver Reed looks on. Despite Kendal's instruction to take them to Manchester

Square (W1), the subsequent view from their hotel room is of Piccadilly, and clearly The Ritz, just a few yards away.

Cathy Tyson buys clothes for Bob Hoskins in **Mona Lisa** (1986) in the Piccadilly Arcade between Piccadilly and Jermyn Street. Jeff Daniels, dragged on his bicycle by Pongo, emerges from the arcade into Jermyn Street in the chase in **101 Dalmatians** (1996). Jonathan Rhys Meyers drives Aria Argento to this entrance for a robbery at no. 13 in **B. Monkey** (1997).

Inside Prince's Arcade, further east off Jermyn Street, Jonathan Pryce attempts to interest distracted publisher David de Keyser with his book on Suez in **The Ploughman's Lunch** (1983). Outside, Miranda Richardson scares two women out of their cab in **Tom & Viv** (1994). In **Being Julia** (2004) Annette Bening emerges from the arcade and crosses to Flores, 89 Jermyn Street. Yul Brynner passes Flores to investigate a bathhouse called the Barrington at 91 Jermyn Street in **File of the Golden Goose** (1969).

Uma Thurman goes to the Reform Club (supposed to be 'Boodles') at 104 Pall Mall and enters – to the shock of the male members – in **The Avengers** (1998). Pierce Brosnan and Toby Stephens enjoy a swordfight here that spills outside in **Die Another Day** (2002). Inside, George Sanders and Robert Helpmann discuss Quiller's progress in **The Quiller Memorandum** (1966). It is a deserted East German mansion in **The Naked Runner** (1967), when Derren Nesbitt gives Frank Sinatra rifle practice. Anthony Hopkins meets Mel Gibson here and successfully invites him to join him on **The Bounty** (1984). Stephen Fry treats James Wilby to lunch in **A Handful of Dust** (1988), and Charlie Hunnan as **Nicholas Nickleby** (2003) confronts Christopher Plummer. Roger Moore walks to his club on the west side of Waterloo Place, south past the equestrian statue of Edward VII, in **The Man Who Haunted Himself** (1970). He's going the wrong way because the next cut shows him entering the Reform Club, and indeed, once inside we receive a privileged tour as Moore searches for the double haunting him.

At the top of the Duke of York steps to the east is 10 Carlton House Terrace, Kirk Douglas's office in **Holocaust 2000** (1977) where Douglas has to run a gauntlet of CND protestors as he makes his way to his car. It is Helena Bonham Carter's house in **The Wings of the Dove** (1997). Here, as Linus Roache is turned away, the whole street is seen converted to the period, complete with cabman's shelter. Uma Thurman arrives here to visit Jeremy Northam in **The Golden Bowl** (2000). Alan Badel's office in **Otley** (1969) is at 14 Carlton House Terrace, and Badel issues instructions to Romy Schneider and Corin Redgrave on the terrace overlooking The Mall. Alan Bates works for Harry Andrews at 16 Carlton House

Terrace in **Nothing but the Best** (1964). Just by the Duke of York's column, Pamela Stephenson joins John Gielgud in a car in **Scandalous** (1984).

In **Charge of the Light Brigade** (1968) David Hemmings walks with companions in Waterloo Place, discussing where the Duke of Wellington's statue should be erected, while Trevor Howard leaves 6 Carlton House Terrace with his dogs.

Left:
Trevor Howard takes his dogs for a walk (top left) past Carlton House Terrace (bottom left) in **Charge of the Light Brigade** (1968).

Ingrid Bergman admires the view from the top of the steps that lead down to The Mall under the credits of **The Inn of the Sixth Happiness** (1958). Michael Bentine walks down the steps as if to go to St James's Park, but actually finds himself in SE21 in **The Sandwich Man** (1966). Donald Pleasence and Dana Andrews walk down the steps in **Innocent Bystanders** (1973). In **Brannigan** (1975) John Vernon and Mel Ferrer walk along The Mall, and on the steps discuss the disposal of John Wayne.

Jeff Daniels cycles down the steps, pulled by Pongo, in **101 Dalmatians** (1996). Vanessa Redgrave as **Mrs Dalloway** (1997) returns home via the steps after buying flowers in EC3. Later John Standing meets Oliver Ford Davies outside 4 Carlton Terrace, renumbered 3 in the film. Cillian Murphy collects some worthless money on the deserted steps in **28 Days Later** (2002).

The grand entrance of the Athenaum, at 107 Pall Mall, is in Waterloo Place. Malcolm McDowell meets Geoffrey Palmer at the entrance in **O Lucky Man!** (1973). Carriages drive up to its porticoed doorway in **Wilde** (1998). Aharon Ipalé visits the club, as the 'Banque Generale', to make a donation to a terrorist group in **Who Dares Wins** (1982). In a separate scene Lewis Collins hops off a no. 24 bus at Lower Regent Street leaving his contact to be killed by Ingrid Pitt's hydrogen cyanide gas. Gabriel Byrne enters the club to investigate his news story in **Defence of the Realm** (1985). In **Goal!** (2005) football hopeful Kuno Becker makes a call to Newcastle after arriving, indirectly, from Los Angeles at Waterloo Place.

David Niven enters the Institute of Directors, 116 Pall Mall (though supposed to be the Reform Club) in **Around the World in Eighty Days** (1956).

Anthony Hopkins and Jim Broadbent visit New Zealand House, on the corner of Pall Mall and Haymarket, to engage the services of solicitor Michael Byrne in **The Good Father** (1985). Gary Lewis and Jamie Draven visit the Theatre Royal on Haymarket to see **Billy Elliot** (2000) playing in *Swan Lake*.

Bernard Lee makes his first treacherous contact at 6½ Suffolk Street, then a gallery, in **Ring of Spies** (1963).

Below:
Ring of Spies
(1963). Bernard Lee awaits his contact for his first foray into treachery at 6½ Suffolk Street.

Bradford Dillman visits John Gielgud and his business partners at Kinnard House, 1 Pall Mall East, in *Gold* (1974). The view from Gielgud's window however appears to be from Canada House, on the west side of Trafalgar Square.

In *The Long Arm* (1956) John Stratton, keeping watch on Peter Burton, hides behind the statue of George III on the triangular pedestrian corner of Cockspur Street and Pall Mall East. In *Train of Events* (1954) Joan Dowling enquires about passage to Canada at 20 Cockspur Street on the triangular intersection of Cockspur Street and Spring Gardens.

A taxi drops off Carol Lynley to meet removal men at Carlton Mews near the start of *Bunny Lake Is Missing* (1965). The mews used to be at the end of Warwick House Street, but have now been destroyed.

In *Howards End* (1992) Vanessa Redgrave and Emma Thompson pass under Admiralty Arch to go to Fortnum and Mason's, accompanied by an impressive Edwardian array of horses and carriages. Bill Travers and William Sylvester drive through the Arch from Trafalgar Square and park to their left outside the Ministry of Defence (Old Admiralty Buildings) to discuss the progress of *Gorgo* (1961), who is wreaking special effects havoc on London. A taxi delivers Michael Caine here in *The Ipcress File* (1965). Kenneth More approaches the sandbagged entrance at the beginning of *Sink the Bismarck!* (1960) and leaves with Dana Wynter at the end.

Amy Ondra, or a double, walks down Whitehall in *Blackmail* (1929). Geoffrey Rush crosses Whitehall greeting passing ladies in *The Life and Death of Peter Sellers* (2004).

Michael Caine drives to Great Scotland Yard, the original police headquarters opposite Scotland Place, in *The Ipcress File* (1965). Clive Owen is chauffered along Great Scotland Yard, past Trafalgar Square and through Admiralty Arch, dressed with barricades, and down The Mall in *Children of Men* (2006).

Both the exterior and interior of the National Liberal Club, 1 Whitehall Place, are seen in *The Wings of the Dove* (1997) as Linus Roache receives an invitation to Venice from Alison Elliott. Ralph Fiennes arrives by taxi at the club to lunch with Bill Nighy in *The Constant Gardener* (2005).

Who Dares Wins (1982) opens with a demonstration through Whitehall Court, cut with other street scenes. Judy Davis and John Duttine arrange for an assassin to fire a crossbolt into a fellow marcher, an undercover agent. The 'Baltic Hotel' is 4 Whitehall Court, seen in *Dirty Pretty Things* (2002), where Chiwetel Ejiofor, Zlatko Buric and Sergi López work.

On the Victoria Embankment Michael Caine runs into Millicent Martin in *Alfie* (1966).

Westminster (see also page 95)

The famous front door of 10 Downing Street appears in film sometimes as an establishing shot with a helpful caption, as for instance in **The Mudlark** (1951), but occasionally actors get in close. Barry Jones watches Prime Minister Ronald Adams posing in front of the door in **Seven Days to Noon** (1950). The area appears at the end of **Operation Crossbow** (1965) as V2 rockets besiege London. In **Casino Royale** (1967) David Niven and Joanna Pettet drive down Downing Street to have a chat outside the door. Oliver Reed and Michael Crawford try to plan an audacious crime right outside the door in **The Jokers** (1966). Peter Cook enters in **The Rise and Rise of Michael Rimmer** (1970). In **The Day of the Jackal** (1973) Tony Britton visits to obtain special licence to hunt the Jackal. These were the security-free days when one could walk up close to the Prime Minister's door, before gates sealed the street off to the general public in 1989. Nevertheless Sacha Baron-Cohen and Michael Gambon pose for photographers in **Ali G Indahouse** (2002).

At the Cenotaph on Whitehall, the end of World War I is celebrated in **This Happy Breed** (1944). In **The Man Who Never Was** (1956) Clifton Webb and Laurence Naismith pass in front of Tweed's statue of Robert Clive, which graces the end of King Charles Street in front of the Foreign and Commonwealth Office while Robert Flemyng awaits them at the bottom of the steps. Michael Byrne drives Lino Ventura to this spot to meet Harry Andrews in **The Medusa Touch** (1977). On Parliament Street Omar Sharif collects Julie Andrews from the Foreign Office, which also used to accommodate the Home Office, for which she works in **The Tamarind Seed** (1974). Near the start of **Permission To Kill** (1975), shot mostly in Austria, Timothy Dalton hails a cab after leaving the Foreign Office. Charles Dance leaves work via the courtyard seen from King Charles Street in **Plenty** (1985). In **The Whistle Blower** (1986) Michael Caine mingles with Remembrance Day crowds. King Charles Street is dressed in early-20th-century style in **The Golden Bowl** (2000).

The headquarters of the Metropolitan Police (the capital's police force) has moved twice, from Great Scotland Yard, off Whitehall (its location until 1890), to New Scotland Yard (the Norman Shaw building on Derby Gate, off Parliament Street just north of Portcullis House) to its current site on Broadway near St James's tube in 1967. The Derby Gate entrance of the Norman Shaw building is seen in **The Blue Lamp** (1950), when Bernard Lee takes charge. In **Seven Days to Noon** (1950) Hugh Cross and Sheila Manahan walk through Derby Gate into Parliament Street to catch a cab. When they reach Trafalgar Square they spot the missing Barry Jones disappearing down the underground entrance at the east end of Cockspur

Left:
Julie Andrews
leaves her work at
the old Home Office
on Parliament
Street (top left) to
be picked up by
Omar Sharif (bottom
left) in *The
Tamarind Seed*
(1974).

Street. Suspect Eric Portman leaves the Victoria Embankment exit in **Wanted for Murder** (1946). New Scotland Yard is relegated to an establishing shot in **Hunted** (1951), and John Mills visits Ronald Culver there to clear his name in **The Vicious Circle** (1957). Jack Hawkins's corner office overlooks Hungerford Bridge and County Hall, a view commented upon in **The Long Arm** (1956). He's back there in **Gideon's Day** (1958) and this time has a view over County Hall and Westminster Bridge in the other corner, visible when he confronts Derek Bond over a charge of bribery. John Gregson works here in **The Frightened City** (1961), while Tony Britton and Donald Sinden are based here in **The Day of the Jackal** (1973).

A popular establishing shot for London is that of Big Ben framed by Thomas Thornycroft's statue of Boudica taken from Westminster Pier steps – **Foreign Correspondent** (1940) and **23 Paces to Baker Street** (1956) for example. But in **Innocent Bystanders** (1973) Donald Pleasence and Dana Andrews feature in the shot.

After opening shots of Boudica and the Norman Shaw building in **The Informers** (1964) Colin Blakely disembarks at Westminster Pier after a chat with detective Nigel Patrick. From the pier, Stanley Baker, Ursula Andress and David Warner take a chilly river trip to discuss the robbery of Baker's bank in **Perfect Friday** (1970). The police capture David Warner at the pier at the end of **The Thirty-Nine Steps** (1978). On a riverboat, John Gielgud arranges for Tony Beckley to kill Bradford Dillman in **Gold** (1974). In **Who Dares Wins** (1982) Lewis Collins ducks into the passageway next to the public lavatories at the bottom of the steps to lose his tail, and jumps onto a Greenwich boat unaware that second tail Ingrid Pitt is watching his every move. In **Sid and Nancy** (1986) police round up the Sex Pistols and their fans as they dock after their riverboat celebrations of the Queen's Silver Jubilee. Gary Oldman and Chloe Webb, however, walk arm in arm untouched by the chaos around them.

In **Defence of the Realm** (1985) Denholm Elliott emerges from the public lavatories by the pier to meet MP Ian Bannen, and they discuss another parliamentary scandal. Elliott then meets Bannen and Greta Scacchi at St Stephen's Tavern in Cannon Row (this pub re-opened in 2004 after an amazing 15-year closure). Above the pier, William Hurt crosses Victoria Embankment to the Yankee Delight Restaurant in **The Accidental Tourist** (1988). In **Percy** (1971) Hywel Bennett and Julia Foster enjoy a romantic walk past the pier.

The final scene of **Seven Days to Noon** (1950) shows Olive Sloane and her dog Trixie heading south on an uncannily deserted Westminster Bridge to complement the many shots of an evacuated London., Similarly, in **28 Days Later** (2002) Cillian Murphy crosses an equally empty Westminster Bridge as he makes his way northwards down Whitehall and across Horse Guards Parade. At the start of *Crossplot* (1969) Claudia Lange is crossing a dawn-deserted bridge with a companion before he is thrown off it into the river at Francis Matthew's instigation.

Kate Hudson and Wes Bentley walk south in front of the Palace of Westminster in a brief shot in *The Four Feathers* (2002).

SW1 (south of Victoria Street): Westminster, Millbank, Pimlico, Chelsea, Knightsbridge, Belgravia, Victoria

Westminster (see also page 92)

In *The Thirty-Nine Steps* (1978) Robert Powell appears to be clinging to the clock hands of the Palace of Westminster's Clock Tower while onlookers in Parliament Square gasp. In *Perfect Friday* (1970) Ursula Andress clumsily parks her car in Old Palace Yard to collect David Warner from the House of Lords. Omar Sharif, and then Jane Seymour, exit taxis in Old Palace Yard in *Oh Heavenly Dog* (1980). Aidan Gillen leaves Old Palace Yard in *Shanghai Knights* (2004), which later also features Owen Wilson emulating Robert Powell's heroics on the clockface. In *Press for Time* (1966) Norman Wisdom, after hitching a lift, enters the House of Commons through New Palace Yard. *Brassed Off* (1996) ends with conductor Pete Postlethwaite's brass band playing an ironic 'Land of Hope and Glory' in an open-topped bus as it passes the Houses of Parliament.

MP Peter Finch attends the House of Commons in *No Love for Johnnie* (1961) enjoying drinks on the members' terrace overlooking the Thames. Rod Steiger wants to blow up the Houses of Parliament in *Hennessy* (1975), taking a tour of the House of Lords as preparation. There is an ingenious mix of stock footage of the state opening of Parliament towards the climax as Richard Johnson attempts to stop Steiger. *Sweeney!* (1976) opens with Ian Bannen leaving the House of Commons. Alun Armstrong briefs Neil Duncan about partner Rutger Hauer on a boat on the Thames in *Split Second* (1992).

Barry Jones buys a paper on St Margaret Street and, seeing his picture, realizes he needs to alter his appearance in *Seven Days to Noon* (1950).

Under the credits of **Blind Date** (1959) Hardy Kruger gets off a no. 170 bus on Victoria Embankment to buy some violets in Parliament Square. Gene Barry and Joan Collins walk in Parliament Square in **Subterfuge** (1969). Collins, again, calls from a traditional red phone box on Great George Street in **I Don't Want to Be Born** (1975). Here Michael Redgrave is forced to attend an important meeting on his way to Parliament in **Goodbye Gemini** (1970). Jane Wyman picks up Michael Wilding from her taxi at this corner in **Stage Fright** (1950). During the titles of **Beautiful People** (1999) a Serb and a Croat take their differences from a bus into a fight around Winston Churchill's statue in Parliament Square. Lee Patterson and Mark Burns hand over diamonds to Michael Caine and Roger Moore in the square at the end of **Bullseye!** (1990). Villain Michael Gambon furiously reads congratulations on his latest job on a billboard positioned in Parliament Square in **High Heels and Low Lifes** (2001). Anna Friel and Sarah Alexander are caught speeding by police outside St Margaret's Church in **Perfect Strangers** (2004).

The Olsen twins tour Westminster Abbey in **Winning London** (2001). Tom Hanks and Audrey Tautou enter Westminster Abbey, though the interior was filmed in Lincoln Cathedral, in **The Da Vinci Code** (2006), while Ian McKellen is bustled into a police car. Paul Nicholls cracks his watch on the postbox on Tothill Street in **If Only** (2004).

As Jesse Spencer leaves Black Rod's Garden Entrance into Parliament, he joins Mary-Kate Olsen on Parliament Green in **Winning London** (2001). Underneath the Green lies Abingdon Street car park, seen in **Johnny English** (2003).

In Great College Street Michael Caine and Ben Kingsley collect a boy spying for them in **Without a Clue** (1988). Despite a carriage trip suggesting otherwise, they live just around the corner at 9 Barton Street. The street previously housed 221a Baker Street, while Christopher Plummer and James Mason live opposite at 3 Barton Street, in **Murder by Decree** (1979). Both films also feature Dean's Yard, the former over the opening credits and the latter when Plummer visits Prime Minister John Gielgud.

In **A Business Affair** (1994) a taxi drops off Jonathan Pryce on Great College Street outside the gates of Dean's Yard to see his lawyer. In Dean's Yard a violinist serenades Peter Sellers as he gets into his car outside the entrance to Westminster School in **The Magic Christian** (1969). He lives in Little Dean's Yard at Grant's, one of the school's boarding houses, and it is to here that he brings his newly adopted son Ringo Starr.

Bag lady Ann Tirard collects her 'bedclothes' (magazines) from outside the Emmanuel Centre on Great Smith Street in **The Chain** (1984).

Opposite:
Innocent Bystanders (1973). Ferdy Mayne leads Stanley Baker to his 'Manhattan' office (top), which is actually at Millbank Tower (centre), disguised as New York with a sign on the stairs (bottom).

In Victoria Tower Gardens Richard Johnson corners Rod Steiger in **Hennessy** (1975). **Looking For Richard** (1996) ends with Al Pacino in the gardens. Trevor Cooper instructs Damian Lewis there on his shady dealings in **Chromophobia** (2005).

Millbank

Bill Shine starts his surveillance on Eric Portman from Lambeth Bridge, jumping to SW3, in **Wanted For Murder** (1946). In **High Heels and Low Lifes** (2001) Kevin McNally throws his mobile phone off the bridge. Just south of the roundabout on Millbank is Thames House, now the headquarters of MI5. Here, next to the east end of Page Street, which ran through the building and was built over when MI5 moved in, Kay Kendall drops off Rex Harrison in **The Constant Husband** (1955). At the rear of this building in Thorney Street, where Ann Tirard huddles down for the night at the end of **The Chain** (1984).

Further south along the Thames on Millbank stands the enormous Millbank Tower, previously known as the Vickers Building. It is established both as home to Rod Taylor's plush flat in **The Liquidator** (1965) and as containing the **Vault of Horror** (1973). The lower level to the north of the tower is the 'Cosmopolitan Hotel' in **The Intelligence Men** (1966). In **Innocent Bystanders** (1973) a shot of the tower from the north is supposed to be New York, seen when Stanley Baker meets Ferdy Mayne. Sticking a sign up by the stairs declaring 'Manhattan Plaza Complex, City of New York' is a nice try. Fiona Richmond drives up to the tower on Millbank in **Hardcore** (1977) for an appointment.

Further south along Millbank again, at Tate Britain, Rowan Atkinson as **Bean** (1997) is seen briefly at the base of the steps being 'very cute'. Richard Roundtree meets his contact inside the Tate in **A Game for Vultures** (1979). Henry Wallis's painting Death of Chatterton in room 9 fascinates John Hurt

in *Love and Death on Long Island* (1996). Daniel Craig and Samantha Morton stroll through the gallery in *Enduring Love* (2004). On the steps Micheline Presle persuades Hardy Kruger to start an affair in *Blind Date* (1959).

In *Swimming Pool* (2003) Charles Dance's publishing office is in Random House, Vauxhall Bridge Road, with views to Parliament and the London Eye to the north.

Behind the old Millbank barracks is Cureton Street. In *A Game for Vultures* (1979) Denholm Elliott lives in a shabby flat in the Landseer building, seen when Sven Bertil-Taube visits the entrance for flats 10–24.

Phil Collins's mother-in-law Sheila Hancock lives at 6 Abady House, Page Street, in *Buster* (1988). Martin Jarvis and Clive Wood arrest Collins here near the end. Inside the Regency Café on the corner of Page Street and Regency Street George Harris beats up Ivan Kaye in *Layer Cake* (2004). The exterior is seen as Daniel Craig leaves.

On the Horseferry Road between Chadwick and Medway Streets is the Richard Rogers-designed Channel 4 building. In *Shooting Fish* (1997) Dan Futterman, Stuart Townsend and the unwitting Kate Beckinsale try a scam in the building, then rush out to beg a warden not to ticket their car parked on Chadwick Street. Anna Massey and Elizabeth Berrington are seen outside the building in *Mad Cows* (1999). Opposite is the Greycoat Hospital School, which Alex Pettyfer and Sarah Bolger attend in *Stormbreaker* (2006).

On the corner of Elveston and Greycoat Streets is the New Royal Horticultural Society Hall, which is an art gallery when Rufus Sewell and Monica Potter visit *Martha, Meet Frank, Daniel and Laurence* (1998). Joseph Fiennes meets up with Potter at the entrance. Just inside the entrance, there is a very brief scene in *Indiana Jones and the Last Crusade* (1989) in which Harrison Ford and Sean Connery catch an airship from 'Berlin Airport'. Equally brief is its appearance further inside in *Richard III* (1995) when Ian McKellen is offered the kingdom. Bob Geldof sings 'In the Flesh' from the balcony at the west end of the hall in *Pink Floyd the Wall* (1982). It is Berlin Templehoff station in *The Saint* (1997) when Val Kilmer meets Rade Serbedzija and Valeri Nikolayev to negotiate the theft of a cold-fusion formula. In *Piccadilly Jim* (2004) it is the Cunard departure hall, with the ingenious effect of a liner towering above the roof as Sam Rockwell and Geoffrey Palmer meet Frances O'Connor. In *Children of Men* (2006) it is the Ministry of Energy, where Clive Owen works.

James Fox is driven up to the Audit Commission at 33 Greycoat Street, set up as a spy centre to monitor Sean Connery's progress in Moscow in *The Russia House* (1990).

In **Operation Amsterdam** (1960) Peter Finch arrives for his briefing at Capital Interiors on the corner of Emery Hill Street and Rochester Row.

The Old Horticultural Hall, on Vincent Square, is the 'Westminster Academy of Music' in **Agent Cody Banks 2** (2004). The New Hall (see above) however provides the entrance lobby and hall where Frankie Muniz and Hannah Spearritt rehearse. Keith Allen lurks at the corner of Elveston Street to begin a chase which, although on foot, cuts quickly to EC3.

In Vincent Square itself Marlene Jobert referees a football game while being spied upon by Patrick Mower, and later Kirk Douglas, in **To Catch a Spy** (1971).

On the corner of Vauxhall Bridge Road and Stanford Street is The Surprise at Pimlico. The games bar off Stanford Street is an Oxford pub in **Iris** (2001) where Judi Dench and Jim Broadbent imbibe after shopping.

Dirk Bogarde tries to sell his coat to a pawnbroker who raises the alarm to police in **Hunted** (1951) at '189 Vauxhall Bridge Road' according to the police radio report. The Peabody Estate opposite the junction with Upper Tachbrook Street is still there, though much of Vauxhall Bridge Road has been rebuilt.

On the corner of Francis and Stillington Streets, no. 29 is a police station in **Scandal** (1988). After the mews shooting scene, Joanne Whalley-Kilmer and John Hurt sit in his car before she gets out into the pouring rain.

Michael Caine enters his office – then Strakers, now part of The Litten Tree – on Artillery Row in **The Whistle Blower** (1986).

From Ashley Place, Jack Birkett enters Westminster Cathedral, standing in as a nightclub, while Ian Charleson sings his praises on the piazza in front in **Jubilee** (1977). Edmund Gwenn appears to fall from the Cathedral tower in **Foreign Correspondent** (1940).

Above:
Vincent Square (above left) is the scene of a football match in **To Catch a Spy** (1971), where Kirk Douglas makes a point to Marlene Jobert (above right).

Robert Mitchum lives at 1–12 Morpeth Mansions, on Morpeth Terrace, in *The Big Sleep* (1978). In *My Beautiful Laundrette* (1985) Derrick Branche watches Gordon Warnecke from the balcony above the entrance to 61–65 Carlisle Mansions as he drives down Carlisle Place.

Pimlico

Just off Grosvenor Road by the river is 119 St George's Square, which contains James Mason's flat in *The Deadly Affair* (1966).

Barry Crocker manages to escape from 'HM Prison Brixton' in a dinghy, using a storm relief duct into the Thames as his escape route in *Barry McKenzie Holds His Own* (1975). This location is easier to view from the other side of the river, from Nine Elms Lane in SW8.

Dolphin Square's entrance on Chichester Street, since altered, and its indoor swimming pool – now with a gallery enclosed by glass and without a diving board – are seen in *The Sorcerers* (1967) when Ian Ogilvy and Elizabeth Ercy sneak in for a swim. Roger Moore and Anton Rodgers take a swim here in *The Man Who Haunted Himself* (1970) and Moore bumps into Olga Georges-Picot.

Opposite is the Pimlico Secondary School, a concrete and glass edifice sunk into the square. From Lupus Street Shirley MacLaine walks a gauntlet of pupils ('Dracula's back') at the start of *Madame Sousatzka* (1988) to attend a concert. Her pianist pupil, Navin Chowdhry, attends the school, called 'Ebury Bridge Comprehensive', and injures his wrist roller-skating in the playground.

Moreton Place provides Meryl Streep's 'Battersea' flat into which Tracey Ullman moves in *Plenty* (1985).

Dirk Bogarde and Jon Whiteley are on Grosvenor Road opposite Claverton Street near the start of *Hunted* (1951). All Saint's Church, which made way for the Churchill Gardens Estate, is seen in the background. Michael Callan visits Keats House on the estate in *You Must Be Joking!* (1965).

On Chelsea Bridge Road is the Chelsea Barracks, which Oliver Reed enters, impersonating an army officer in his plan to steal the Crown Jewels in *The Jokers* (1966). In *Diamond Skulls* (1989) the police investigate Douglas Hodge's Jaguar here.

On the south corner of Ebury Bridge Road and Warwick Way is the 'Westminster Hospital' where Michael Caine as *Alfie* (1966) chauffeurs himself to check on a 'problem with my X-ray'. Orlando Bloom as **The Calcium Kid** (2003) trains on the path running alongside the tracks to Ebury Bridge.

Chelsea

Bill Travers lives on Lower Sloane Street in **Ring of Bright Water** (1969). When Peter Jeffrey presses the bell at no. 18, Travers throws the key down from the window on the second floor above no. 20.

Susan George and her cycling friends tease schoolboys at the zebra crossing in Sloane Square in **Twinky** (1969). John Stratton follows Peter Burton to Peter Jones in Sloane Square in **The Long Arm** (1956). Jonathan Rhys Meyers catches a taxi outside Holy Trinity Church, Sloane Street, in **I'll Sleep When I'm Dead** (2003). Oskar Werner and Barbara Ferris cross onto the square in **Interlude** (1968). When Werner recognizes a friend, Ferris has to take refuge quickly in the doorway of the post office on King's Road to keep their affair a secret. Yvan Attal buys flowers on the north side of the square in **Ma Femme est une Actrice** (2001).

In **Oh Heavenly Dog** (1980) Jane Seymour and Benji visibly ride through London, including Belgrave Square, and pass the Royal Court Theatre on Sloane Square, even though Montreal is used as London in the next shot. Michael Caine and Sigourney Weaver leave the Royal Court in **Half Moon Street** (1986). The theatre is part of Ayub Khan Din and Frances Barber's 'perfect day' in **Sammy and Rosie Get Laid** (1987). Jonathan Rhys Meyers sits on the square's memorial while waiting for Scarlett Johansson's audition at the theatre in **Match Point** (2005).

On the north side of Cadogan Square Angela Lansbury finds a lost piece of jewellery in **Mrs 'Arris Goes to Paris** (1992) on her way to work at 6 Cadogan Square. Yvan Attal visits Charlotte Gainsbourg on location in **Ma Femme est une Actrice** (2001). 13 Cadogan Square is George Peppard's hideout in Vienna in **The Executioner** (1970). 'Back' in England, Peppard drives from Clabon Mews across Cadogan Square and into Shafto Mews. He lives at the far end, no. 13, up the iron stairs, and is later attacked in his garage below. Claire Forlani leads brother Elijah Wood along Cadogan Square to her and husband Marc Warren's flat in the south-east annex in **Green Street** (2005).

In **You Must Be Joking!** (1965) Gabriella Licudi steals a Silver Lady from pop stars The Cavemen's Rolls Royce parked in Pavilion Road near Herbert Crescent. Michael Callan drives her away as the group gives chase.

On Pont Street, at the cabman's shelter just beyond Sloane Street, a taxi driver recognizes a victim of **The Sorcerers** (1967) in a paper. In **The Servant** (1963) James Fox escorts Wendy Craig to a taxi after lunch in a restaurant at 12 Lowndes Street.

At 24 Motcomb Street is Lowe's, the hatter visited by Diana Rigg, cited as being in Piccadilly in **The Assassination Bureau** (1968). Rigg's carriage conveys her soon after into Wilton Crescent (see below). Lowe's is now the Mathaf Gallery.

Knightsbridge

Rita Tushingham tries on a dress in a shop on Brompton Road, in a block since rebuilt, in **The Knack** (1965). Barbara Hershey (calling herself Barbara Seagull at the time) collects a cheque from Robert Shaw at Graffs, formerly 35 Brompton Road, in **Diamonds** (1975).

In Park Close at Wellington Court, between Knightsbridge and South Carriage Drive, is Miranda Richardson's nightclub, which Ian Holm visits at the start of **Dance with a Stranger** (1985).

In **Victim** (1961) Dirk Bogarde drives under the office block Bowater House, built over Edinburgh Gate, while sinister Derren Nesbitt looks on. In **Otley** (1969) Romy Schneider leaves her car to let Tom Courtenay battle with the traffic in front of Bowater House. The building is seen from the north in **Sebastian** (1968) when Susannah York argues from her jeep with Dirk Bogarde in front of Epstein's Pan sculpture on South Carriage Drive. Bowater House was demolished in 2006.

In **The L-Shaped Room** (1963) Tom Bell and Leslie Caron are more concerned to enter Hyde Park through Albert Gate, passing the French embassy, than join in the CND march on Knightsbridge.

In **The Golden Lady** (1978) David King and Richard Oldfield check into the Hyde Park Hotel, now the Mandarin Oriental, on Knightsbridge. Soon after, June Chadwick picks up Oldfield outside. Michael Peña and his entourage book the Presidential Suite in **The**

Calcium Kid (2003). In **Ring of Bright Water** (1969) Bill Travers is disappointed to see an otter-fur coat for sale in a shop window at 36 Knightsbridge, now home to Aesthetique.

John Mills ducks into Knightsbridge tube to evade the law in **The Vicious Circle** (1957). It's seen again in **Londinium** (2001) when Mariel Hemingway and Mike Binder dine at the One-O-One restaurant in the Sheraton Park Tower with Colin Firth and Irène Jacob.

Belgravia

Susan Penhaligon returns to parents Kenneth More and Billie Whitelaw, who live at 28 Eaton Terrace in **Leopard in the Snow** (1977).

13 South Eaton Place, on the north corner of Chester Row, is the upmarket flat of Julie Andrews in **The Tamarind Seed** (1974). Andrews and Omar Sharif take a walk from the flat down Chester Row.

11 Eaton Square, close to Belgrave Place, is Joan Collins and Walter Gotel's house in **The Stud** (1978). Collins is on the balcony when Oliver Tobias calls round in an early scene. In **Touch And Go** (1955) Jack Hawkins and Roland Culver, driving a Vauxhall Cadet, give John Fraser a lift to his college at 114 Eaton Square, near St Peter's church.

On the north-west side of the square, a taxi drops off Doris Day outside no.s 74–80, before she moves to the country in **Do Not Disturb** (1965).

Jeremy Irons and Annette Bening live at 7 West Eaton Place, on the corner with West Eaton Place Mews, in **Being Julia** (2004). Peter Cushing and Sue Lloyd drive to Kate O'Mara's house at 21 Eaton Place in **Corruption** (1967). Kirk Douglas takes Agostina Belli to Geoffrey Keen, a gynaecologist-cum-abortionist, at 65 Eaton Place in **Holocaust 2000** (1977). During the planning to assassinate judge Brian Coleman outside 100 Eaton Place in **The Crying Game** (1992), Stephen Rea and Miranda Richardson sit on a bench outside The Lowndes Arms while Jaye Davidson, who has followed them by taxi, waits inside. The pub was in a small cul-de-sac off Chesham Street, but it has since been converted into a private house and is now simply 37 Chesham Street. Adrian Dunbar later shoots the judge and is himself gunned down by a bodyguard at the junction of Eaton Place and Chesham Street.

Anton Rodgers lives at Chesham House, Chesham Close, next to Lyall Mews in **The Fourth Protocol** (1987).

Richard Todd lives at 12a Eaton Mews North in **Stage Fright** (1950) and when the police pick him up, they drive under the arch leading to Lowndes Place. John Justin as **The**

Man Who Loved Redheads (1955) lives at Lowndes House, on Lowndes Place next to Robert's Mews.

In **The Fallen Idol** (1948) Bobby Henrey follows Ralph Richardson into Belgrave Mews West. Henrey swings under the cross railings in front of the The Star Tavern, and although they now wobble, they are still there. In **The League of Gentlemen** (1960) Bryan Forbes lives at no. 2.

On the east corner of Belgrave Square, where Chapel Street meets Upper Belgrave Street, is Seaford House, 37 Belgrave Square, which is Stewart Granger's grand house (to which Richard Burton is driven) in **The Wild Geese** (1978). David Niven lives at 42 Belgrave Square in **Around the World in Eighty Days** (1956), seen as he and Cantinflas hail John Mills's carriage. Outside 47 Belgrave Square drifter Gregory Peck is invited in by brothers Wilfrid Hyde-White and Ronald Squire to receive **The Million Pound Note** (1954). Although Peck looks straight up, the brothers are hailing him from the balcony of no. 43, which is architecturally more ornate with its pilastered columns. Peck follows the note as it is blown down Chapel Street past Montrose Place. Roger Moore helps himself to a pint of milk as he drives his Alfa Romeo past a milk float on the north-west side of Belgrave Square in **Crossplot** (1969). Dirk Bogarde joins his plush new practice at no. 6, on the same side, in **Doctor At Large** (1957). On the northern corner a Jaguar, with Gabriel Byrne at the wheel, knocks down a cook in **Diamond Skulls** (1989). Later Douglas Hodge, jogging there, pauses guiltily at the corner, dubbed 'Chesham Street' in the film. Near the same corner, 49 Belgrave Square appears as '117 Belgrave Square', the address quoted in **Fanny By Gaslight** (1944) and seen when Phyllis Calvert visits Stuart Lindsell. In **Perfect Friday** (1970) Ursula Andress drives past David Warner as he waits expectantly on the corner outside no. 49 for her to pick him up.

In the same corner, where Grosvenor Crescent meets Wilton Crescent, is 1–2 Grosvenor Crescent, which plays an embassy at '48 Chesterton Square' in **The Fallen Idol** (1948). Ralph Richardson and Bobby Henrey use the door in Wilton Crescent. The pavement in front of the building has, since 1998, been graced with a statue of Sir Robert Grosvenor. In an establishing shot, Alida Valli lives at 33 Wilton Crescent in **The Paradine Case** (1947). Lesley-Anne Down and daughter Patsy Kensit cross the road to home at 4 Wilton Crescent in **Hanover Street** (1979). In **Crossplot** (1969), Roger Moore visits Claudia Lange, who is staying with her aunt Martha Hyer, at 23 Wilton Crescent, despite a misleading Belgrave Place sign.

Colin Firth lives at 27 Wilton Place, at first with Mariel Hemingway, then Irène Jacob, in *Londinium* (2001). At the end of *Lassiter* (1986) Joe Regalbuto and Jane Seymour chat outside no. 20 when a triumphant Tom Selleck and Ed Lauter drive up to collect Seymour.

Hardy Kruger dances excitedly through Wilton Row on his way to a date, taking the side alley next to The Grenadiers in *Blind Date* (1959). His date lives up the iron steps at 16 Old Barrack Yard. Dirk Bogarde visits the same flat to meet Dennis Price in *Victim* (1961). In *The Fallen Idol* (1948) Bobby Henrey flees into the rainy night down Old Barrack Yard and is found by policeman Torin Thatcher.

Forbes Place, on Halkin Street – now a one-way street – is the embassy that Sean Young leaves before her abduction in SE1 in *Blue Ice* (1992).

In *Perfect Friday* (1970) Ursula Andress, David Warner, and Stanley Baker's plan to rob the bank where Baker works involves hiring a flat at 12 Grosvenor Crescent. The 'National Metropolitan Bank Ltd.' is 1 Grosvenor Place, opposite what was St George's Hospital and is now the Lanesborough Hotel, inside which Stanley Kubrick shot scenes for *Eyes Wide Shut* (1999). Here too Joan Allen drinks too much after her eldest daughter's degree ceremony in *The Upside of Anger* (2004). Donald Pleasence arrives for work at the hospital entrance off Grosvenor Crescent, now restructured, in *I Don't Want to Be Born* (1975).

On the other side of the hotel is the Hyde Park Corner underpass in which Rhys Ifans suffers a brief road rage incident in *Rancid Aluminium* (2000).

Above:
Hardy Kruger catches the attention of a policeman (above left) on his way to a date in *Blind Date* (1959). The location is Old Barrack Yard (above right), also seen in *The Fallen Idol* (1948) and *Victim* (1961).

Stanley Baker and Ursula Andress have to sneak out of a back window, supposed to be the rear of 17 Chester Street but actually 6 Groom Place, in *Perfect Friday* (1970). Baker then hails a taxi on Chester Street to spirit Andress away from under the nose of the chap at the front door.

In *A Touch of Class* (1973) George Segal and wife Hildegard Neil live at 16 Upper Belgrave Street, now with much altered frontage, 'just around the corner from Disraeli'.

At the corner of Grosvenor Gardens and Ebury Street is 'The Danby Domestic Employment Agency', which Michael Caine and Guy Doleman visit in *The Ipcress File* (1965). Nigel Green's office is on the first floor of 28 Grosvenor Gardens.

Joanna Pettet and Stanley Baker step out from Victoria Station into Terminus Place in *Robbery* (1967). Baker puts Pettet into a taxi, buys a paper and crosses Buckingham Palace Road towards the Marshall Foch equestrian statue in Grosvenor Gardens.

Victoria

Victoria Station is a major location for *Runners* (1983). In his obsessive search for his errant daughter, James Fox takes a room at the Grosvenor Hotel. Fox wanders around the station showing various characters photographs of his daughter. He and Jane Asher chase through the station in pursuit of a false alarm and also meet nutcase Bernard Hill. Near the end, Fox weeps into a phone on the right-hand side of the exit opposite platforms 7 and 8 as his daughter Kate Hardie looks on. The Grosvenor Hotel provides the lobby of the 'Bucharest' hotel into which Patrick Mower and Marlene Jobert check in *To Catch a Spy* (1971).

After her arrival from Las Vegas, Elizabeth Daily passes through the exit opposite platform 8 of Victoria Station to catch a taxi in *Funny Money* (1983). Bill Travers approaches here with his pet otter in *Ring of Bright Water* (1969). In *The Lady Vanishes* (1938) Alfred Hitchcock makes a cameo appearance on platform 1 as Michael Redgrave and Margaret Lockwood arrive from the Continent along with Basil Radford and Naunton Wayne. The establishing shot of the façade outside is taken from the same angle on Wilton Road as that of *The Big Money* (1955), when Ian Carmichael steals a suitcase full of counterfeit money. In *Forbidden Cargo* (1954) Terence Morgan goes to the station with a drugs package, prompting Jack Warner and Nigel Patrick's search of the left luggage office. The boat train with Laurence Olivier's school party, including Sarah Miles and Terence Stamp, arrives at the station in *Term of Trial* (1962). Michael Caine takes the London–Paris train in *The Ipcress File* (1965), during which he is abducted. Helmut Berger calls Caine from a box on platform 1 in *The Romantic Englishwoman* (1975). Phil Daniels takes a train to Brighton from the same platform in *Quadrophenia* (1978). Sam Waterston as *Sweet William* (1980) sees off Jenny Agutter at the station. Joseph Long and family meet his father Vittorio Duso in *Queen of Hearts* (1989). On the top level of 'Victoria Island' in the centre of the concourse, Jason Patric and Irène Jacob emerge from a photo booth in *Incognito* (1997). Patric then pickpockets passports from a passer-by before catching the Orient Express on platform 8. Michael Caine and Roger Moore take the Orient Express for a tour of stately homes in *Bullseye!* (1990). Chris Rea stashes his gun in a locker at Victoria in *Parting Shots* (1998). Chen Hsiau Hsuan seeks directions from Harrison Liu in *Foreign Moon* (1995). In *High Heels and Low Lifes* (2001) Minnie Driver arranges for Kevin McNally and Len Collin to take a train to Brighton.

South along Buckingham Palace Road is the Victoria Coach Station. The exit on Elizabeth Street is seen when David Knight and Julia Arnall follow a false lead to find their son in *Lost* (1955). Out-of-towner Rita Tushingham arrives at the coach station in *The Knack* (1965). Here also Anton Rodgers playfully sets Kenneth Griffith on fire in *Rotten to the Core* (1965) when he tries to pickpocket him.

In *The Deadly Affair* (1967) Simone Signoret gets off a coach, watched by Harry Andrews, who follows her to see her catching a bus in Buckingham Palace Road.

Oliver Reed and Ian McShane visit Frank Finlay and Jill Townsend at 77 Eccleston Square Mews, off Warwick Way, in *Sitting Target* (1972). Between Warwick Way and Warwick Square on Belgrave Road is a set of four telephone boxes, from where Rufus Sewell calls Joseph Fiennes in *Martha, Meet Frank, Daniel and Laurence* (1998).

SW3: Chelsea, Brompton

Chelsea (see also page 101)

Just east of Park Walk, 372 King's Road, is La Bersagliera, 'The Cavern' coffeehouse in *Dracula A.D. 1972* (1972) where Christopher Neame suggests a séance to his fellow revellers. The alleyway supposedly leading to the rear, taken by Stephanie Beacham and Philip Miller, and later Peter Cushing, is called The Porticos.

In *Theatre of Blood* (1973) Jack Hawkins and wife Diana Dors live at 8 Cheyne Walk. Hawkins jealously watches Vincent Price leaving his house from Chelsea Embankment

Gardens. Martin Potter and Judy Geeson arrive at 9 Cheyne Walk next door, with its distinctive first floor bay windows, in **Goodbye Gemini** (1970). Here too lives Robert Hays in **Scandalous** (1984). Pamela Stephenson poses for photographers at the doorway. In front of Cheyne Court on Christchurch Street a Sloane Ranger orders her supply of cocaine in **The Business** (2005). Bill Murray kisses Joanne Whalley by the river on Cheyne Walk in **The Man Who Knew Too Little** (1997). On the corner of Lawrence Street, close to All Saints' Church, is 60–61 Cheyne Walk, a police station, now converted to flats, to which Hardy Kruger is taken in **Blind Date** (1959). When Stanley Baker and Kruger leave later, Kruger crosses the road to the Thames, drops his bunch of violets into the river, and catches a bus west to Battersea Bridge. Ayub Khan Din, Frances Barber and Shashi Kapoor return to their car parked in Cheyne Walk after their blazing restaurant row in **Sammy and Rosie Get Laid** (1987).

Jack Hawkins's house and street in **Touch and Go** (1955) look like a set, but the scenes as he drives off from Cheyne Row into Cheyne Walk are real enough. On Cheyne Walk opposite Cheyne Row is the statue of Thomas Carlyle seen during a happy interlude between Charles Bronson and Susan George as *Twinky* (1969). In *Around the World in Eighty Days* (1956) Cantinflas rides his penny-farthing from Cheyne Row east into Upper Cheyne Row to look for a job in SW1.

Just north is 35 Glebe Place, grandly positioned in the corner, seen briefly in *Withnail & I* (1987) when Richard E Grant and Paul McGann call on Richard Griffiths to borrow the keys to his house in the Lake District. In *There's a Girl in My Soup* (1970) Nicky Henson and Goldie Hawn live in the basement of 15 Glebe Place; Peter Sellers picks up Hawn outside on his way to a party upstairs with Tony Britton.

Tom Courtenay as *Otley* (1969) shelters in the alley, now blocked off, next to The Cross Keys, 1 Lawrence Street, opposite Lordship Place, while waiting for clothes to be delivered by James Maxwell.

2 Bramerton Street, the last door on the east side at the corner of King's Road, is the 'Green Door', celebrated in song, leading down to Gateways, the now-closed club where Beryl Reid suggests Coral Browne meet her in *The Killing of Sister George* (1968). Only interiors are seen.

In *A Clockwork Orange* (1971) Malcolm McDowell, now rehabilitated, walks along Chelsea Embankment to the underpass of Albert Bridge, where he re-encounters tramp Paul Farrell, whom he beat up earlier. Peter Sellers extols the value of dogs to Donna Mullane and John Chaffey by the underpass, before crossing the bridge, in *The Optimists* (1973). Jared Harris follows Aria Argento across Albert Bridge and through the underpass to make a date in *B. Monkey* (1996). Joss Ackland and Andrew Connolly investigate Elizabeth Hurley's plunge into the Thames here in *Mad Dogs and Englishmen* (1995).

Albert Bridge itself is a big feature of *Sliding Doors* (1999), where Gwyneth Paltrow goes to console herself in times of trouble, joined at the end by John Hannah. Dirk Bogarde and Renee Asherson enjoy a date on the bridge in *Once a Jolly Swagman* (1948). John Fraser rescues June Thorburn's cat, trapped on one of the east side's supports, in *Touch and Go* (1955); later he and Thorburn meet for a date at the underpass.

In *The Thirty-Nine Steps* (1978) Donald Pickering and Ronald Pickup try to assassinate John Mills at Cadogan Pier. Under the credits, Mills exits a carriage and walks through the underpass to meet Timothy West and William Squire in a boat. He avoids death after the meeting by running along the Thames riverbank, fortunately at low tide. Tom Selleck as *Lassiter* (1986) and Ed Harris rescue Joe Regalbuto from his boat moored at Cadogan Pier when Warren Clarke chucks a grenade into it.

The opening shot of **Captives** (1994) pans Albert Bridge and tilts to Julia Ormond's flat between Royal Hospital Road and Swan Walk on Chelsea Embankment. Eric Portman lives with mother Barbara Everest at Garden Corner, 13 Chelsea Embankment, in **Wanted For Murder** (1946). In **The Small Back Room** (1949) Kathleen Byron catches up with David Farrar on Chelsea Embankment.

At Burton's Court's cricket pavilion, where Ormonde Street meets St Leonard's Terrace, Michael Crawford and Oliver Reed as **The Jokers** (1966) watch a cricket match with parents Peter Graves and Rachel Kempson, sister Ingrid Brett and her boyfriend Edward Fox. Alex Pettyfer cycles alongside Burton Court to his house at 17 St Leonard's Terrace in **Stormbreaker** (2006).

David Warner as **Morgan** (1966) rides down Smith Terrace on a motorbike wearing a gorilla suit, travelling from W1 to SW10.

The Servant (1963) opens with a shot facing south along Royal Avenue, then tilting north to Dirk Bogarde crossing King's Road in front of no. 120, Thomas Crapper, now The Vestry. He goes to 30 Royal Avenue on the west side for a successful interview with James Fox. Oskar Werner and Barbara Ferris share a romantic **Interlude** (1968) in front of no.s 42 and 44 Royal Avenue. On the corner of King's Road and Royal Avenue is the site of the Chelsea Drug Store, where Malcolm McDowell picks up two girls at the record counter in **A Clockwork Orange** (1971). The shop is now a McDonalds.

8 Blacklands Terrace, on the corner with Bray Place, is Andreas, now slightly altered and called El Blason, the restaurant where David Hemmings has lunch with publisher Peter Bowles in **Blow Up** (1966).

Across King's Road is the Duke of York's HQ, best seen from Cheltenham Terrace. Peter Vaughan surreptitiously receives information from an officer in the portico in **The Naked Runner** (1967). In **Diamond Skulls** (1989) Douglas Hodge betrays his feelings of guilt to fellow officers Ralph Brown and David Delue after a drill on the west side of the field.

In **I Don't Want to Be Born** (1975) Joan Collins and Ralph Bates live at 32 Wellington Square, just off King's Road.

St Luke's Church on Sydney Street is the wedding venue of Jeff Daniels and Natasha Richardson in **101 Dalmatians** (1996).

Opposite:
Garden Corner,
Chelsea
Embankment (top)
provides a location
for **Wanted for Murder** (1946). Eric
Portman leaves
Garden Corner
(bottom left) while
mother Barbara
Everest watches
from the balcony
(bottom right).

Brompton

Dirk Bogarde takes Delphine Seyrig out to supper to 19 Mossop Street in *Accident* (1967).

Jonathan Rhys Meyers exits Ralph Lauren, 105–09 Fulham Road on the corner of Elystan Street, and bumps into Scarlett Johansson in *Match Point* (2005). At Bibendum, 81 Fulham Road opposite Pelham Street, Aria Argento as *B. Monkey* (1996) is late for a date with Jared Harris. On the corner, since rebuilt, of Draycott Avenue and Brompton Road is the pet shop where Oliver Reed admires tropical fish in *Castaway* (1987).

Christina World as *The Golden Lady* (1978) operates from her base at 30 Egerton Crescent. She dines with June Chadwick at La Brasserie, now enlarged, at 272 Fulham Road close by.

Natasha Richardson lives at 23 Egerton Terrace, close to Egerton Place, known as '7 Pembroke Green' in *The Parent Trap* (1998). The Rolls, bringing in Lindsay Lohan from the airport via London's landmarks, arrives from the dead end of Egerton Terrace.

The all-night party in *The Jokers* (1966) spills out onto North Terrace, off Fulham Road.

Deborah Kerr drives Roger Livesey to 15 Ovington Square in *The Life and Death of Colonel Blimp* (1943), while John Laurie unfurls the Union Flag from a top floor window in greeting. Later Kerr in her third character picks up Anton Walbrook, while Livesey and Laurie, now elderly, see him off. The house appears to be blitzed soon after, with a gap between nos. 13 and 17.

In *To Catch A Spy* (1971) Marlene Jobert sends a drink out from San Lorenzo, 22 Beauchamp Place, to her tail Tom Courtenay, who's skulking by the stairs of a shop called Little Things, now Magaschoni.

In *Ring of Bright Water* (1969) Bill Travers crosses the road from the Barclays Bank at 137 Brompton Road. The hairdresser's Robert Fielding of Regent Street, no longer there, appears in *Theatre of Blood* (1973); Coral Browne visits. She is dropped off on Brompton Road opposite Harrods and enters, to her doom. Genevieve Waite and Glenna Forster-Jones walk down Brompton Road and imagine themselves astride an elephant outside Harrods in *Joanna* (1968).

Under the titles of *To Catch A Spy* (1971) Marlene Jobert leads her school children to Vincent Square (SW1) via Harrods. Sidney Poitier shops at Harrods in *A Warm December* (1973). Anne Bancroft breaks down inside in *The Pumpkin Eater* (1964). Sinead Cusack and Peter Sellers shop for meat there in *Hoffman* (1969). Mohamed Al-Fayed, playing a doorman in his own store, gives directions to Anna Friel in *Mad Cows* (1999).

SW7: Brompton, South Kensington, Knightsbridge

Brompton

In *Goodbye Mr. Chips* (1969) Peter O'Toole and Petula Clark gaze at each other adoringly at the south-east end of Pelham Crescent. In *Around the World in Eighty Days* (1956) Cantinflas fetches a padre from 12 Pelham Crescent before realizing that they 'gained' a day by crossing the International Dateline. Corey Cooper throws cross-dressing husband Adrian Pasdar out of 26 Pelham Crescent in *Just Like a Woman* (1992), and later the family moves out altogether.

Left:
Corey Cooper throws out Adrian Pasdar's dresses from a balcony on Pelham Crescent in *Just Like a Woman* (1992).

Richard Burton exits South Kensington tube and crosses Pelham Street in an effort to lose his tail in **The Spy Who Came in from the Cold** (1965). Miranda Richardson waits on Pelham Street to be picked up by fellow assassins in **The Crying Game** (1992).

At the beginning of **Repulsion** (1965) Catherine Deneuve crosses Harrington Road, then confusingly passes the Hoop and Toy pub, 34 Thurloe Place (where John Fraser tries to attract her attention) and heads onto the triangular island between Brompton Road and Onslow Square, where she is hassled by workman Mike Pratt. John Fraser joins her for lunch at Dino's next to South Kensington tube. He then escorts her back to the beauty parlour, Madame Denise's at 31 Thurloe Place, where she works. This is now Thurloes, still a beauty parlour. Juliette Caton and Kirsten Parker emerge from Daquise Restaurant, 20 Thurloe Place, in **Small Time Obsession** (2000).

South Kensington

The house vacated by Leo McKern for Judy Parfitt and John Rowe to move into in **The Chain** (1984) is 80 Onslow Gardens. 69 Onslow Gardens plays the in-joke '69 Basil Street' in **A Fish Called Wanda** (1988). Michael Palin finally manages to rub out Patricia Hayes outside after mistakenly knocking off her terriers one by one.

Simon Callow lives at the south end of Cranley Mews, seen briefly under the titles of **Four Weddings and a Funeral** (1994).

14 Wetherby Place is the embassy visited by Jenny Runacre in **The Passenger** (1975).

John Thaw goes to the Gloucester Hotel, 4 Harrington Gardens, in **Sweeney!** (1976) to meet Diane Keen. They are forced to flee Keen's room when assassins attempt to shoot them. New building now encloses the outdoor fire escape they use in the central courtyard.

Knightsbridge

Across Cromwell Road is Emperor's Gate. In the corner just next to the arch to Osten Mews is no. 36. This is where, on the first floor, Julie Christie and Dirk Bogarde set up their love nest in **Darling** (1965). Lee Remick lives at the same address, flat 8, in **Hennessy** (1975). She harbours Rod Steiger until he is forced to flee via Osten Mews after an attack by Eric Portman and his IRA colleagues.

In **The Jokers** (1966) Oliver Reed lives at 19 Cornwall Gardens. Reed and brother Michael Crawford watch as the police surround the area from the first floor balcony.

In **The Big Sleep** (1978) Derek Deadman, followed by Robert Mitchum, emerges from the dead end of the western branch of Kynance Mews and takes the stairs by the church. Here Mitchum's prey hides in a bush at the base of Victoria Road but, panicking, he runs up Victoria Road into W8, leaving his porn book in the bush. Janet Suzman runs down the stairs and towards the dead end of the mews to evade her tail in **The Black Windmill** (1974). Michael Craig escorts Julie Andrews home to Bell Cottage, 13 Kynance Mews, on the north side, in **Star!** (1968). A later scene squeezes a period bus into the mews to collect enthusiastic revellers for an excursion. 25 Kynance Mews is Lewis Collins's house in **Who Dares Wins** (1982). Ingrid Pitt and an accomplice come down the Victoria Road steps, overpower the police guard and hold Collins's wife Rosalind Lloyd and baby hostage until the SAS intervene from no. 26. 23 Kynance Mews is Pamela Stephenson's house, to which she brings Robert Hays in **Scandalous** (1984). Susan George cycles off to school from roughly in front of no. 21 under the credits of **Twinky** (1969). John Thaw and Diane Keen, chased by a car, run through the arch of the west entrance in **Sweeney!** (1976).

Across Launceston Place is the east part of Kynance Mews. Next to the arch, on the south side, is no. 10, Juliette Binoche's house in **Damage** (1992). Jeremy Irons meets her here for some passion. The signs next to this arch, Launceston Place and Kynance Mews, are renamed Kenton for a scene with a taxi arriving in **Crooks Anonymous** (1963). Leslie Phillips lives with Julie Christie at no. 4, but look carefully at the night shots featuring the actors on the street: it's a near accurate studio mock-up.

Across Gloucester Road on the south-east corner of Elvaston Place and Elvaston Mews is 23a Queen's Gate Lodge. This is 'Keeley's Foundation For Science' in **The Satanic Rites of Dracula** (1973). Peter Cushing enters through a side door just under the mews's very distinctive arch.

In **Performance** (1970) a chauffeur receives a head shave and James Fox ruins a Rolls Royce's paintwork in a garage next to 35 Queen's Gate Mews, while a milkman delivers to no. 37. Daniel Craig lives to the east at no. 7 in **Layer Cake** (2004).

Along Cromwell Road is the Natural History Museum. The steps to the main entrance, and the hall inside with its notable staircase, feature in **One of Our Dinosaurs Is Missing** (1976). Derek Nimmo hides a piece of microfilm inside, and is aided by nannies Helen Hayes and Joan Sims, who take on Nimmo's pursuers. In **Seven Days to Noon** (1950) Barry Jones listens to the prime minister's plans for the evacuation of central London inside the museum. He leaves by the main door and, panicked by seeing his face on 'Wanted' posters, crosses Cromwell Road and seeks refuge in South Kensington tube. In **Greystoke** (1984) Andie MacDowell and Christopher Lambert ascend the staircase in the main hall of the museum. Lambert finds his ape father imprisoned within the museum, and they escape to clamber over the Albert Memorial, north of the museum, and thence to a tree, where the ape is shot. Harvey Keitel meets Craig Kelly on a bench to the west of the staircase in **The Young Americans** (1993). At the end of **Loch Ness** (1994) a conference gathers in the hall and ascends the stairs, where Ted Danson and James Frain fail to produce evidence of Nessie, to Harris Yulin's dismay. David Morrissey visits ex-wife Indira Varma at her workplace here in **Basic Instinct 2** (2005).

Behind the museum on Exhibition Road is the Science Museum, the interior of which is seen when Derren Nesbitt and Deborah Barrymore brief Michael Caine and Roger Moore in **Bullseye!** (1990). Prime minister Robbie Coltrane meets Mickey Rourke here to activate Rourke's project called **Stormbreaker** (2006). June Thorburn and John Fraser visit in **Touch and Go** (1955).

In **The Ipcress File** (1965) Michael Caine escorts Aubrey Richards from the Victoria and Albert Museum into a car. Dirk Bogarde interviews Julie Christie in front of the Cromwell Gardens entrance of the V&A in **Darling** (1965). The interior is seen when Oliver Reed, Michael Crawford and Lotte Tarp visit a copy of Trajan's column in **The Jokers** (1966).

In **Against the Wind** (1948) Robert Beatty approaches the entrance of the Imperial Institute on the north side of Imperial Institute Road, guarded by four sedentary lions, to receive training for a World War II operation in Belgium. Villagers steal **The Titfield Thunderbolt** (1953) from the institute under the direction of John Gregson, Naunton Wayne and George Relph. The institute was demolished and the site swallowed up by Imperial College years ago, and the road renamed Imperial College Road.

On the corner of Kensington Road and Queen's Gate is 25 Kensington Road, now part of the College of Art, the house seen in **23 Paces to Baker Street** (1956) when a nursemaid wheels an invalid through Queen's Gate. Van Johnson, Vera Miles and Cecil Parker help inspector Maurice Denham, who finds the chair abandoned in nearby shrubbery.

In **The Million Pound Note** (1954) starving Gregory Peck watches a family picnic in front of the Albert Memorial on South Carriage Drive. Here Jean Kent as **Trottie True** (1948) invites Hugh Sinclair to join her in her carriage. Peter Lawford's carriage passes by the memorial in **The Hours of 13** (1952), but this is a back projection. The memorial is the first target of the fake bombers in **The Jokers** (1966). Oliver Reed watches James Donald defusing the bomb from a deckchair to the east. Disguised as a bear-skinned guard Reed, again, meets Diana Rigg just to the west in *The Assassination Bureau* (1968). Adam Ant enjoys a bottle of milk on the south steps of the memorial in *Jubilee* (1977). Bob Hoskins appeals for help from Jane Seymour sitting in the rain on the south steps of the memorial in *Lassiter* (1986). Anna Friel catches a bus on Kensington Gore in front of the memorial in *Mad Cows* (1999). The band led by Pete Postlethwaite and including Ewan McGregor, Tara Fitzgerald and Stephen Tompkinson in *Brassed Off* (1996) pose in front of the Royal Albert Hall to the south of the memorial. The same view appears briefly in *Leopard in the Snow* (1977). Paul Nicholls walks past the memorial on his way to a concert in *If Only* (2004). In *To Catch a Spy* (1971) Marlene Jobert and Angharad Rees split up at the north end of the Albert Memorial. Tom Courtenay chases Jobert around the Albert Hall but loses her at the south end when she hides in entrance no. 2, near Albert Hall Mansions.

In *The Man Who Knew Too Much* (1955) Doris Day hurries through entrance no. 6 of the Albert Hall to avert an assassination. In the 1934 version, Edna Best follows the would-be assassin as he escapes. Margaret Lockwood plays the 'Cornish Rhapsody' at the end of *Love Story* (1944). In *Interlude* (1968) Oskar Werner draws up to the north-west side of the hall to sign autographs while Barbara Ferris looks on. Werner rehearses inside and Virginia Maskell, Werner's wife, sees evidence of his affair with Ferris. She catches a taxi on Prince Consort Road. Paul McCartney plays 'Eleanor Rigby' to an almost deserted auditorium in *Give My Regards to Broad Street* (1984). A tracking shot follows Julie Andrews and Rupert Everett from behind the stage to a packed house, including Alan Bates, in *Duet For One* (1986). Leigh Lawson takes Navin Chowdhry to the hall where Chowdhry plays piano to an empty auditorium in *Madame Sousatzka* (1988). Christopher Walken, Jonathan Pryce and Carole Bouquet enjoy a concert inside in *A Business Affair* (1994).

Michael Caine follows a suspect down the steps from the south end of the Albert Hall to the 'Science Museum Library', actually the Royal School of Mines and now part of Imperial College, in *The Ipcress File* (1965). Inside he makes contact with Frank Gatliff. After telephoning a dud number in a phone box on Prince Consort Road, he fights with Gatliff's minder Thomas Baptiste on the steps (all stylishly shot through the phone box windows) but the two get away. Later at the same location Caine asks Gatliff for his money back.

The Royal School of Mines is a registry office in *Jack & Sarah* (1995). Thanks to clever cutting, it appears to be the view from Richard E Grant's office as he watches what he interprets as Samantha Mathis' wedding.

Michael Crawford and Donal Donnelly carry a bedstead with Rita Tushingham on it down the steps from the Royal Albert Hall in *The Knack* (1965). Later Ray Brooks fantasizes about queues of women, including a then unknown Jacqueline Bisset, outside the concert hall.

In *Quest For Love* (1971) Tom Bell shows his driving licence, revealing his address as '7 Albert Court', and indeed he gets out of Sam Kydd's taxi in front of Albert Court. Later he and Joan Collins walk up the Kensington Gore steps. In *The Thirty-Nine Steps* (1978) John Mills and Robert Powell live in Albert Court. Mills has a corner flat, looking both north and west over Albert Hall, above Powell's. When Ronald Pickup and Ronald Pickering come to kill Mills, he slips down the emergency stairs, comes round the front, posts a letter in a box on Prince Consort Road and hails a cab just before being recognized. Albert Court is established as Alan Shearman's residence in *Bullshot* (1988).

Peter Cushing descends the steps leading from the south end of the Hall to Prince Consort Road on his way to Elvaston Mews in *The Satanic Rites of Dracula* (1973). George Segal, leaving wife Hildegard Neil to enjoy Beethoven in the Albert Hall, rushes down the steps to catch a taxi and squeeze in some extra-marital business in *A Touch of Class* (1973). On the steps Rod Steiger as *Hennessy* (1975) records politician Hugh Moxey talking about pollution so he can learn to impersonate his voice. In *The Fourth Protocol* (1987) Joanna Cassidy gets off a bus from Heathrow, which parks on Kensington Gore between the hall and the steps. She descends the steps and is met by Pierce Brosnan. They get into Brosnan's car parked on Albert Court opposite Albert Hall Mansions.

In *Success Is the Best Revenge* (1984) an enraged motorist punches Michael York on the pedestrian crossing after York descends the steps with his family. Jonathan Ross interviews the Spice Girls in *Spice World* (1997) in front of the Royal Albert Hall, where manager Richard E Grant is planning a concert. Later the Spice Bus parks in Prince Consort Road and the Spice Girls disembark. They run up the steps and are accosted at the top by two policemen who receive free tickets for their concert.

From a window in the Royal College of Music overlooking Prince Consort Road, John Gielgud watches student Noah Taylor drop his sheet music over the steps while contemplating his 'fantastic hands' in *Shine* (1996).

In the middle of *The X-Files* (1998) there is a brief London scene when John Neville is driven to Queen Alexandra's House on Kensington Gore, to the west of the hall. Genevieve Waite as *Joanna* (1968) studies at the Royal College of Art, just to the north.

In **Maybe Baby** (2000) Hugh Laurie and Joely Richardson chat on their favourite bench in Ennismore Gardens, quite a way from their flat in SW11. It is here that Laurie comes up with the idea of basing a film script on their life together, causing serious friction for their marriage.

John Mills lives at 33 Ennismore Gardens Mews in **The Vicious Circle** (1957) with the distinctive arch separating the mews from Ennismore Street visible. In **Frenzy** (1972) Jon Finch escorts Barbara Leigh-Hunt to her house at no. 31, just to the west.

On the north side of Ennismore Street is Clock House in Rutland Mews West where, in **Sexy Beast** (2000), James Fox lives briefly until Ian McShane kills him, much to Ray Winstone's surprise. John Gregson and Dinah Sheridan live at 17 Rutland Mews South, opposite the garage for **Genevieve** (1953). Kenneth More pops in for lunch. Beryl Reid and Susannah York live in the upper flat of 10 Rutland Mews South in **The Killing of Sister George** (1968). Reid goes to her neighbours at 19 Grafton Cottage, opposite, for a cry. No. 10 was completely demolished and rebuilt in 2004.

26 Rutland Gate, next to Rutland Gate Mews, is Jeremy Brett's house in **Mad Dogs and Englishmen** (1995), which is under surveillance by Joss Ackland and Andrew Connolly. At the basement level Ackland attacks Elizabeth Hurley.

SW5: Earl's Court

In **Success Is the Best Revenge** (1984) Michael Lyndon crosses Lillie Road to West Brompton tube. At the station a killer slashes a victim in Ben Keyworth's young imagination in **Afraid of the Dark** (1991). Keyworth trips over on Old Brompton Road opposite Kramer Mews while following Paul McGann into the north end of Brompton cemetery (SW10). This entrance is also seen in **Johnny English** (2003) when Rowan Atkinson, chasing the wrong hearse, slips in via the chapel next to the main gate. In **Melody** (1971) Mark Lester and Tracy Hyde enter here for a picnic.

The ballroom scene at the start of **Richard III** (1995) is in the church of St Cuthbert in Philbeach Gardens. Later Ian McKellen is invited to take the crown of England in the basement of Earl's Court Exhibition Centre on Warwick Road. Laura Fraser and Luke de Lacey cross Warwick Road to the Exhibition Centre hosting a Virtual Reality exposition in **Virtual Sexuality** (1999).

15 Kensington Mansions on Trebovir Road, which the kitchen overlooks, houses Catherine Deneuve's flat, shared with sister Yvonne Furneaux, in **Repulsion** (1965). John Fraser drives Deneuve home from work to the entrance.

In **Sweeney!** (1976) Dennis Waterman lives at 24 Longridge Road on the corner of Templeton Place. John Thaw hides Diane Keen in this flat, trying in vain to protect her from hit men.

Joan Collins visits Oliver Tobias as **The Stud** (1978) at his pad in 250 Earl's Court Road. Rita Tushingham exits Earl's Court tube in **Straight On Till Morning** (1972). She bumps into Shane Briant outside a newsagent's, which is still in business, at 214 Earl's Court Road.

Colin Firth and Irène Jacob discuss their counselling session with Stephen Fry in **Londinium** (2001) while walking along Bramham Gardens towards the corner of Collingham Gardens.

Opposite:
121 Earl's Court Road provides the setting for **Straight On Till Morning** (1972).

Left:
Straight On Till Morning (1972). Shane Briant parks in Hogarth Road (top left) to enter a newsagent's on Earl's Court Road (bottom right).

SW10: West Brompton

As **Morgan** (1966) David Warner in a gorilla outfit rides a stolen motorbike into the Thames, launching from Cremorne Wharf. Coming to just north of Chelsea Basin, he hallucinates that Bernard Bresslaw straightjackets him, Robert Stephens hooks him up onto a crane and Vanessa Redgrave and revolutionaries surround him. The goods sheds and railway lines have now been replaced by the Chelsea Harbour development.

Aria Argento as **B. Monkey** (1996) moves into Jared Harris's houseboat moored near Chelsea Creek. In **The Optimists** (1973) Peter Sellers lives up some steps in a warehouse – still there though the canal has been filled in – off Lots Road, overlooking Chelsea Creek and Sand's End gasworks.

In **The Deadly Affair** (1967) James Mason and Harry Andrews visit Roy Kinnear for questioning at his garage. The garage is overshadowed by Lots Road Power Station, with its distinctive four chimneys. Only two of the chimneys remain now. Kinnear lives at 116 Lots Road, next door to The Balloon Tavern. After a thug breaks Mason's hand, Andrews dishes out a beating to Kinnear outside the pub. Mason's attacker returns later and kills Kinnear, dumping his body into Chelsea Creek. As The Ferret and Firkin in the Balloon up the Creek, the same pub is Oliver Reed's drinking hole in **Castaway** (1987). It is now called Lots Road Pub and Dining.

Donna Mullane and John Chaffey live with their parents in the basement of Carlisle House, 64 Uverdale Road, in **The Optimists** (1973). Cecil Parker walks down Uverdale Road towards the power station in **I Believe in You** (1952).

In **The Deadly Affair** (1967) Harry Andrews follows Maximilian Schell to his houseboat base at the Chelsea Yacht and Boat Company at the western end of Cheyne Walk. After calling James Mason for help, Andrews is shot by Schell before he is dispatched into the Thames by Mason and crushed by a boat.

Dennis Price lives at the east end of Cheyne Walk in **The Naked Truth** (1957). One of his blackmail victims, Shirley Eaton, visits, and then another, Peter Sellers, 'barges in' followed by yet another, Terry-Thomas. Later Sellers steals Price's files from his car parked across Cheyne Walk. In **I'll Never Forget What's'isname** (1967) Orson Welles visits Oliver Reed on a houseboat to woo him back to his job. Here Reed picks up Carol White for a day in Cambridge. At the end Reed tosses his advertising award into the river from Battersea Bridge. Roger Moore finds Claudia Lange on a houseboat here in **Crossplot** (1967). Tom

Courtenay as *Otley* (1969) takes refuge on James Bolam and Fiona Lewis's houseboat until his pursuers catch up with him. He escapes by jumping into the mud and scrabbling over the wall opposite The King's Arms, 114 Cheyne Walk, now converted. Courtenay then runs down Blantyre Street, since completely redeveloped as the World End estate. Martin Potter and Judy Geeson encounter Michael Redgrave and Alexis Kanner on a houseboat party in *Goodbye Gemini* (1970). In *Twinky* (1969) Charles Bronson lives on the second floor of 91 Cheyne Walk, on the corner of Beaufort Street. Susan George moves in with him after their marriage.

On the bend of King's Road, on the corner of Milman's Street, was the site of the police station where David Farrar operates the investigation of baby Simon's disappearance in *Lost* (1955). In *Sapphire* (1959) outside the station Michael Craig watches Gordon Heath drive off. In *Victim* (1961) John Barrie and John Cairney take Peter McEnery here for questioning, and later summon Dirk Bogarde. Just to the east of Milman's Street, Anthony Bourke and John Rendall exercise *The Lion at World's End* (1971) in an enclosed old burial ground.

At the north end of Park Walk is Salvadors, now a tapas bar, where Julie Walters is so late for a date in *Personal Services* (1986) that she hides opposite 9 Park Walk under the arch of Stanley Studios.

At Chelsea and Westminster Hospital on Fulham Road, Richard E Grant is shocked when Imogen Stubbs dies after giving birth to Sarah in *Jack & Sarah* (1995). Naoko Mori gives birth in *Spice World* (1997). John Hannah meets the other Gwyneth Paltrow in *Sliding Doors* (1998). Lena Headey works here in *If Only* (1998). In *Five Seconds to Spare* (1999) Max Beesley visits rape victim Sarah Jane Potts. In *Eyes Wide Shut* (1999) Tom Cruise enters through the revolving doors and finds out at the information desk that his saviour Julienne Davis has died.

In the middle of Brompton Cemetery, Eileen Atkins mourns her daughter in *Jack & Sarah* (1995). Helena Bonham Carter scrubs her mother's grave in *The Wings of the Dove* (1997). Alex Pettyfer, Alicia Silverstone, Bill Nighy, Sophie Okonedo and Jimmy Carr attend Ewan McGregor's burial in *Stormbreaker* (2006). Ben Keyworth spies on photographer Paul McGann in *Afraid of the Dark* (1991). His bedroom overlooks the cemetery, though some scenes are actually in NW10. Michael York jogs here with son Michael Lyndon in *Success Is the Best Revenge* (1984). The exterior of the Russian church in *Golden Eye* (1995) where Izabella Scorupco hides before her betrayal is the chapel to the south side.

Jude Law returns a crucifix to Timothy Spall as they walk along Central Avenue to Spall's car in *The Wisdom of Crocodiles* (1998). Rowan Atkinson as *Johnny English* (2003) drives up Ifield Road, pauses at the junction with Cathcart Road, sees – and follows – a hearse driving up Finborough Road, which runs parallel, while his real quarry goes down Redcliffe Gardens. In the cemetery he makes a fool of himself at the burial before Ben Miller's rescue.

On the corner of Lillie Road and Finborough Road is Princess Beatrice House, where after being attacked David Naughton wakes up to the nursing charms of Jenny Agutter in *An American Werewolf in London* (1981). Agutter invites Naughton to recuperate at 64 Redcliffe Square, opposite St Luke's Church.

On the west corner of Westgate Terrace, John Collin, drunk, arrives home at 49 Redcliffe Square with his baby, to the fury of Julie Andrews in *Star!* (1968). In *Defence of the Realm* (1985) Gabriel Byrne stakes out a flat for a possible news story outside 20 Redcliffe Square.

Outside 241 Fulham Road, on the corner with Elm Park Gardens, is the flower stand run by Dan Mead, who is unimpressed by Danny Dyer's stories of hooliganism in *The Football Factory* (2004).

SW6: Fulham, Sands End

Fulham

In *The Omen* (1976) Patrick Troughton arranges to meet Gregory Peck at Bishop's Park. After the meeting Troughton makes his way against increasing wind across an avenue of plane trees and heads for All Saints' Church near Putney Bridge Approach, where he is skewered by a lightning rod. Peter Sellers, Donna Mullane and John Chaffey walk back home after an afternoon's busking outside Craven Cottage, home to Fulham FC, in *The Optimists* (1973).

Left:
Gregory Peck confronts Patrick Troughton in *The Omen* (1976).

Left:
Bishop's Park, as seen in *The Omen* (1976).

The café seen at the beginning of *Poor Cow* (1967) in a visit by Carol White is George's Snack Bar, 623 Fulham Road. A Waitrose has replaced the ABC cinema on North End Road seen opposite through the café's window. The interior of Fulham Pools, at 368 North End Road near Dawes Road, appears in *Deep End* (1972) – though it's called Newford Baths – where John Moulder-Brown takes a shine to Jane Asher.

At the corner of Walham Grove and Farm Lane is The Harwood Arms, where cabbie Jamie Foreman collects Dudley Sutton and John Junkin in *The Football Factory* (2004).

Diane Keaton exits Fulham Broadway tube in *The Little Drummer Girl* (1984). East of the tube is Stamford Bridge, home to Chelsea FC, where Eric Idle and Robbie Coltrane steal a car in *Nuns on the Run* (1990). The site has since been extensively redeveloped into the Chelsea Village complex. Opposite, 469 Fulham Road is Anthony Valentine's betting office in *Performance* (1970). After it is trashed, James Fox comes to collect him. It is now Hair Brazil.

Mark Lester and his family live at 11 Musgrave Crescent in *Melody* (1971). Jack Wild and Lester walk beside the railings and down the path onto Eel Brook Common.

Sands End

Sands End Gas Works, south-east of Fulham Broadway, is the setting for the armoured car robbery that the flying squad foils near the beginning of *Sweeney!* (1976). This area has changed quite a bit, but the five gasholders are still there and can be briefly caught in later scenes featuring Joe Melia's breaker's yard.

In *Eye of the Needle* (1981) two of these gasholders – the ones alongside Imperial Road – are seen several times when enemy spy Donald Sutherland meets his contact in a 1940s-period cab. After the contact is apprehended, Sutherland is chased across town to Marylebone Station (NW1).

Bob Hoskins is furious with Tom Selleck as *Lassiter* (1986) for visiting him at his house at 37 Querrin Street on the corner of Kilkie Street. There is a good view of the four chimneys of Fulham Power Station, now demolished, across Townmead Road as Hoskins and Selleck walk up Kilkie Street. After crossing Wandsworth Bridge Stanley Baker and fellow ne'er-do-wells swap cars on Townmead Road, to the west of the power station, in *The Criminal* (1960).

The parade of shops seen in *Thunderpants* (2002), where Bruce Cook has his photo taken with Rupert Grint and later chases a bully, is at the north end of Sullivan Court off Peterborough Road. New doors leading to upstairs flats have enclosed the location of the photo booth.

SW8: Clapham, Battersea, Nine Elms, Vauxhall

Clapham

In *My Beautiful Laundrette* (1985) Saeed Jaffrey walks from Ravenet Street to visit Roshan Seth, who lives with son Gordon Warnecke at 239 Queenstown Road. The balcony at the back is from a house further north as it overlooks the intersection of the mainline tracks from Victoria and Waterloo, and London Stainless Steel, still there. Mark Rylance drives north up Queenstown Road to go to work in WC1 from SE14 in *Intimacy* (2000), somewhat off the most direct route.

Alex Pettyfer cycles over the Queen's Circus roundabout in pursuit of a van in *Stormbreaker* (2006). On Queenstown Road is Marco Polo House, currently the headquarters of QVC, although renamed 'Presm Medical Centre' for the purposes of *Leon*

Opposite:
Saaed Jaffrey walks along Ravenet Street (top) in *My Beautiful Laundrette* (1985). This scene takes place in Ravenet Street (bottom left), while Queenstown Road (bottom right), seen as Gordon Warnecke and Roshan Seth's flat, is just around the corner.

the Pig Farmer (1992). Here Mark Frankel delivers kosher food round the back and ends up in Annette Crosbie's office overlooking the power station. Aria Argento as **B. Monkey** (1996) works here. Eighties yuppies order cocaine on their brick-like mobile phones in **The Business** (2004). A Rolls crosses Chelsea Bridge to drop off Suzy Kendall on Queenstown Road in **Up the Junction** (1967).

Battersea

In **The Day the Earth Caught Fire** (1961) after their trip to the fair (SW11) Edward Judd and Janet Munro go to the embankment to watch a mysterious fog swirl around Chelsea Bridge. Later, behind the gates leading from Carriage Drive North to Queenstown Road, water rations are distributed and Judd says goodbye to his estranged family. Here at this gate Meryl Streep meets Sting in **Plenty** (1985) and they embrace on Chelsea Bridge. Just inside the park, police pull over Adrian Pasdar in his transvestite gear after he crosses the bridge in **Just Like a Woman** (1992).

Battersea Power Station (started in 1928, finished in 1953 and closed in 1983) gained immortality in the popular world by being featured along with a flying pig on Pink Floyd's album *Animals*, reproduced in **Children of Men** (2006) along with CGI trickery, but the station is currently just a shell and still awaiting redevelopment more than two decades after closure. In his first act of **Sabotage** (1936) Oscar Homolka causes London to plunge into temporary darkness by attacking the station. The opening titles of **Eye of the Needle** (1981) feature over the South Lambeth Goods Depot, standing in for a busy railway station. In **1984** (1984) John Hurt uses the station to take a train into the countryside for a rendezvous with Suzanna Hamilton. Most of the tracks and buildings south of the power station have now been razed. As **Richard III** (1995) Ian McKellen rests his troops between the river and the power station before the Battle of Bosworth ensues. Dominic West's tank pursues McKellen's jeep into the roofless power station. Within the empty shell of the station cop James Faulkner shows a body to Stephen Baldwin, who's promptly sick, in **Crimetime** (1996). The shell is also seen in **If Only** (1998) when Douglas Henshall spins himself around. Tom Hollander is filming an advert between the station and the crane in **Maybe Baby** (2000) and accepts the directing job of Hugh Laurie's film script. Later Laurie has second thoughts, since he has based it on his personal life with his wife. He tries to regain control of his script inside the shell while Adrian Lester and Matthew MacFayden look on and Hollander tries to reassure him. In the extensive car park there is an assassination in **Three Blind Mice** (2002).

In the car chase of **Sitting Target** (1972) Oliver Reed forces Ian McShane and Jill St John into the area north of the gasworks off Queenstown Road. After McShane's car crashes, there is a showdown on the grass embankment south-west of the station. Policeman Edward Woodward arrives too late to make a difference.

Peter Sellers, Donna Mullane and John Chaffey visit Battersea Dogs' and Cats' Home (cats being a recent addition) on Nine Elms Lane to choose a dog in **The Optimists** (1973). They take the footbridge to Stewart's Road alongside the railway lines.

In **The Low Down** (2001) within the arch unit 696 off Havelock Terrace, under the line that runs from Victoria to Beckenham, Aidan Gillen runs his prop-making business with Dean Lennox Kelly and Tobias Stephens.

Just on the other side was Gladstone Terrace where Adrienne Posta and Maureen Lipman live with mother Liz Fraser in **Up the Junction** (1967), but the area is now unrecognizable. Still standing however is The Pavilion, on Bradmead, outside which bikers pick up the girls, including Suzy Kendall.

Nine Elms

In **My Beautiful Laundrette** (1985) Gordon Warnecke meets old school friend Daniel Day-Lewis on Stewart's Road as his gang, including Richard Graham, threaten motorists under the railway bridge. Later Derrick Branche drives from Ascalon Street into Stewart's Road, running over gang member Stephen Marcus's foot.

In **Melody** (1971) Mark Lester follows a gang of schoolboys he wants to befriend over desolate ground. He picks his way past Vauxhall Cold Store, which was demolished in 1999, and ends up 'spying' on the gang as they experiment with a firework by the railway lines of Nine Elms. This is where, later, Jack Wild arranges for Lester to 'marry' Tracy Hyde in front of several schoolchildren, who riot when their teachers attempt to stop them. The waste area has now been developed and the site, unrecognizable except for the arches (now blocked up) under the railway line from Waterloo, is at the end of Ponton Road, now occupied by Christie's depot.

Vauxhall

On the other side of the tracks is New Covent Garden Fruit and Vegetable Market, but at the climax of **Villain** (1970) Richard Burton takes Joss Ackland to the site cleared in preparation for the market.

Gina McKee lives at the high-rise Bannerman House on Lawn Lane next to Vauxhall Park in **Wonderland** (1999). The flat has a great view of the Oval cricket ground.

Richard Graham's gang hand out leaflets to motorists entering Sainsbury's car park on Wandsworth Road in **My Beautiful Laundrette** (1985). The laundrette itself, called 'Powders', is at 11 Wilcox Road. Here Saeed Jaffrey entrusts Gordon Warnecke and Daniel Day-Lewis with the running of the laundrette. The parade is much the same now though no. 11, after a while as Low Gear, is now Magic T-Shirts. Trend, the dry cleaners next door, recently became the restaurant Legends. Charles A Perry, outside which Jaffrey and Shirley Anne Field have a row, is now a branch of bookmakers William Hill, and the doors at the rear of the parade, where there used to be parking, have been bricked up.

In **The Good Father** (1985) Simon Callow, Anthony Hopkins and Jim Broadbent, taking a break from court (SW18), discuss the dustmen's strike as they walk past The Gladstone along Wilcox Road, piled up with rubbish bags.

In **Intimacy** (2000) Mark Rylance follows Kerry Fox through Fosbrooke House off Wandsworth Road and across Thorncroft Road to her home in Sheldon Court. The second laundrette Gordon Warnecke and Derrick Branche inspect in **My Beautiful Laundrette** (1985), while Daniel Day-Lewis sits sulking in his car outside, is on Wandsworth Road, near Thorncroft Street.

Towards the end of **Janice Beard 45 wpm** (1998) Eileen Walsh meets Rhys Ifans in Pensbury Place to prevent a car being crushed in a wrecking yard. Supposed to be in Rotherhithe, the two Richard Seifert-designed tower blocks seen are indeed similar to a couple near Canada Water tube (SE16).

Oliver Reed visits a scrapyard just north of Clyston Street in his imagination, while hallucinating on his tropical island in **Castaway** (1987). Alex Pettyfer chases the van into a junkyard at the north end of Pensbury Place before a cut to Colindale in north-west London in **Stormbreaker** (2006).

SW9: Stockwell, north Brixton

The curious concrete structure in the middle of Ackerman Road makes an appearance when Gary Oldman is clinging to a van's roof at high speed in **Dead Fish** (2004).

On the corner of Evandale Road and Loughborough Road, the Loughborough Hotel provides the interiors of the 'St Paul's' salsa club in **Born Romantic** (2000).

In *The Long Good Friday* (1980) Bob Hoskins, Derek Thompson and PH Moriarty pay a visit to 33 Villa Road, east of Brixton Road, to interview grass Paul Barber. 'This used to be a nice area. No scum.' At the time Villa Road was in fact a white, middle-class-dominated squat, whose barricading in 1976 prevented demolition of the north side of the Victorian terrace, but did not save the south side. In *Black Joy* (1976) a local urchin mugs Norman Beaton on that south side, now occupied by a park. He has just arrived at Brixton tube, further south on Brixton Road. Much of the action takes place in the market and shops of Brixton Station Road and Atlantic Road. Trevor Thomas's local is The Atlantic, 389 Coldharbour Lane on the corner of Atlantic Road, where Floella Benjamin works. Jonathan Pryce's closest tube to home is Brixton in *The Ploughman's Lunch* (1983).

South West 9 (2001) opens to a small park on the corner of Stockwell Road and Stockwell Park Walk where Wil Johnson introduces himself. Stuart Laing and Mark Letheren are first seen in Brixton Station Road, close to no. 28 Ashok Supermarket. Characters assemble in The Dogstar, formerly The Atlantic. While Orlessa Edwards watches an argument with traffic wardens outside Michael's Meats diagonally opposite, Amelia Curtis steals her case and takes it to her squat at 70 Wiltshire Road, outside which she meets old boyfriend Stephen Lloyd. A mass eviction takes place there at the end of the film.

Johnson runs errands for Robbie Gee, reporting at 'Sid Cars' just south of Ichiban Sushi, still there at 58a Atlantic Road. After collecting a film can he takes an extraordinary route to get to 'The Smokehouse'. He enters a boarded-up 372 Coldharbour Lane through the derelict area behind, and is then seen alongside a railway viaduct filmed further to the east in Belinda Road; finally he arrives back at Saltoun Road, location of 'The Smokehouse' (SW2).

Opposite 372 Coldharbour Lane is Southwyck House, part of the Moorlands Estate seen in the same film when Edwards is waiting at a phone box unaware that Curtis is passing by with her stolen case. Along with Frank Harper, sister Nicola Stapleton and Edwards's sister Zebida Gardener-Sharper, all congregate at St John's Angell Town (where Wiltshire Road meets Villa Road) for a techno-trance rave.

In *Date With a Dream* (1948) Bill and Len Lowe walk along Barrington Road, past the long-closed East Brixton station. In *I'll Sleep When I'm Dead* (2003) Jonathan Rhys Meyers is dropped off by taxi under the railway bridge. As he makes his way east along Coldharbour Lane, Malcolm McDowell's heavies drag him into an alleyway, opposite Loughborough Park, that runs alongside Coldharbour Lane. Just to the east is The Junction Bar, now converted to flats, outside which Brian Coucher threatens Clive Owen.

Round the corner in the same film, Jamie Foreman lives in Woolley House on Loughborough Road. He is picked up by Ross Boatman in the AB News shop on the corner of Loughborough Road and Barrington Road, bundled into Ken Stott's car parked in Featley Road and taken for a questioning session before being dropped off at the old Russell Hotel on the corner of Caldwell Road and Brixton Road.

During the abortion scene in *Alfie* (1966) Michael Caine wanders along Brixton Station Road heading east. In the next shot he is heading east on Atlantic Road, opposite Electric Avenue. Trevor Thomas walks west along Brixton Station Road after Floella Benjamin has thrown him out in *Black Joy* (1976).

The Brixton Academy on the corner of Stockwell Road and Astoria Walk is seen as 'The Lyceum' in *Velvet Goldmine* (1998), where Jonathan Rhys Meyers appears to be assassinated. Here Kieran O'Brien meets Margo Stilley in *Nine Songs* (2004). David Hemmings drives south down Stockwell Road in *Blow Up* (1966).

Carve Her Name with Pride (1958) opens with Virginia McKenna leaving 3 Burnley Road, turning into St Martin's Road and catching a bus on Stockwell Park Crescent. The house no. 3 is renumbered 18 (the number is seen as Paul Schofield drops her off after her first mission), since Violette Szabo, the film's real-life subject, had lived opposite at the blue-plaqued 18 Burnley Road.

SW4: Clapham Park

Norman Beaton unwisely forks out rent in advance for a flat in Langham House on Worsopp Drive, only to find it's already occupied in *Black Joy* (1977).

The Winslow family, headed by Nigel Hawthorne and Gemma Jones, live at 21 Clapham Common West Side, on the corner with Thyleigh Road, in *The Winslow Boy* (1999).

In *This Happy Breed* (1944) Celia Johnson pushes a pram by the pond alongside Clapham Common South Side, opposite Narbonne Avenue.

Anthony Hopkins as *The Good Father* (1985) sits on a bench with son Harry Grubb just west of Clapham Common tube during the opening credits. Hopkins and Jim Broadbent visit Miriam Margolyes at the 'Clapham Law Centre' opposite the tube on Clapham Common South Side. The two also share scenes in the bandstand in the middle of the common, and on the roughly surfaced football fields where Hopkins finally admits

that 'I wanted to do some damage'. John Shea plays football with Daniel Chasin while Helen Mirren looks on from the bandstand area in **Hussy** (1980).

Paul Angelis steals a car on the south side of Grafton Square, driving it off when its owner stops to untie the cans attached to its rear. On the south-west corner of Cubitt Terrace, clearly signed, Paul Angelis equally ingeniously steals another car by kicking it as it passes and when the enraged driver gets out to remonstrate he overpowers him and drives off.

On the corner of Larkhall Lane and Priory Grove is the Larkhall Tavern, hired just before conversion into flats for interior scenes in **Last Orders** (2001). Bob Hoskins, Ray Winstone, Tom Courtenay and David Hemmings meet there before setting off to scatter Michael Caine's ashes. The exterior of the pub is in SE15.

Above:
Clapham Common South Side (above left) is featured in ***This Happy Breed*** (1944), where Celia Johnson pushes a pram in war-torn London (above right).

SW11: Battersea

Carol White crosses Plough Road from Harbut Road in **Poor Cow** (1967). The demolished Fulham Road Power Station (SW6) is seen in the background. In **The Good Father** (1985) Anthony Hopkins crosses Plough Road to his new flat at 1 Cologne Road, on the corner of Plough Terrace.

On the Thames, off Bridges Court, is the London Battersea Heliport, formerly Westland. Judy Garland and Gregory Phillips take off for an aerial sightseeing tour in *I Could Go On Singing* (1963). Fans gather here to greet a swami landing in *The Strange Affair* (1969). Ian Bannen and John Paul land here in *Doomwatch* (1972). In *A Warm December* (1973) Sidney Poitier, his daughter and Esther Anderson take a trip interrupted by Anderson feeling an attack of sickle cell disease. The waiting room where Anderson gives her host the slip is largely unchanged. Michael Caine lands here in *Half Moon Street* (1986). Richard Johnson catches a helicopter in pursuit of David Niven in *A Nightingale Sang in Berkeley Square* (1979). Andy Garcia leaves for home, waved off by Robert Stephens and Kitty Aldridge, in *American Roulette* (1988). In *The Innocent Sleep* (1995) Franco Nero is questioned at the gates (since replaced by taller ones) by hordes of reporters, including Annabella Sciorra.

In *Mona Lisa* (1986) Robbie Coltrane lives by the river off Vicarage Crescent, just north of the railway bridge. Peter Sellers plays a little ditty to his two youthful assistants in the small open area off Vicarage Crescent in *The Optimists* (1973), and the children walk by the riverside just to the north.

Dana Andrews chases after Peggy Cummins to Clapham Junction Station in *Night of the Demon* (1957). Suzy Kendall arrives at the station in *Up the Junction* (1967). She finds digs on Ingrave Street, a once-terraced street now cleared for the huge Surrey Lane Estate.

Jill St John lives near the top of the enormous Sporle Court tower on the corner of Darien Road and Winstanley Road in *Sitting Target* (1972). Oliver Reed leaves Clapham Junction, has a fight with Edward Woodward on St John's balcony but escapes and is rescued by Ian McShane at Ganley Court. Later they return, cause an explosion near the railway line off Grant Road, and with a telescopic sight fixed to his Mauser, Reed has another go at St John from the estate south of Sporle Court. Here McShane beats up Reed and rushes off to join St John.

Near Clapham Junction on the corner of Lavender Hill and St John's Road, opposite Falcon Road, is the department store of Arding & Hobbs. In *Nighthawks* (1981) Rutger Hauer plants a bomb there and when it explodes he phones the news service to prove his terrorist credentials. Arding & Hobbs changed its name to Allders in 2004, and soon after it became a Debenham's. The store is 'Platts' in *All the Little Animals* (1998), where it is visited by John Hurt and Christian Bale in a taxi that drops them off in St John's Road.

On Battersea High Street is The Woodman, the interior of which is seen as a Norfolk pub in *The Low Down* (2001) when a bully threatens Aidan Gillen and Tobias Menzies.

Overlooking the Thames off Battersea Church Road is St Mary's Church. Here in **Alfie** (1966) Julia Foster meets Graham Stark for a picnic. Michael Caine later makes an appearance at the church to watch his child's baptism. In **Melody** (1971) Mark Lester and Jack Wild parade in front of the church as members of the Boys' Brigade. Lester's mother Sheila Steafel picks the two up and they drive off to SE11. On the muddy littoral just west of the church police marksmen shoot Jack May in **Night, After Night, After Night** (1969).

In **Lock, Stock and Two Smoking Barrels** (1999) Jason Flemyng goes to Battersea Bridge to dump the shotguns. In **Maybe Baby** (2000) Hugh Laurie and Joely Richardson live in a modern riverside flat just to the west of Albert Bridge, over which Laurie bikes to his work at the BBC. In **24 Hours in London** (1999) Gary Olsen has an apartment in Waterside Point overlooking the bridge. He and sidekick Tony London entertain various villains as they plan their attack in EC2.

On Battersea Bridge itself, on the east side, Julie Christie and Roland Curram drop a goldfish into the Thames in **Darling** (1965). It is a popular bridge for driving-over-the-river shots seen in, for example, **A Ploughman's Lunch** (1983), **Half Moon Street** (1986), **Bright Young Things** (2003), **Love Actually** (2004) and **Stormbreaker** (2006).

Above:
Vicarage Crescent (above left) provides a location for **The Optimists** (1973) (top right). Peter Sellers entertains his young charges by the Thames (bottom right).

In 1951 Battersea Park celebrated the Festival of Britain by providing gardens, a children's zoo and a funfair, of which little trace now remains. Dirk Bogarde takes Muriel Pavlow to the fair on a date in **Doctor in the House** (1954). Edward Judd takes Janet Munro here in **The Day the Earth Caught Fire** (1961) and they watch a mysterious fog enshroud Chelsea Bridge from the embankment. The funfair is an, albeit brief, home of **Gorgo** (1961). In **The Wrong Arm of the Law** (1963) villains Peter Sellers and Bernard Cribbins agree 'no crime for 24 hours' with police John Le Mesurier, Lionel Jeffries and Raymond Huntley as they ride the merry-go-round. Yul Brynner, leaving the fair, takes a boat east from the Festival Garden Pier – no longer extant but which used to be halfway between the two bridges – in **File of the Golden Goose** (1969).

In **Piccadilly Jim** (2004) Sam Rockwell's game is nearly given away when he is recognized by Nitin Ganatra when walking here with Frances O'Connor.

Below:
The Henry Moore sculpture in Battersea Park (below left). Esther Anderson hides from Sidney Poitier (below right) in **A Warm December** (1973).

Sidney Poitier and Esther Anderson distribute balloons to children at the top of the stairs north of the funfair in *A Warm December* (1973). Anderson playfully hides in the Henry Moore sculpture just south of the bowling green. In *Robbery* (1967) joggers Stanley Baker and William Marlowe meet up at a water fountain, since removed, between the football fields and bowling green. They jog down the west side of the boating lake, splitting up as they approach Carriage Drive South. In *The Leading Man* (1995) Jon Bon Jovi and Lambert Wilson meet in front of the wooden bridge, now rebuilt, over the boating lake, to arrange for the former to seduce the latter's wife.

On a bench overlooking the south-east point of the lake near Carriage Drive South, Helena Bonham-Carter and Paul Bettany enjoy some romantic poetry reading in *The Heart of Me* (2002). In *The Squeeze* (1977) Edward Fox drops off wife Carol White, son and dog to watch toy boats on the lake from Carriage Drive South. However kidnappers David Hemmings and his gang soon bundle them into a van.

The mansions on the Prince of Wales Drive can be glimpsed through the rain in *The End of the Affair* (1999) when Ralph Fiennes meets Stephen Rea.

In *Scandal* (1989), on his recall to Moscow, Jeroen Krabbé bids farewell to John Hurt in front of the rock formation on a peninsula of the boating lake. In *The Spy Who Came in from the Cold* (1965) Michael Hordern catches up with Richard Burton here.

The café, out of shot in the above, features in *Martha, Meet Frank, Daniel and Laurence* (1998) when Monica Potter and Rufus Sewell shelter from the rain. Then it was simply called the Park Café; it became Café Lakeside and is now La Gondola. Watch carefully as Potter leaves and Sewell chases after her. These scenes are filmed in St James's Park (SW1). Joseph Fiennes later follows the same route. Potter hangs around the bandstand, dressed with cars and chess-playing winos, on Central Avenue. Sewell chats her up and they walk to the embankment.

In *Spice World* (1997) the Spice Girls eat fish and chips on a bench on the mile-long embankment. Greg Henry and Elizabeth Daily pause here after running out of a restaurant without paying in *Funny Money* (1983). Adrian Dunbar and Susan Vidler share a bench in *The Wedding Tackle* (1999).

In *Maybe Baby* (2000), when Hugh Laurie and Joely Richardson split up, Richardson moves not too far away to a first-floor flat with balcony in Overstrand Mansions on Prince of Wales Drive, between Beechmore Road and Alexandra Avenue. Here James Purefoy picks her up for a première. Judy Geeson drives John Wayne to 61–80 York Mansions, between

Forfar Road and Macduff Road, in ***Brannigan*** (1975). When the bathroom in his flat blows up, destroying the outside wall, the impossible view of the Albert Memorial (SW7) is exposed. In a separate scene, the car chase starts on the corner of Beechmore Road and Brynmaer Road as Wayne commandeers a Capri to chase James Booth down Warriner Gardens. Ian McShane lives at 81–100 York Mansions in ***Villain*** (1970). Lucy Davenport lives in the same block in ***If Only*** (2004).

Chris Rea and Diana Rigg are forced to move to 14 Alexandra Avenue, on the corner of Warriner Gardens where the entrance is, when times get hard in ***Parting Shots*** (1998). Later, when Rea slips away from policeman Gareth Hunt, his nearest tube appears to be Latimer Road (W10).

On the corner of Culvert Road and Rowditch Lane is The British Flag, seen in ***Saturday Night and Sunday Morning*** (1960). A drunk hurls his pint glass into a shop window on the corner opposite, much to the amusement of Albert Finney. The pub, rechristened Carey's for a short while, is all that has survived in an area so heavily rebuilt that Sheepcote Lane no longer runs east into Rowditch Lane but meets Culvert Road a little further south. The scene was set in Nottingham, where it was mostly filmed. In ***Sitting Target*** (1972) this corner is seen at least twice during the car chase as Oliver Reed pursues Ian McShane and Jill St John. They take the tunnel that leads from Culvert Road into Culvert Place; it then cuts to SW8. In Culvert Place to the east is arch no. 3, where the gang hides the diamonds in ***A Fish Called Wanda*** (1988). Kevin Kline waits for Jamie Lee Curtis just inside the tunnel.

Below:
*In **A Fish Called Wanda** (1988) Kevin Kline keeps an eye on his fellow diamond thieves (below left) from an archway in Culvert Place (below right).*

Two sets of railway lines cross Latchmere Road. The northern bridge is seen as Cecil Parker visits 'Lewisham' in *I Believe In You* (1952), during the car chase in **Brannigan** (1975), and when Julia Ormond drives under the southern one to Wandsworth Prison (SW18) in *Captives* (1994).

SW12: Balham

The street with the school at the south end, seen as Robert Newton and Celia Johnson move into their new house, in which they spend most of the time in **This Happy Breed** (1944), is Alderbrook Road. In the film there's a no. 17 on the door seen when John Mills leaves, but it's actually no. 53, on the east side.

SW2: Streatham Hill, south Brixton, west Tulse Hill

In *Greenwich Mean Time* (1999) Georgia Mackenzie works in the 'Meridian Building Society' on the corner of Streatham Hill and Wyatt Park Road. Ben Waters is shot at the doorway of the same building by police marksmen positioned in front of 76–80 Streatham Hill.

Some of **South West 9** (2001) was filmed in SW2, including 'The Smokehouse' inside which Wil Johnson has dealings with Robbie Gee. The derelict building is on Effra Road on the corner of Saltoun Road. Trevor Thomas lives on the other end of Saltoun Road, close to Atlantic Road in **Black Joy** (1977).

SW16: Furzedown, Streatham Park, Streatham Vale

Korona, 30 Streatham High Road, is the delicatessen where Alex King works under father Jurek Janosk in **Small Time Obsession** (2000).

Daniel Craig and Kelly MacDonald enjoy a swim at Tooting Bec Lido in **Some Voices** (2000). The lido, with its colourful cubicles and fountain at the north end, is on the common, off Tooting Bec Road opposite Aldrington Road.

SW17: Summerstown, Upper Tooting, Tooting Graveney, Colliers Wood

Wimbledon Stadium on Plough Lane hosts the dog track visited by Clive Owen before he catches a bus to meet Julianne Moore in **Children of Men** (2006).

SW18: West Hill, Southfields, Wandsworth

The main doors of Her Majesty's Prison Wandsworth, opposite Heathfield Avenue, are seen in **Law And Disorder** (1958), during which Michael Redgrave is released after serving various terms. Stanley Baker as **The Criminal** (1960) is released temporarily. In **Poor Cow** (1967) Carol White visits Terence Stamp, and again the doors are seen in **Ooh…You Are Awful** (1972). Julia Ormond parks in Heathfield Avenue to supply dentistry to the inmates, especially Tim Roth, in **Captives** (1994). In **Mad Cows** (1999) Joanna Lumley smuggles out Anna Friel's baby.

Orlando Bloom visits father Frank Harper at 'Halmsworth Prison' in **The Calcium Kid** (2003). Since the mid-1990s a large brick wall has surrounded the entrance to provide further security.

5 Spencer Park is the house of Frank Windsor and Vivien Pickles, mutual friends of Glenda Jackson and Peter Finch, in **Sunday Bloody Sunday** (1971). Jackson and Finch finally meet each other at the end outside.

The old Wandsworth Gasworks on the river Wandle appears in **Theatre of Blood** (1973) when Ian Hendry meets Diana Rigg at The Causeway, located next to the tunnel under the railway line. After down-and-outs overpower Hendry, Rigg drives off in his car, with Eric Sykes trapped in the boot. The same gasholders and tunnel are seen in **The Optimists** (1973) as Peter Sellers, Donna Mullane and John Chaffey wander along the Thames. The gasholders on Smugglers Way are no longer there, but the tunnel with a view of the Arndale Centre, which has now been renamed Southside, can still be seen in this location and continues to thrive.

After driving over Wandsworth Bridge, James Fox makes a call to find somewhere to lie low in **Performance** (1970). Then he drives from Podmore Road into Bramford Road and dyes his hair red underneath the Bramford Road tunnel, which is now pedestrianized. He

Left:
The Causeway (top left), seen in ***The Optimists*** (1973) and ***Theatre of Blood*** (1973). Ian Hendry drives to meet Diana Rigg (bottom left and right) in ***Theatre of Blood*** (1973).

calls his mother from a phone box nestling just outside Wandsworth Town Station. The station entrance on Old York Road was revamped as a millennium project.

At Wandsworth gyratory there are four concrete subways leading into the green space in the middle. All are labelled 'Structure 17' followed by the subway number. They all look identical, but no. 1 is where Malcolm MacDowell and his droogs beat up tramp Paul Farrell in ***A Clockwork Orange*** (1971).

South of the gyratory is Trinity Road, seen during the car chase in ***Brannigan*** (1975). To the west, on the corner of Fairfield Street and Wandsworth High Street, is Wandsworth Town

Hall, which is 'Battersea Court' where Anthony Hopkins helps Jim Broadbent gain custody of his son in *The Good Father* (1985). On the corner of Wandsworth High Street and Ram Street is The Brewery Tap. In *The Amsterdam Kill* (1977), filmed mostly in Holland and Hong Kong, Robert Mitchum enters his flat above the pub on Ram Street.

The second robbery in *Sweeney 2* (1978) takes place in the Arndale Centre, remodelled in 2002. Villain Ken Hutchison drops his gold-plated Purdy sawn-off shotgun, to be picked up by a passing skateboarder, on Neville Gill Close, where John Thaw and Dennis Waterman park to investigate.

SW19: Wimbledon, Merton Park

The All England Wimbledon Lawn Tennis and Croquet Club hosts the tennis scenes in *Nobody Runs Forever* (1968), during which Rod Taylor prevents Derren Nesbitt from shooting Christopher Plummer.

In *Players* (1979) the final between Dino-Paul Martin and Guillermo Vilas is staged on the Centre Court. Coach Pancho Gonzalez, brother Steve Guttenberg and Ali MacGraw support Martin. At the end of the match, MacGraw leaves through the gates on Somerset Road. In *Wimbledon* (2004) Paul Bettany and Kirsten Dunst play their matches on the fringe courts until Bettany reaches the final and Centre Court.

In *Hoffman* (1969) Peter Sellers and Sinead Cusack walk on Wimbledon Common, strolling by King's Mere, admiring the Wimbledon Windmill and following Beverley Brook. In *Felicia's Journey* (1999) Bob Hoskins takes Elaine Cassidy to his house, supposedly in Birmingham, at 5 Southside Common, opposite Rushmore Pond in the south-east corner of Wimbledon Common.

41 Marryat Road, on the west corner with Burghley Road, is Richard Attenborough and Kim Stanley's house in *Séance on a Wet Afternoon* (1964). The house, with its wall lower than now, is best seen when the séance members arrive. The postbox diagonally opposite is still there.

Colin Campbell and Rita Tushingham are married at Bethel United Church in Kohat Road, and hop onto a no. 49 bus to their reception in *The Leather Boys* (1963). Tushingham later has her hair done and peruses the parade of shops in Durnsford Road, which turns into Haydon's Road just north of Cromwell Road and Kohat Road.

SW15: Putney Heath, Putney Vale, Roehampton

Robbie Coltrane and Eric Idle spring Camille Coduri out of the now-closed Putney Hospital, alongside Commondale, in **Nuns on the Run** (1990).

At the northern end of Embankment, where it turns into the Thames Path, Anna Nygh parks a decoy car in **Sweeney 2** (1978), where it duly attracts the attention of John Thaw and Dennis Waterman. Opposite here is Beverley Brook, where Ioan Gruffud and Ben Crompton run the 'Second Chance' dogs' home in **102 Dalmatians** (2000). Mostly the rear is seen, especially when Jim Carter arrests Gruffud, to Glenn Close's delight. Tim McInnerny slips in through the riverfront entrance to incriminate Gruffud.

On the corner of Embankment and Festing Road is Leaders Gardens, a small park with swings where Frank Finlay's child plays under the watchful eye of a plain-clothes detective in **Robbery** (1967). Stanley Baker and Finlay discuss details of the impending train heist by the river.

Between Festing Road and Rotherwood Road is the Imperial College Boat Club. Here in **The Big Sleep** (1978) Robert Mitchum follows, by taxi, a suspect white van (W8) and meets up with Edward Fox, who has a flat on the first floor. On a second visit he ends up in a fight with Joan Collins and sees Fox shot by Simon Turner in the flat. Mitchum chases Turner into Festing Road and grabs him approximately in front of no. 57. Much of this area, with its boathouses, is seen in **True Blue** (1996) as Oxford train to win the Boat Race of 1987. A taxi delivers Sinead Cusack to Peter Sellers's flat in Ruvigny Mansions, Embankment in **Hoffman** (1969).

On a slipway off Embankment, Peter Sellers and Ringo Starr bribe Richard Attenborough to sabotage the Oxford–Cambridge boat race in **The Magic Christian** (1969). Sellers then pays traffic warden Spike Milligan to eat a penalty notice affixed to his car parked further south in Thames Place outside The Duke's Head.

This area overlooks Putney Pier, which is where Michael Bentine and Suzy Kendall await a river bus in **The Sandwich Man** (1966). David Buck offers the two a lift in his car, then proceeds to drive down the ramp into the river, floating home to E16.

In **10 Rillington Place** (1970), a thriller that tells the story of serial killer John Christie, Richard Attenborough walks down from the Star & Garter, now Bar M, to Putney Pier. A passing policeman recognizes him and apprehends him, as indeed happened to the real-life John Christie.

Sweeney 2 (1978) opens at a café called Riverside Snacks, where Waterman and the rest of the Flying Squad congregate on the corner of Embankment and Lower Richmond Road. There is now a much plusher establishment.

Putney Bridge appears as Westminster Bridge in *Chaplin* (1992), a clever matte shot that replaces Bishop's Park (SW6) with the Houses of Parliament.

Close to the corner of Putney High Street on Felsham Road stood the Putney Hippodrome, which starred as the *Theatre of Blood* (1973). The old theatre has now been replaced by housing, but the building to the east, now a bar, is still there. Diana Rigg leads Dennis Price down an alleyway called Walker's Place between an old school and brewery, both also rebuilt. Ian Hendry and Milo O'Shea join the onlookers to watch Vincent Price's fiery demise on the roof. Oliver Reed collects his stashed loot from the Hippodrome in *Sitting Target* (1972). Hugh Grant takes Martine McCutcheon to Elliott School, Pullman Gardens, where most of the cast assemble towards the end of *Love Actually* (2003).

In *Sweeney 2* (1978) the squad tracks a Mercedes, which turns from Roehampton Lane into Danebury Avenue at the eastern edge of the vast concrete housing and shopping sprawl of the Alton Estate, and then right again into a circular parking area in front of Allbrook House. The west front of Allbrook House faces Harbridge Avenue, where the diamond thieves in *Robbery* (1967) abandon their ambulance and swap it for a car, an exchange witnessed by police parked on Danebury Avenue.

Warren Mitchell and the rest of the Garnett clan are relocated to the towering Denmead House on Highcliffe Drive in *Till Death Us Do Part* (1969). Some angles are filmed from the neighbouring Dunbridge House.

SW13: Barnes

A walk on the Thames Path just west of Castelnau forms part of Ayub Khan Din and Frances Barber's perfect day in *Sammy and Rosie Get Laid* (1977).

In *Blue Ice* (1992) Bob Hoskins leaves by the Arundel Terrace exit of The Bridge, on the corner of Castelnau, where a red van menacingly approaches him.

34 The Crescent is home, supposedly in the Oxfordshire town of Wallingford, for Simone Signoret in *The Deadly Affair* (1967). James Mason visits twice to interview her over her husband's death. Mason arranges for local cop Harry Andrews to follow her as she crosses

Barnes Green. Passing by the Barnes Methodist church, she hails a bus on Station Road for Victoria Coach Station. Julie Walters takes in lodger Adrian Pasdar next door at 33 The Crescent in *Just Like a Woman* (1992), supposed to be Twickenham. Pasdar visits a shrink at The Tower on the corner of The Terrace and Elm Bank Gardens.

76 Church Road, now The Blue Door, is the Barnes Vet seen in *Are You Ready For Love?* (2006).

Jenny Seagrove walks over Barnes Railway Bridge to play with her dog on the littoral by The Terrace in Kiki Dee's 'Loving And Free' interlude in *Don't Go Breaking My Heart* (1998). The area and views underneath the bridge are sufficiently convincing for Elizabethan times to appear in *Shakespeare in Love* (1998).

SW14: East Sheen, Mortlake

The off-screen crash between three vehicles in *Sweeney 2* (1978) occurs on the intersection of Church Avenue and Thornton Road. Dennis Waterman guides John Thaw through the events, leading him into Chestnut Avenue, through a house and into its garden. They jump, in a cut, to a bridge leading across a railway line from South Worple Way opposite Queen's Road to North Worple Way, from where they see a lollipop man lying dead in Ripley Gardens because 'he got in the way'.

In *Vault of Horror* (1973) Tom Baker desperately tries to hail a taxi by the war memorial at Sheen Lane and Milestone Green Corner. Spotting one across the road on Leinster Avenue, he rushes in front of an oncoming lorry and meets a rather messy death on Upper Richmond Road West.

south-east london

Riverside views of the Thames abound as old docks and wharves give way to smart galleries and offices. South-east London reaches east beyond Greenwich, towards Kent and south through hilly parks to Surrey.

SE1: Lambeth, South Bank, Waterloo, Bankside, Borough

Lambeth

A bomb appears to explode in Terry Farrell's green-glassed MI6 in *The World Is Not Enough* (1999). Pierce Brosnan pursues Maria Grazia Cucinotta's speedboat in Q's latest aqua-invention, a powerboat, ejected east of the rotunda from where a computer image extends the building. In reality this is a ramp to the river, where Paul Bettany sorts out his guns in *Kiss Kiss (Bang Bang)* (2000). Tim Vincent falls from the roof of Camelford House next door in *Sorted* (2000). Matthew Rhys collects Vincent's BMW parked underneath and later contemplates the spectacular view of his brother's death.

At 93 Albert Embankment is Peninsula Heights, formerly known as Alembic House, prized for its views of Parliament used for the credits of *The Night Caller* (1965). The building also contained Frank Sinatra's flat in *The Naked Runner* (1967), Calvin Lockhart's flat in *Joanna* (1968), the venue for the planning of the Turin job in *The Italian Job* (1969), Michael Caine's office in *X, Y and Zee* (1972), George Segal's office in *A Touch of Class* (1973), Vincent Price's suicide in *Theatre of Blood* (1973), Lee Grant's office in *The Internecine Project* (1974), Barry Foster's office in *Sweeney!* (1975), a murder in *The Awakening* (1980), the briefing of Pierce Brosnan in *The Tailor of Panama* (2001) and James Laurenson's flat in *Three Blind Mice* (2002).

Across the road, Robert Powell meets Laurence Olivier in his first-floor office at the corner of Tinworth Street in *The Jigsaw Man* (1984). The offices of *The Intelligence Men*

Opposite:
Southwark House, on the corner of Lambeth High Street and Black Prince Road (bottom) seen in *Hot Enough for June* (1964) and *Just Ask for Diamond* (1988). The building doubles as a 'Turkish Baths', visited by Dursley Linden and Colin Dale in *Just Ask for Diamond* (1988) (top).

(1966) are on the opposite corner of Tinworth Street.

Brenda de Banzie checks into the 'Ritz Tower Hotel', actually Eastbury House, in *A Pair of Briefs* (1961).

Dirk Bogarde visits Prince Consort House, an employment exchange office, in *Hot Enough for June* (1964).

Rachel Ward drops off Richard E Grant at Hampton House in *How to Get Ahead in Advertising* (1989) though his office view suggests a shot from Westminster Tower. Across the road Grant tosses his poetry into the river in *Keep the Aspidistra Flying* (1997). At Westminster Tower, 3 Albert Embankment, James Fox has his office in *The Russia House* (1990). Rex Harrison works next door in a site now rebuilt as Parliament View Apartments in *Midnight Lace* (1960). Newlyweds Jonathan Rhys Meyers and Emily Mortimer move into one of the penthouses in *Match Point* (2005). Later Rhys Meyers has to bundle confrontational Scarlett Johansson into a taxi outside before chauffeur John Fortune arrives with his Rolls. *George and Mildred* (1980) circle the roundabout while lost in London. In *National Lampoon's European Vacation* (1985), the Griswald family, headed by Chevy Chase, drive round the roundabout until night falls, ineptly unable to escape. The roundabout was redesigned in 2001. In *Blue Ice* (1992) a crash into Sean Young's bodyguards' car is staged at the roundabout, so that her crooked chauffeur can whisk her away in hers. *Velvet Goldmine* (1998) opens with fans rushing over Lambeth Bridge to meet others coming through the underpass. Under the opening titles of *The Innocent Sleep* (1995) Rupert Graves staggers along the bridge and nearly gets run over.

On the corner of Lambeth Road and Lambeth High Street is The Royal Pharmaceutical Society, where Chiwetel Ejiofor makes a delivery in *Three Blind Mice* (2002). Dirk Bogarde goes to Southbank House on the corner of Lambeth High Street and Black Prince Road to receive a job from Robert Morley in *Hot Enough for June* (1964). It is a Turkish baths in *Just Ask for Diamond* (1988), seen when Dursley McLinden and Colin Dale visit Michael Robbins. At Salamanca Place, now rebuilt, Ade is cornered in *Snatch* (2000).

At the corner of Hercules Road and Cosser Street is The Pineapple, outside which Jack Wild and Mark Lester join a huge queue of schoolchildren at a bus stop before crossing the road to catch a bus for the West End in **Melody** (1971). Further down Lambeth Road, on the north-west corner of Kennington Road, Tracy Hyde temporarily releases her goldfish for a swim in the cattle trough. At the north end of Hercules Road, Kenneth More and John Gregson are temporarily held up by policeman Harold Siddons at the intersection with Kennington Road. Old gentleman Arthur Wontner delays Gregson in conversation about his Darracq in **Genevieve** (1953).

Charlie Creed-Miles makes a call for heroin from a phone box outside Elephant and Castle tube in **Nil By Mouth** (1997). The interior is seen briefly in **Intimacy** (2000) as Mark Rylance trails Kerry Fox. In **Empire State** (1987) Jamie Foreman and Elizabeth Hickling's flat in Draper House overlooks the Elephant and Castle roundabout. Jeremy Kemp keeps police suspect Artro Morris under surveillance at the Elephant and Castle Shopping Centre in **The Strange Affair** (1969).

The Knack (1965) ends with Michael Crawford and Rita Tushingham walking south along the riverside walk. Michael Caine and Murray Melvin discuss careers in tourism

Above:
The Pineapple on Hercules Road (above left) provides the backdrop as Mark Lester and Jack Wild join a high-spirited bus queue of schoolchildren (above right) in **Melody** (1971).

photography in *Alfie* (1966). Lance Percival busks with spoons in ***Mrs Brown, You've Got a Lovely Daughter*** (1967).

Joanne Whalley-Kilmer and Bridget Fonda stroll in ***Scandal*** (1989) as do Fiona Allen and Sophie Thompson as ***Fat Slags*** (2004). Carmine Canuso and Celia Meiras begin their brief affair by the embankment in ***Day of the Sirens*** (2002).

Further north on the pathway, Michael Caine and Sean Young leave St Thomas's Hospital by the river exit in ***Blue Ice*** (1992). Colin Fox offers Rob Lowe a commission in ***Perfect Strangers*** (2004). Jon Bon Jovi walks on the embankment under the titles of ***The Leading Man*** (1995). In ***Genevieve*** (1953) Kenneth More has an argument with a fruit stallholder just north of the roundabout on Lambeth Palace Road as he drives his Spyker into the stall. Sure that he will win the race between the two, John Gregson cheerfully passes him towards St Thomas's Hospital before he gets a puncture. In ***School for Scoundrels*** (1960) Ian Carmichael runs after a bus, hops on and falls off with Janette Scott, whom he chats up opposite Lambeth Palace.

The north-west corner of St Thomas's Hospital houses Richard Attenborough's New Scotland Yard office in ***Brannigan*** (1975), a bit cheeky since an establishing shot shows the rotating sign in SW1. Ian Holm's shipping office has the same view in ***Juggernaut*** (1974). Bob Hoskins and Helen Mirren share memories of Michael Caine in ***Last Orders*** (2001) outside the north-west corner and move into a small pavilion, a prop, when it starts to rain. The hospital provides exteriors when Cillian Murphy wakes up after a coma to find a deserted London in ***28 Days Later*** (2002).

Westminster Bridge is the finishing post for the two vintage cars in ***Genevieve*** (1953). The bridge is also the setting for the rain-soaked march, led by Hugh Griffith, Wylie Watson, Stephen Murray and Susan Shaw, to the Home Office in ***London Belongs to Me*** (1948). When the march is abandoned on the bridge, there is a glimpse of the old St Thomas's Hospital building, some of which survives to the south. Dennis Quaid pokes his head out of a taxi to read an unfavourable headline on a newsvendor's board as he leaves England in ***Great Balls of Fire!*** (1989). On the north-east side of the bridge Howard Keel and Janina Faye take an abandoned car in ***The Day of the Triffids*** (1962).

In ***102 Dalmatians*** (2000) Alice Lewis's probation office is in the north-west corner of County Hall. Glenn Close wanders outside onto the bridge when the strike of Big Ben causes her to see everything, including Tim McInnerny, in Dalmatian spots. On this corner Pierce Brosnan walks down the steps to a door underneath the Coade stone lion in ***Die***

Another Day (2002) to meet Judi Dench. By the lion Jeremy Irons returns money to a vendor from whom he stole as a child in **And Now … Ladies and Gentlemen** (2003). The plinth, minus its lion, is seen in **Night and the City** (1950) when Richard Widmark hands Googie Withers a fake nightclub licence.

Romola Garai and Henry Cavill sit on a nearby bench in **I Capture the Castle** (2003). *Oh Heavenly Dog* (1980) opens with a drenched Chevy Chase, or possibly a stand-in, making his way through the rain. Jonathan Rhys Meyers and Emily Mortimer leave the Saatchi Gallery in County Hall in **Match Point** (2005). In an internet set-up, Jude Law sends Clive Owen to meet Julia Roberts at the Aquarium in County Hall in **Closer** (2004). John Boxer's speech on cleaning up the river in front of County Hall is interrupted in **Frenzy** (1972) when another necktie murderer's victim is pulled from the Thames, using the steps to the north in front of the building's crescent. Alfred Hitchcock makes his usual cameo appearance as one of the crowd ghoulishly looking on. Gregory Phillips phones mother Judy Garland from a box in **I Could Go on Singing** (1963) in front of the crescent. Andy Garcia gives a press interview there under Alfredo Michelsen's supervision in **American Roulette** (1988). Celia Meiras stays at the Marriott Hotel within County Hall in a room overlooking the Millennium Wheel in **Day of the Sirens** (2002).

The roof on the north-east corner is transformed into a garden for the end of **The Avengers** (1998). Cinematic trickery also places the swinging pad of **Austin Powers in Goldmember** (2002) on the roof. The interior is seen in **Mission Impossible** (1996) as the corridors of the Pentagon. The exterior, seen briefly, is the Lord Protector's Office in **Richard III** (1995), with the interiors being shot at Senate House (WC1). At Yo! Sushi on Belvedere Road Natalie Imbruglia watches Rowan Atkinson's tie getting stuck in the food conveyor belt in **Johnny English** (2003).

The police station where Bernard Lee operates, and to which Stewart Granger is taken in **The Secret Partner** (1961) was in Addington Street. The site was demolished and became Waterloo International.

South Bank

Unimpeded views of Parliament were possible from Jubilee Gardens until the Millennium Wheel, or London Eye, was raised in 1999. In **Endless Night** (1972) Hywel Bennett meets Hayley Mills feigning a sulk over her millions. Sidney Poitier and his daughter drive into the South Bank Gardens, as the Jubilee Gardens were known, to meet Esther Anderson for some ice creams in **A Warm December** (1973). Robert Hayes and Pamela Stephenson walk along the gardens at night in **Scandalous** (1984). Irène Jacob meets Jason Patric here towards the end of **Incognito** (1997). Anne Reid, as **The Mother** (2003), takes a 'flight' on the British Airways London Eye. Lieran O'Brien and Margo Stilley visit the Eye in **Nine Songs** (2004). The press await Paul Bettany and Kirsten Dunst at the bottom in **Wimbledon** (2004). Frankie Muniz, Anthony Anderson and Rod Silvers walk from the new Hungerford footbridges to enjoy the Eye in **Agent Cody Banks 2** (2004). Paul Nicholls and Jennifer Love Hewitt also take the wheel and cross the bridge in **If Only** (2004). In **Thunderbirds** (2004) a hijacked Thunderbird 2 lands in the gardens followed by Thunderbirds 1 and 3. Special effects had a big hand in these scenes, which include a fake monorail built above the Thames.

Between Hungerford Bridge and Waterloo Bridge, Richard Widmark flees for his life in **Night And The City** (1950). A Howley Terrace sign betrays the area, but all the roads named Howley have now been subsumed by post-war development. The 19th-century shot tower where Widmark hides was incorporated into the Festival of Britain site in 1951, but was demolished in 1967 to make way for the Queen Elizabeth Hall.

On the north side of Hungerford Bridge at the Royal Festival Hall, Jack Hawkins and John Stratton catch their man Richard Leech red-handed at a safe in **The Long Arm** (1956). Leech makes a break for it when Ursula Howells drives a car at them as they leave the main entrance. Stratton recaptures Leech while Hawkins clings onto the car's bonnet. There was a lot more space then before the eastern additions of the Queen Elizabeth Hall, Purcell Room and Hayward Gallery appeared in the 1960s.

In **The Vicious Circle** (1957) John Mills attends a concert at the Festival Hall. Barbara Ferris watches conductor Oskara Werner in concert in **Interlude** (1968). In the café Suzanne Leigh uses a poisoned handbag to kill Gene Barry's contact before fleeing for Hungerford Bridge in **Subterfuge** (1969). Charles Gray leads Edward Woodward out after dining in the restaurant in **File of the Golden Goose** (1969). Anthony Hopkins and Judi Dench enjoy al fresco dancing in **84 Charing Cross Road** (1986) commenting on the Shell-Mex building across the Thames. Glenda Jackson sits outside the Hall and looks up as a train passes on Hungerford Bridge in **Turtle Diary** (1985).

Andy Garcia and Kitty Aldridge leave the Hayward Gallery to be offered financial aid by Christopher Rozycki and Boris Isarov on the Embankment in **American Roulette** (1988). Later they flee a fund-raising auction on the south-west side to an awaiting ice cream van driven by Robert Stephens. Here Rita Tushingham kidnaps Shane Briant's dog, much to his amusement as he watches from above in *Straight on Till Morning* (1972).

At the Festival Pier, Phil Collins and Julie Walters run a flower-selling business after Collins has served his time in *Buster* (1988). Here market stalls are put up for Amanda Bynes and Oliver James's date in *What a Girl Wants* (2003). Later Bynes takes Colin Firth to the same 'market'. Bill Paxton and his family gather here in *Thunderbirds* (2004).

Outside the café fronting the riverside entrance to the National Film Theatre (NFT) Rupert Graves tells Graham Crowden about the murder he witnessed in *The Innocent Sleep* (1995). Orson Welles enters the NFT to attend an advertising film award ceremony in *I'll Never Forget What's'isname* (1967). Glenda Jackson and Michael Murphy enjoy part of a horror film season in *The Class of Miss MacMichael* (1978). As *Joanna* (1968) Genevieve Waite slaps a poster of Peter Sellers at the NFT before ascending to Waterloo Bridge. David Hemmings and Samantha Eggar exit to his car parked under the bridge in *The Walking Stick* (1970).

In *Truly, Madly, Deeply* (1991) Juliet Stevenson and Michael Maloney introduce themselves to each other hopping from outside the National Theatre to underneath Waterloo Bridge, where Stevenson catches sight of her ghost husband Alan Rickman playing the cello.

At the other entrance to the NFT, deaf brother David Bower waits for Hugh Grant, who arrives late with Andie MacDowell in *Four Weddings and a Funeral* (1994). MacDowell leaves up the concrete stairs leading to Waterloo Bridge. Grant catches up with her under Waterloo Bridge to profess his love. Lewis Collins meets his contact in the concrete skateboarders' paradise underneath the Queen Elizabeth Hall in *Who Dares Wins* (1982). The contact makes a phone call from a telephone box under Waterloo Bridge, unaware that Ingrid Pitt is watching his every move. Under Waterloo Bridge Stellan Skarsgård and Paul Bettany enter through one of its river arches into a different world in *Kiss Kiss (Bang Bang)* (2000).

Rufus Sewell walks out of an audition at the National Theatre and throws his script into the river in *Martha, Meet Frank, Daniel and Laurence* (1998). Daniela Nardini refuses to go in with Mark Strong until he removes his shoes in *Elephant Juice* (2000). Patrick Drury takes Stephanie Zimbalist to the Cottesloe Theatre in *The Awakening* (1980) and they exit onto the Baylis terrace. Before the theatre was built, the cleared site is seen in *The Magic Christian* (1969), where Peter Sellers and Ringo Starr entice commuters on Waterloo Bridge to collect free money from a stinking vat.

In **About A Boy** (2002) Hugh Grant is kept waiting by Isabel Brook at the IMAX cinema, which replaced the cardboard city of the homeless in the 1980s under the Waterloo Road roundabout.

Waterloo

Waterloo station features appropriately in **Waterloo Road** (1944) when John Mills evades the Military Police by running across the tracks. **The Gentle Sex** (1943) opens with the station's four-faced clock as the seven main characters catch their train. Deborah Kerr sees off Robert Donat in **Perfect Strangers** (1945). Joyce Carey meets Celia Johnson under the clock in **The Astonished Heart** (1949). Bernard Miles asks for directions near platform 11 in **Chance of a Lifetime** (1950). Watched by police and bent on revenge, John Mills arrives at Waterloo in **The Long Memory** (1952). Later a taxi drops off Elizabeth Sellars at Station Approach, and she sits under the clock. Gary Cooper arrives at the station and leaves via the grand exit near Mepham Street in **The Wreck of the Mary Deare** (1960). Melvin Murray meets Michael Caine as **Alfie** (1966) returning from recuperation. Girlfriend Ingrid Brett meets Michael Crawford, and they join their car and chauffeur Peter Gilmore, in **The Jokers** (1966). Gregory Peck arrives back from Ascot at the station in **Arabesque** (1966). Keith Bell collects Jane Merrow in **Hands of the Ripper** (1971). Robin Askwith catches the train from Waterloo for **Horror Hospital** (1973). Dick Emery visits his announcer girlfriend in **Ooh... You Are Awful** (1972). In **Londinium** (2001) Colin Firth and Irène Jacob, stood up by their respective partners, board their scheduled train. Later they meet and embrace on platform 14. In **The Good Die Young** (1954) John Ireland goes AWOL while descending the steps.

At the underground station Jude Law saves Kerry Fox from suicide in **The Wisdom of Crocodiles** (1998). Heather Graham catches the tube for work and, later, for High Barnet in **Killing Me Softly** (2002).

Jared Harris meets Aria Argento as **B. Monkey** (1996) for a Eurostar trip to Paris from Waterloo's International Terminal, designed by Nicholas Grimshaw. Yvan Attal arrives from Paris in **Ma Femme est une Actrice** (2001). Edward Furlong descends the escalator to the International Terminal in **Three Blind Mice** (2002). Ralph Fiennes catches the Eurostar there in **The Constant Gardener** (2005).

In **File of the Golden Goose** (1969) Charles Gray walks from Leake Street to what was then a camera shop, now Prophecy, at 11 Lower Marsh Street. Later he makes a phone call from a box on Baylis Road, diagonally opposite the Old Vic Theatre. In **Snatch** (2000)

Vinnie Jones confronts Ewen Bremner outside 18 Lower Marsh Street, Guys and Dolls. Jones winds up his car window trapping Bremner's head and starts driving down the street to encourage a release of information.

In *Trauma* (2004) Colin Firth watches a police reconstruction of a murder outside the Card Shop, 103 Lower Marsh Street, arousing the suspicions of Kenneth Cranham, while an enormous poster of the victim Alison David is draped on the side of no. 140 further down the street.

In the gardens opposite the Old Vic, between Waterloo Road and Cornwall Road, detectives capture Bernard Lee, Margaret Tyzack and William Sylvester to break the *Ring of Spies* (1963).

Daniel Lapaine goes to Webber Street for credit card sex in *Elephant Juice* (2000). He parks his car outside Dauncey House to visit 10 Algar House and is caught there by fiancée Emmanuelle Béart. On Gaunt Street is the Ministry Of Sound – 'The Institute' in *Sorted* (2000) – where Matthew Rhys forks out £30 to doorman Stephen Marcus to gain entry.

At the junction of Treveris Street and Chancel Street under a railway tunnel is the ambush and kidnap site in *The Whistle Blower* (1986).

On Great Suffolk Street are the Ewer Street arches which house 'St Mary's Apartments' in *Trauma* (2004).

Jonathan Pryce visits the office of London Weekend Television on Upper Ground in *The Ploughman's Lunch* (1983).

Bankside

Liam Neeson and Thomas Sangster share thoughts on a bench overlooking the river just to the west of Gabriel's Wharf in *Love Actually* (2003). Here Mariel Hemingway and Mike Binder walk together in *Londinium* (2001), and Clive Owen and Julia Roberts chat in *Closer* (2004).

In *The Innocent Sleep* (1995) Rupert Graves and Annabella Sciorra pour Graham Crowden's ashes into the Thames from the wooden jetty just east of Gabriel's Wharf.

In *Love Actually* (2003) Andrew Lincoln, embarrassed by his video devoted to Keira Knightley, storms out of his flat in Barge House Street, the middle door on the north side, through Oxo Tower Wharf to the river.

Just east of Blackfriars Railway Bridge Jonathan Rhys Meyers throws evidence of his crime into the river in *Match Point* (2005). Earlier in the film, he approaches Tate Modern from Holland Street to meet Emily Mortimer and bumps into femme fatale Scarlett Johansson inside.

Ned Beatty's helicopter is able to take off from a riverfront location quoted as 'Lambeth Heliport' just in front of the Falcon Point development in **Hopscotch** (1980).

Tate Modern is the old Bankside power station, which serves as the Tower of London in Ian McKellen's 1930s-set **Richard III** (1995) where Nigel Hawthorne is incarcerated. At Gate C, off Sumner Street, Annette Bening, Maggie Smith, Kristin Scott-Thomas and Kate Stevenson-Payne try to visit the doomed princes. Sean Bean's police escort transferring him from prison passes through this gate in **Patriot Games** (1992). Yvan Attal calls his sister from inside while admiring the exhibits in **Ma Femme est une Actrice** (2001). Anne Reid as **The Mother** (2003) visits the cavernous exhibit hall known as the turbine room. Clive Owen is chauffered into this hall in **Children Of Men** (2006). Keith Allen's office is the East Room in **Agent Cody Banks 2** (2004). Frankie Muniz and Anthony Anderson approach Tate Modern, dressed in 'Kenworth Laboratories' uniforms, from the Millennium Bridge. The same room is Jerry O'Connell's office in **Fat Slags** (2004) though the exterior is not the Tate. It also appears briefly in **Incognito** (1997). Rachel Weisz asks Ralph Fiennes awkward questions at a lecture there in **The Constant Gardener** (2005). Amanda Bynes and Oliver James cross the Millennium Bridge in **What a Girl Wants** (2003), as does newly unemployed Rob Lowe in **Perfect Strangers** (2004). Daniel Craig crosses the bridge to have his lunch inside the Tate disturbed by Rhys Ifans in **Enduring Love** (2004).

Al Pacino visits the Globe Theatre, then still under construction, in **Looking for Richard** (1996). The Olsen twins enjoy mock sword fights with their prospective boyfriends in the finished theatre in **Winning London** (2001).

On Bankside Jetty, journalist Annabella Sciorra asks CID man Crispin Redman to investigate a potentially incriminating button for her in **The Innocent Sleep** (1995). Ed Byrne films his dating video on the jetty in **Are You Ready for Love?** (2006), the opening titles of which appear over the Millennium Bridge.

At the corner of Southwark Bridge was a flattened site called 'Ballard's Wharf' in **Hue and Cry** (1947). Here hundreds of children chase after thieves at the climax. This corner, now built on, is Roger Moore's office, situated in Globe House, Bankside, with a view of St Paul's, in **The Man Who Haunted Himself** (1970). Under the opening credits Moore takes a car journey home beginning with his crossing of Southwark Bridge. The offices were rebuilt in 2001.

In **Goodbye Gemini** (1970) Judy Geeson wanders between Southwark Bridge and the rail-only Cannon Bridge, also called Alexandra Bridge, next to which is The Anchor Inn. On a very rainy day Jon Bon Jovi and Anna Galiena picnic on the tables outside the pub in **The Leading Man** (1995). Leslie Philips and Renée Asherson stroll here when it was all wharves and cranes in **Pool of London** (1950). Here also Tom Cruise and Ving Rhames relax with a pint at the end of **Mission Impossible** (1996) but they eschew the riverside views by sitting to the pub's side on Bank End. It is a biker hangout in **Different for Girls** (1997), where Rupert Graves walks with girlfriend Nisha K. Nayar.

Borough

East of Cannon Bridge is Clink Street, which stands in for the backstreets of Soho in **An American Werewolf in London** (1981). The police run through the tunnel under Cannon Bridge and corner werewolf David Naughton. Jenny Agutter pushes through the cordon set up at the junction of Clink Street and Stoney Street and appears to continue east along Clink Street. In fact it is Winchester Walk, with a false end where police marksmen shoot the werewolf dead. On Clink Street is Hugh Grant's flat in the second block east of the bridge in **Bridget Jones's Diary** (2001), while on the rooftop of the first block Sean Gallagher and Emmanuelle Béart's marriage is celebrated in **Elephant Juice** (2000). After the ceremony Mark Strong and Daniela Nardini catch a taxi at the corner of Winchester Square and Cathedral Street.

On Stoney Street, corrupt cops Dave Duffy and Geoffrey McGivern drop off Harvey Keitel in **The Young Americans** (1993), while they pick up their kickbacks and get petrol-bombed for their pains. Keitel, returning from a wander by The Market Porter, sees the car explode from the arched tunnel carrying trains to Cannon Street station.

In **101 Dalmatians** (1996) Hugh Laurie and his sidekick pick up a Siberian White Tiger fur from one of the warehouses, now belonging to Vinopolis, on Stoney Street. Here too is Vittorio Amandola's shop visited by Joseph Long in **Queen of Hearts** (1989). Ewen Bremner cycles under the tunnel in **Mojo** (1997).

Peter Wight and David Thewlis go to the Jubilee Café on Winchester Walk in **Naked** (1993), where Thewlis sweet-talks waitress Gina McKee. The café is now called The Rake.

Under the titles of **Lock, Stock and Two Smoking Barrels** (1999) Jason Statham and Nick Moran have to break off from selling dodgy gear to leg it down Rochester Walk through the west side of Borough Market, pursued by a couple of cops.

Lee Ross and Ross Boatman drive past The Market Porter, 9 Stoney Street on the corner of Park Street, looking for Vincent Regan in **Hard Men** (1996). Next door to the pub is 8 Stoney Street, the 'Third Hand Book Emporium,' and next to that, directly under the railway bridge, at 7 Stoney Street, the door to 'The Leaky Cauldron' seen when Daniel Radcliffe is dropped off by triple-decker bus in **Harry Potter and the Prisoner Of Azkaban** (2004). Radcliffe's room at the top of no. 8 has a view of Southwark Cathedral.

In **Entrapment** (1999) Sean Connery drives Catherine Zeta-Jones to the Haas Gallery at 5 Park Street to pick up a vase. Connery has to drive off in a hurry down Park Street and under the bridge at the end where the road doglegs, while Zeta-Jones has to avoid a knife attack coming through the roof of their car.

In **Lock, Stock and Two Smoking Barrels** (1999) Jason Flemyng, Nick Moran, Dexter Fletcher and Jason Statham live at 15 Park Street by the bridge, and Frank Harper's gang are next door at no. 13. At no. 15 Vas Blackwood's gang shoots it out with Harper's gang. Harper jumps out of the double doors above the window only to be head-butted by Vinnie Jones, who takes the pair of shotguns. Steven Mackintosh leaves no. 15 as the only survivor. Harper recovers and steals a car to pursue Jones. 'This is not a photo opportunity', a stencil by the elusive artist Banksy, now adorns no. 15.

At the Borough Café, 11 Park Street, renamed 'Bridge Café', Ralph Fiennes as **Spider** (2002) enjoys solitude and a cup of tea. From here he sees a Kitchener Road E1 sign, a prop on the wall just before the railway bridge under which Gabriel Byrne and Miranda Richardson pass earlier. The café is now called Little Dorrit. Opposite the café is Alice Lewis' flat, 12 Park Street, in **102 Dalmatians** (2000). Ian Hawke and Tat Whalley run under the tunnel and Hawke, slipping, cuts his hand on glass in **Queen of Hearts** (1989). Sam West lives with Nicola Duffett at 13 Park

Street in **Howards End** (1992). No. 13 is a funeral business and no. 15 is 'Eldridge Books', where Richard E Grant works, much to the disappointment of sister Harriet Walter and Helena Bonham Carter in **Keep the Aspidistra Flying** (1997). 'My God, Lambeth.' 'Quite so.' Actually it's Southwark. When Julian Wadham visits, Grant walks with him to Stoney Street, where Grant washes away his poetical aspirations in the Market Porter, turned briefly into public baths. **Mojo** (1997) opens with Andy Serkis and Martin Gwynn-Jones walking up Park Street past no. 15. No. 13 is 'Flash' dispatch riders where Rupert Graves works as a courier in **Different for Girls** (1997). In **What a Girl Wants** (2003) Park Street is dressed as New York's Chinatown, with Brooklyn Bridge superimposed on the skyline.

At the corner of Redcross Way and Park Street, described as the 'East End' in **O Lucky Man!** (1973), Malcolm McDowell argues with a temperance troupe. Craig Kelly lives in the Cromwell Buildings in **The Young Americans** (1993). He takes Thandie Newton to the roof for views over the railway lines leading to London Bridge. Underneath the bridge is the cab firm, now called London Bridge Cars, 28 Southwark Street, for which Chiwetel Ejiofor works in **Dirty Pretty Things** (2002). The interior of the Hop Exchange appears in **Spice World** (1998).

On Bedale Street outside The Globe, Bonar Colleano is dropped off after hitching a ride in **Pool of London** (1950). In **Blue Ice** (1992) The Globe is the 'Critchley Hotel'. Michael Caine and Alun Armstrong keep an eye on Todd Boyce as he leaves an Italian restaurant, now Quinlan's Opticians, to enter the hotel. Soon Caine ends up on the roof of the pub, finds two bodies and chases the assassin over the railway lines. This area is also seen in the sniper scene in **The Criminal** (1999). Tom Selleck as **Lassiter** (1986) loses his tail by walking down the steps next to 2 London Bridge leading to Montague Close, round Southwark Cathedral, through the market and then tracking back to hide in the beer delivery hatch on the pavement outside The Globe.

Renée Zellweger lives at the top of The Globe in **Bridget Jones's Diary** (2001). Hugh Grant and Colin Firth's fight occurs outside and inside the restaurant 'Kalispera' at 5 Bedale Street. In the sequel **Bridget Jones: The Edge of Reason** (2004) there is an impressive pull-back from her alone in her window to show happy couples enjoying each others' company. The pub is 'Great Britain Grand Hotel' which is Amanda Bynes' first port of call in **What a Girl Wants** (2003).

Jeremy Irons looks for Meryl Streep underneath the railway lines between Green Dragon Court and Southwark Cathedral in **The French Lieutenant's Woman** (1981). Here Rupert Everett tries to win back Miranda Richardson in **Dance with a Stranger** (1985). In **Murder by Decree** (1979) Christopher Plummer chases after Susan Clark from Cathedral Street to Clink Wharf. Interiors and exteriors of Southwark Cathedral are seen in **Pool of London** (1950) when Bonar Colleano meets Max Adrian. In **The Slipper and the Rose** (1976) Annette Crosbie interrupts Richard Chamberlain's wedding inside by heralding Gemma Craven's arrival. **Brimstone and Treacle** (1982) opens with Sting at the south side of the cathedral attempting a scam in the underpass linking Green Dragon Court and Borough High Street. Unsuccessful in this, he walks north along Borough High Street and down the steps east of the cathedral. At the base of the stairs he 'accidentally' bumps into Denholm Elliott, whose office overlooks the cathedral, to inveigle himself into Elliott's house.

In **Tom Brown's Schooldays** (1950) the George Inn off Borough High Street is the stagecoach station when Francis de Wolff sees off son John Howard Davies to begin his first term at Rugby.

On Trinity Church Square Renée Zellweger catches a taxi in **Bridget Jones: The Edge of Reason** (2004) after being kissed by Jacinda Barrett outside Colin Firth's house, which is over in Richmond.

Hugh Grant ponders Christmas while walking on London Bridge against the flow of commuters heading to the jobs in the City he doesn't need to have in **About a Boy** (2002).

In **The Rachel Papers** (1989) Dexter Fletcher and Ione Skye part for the final time at the Hays Galleria.

In **Pool of London** (1950) the ship containing Earl Cameron, Bonar Colleano, Leslie Philips and James Robertson Justice docks at Battle Bridge Wharf just west of Tower Bridge. Philips and Cameron separately catch trams from Tooley Street on the corner of Battle Bridge Lane.

Opposite:
The Globe, Bedale Street, seen in **Pool of London** (1950), **Lassiter** (1986), **Blue Ice** (1992), **The Criminal** (1999), **Bridget Jones's Diary** (2001), **What a Girl Wants** (2003) and **Bridget Jones: The Edge of Reason** (2004).

Left:
Bermondsey Street
(far left), where
Clive Powell looks
sinister under
Bermondsey
Street's tunnel
(right) in *Children
of the Damned*
(1964).

At the corner of Bermondsey Street and 88 Tooley Street, Ian Hendry receives directions
from a cabbie while following Barbara Ferris on foot from W2 in *Children of the Damned*
(1964). He then sees her at the other end of Bermondsey Street tunnel. This is the same
angle – the corner of Holyrood Street and Bermondsey – seen in the opening titles
featuring a sinister still of Clive Powell. Just to the west is the Weston Road tunnel on St
Thomas Street, into which Powell's mother walks against the traffic under his hypnosis.

Todd Boyce contacts Sean Young from a callbox in *Blue Ice* (1992) while a Royal Mail
van, parked in front of Devon Mansions on the corner of Tooley Street and Druid Street,
observes him.

The area immediately west of Tower Bridge was once wharves, then was cleared for a
coach park and heliport and from 1977 to 1985 was the William Curtis Ecological Park. It is
now the site of the new City Hall. In the park three tramps become victims of *An
American Werewolf in London* (1981). In *Just Like a Woman* (1992) Paul Freeman
welcomes Togo Igawa at the heliport. In *Mission Impossible* (1996) Henry Czerny arrives at
the heliport. Here the Spice Girls film the end credits in *Spice World* (1997). At City Hall,
Bill Nighy discovers he's no. 1 in the charts in *Love Actually* (2003).

Outside on the riverfront Renée Zellweger argues with Colin Firth in *Bridget Jones: The
Edge of Reason* (2004).

John Wayne and his commandeered Capri end up in a skip on the south-east side of Tower Bridge Road after jumping the half-raised bascule section of Tower Bridge in pursuit of James Booth in **Brannigan** (1975). No such luck for Terence Morgan, who tries the same jump and ends up in the Thames in **Forbidden Cargo** (1954).

Bermondsey

Shad Thames, on the east side of the bridge, was once warehouses, complete with overhead walkways across the narrow street, now converted into flats, shops and restaurants. In **The Long Memory** (1952) first Elizabeth Sellars, then John Mills, visit scrap metal dealer John Chandos at the building, slightly altered, now called Courage Brewery Horsleydown. As cop John McCallum, reporter Geoffrey Keen and Eva Bergh arrive on Tower Bridge, Mills, shot by Chandos, escapes from Butler's Wharf. In **Callan** (1974) Kenneth Griffith warns Carl Mohmer about Edward Woodward's 'previous form' at a wharf window on Shad Thames. Paul McCartney rehearses with Ringo Starr, Dave Edmunds and Chris Spedding at Butler's Wharf in **Give My Regards to Broad Street** (1984).

Left:
John Mills visits John Chandos (top and centre) in **The Long Memory** (1952), set in Shad Thames (bottom).

Paul McGann invites Rebecca De Mornay to his seaplane moored at Butler's Wharf Pier in **Dealers** (1989). The Dixie Queen is moored here to host a singles' party and launch true love for Andy Nyman, Lucy Punch and Ed Byrne in **Are You Ready for Love?** (2006).

Peter Capaldi has his children's book rejected by Frances Barber in offices overlooking the bridge in **Soft Top Hard Shoulder** (1992). A concerted effort to break a computer system by a team of **Hackers** (1995) includes a British representative who operates from the outside seating area of Le Pont de la Tour. Hugh Grant takes Renée Zellweger to a riverside restaurant in **Bridget Jones's Diary** (2001). They walk into Shad Thames with the camera overhead on one of the higher walkways. Rob Lowe and Sarah Alexander dine in this area in **Perfect Strangers** (2004).

By the Paolozzi sculpture on Butler's Wharf, opposite the Design Museum, Helen Slater and Alfred Molina check out an inlet (in fact in W6) to gain access to a bank (EC3) in **The Steal** (1994). In **The French Lieutenant's Woman** (1981) Jeremy Irons is conveyed by carriage under the walkways of Shad Thames to meet Peter Vaughan at his offices at Cinnamon Wharf. Shad Thames used to run right round but is now broken off by Maguire Street, so Irons's journey is no longer possible.

When Anthony Hopkins looks for **The Elephant Man** (1980), he appears to be in the Shad Thames area. In **Young Sherlock Holmes** (1985) Nicholas Rowe, Alan Cox and Sophie Ward flee from cult worshippers through the area. In **Virtual Sexuality** (1999), in a sudden cut from SE16, Laura Fraser and pals escape from Rupert Penry-Jones' kidnappers.

On the extremity of Butler's Wharf, by St Saviour's Dock, Joe Regalbuto and Bob Hoskins find a body in **Lassiter** (1986). Later, Hoskins's car is ambushed and his prisoner Tom Selleck is abducted on what may be the corner of Gainsford Street and Lafone Street. Shortly after, fire swept through the area and its character changed after rebuilding.

In **Jubilee** (1977) Jenny Runacre, Little Nell and Toyah Willcox dump a body from Cinnamon Wharf into St Saviour's Dock. Later Willcox and Jordan kill a policeman to the south of this spot. In **The World Is Not Enough** (1999) during the speedboat chase a clever cut connects the dock, in reality a dead end, to E14.

Jon Bon Jovi takes Anna Galiena to his plush flat, with its deep-blue exterior, in **The Leading Man** (1995). This is in The Circle, a development embracing both sides of Queen Elizabeth Street with a statue of a horse, called Jacob, in the middle. In **Mad Dogs and Englishmen** (1995) C. Thomas Howell delivers a package to Elizabeth Hurley, whose office (until she is fired) is in The Circle, and asks her for a date. In **Loop** (1997) Andy Serkis drives up to The Circle to join Emer Court to dump her. Lucy Punch walks east along Tooley Street from Boss Street in *Are You Ready for Love?* (2006).

In *A Fish Called Wanda* (1988) John Cleese invites Jamie Lee Curtis to '2B St Trevor's Wharf, E1' for an assignation. Curtis crosses the bridge from Butler's Wharf and finds her way further east to Reed's Wharf, from where Kevin Kline later suspends Cleese out of the window.

Lynn Redgrave's penthouse, where she hosts a party and meets Jesse Birdsall in *Getting It Right* (1989), is in New Concordia Wharf on Mill Street.

At The Fleece, 160 Abbey Street, Steven Berkoff foolishly rails at Gary Love in *The Krays* (1990). Later Tom Bell creates a disturbance by drunkenly pulling out a sawn-off shotgun. Love escorts Bell to his eventual death after dancing a little jig with him under the railway bridge over Gelding Place. The Fleece is now Sidney House, a block of flats.

Reece Dinsdale reveals his hooligan tendencies to Richard Graham as he drives recklessly around the roundabout of Bermondsey Square in *I.D.* (1994).

In *The Football Factory* (2003) Frank Harper leads the fighting outside The Star, now demolished, on the corner of Willow Walk and Alscot Way. It is supposed to be near Tottenham's White Hart Lane, and curiously the pub is renamed The Start.

The house that is shared by Joe Absalom, Lara Belmont, Melanie Cutteridge, Lukas Haas, Alec Newman and Mel Raido in *Long Time Dead* (2000) is on Lynton Road, opposite Camilla Road.

SE16: Bermondsey, Rotherhithe, Surrey Quays

Bermondsey

In *The Business* (2005) Tamer Hassan's security van robbery takes place on the east of the tunnel formed by the viaduct over Dockley Road.

In *Nil by Mouth* (1997) Ray Winstone punches a man exiting a Wimpy, situated at 251a Southwark Park Road, close to St James's Road. Just to the east at no. 283 is Times Kebab, where Sophie Thomson relishes her kebab while Jerry O'Connell has reservations in *Fat Slags* (2004).

Jesse Birdsall attends a party (in SE1) hosted by Lynn Redgrave in *Getting It Right* (1989), parking his scooter on the promontory on Bermondsey Wall West. Here he meets

Helena Bonham-Carter. In *Hennessy* (1975), while fellow policeman Peter Egan looks away, Richard Johnson drives into David Collings's taxi parked outside Chamber's Wharf on Bermondsey Wall West to get information. The wharf has changed and no longer provides a view of Tower Bridge, but St Catherine's House is still there. Paul McCartney goes to the Old Justice, 94 Bermondsey Wall East, to see Ralph Richardson, who lives above the pub in *Give My Regards to Broad Street* (1984).

On West Lane is 39–77, home to *Sid and Nancy* (1986). Gary Oldman and Chloe Webb have a brief row on the street as they walk south past The Two Brewers at 35 West Lane, now closed and remodelled as flats with an additional storey.

The finale of *Mad Cows* (1999) takes place north of Jamaica Road. Greg Wise crashes his car as he follows Anna Friel along Paradise Street to King's Stairs Gardens. Friel, Joanna Lumley and Phyllida Law pass The Angel on Bermondsey Wall East and see off Friel on her boat bound for Australia.

In *Virtual Sexuality* (1999) Laura MacCauley and Steve John Shepherd's base is at Prince's Wharf near Elephant Lane, along the Thames Path. Here Laura Fraser and Luke de Lacey free the kidnapped Rupert Penry-Jones and flee to SE1.

Rotherhithe

Further along the path towards Rotherhithe Street, between riverside buildings, is a small viewing point for the river. Here Jamie Lee Curtis and Kevin Kline discuss Kline's apology to John Cleese in *A Fish Called Wanda* (1988).

Further east, opposite Isambard Place, Harvey Keitel and Iain Glen view James Duggan's washed-up body on the Thames littoral in *The Young Americans* (1993).

In *Pool of London* (1950) diamond thieves, chased by police, enter the Rotherhithe tunnel going northbound. After their car crashes Bonar Colleano flees up the stairs leading to Rotherhithe Street near Surrey Water. Max Adrian shoots Colleano outside at the top of the stairs, then suffers a messy death when he falls into the traffic of the tunnel. Meanwhile the wounded Colleano struggles into a boat on the Thames. In *Dead Fish* (2004) the van with Gary Oldman dangling from it both enters and then exits the northbound entrance.

Steven Mackintosh lives at 4 Deauville Court, next to Surrey Water at the end of Eleanor Close, in *Different for Girls* (1997).

Just inland off Salter Road is Leydon Close, a branch of Lagado Mews. In *I.D.* (1994) undercover cop Reece Dinsdale and wife Claire Skinner live at 37 Leydon Close.

In *24 Hours In London* (1999) Gary Olsen arranges a meeting on Stave Hill in the Russia Dock Woodland with a rival gang and, with the help of Sara Stockbridge, Luke Garret and David Sonnnenthal, slaughters the lot of them along with any unlucky innocent witnesses. Anjelica Lauren-Smith is the only survivor of the outrage, apart from the children in the local secondary school playing outside who are, apparently, blissfully oblivious to the roar of gunplay.

364 Rotherhithe Street, with its front garden decorated by all kinds of paraphernalia, makes a brief appearance in *Jubilee* (1977) when Linda Spurnier visits Neil Kennedy.

Surrey Quays
In *The Steal* (1994) there is clever cutting impressively condensing London's geography, when a van hurtles along Mount Vernon (NW3), down some steps, onto Elgar Street, and heads towards the Ship & Whale before turning into Gulliver Street and plunging into the Thames. Its occupants are next seen drenched at Hammersmith Bridge (W6).

Trisha Mortimer lives on a barge visited by Doug Cockle, in South Dock Marina, in *London Voodoo* (2004).

In *The Football Factory* (2004) Danny Dyer and fellow Chelsea hooligans exit Surrey Quays tube on Rotherhithe Old Road. They meet up with leader Frank Harper and walk down Oldfield Grove to connect with a wide path that leads past Sketchley Gardens and Silwood Street. They pass under two bridges and meet the Millwall 'firm' led by Tamer Hassan, who passes under a third bridge, where Dyer is badly beaten up in the ensuing fight.

Left:
Just southeast of Millwall's New Den gangs gear up for a fight in *The Football Factory* (2004).

165

SE11: Kennington, Lambeth

Kennington

Ralph Fiennes as *Spider* (2002) pauses by the bricked-up Oval Mansions on the north cusp of Kennington Oval on his way to the fictitious '71 Pegge Street, E1'. He walks along the back of Kilner House, accessible from Pegasus Place with a gasholder in the background. This is the same gasholder that appears to be directly behind a wall outside the front door of 'Pegge Street', but this is trick photography. The angle used in the shot can be seen at the western end of Mountford Place.

At the Oval cricket ground, Jack Warner and England try to prevent another Australian victory in *The Final Test* (1953).

In *Snatch* (2000) Vinnie Jones staggers from a car crash into The Jolly Gardener, 49 Black Prince Road on corner of Tyers Street, to be confronted by Robbie Gee and his replica gun.

Orlando Bloom as *The Calcium Kid* (2003) lives at 5 Vauxhall Walk. He signs Lyndsey Marshal's panties on the corner of Salamanca Street. His milk round includes Courtney Street and 5 Courtney Square – where flirtatious Tamsin Griffin lives – and Dolland House on Vauxhall Street overlooking Tesco's on Kennington Lane. His training includes punching a bag on a milk-cart passing The John Bull, 64 Tyers Street, now closed, where Rafe Spall gets into a fight inside. Spall performs his rap in front of Hayman's Point on Tyers Street. His training takes Bloom along Lambeth Walk and into a park, Lambeth Walk Doorstep Green, along Fitzalan Road. Billie Piper leads her cheerleaders outside Ravi's, 20 Vauxhall Street, on the corner with Jonathan Street. Omid Djalili's gym is the Vauxhall Street entrance of Lilian Baylis Secondary School.

Lambeth

South of Lambeth Road, on the corner of Sail Street, lie the estates of Copeland House and Ferrybridge House. In World War II it was bombed, so a street was built on the cleared site for the filming of *Passport to Pimlico* (1949), Lambeth standing in for the area just opposite across the river. Occasional glimpses can be seen in the background of surviving buildings on Lambeth Walk; and the buildings, especially the Grub Shop, now the Corner Café, on the corner of Hercules Road and Lambeth Road (SE1) are unmistakable, as is the railway bridge from which well-wishers throw food to help the beleaguered 'Burgundians' as they pass by on trains from Waterloo. The border post is set up opposite Hercules Road.

Opposite:
The Calcium Kid
(2003). Omid
Djalili's boxing gym
(top right) is situated
on Vauxhall Street
(left) and Orlando
Bloom steps out on
Vauxhall Walk
(bottom right).

In *Melody* (1971) Jack Wild pretends to Mark Lester's mother Sheila Steafel that he lives at 169 Kennington Road when she offers him a lift from Battersea. As soon as the car leaves, he jumps over the wall and rounds The Ship into Bishop's Terrace. The Ship is Roy Kinnear's local, though the doorway has since been moved. Under the titles a cinematic shot from Fairford House sweeps the area and zooms to a Boys Brigade troop marching down Kennington Lane from Kennington Road.

On the corner of Walcot Square and Sullivan Road is Walcot Stores, visited by Martin Kemp in *The Krays* (1990). Seeing a couple of young men he thinks are admiring both car and wife Kate Hardie too much, he gives them a thorough beating. During this fight the Sullivan Road sign is seen with the 'S' postcode covered up to disguise the location as E11.

The site of the old Lambeth Hospital, roughly where Castlebrook Close is today, stood in for the Bronx in *Death Wish 3* (1985).

SE17: Walworth

The towers of Walton House, Cruden House (obscuring Brawne House) and Prescott House are seen in a brief establishing shot in *The War Zone* (1998) as Ray Winstone's children walk across the extensive piece of grass between Bolton Crescent and Hillingdon Street towards the Brandon Estate. Rafe Spall 'motivates' Orlando Bloom as *The Calcium Kid* (2003) on the same patch of grass, and Bloom trains along St Agnes Place.

Now closed, the police station alongside the elevated railway track in Carter Place off Walworth Road is seen briefly in *Incognito* (1997).

SE5: Camberwell

In *For Queen and Country* (1988) Denzel Washington, Amanda Redman and her daughter, parking on the higher level of Hanworth House, on the corner of Camberwell New Road and John Ruskin Street, witness an attack by Geff Francis, who pushes a lump of concrete onto a police car on the lower level, killing Brian McDermott and injuring George Baker.

Bob Hoskins spies on and later picks up daughter Zoë Nathenson from her school on Farmers Road, just off Camberwell New Road, in *Mona Lisa* (1986).

Opposite:
Blow Up (1966).
David Hemmings makes his way from Consort Road (top) to Copeland Road (centre and bottom) after a night's photography.

Rupert Graves leaves Camberwell Magistrates Court on D'Eynsford Road with lawyer Lia Williams in **Different for Girls** (1995).

Camberwell Palace used to stand on the corner of Denmark Hill and Orpheus Street near Camberwell Green. In **Pool of London** (1950) Earl Cameron intends to meet Susan Shaw but is too shy when he sees her surrounded by friends. He turns away back south down Denmark Hill as trams trundle past in a bygone age.

In **Nil by Mouth** (1997) Ray Winstone, Charlie Creed-Miles and Jon Morrison drive past a dead-looking motorcyclist outside The Joiners' Arms, 35 Denmark Hill.

In **I'll Sleep When I'm Dead** (2003) Charlotte Rampling lives at 91 Knatchbull Road overlooking Myatt's Fields park, where Marc O'Shea lurks in wait for her after her visit to Clive Owen's camper van parked just west of the railway bridge over Gordon Grove near Lougborough Junction.

SE15: Peckham, Nunhead

Blow Up (1966) opens with David Hemmings emerging after a night photographing down-and-outs in a doss house, roughly where Nazareth Gardens now is. Hemmings chats to a few companions underneath one of the railway tunnels at Consort Road and then moves west to his Rolls, parked in Copeland Road.

Michael Caine's butcher shop, 'Dodds And Son' in **Last Orders** (2001) is 194 Bellenden Road, now Lucius And Richards near Danby Street. Opposite is

Left and opposite:
Darrell Road (left),
where Bob Hoskins
attempts to visit his
estranged family
(opposite) in ***Mona
Lisa*** (1986).

Tom Courtenay's funeral director business, 'Tucker And Son', at 157, and just to the north on the corner with Chadwick Road is The Wishing Well Inn, seen when Bob Hoskins approaches and later consoles Denise Black. The interiors of the pub are in SW4. Since filming, oddly shaped bollards have appeared on the pavements.

SE22: East Dulwich, west Honor Oak

In ***Mona Lisa*** (1986) Bob Hoskins goes to 286 Crystal Palace Road, on the corner of Goodrich Road, to buy some flowers. With these he visits 16 Darrell Road to see daughter Zoë Nathenson. Estranged wife Pauline Melville is having nothing of this and Hoskins is thrown out onto the street, where after kicking over a dustbin he picks a fight with a local. Robbie Coltrane rescues him and leads him north over North Cross Road into Upland Mews, where his Jaguar is waiting. Later Hoskins drops off Nathenson from school at the same corner on Crystal Palace Road. The shops are now private housing.

Entertaining Mr Sloane (1970) opens with Beryl Reid enjoying an ice lolly and a burial in Camberwell Old Cemetery, south of Peckham Rye Park. She finds Peter McEnery sunbathing on a grave and invites him into her house, which is at the entrance to the cemetery. During these scenes one can glimpse the Roman Catholic mortuary chapel by Wood Vale, demolished in the 1970s, matching the fate of the other two chapels. The house itself is largely unchanged, but the conservatory at the back, where Alan Webb stabs McEnery with a pitchfork, has gone, and the garden is no longer so open to prying eyes. The shed at the front over the driveway has disappeared as well. The gates lead into Forest Hill Road, seen when Harry Andrews in his car chases Webb on his bicycle. The SPAR corner shop opposite, next to Marmora Road, has closed down.

SE24: Herne Hill

In **Love Actually** (2003) Hugh Grant – with police escort – sweeps into Poplar Road to look for Martine McCutcheon. After trying several doors – including no. 89, and no. 100 where Heike Makatsch lives – he strikes gold at no. 102.

Jonathan Rhys Meyers lives at 94 Shakespeare Road in **I'll Sleep When I'm Dead** (2003). Here Jamie Foreman and landlady Sylvia Syms discover his body, and brother Clive Owen investigates later. On the corner of Hinton Road and Wellfit Street, outside the Ackee Café (surmounted by a big baked beans tin captioned 'Fill Your Tummy for Less Money') Ken Stott picks up hitman Marc O'Shea.

Left:
Poplar Road, where Martine McCutcheon lives in **Love Actually** (2003).

SE21: Dulwich Village

Dulwich Park has its moment of fame in **The Sandwich Man** (1966). Michael Bentine walks down the Duke of York steps (SW1) and in the next cut is standing on a bridge, since rebuilt at the top, watching drunk city gent Ronnie Stevens trying to adjust a sundial to conform with his watch. This bridge is just west of the small lake. Bentine then sits down to admire a floral display at the south-east edge of the lake. Here Bernard Cribbins photographs Suzy Kendall until jealous boyfriend David Buck attacks him. Toy yachtsman Alfie Bass is attacked by a runaway lawnmower, and both flowers and toy boat are destroyed in the chaos. Meanwhile the lawnmower leaves Dulwich Park by Roseberry Gate, which leads onto Dulwich Common – part of the South Circular – and ends up in Green Park (W1).

In **Legally Blonde** (2001) Reese Witherspoon gives her Harvard Law College graduation speech in the Great Hall of Dulwich College.

SE19: Norwood New Town, Upper Norwood, Crystal Palace

Don't Go Breaking My Heart (1998) opens with Anthony Edwards timing Linford Christie and being fired for his trouble at the running stadium in Crystal Palace.

Before the track was there, Michael Caine utters the immortal line 'You're only supposed to blow the bloody doors off' in **The Italian Job** (1966). One can just make out the TV mast that dominates the skyline.

SE20: Anerley

In **Our Mother's House** (1967) Dirk Bogarde takes his family rowing in the Lower Lake of Crystal Palace alongside Thicket Road. Life-size concrete and stonework dinosaurs built in 1852–54 after the Crystal Palace was moved here from Hyde Park still grace the lake.

SE10: Greenwich

Just south of Blackheath Hill is Dartmouth Terrace. In *The Crying Game* (1992) IRA man Stephen Rea gets a job on a building site run by Tony Slattery. The site overlooks a cricket match being played on Blackheath across Wat Tyler Road, and Jaye Davidson causes a stir when visiting Rea.

The New Haddo Estate, on which Timothy Spall and Lesley Manville, as well as Ruth Sheen, live in *All or Nothing* (2003), is on Tarves Way just next to Greenwich station. The whole complex, including Abercorn House, Gordon House and Haddington Court, was boarded up in September 2003 awaiting demolition and replacement by a new, upgraded housing estate.

In *Beautiful Thing* (1996) Glen Berry and Scott Neal, followed by Berry's mother Linda Henry, visit The Gloucester (now The Park), 1 King William Walk, for answers regarding their sexuality.

Glenda Jackson and Murray Head escort the children they are looking after down St Alfege Passageway in *Sunday Bloody Sunday* (1971), while a young Daniel Day-Lewis and a couple of his pals run broken glass along the sides of cars of the Sunday worshippers inside the church.

Peter Finch and Mary Peach sit in the colonnade of the Queen's House in Greenwich Park in *No Love for Johnnie* (1961). Richard Chamberlain and Glenda Jackson walk along the colonnade in *The Music Lovers* (1971). It is a London street in *Sense and Sensibility* (1995). Toby Stephens is led along it to his gruesome execution by hanging in *Photographing Fairies* (1997).

Bob Hoskins as *The Secret Agent* (1996) sends Christian Bale to plant a bomb at the Old Royal Observatory, with tragic consequences. Earl Cameron and Susan Shaw walk up to the main observatory building, known as Flamsteed House, in *Pool of London* (1950) after a visit to the Neptune Hall in the National Maritime Museum. Glenda Jackson and Murray Head spy on their charges, who are playing in the park, from the observatory in *Sunday Bloody Sunday* (1971). Under the titles of *Greenwich Mean Time* (1999) the group of friends play with water pistols between the observatory and the Queen's House. Daniel Craig receives his call from 'Dragon' in *Layer Cake* (2004) in front of the statue of General Wolfe, just outside the observatory. Later on in the film, sniper Paul Orchard is shot in the same location.

Bob Newhart drives Maggie Smith through the south exit from Greenwich Park in **Hot Millions** (1968). Just west of this exit is the pond seen during the voodoo ceremony at the climax of **London Voodoo** (2004).

On the Cutty Sark, at the northern end of King William Walk, Alun Armstrong hosts a concert in **Greenwich Mean Time** (1999) while Ben Waters first meets Georgia Mackenzie below decks. Beyond the ship at Greenwich Pier, Peter Finch and Mary Peach's pleasure boat arrives in **No Love for Johnnie** (1961). Here Lynn Redgrave as **Georgy Girl** (1966) finally leaves Alan Bates.

Trisha Mortimer cycles past Coltman House on the way to her barge in SE16 in **London Voodoo** (2004). Oliver James makes a phone call from a prop phone box on King William Walk in **What a Girl Wants** (2003).

The Old Royal Naval College, parts of which now house Greenwich University and Trinity College of Music, is a regularly used location. The area under the colonnade of King William's Court, the west wing, is transformed into an outdoor café in **The Music Lovers** (1971), where Richard Chamberlain and Glenda Jackson decide what to do on their first day of marriage. A little further south the colonnade becomes a fencing gym in **An Ideal Husband** (1999), where Simon Russell Beale tries to discover the truth over the 'Argentine affair' from Jeremy Northam. The Olsen twins play with pedal scooters along the colonnade on Queen Mary's Court, the east wing, in **Winning London** (2001).

The East Gate on Park Row is the entrance to Buckingham Palace when John Goodman as **King Ralph** (1991) sneaks out disguised as a trooper. Here photographers gather to capture Camille Coduri as she leaves by taxi.

The exterior of Queen Anne's Court, the east building on the riverfront, provides the setting for Anthony Hopkins' court martial by Laurence Olivier and Edward Fox at the beginning of **The Bounty** (1984). Here Heath Ledger resigns his commission in **The Four Feathers** (2002).

In **Sunday Bloody Sunday** (1971) Glenda Jackson and Murray Head walk round the riverfront of the Old Royal Naval College on the Five-Foot Walk, where Head half climbs the Water Gate to release some balloons.

In **Patriot Games** (1992) the buildings stand in for both the college and Buckingham Palace. After a quick establishing shot of the actual Buckingham Palace, James Fox's car leaves through East Gate on Park Row. Harrison Ford walks through the colonnade and down the steps towards the octagonal piece of grass with its statue of George II in front of the Thames to greet wife Anne Archer and daughter Thora Birch, who are standing in front of Queen Anne's Court. There he springs into action to foil Sean Benn's attempted assassination of Fox. In **Charge of the Light Brigade** (1968) Trevor Howard disrupts an anti-war protest held at the top of the steps. In **Shining Through** (1992) Melanie Griffiths tries to persuade Michael Douglas to let her be a spy; the Naval College is here standing in for the Pentagon.

Just to the east of the steps at Queen Anne's Court, Nicole Kidman first arrives in London to meet Mary-Louise Parker in **The Portrait of a Lady** (1996). The court is 'Charing Cross Station' in **Shanghai Knights** (2003) for Jackie Chan and Owen Wilson's arrival. Aaron Johnson steals Wilson's watch while the background shows a digitally imposed Big Ben.

In **Murder by Decree** (1979) the same area is used for no less than three different scenes. First, Donald Sutherland, accompanied by Tiddi Moore on a bus, thinks he spots the Ripper; a fake St Paul's is in the background. Second, a carriage conveys Christopher Plummer and James Mason, after the latter's brief spell in gaol, heading east. Third, the same pair is conveyed around the square heading apparently for the Thames. Bob Hoskins crosses this area east of the steps on his way to Somerset House (WC2) in **The Secret Agent** (1996). In a separate scene, Julian Wadham awaits Eddie Izzard at the portico just east of the steps. For **Charlotte Gray** (2001) the area is transformed into 1940s 'Southerby Square, SW3' where Cate Blanchett is invited to a book signing and meets Rupert Penry-Jones. To the west of the steps Helena Bonham Carter spots Allison Elliott from her period bus in **The Wings of the Dove** (1997). Here chauffeur Stephen Fry picks up Emily Mortimer and Stephen Campbell Moore in **Bright Young Things** (2003).

Nigel Hawthorne causes a rumpus at a Handel concert in **The Madness of King George** (1994). The orchestra is sitting in front of Thornhill's *trompe l'oeil* in the Painted Hall in King William's Court. The hall plays a 'Venice church' in **Lara Croft: Tomb Raider** (2001), seen when Iain Glen and Angelina Jolie meet after finding the first part of the triangle. Sean Connery addresses the World Council ('Now is the winter of your discontent') there in **The Avengers** (1998). Patrick Malahide reads out passages from de Sade's *Justine* to the Dauphin in **Quills** (2000). The news of a posting to the Sudan is announced to the regiment in **The Four Feathers** (2002), to the delight of all except Heath Ledger. In **Stage Beauty** (2004), at a banquet attended by Billy Crudup and Claire Danes, Rupert Everett as Charles II proclaims that women may take to the stage. The exterior of the Royal Fashion Show is the east side of King Charles' Court in **What a Girl Wants** (2003). When Amanda Byrne is turned away at the entrance, she sneaks in through the Admiral House's door. The interior turns out to be the Painted Hall. On the west side of Trinity College is an open space on which West Wycombe Park is cleverly superimposed as Colin Firth's grand residence. Its view overlooks King William's Court and beyond to the National Maritime Museum.

Rowan Atkinson nervously joins together David Haig and Sophie Thompson in the chapel in Queen Mary's Court in the second wedding in **Four Weddings and a Funeral** (1994). Tim Pigott-Smith welcomes Heath Ledger home in the chapel at the end of **The Four Feathers** (2002) while Wes Bentley gives a rousing speech. In **What a Girl Wants** (2003) Colin Firth resigns his candidacy in the chapel and on the steps of the entrance slugs Jonathan Pryce and dumps Anna Chancellor. The colonnade stands in for Oxford in the closing scenes.

In **Crimetime** (1996) Stephen Baldwin meets girlfriend Sadie Frost at the river end of Park Row, and they turn past The Trafalgar Tavern into Crane Street. The fleet leaving for the Sudan departs from here in **The Four Feathers** (2002).

In **All Or Nothing** (2002) Timothy Spall works at a car hire firm, now Article7.co.uk, at 73 Lassell Street near Old Woolwich Road.

On Ballast Quay Robert Mitchum in a wheelchair leaves the Cutty Sark pub in **The List of Adrian Messenger** (1963). After Kirk Douglas dispatches Mitchum into the Thames, George C Scott and Raoul Le Beerg discuss the case on the promenade in front of the pub across the road. Linda Henry is assigned to a new post managing The Cutty Sark in *Beautiful Thing* (1996).

In *Greenwich Mean Time* (1999) Georgia MacKenzie, followed by Charles De'Ath, leaves the pub and they start to argue outside. Steven John Shepherd intervenes and exchanges blows with De'Ath, who leaves beaten. Later MacKenzie also rejects Shepherd on her doorstep at 9 Ballast Quay just around the corner. Just to the west, Alec Newman photographs the band members (Chiwetel Ejiofor, Ben Waters and Alice Eyo) on the promontory on the Thames at the bottom of Hoskins Street. Later, in the same place, Ejiofor and Shepherd have to change Newman's catheter.

In *The Secret Partner* (1961) Norman Bird's dentistry is at Harbour House, 21 Ballast Quay, on the corner of Pelton Road. Stewart Granger approaches from Lovell's Wharf.

In *The Krays* (1990) 30 Caradoc Street, cobbled at the time opposite Thornley Place, is the Kray family home run by Billie Whitelaw, standing in for Bethnal Green's Vallance Road.

In *Plenty* (1985) Sting walks down Caradoc Street past Thornley Place, where the streets are host to 1953 coronation celebrations.

Below:

In *The Secret Partner* (1961) Stewart Granger makes his way to Ballast Quay (below right) from Lovell's Wharf (below left).

The isolated house surrounded by wasteland in **The Cement Garden** (1993) was just to the east of the still surviving gasholder and Blackwell Lane. But the gasworks had been taken out, and after decontamination the Millennium Dome project was realized. Look carefully at the background and one can make out across the river the two tower blocks at the end of Evelyn Road, the Millennium Mills (E16) and Reuters, during construction.

In **Spivs** (2004) Kate Ashfield takes Jack Dee to Fatboy's Diner (temporarily transported from E1) isolated at Dee's building site at the Tunnel Avenue Trading Estate.

Timothy Spall drives French visitor Kathryn Hunter to her hotel in WC1 via the northbound approach to the Blackwall Tunnel in **All or Nothing** (2002).

The Millennium Dome on the northern tip of the Greenwich peninsula makes a timely appearance in **The World Is Not Enough** (1999). At the climax of the speedboat chase, Maria Grazia Cucinotta attempts to escape by hot air balloon over the dome, but blows herself up rather than be caught, allowing Pierce Brosnan to fall onto the roof of the dome with a resounding thud as the credits start.

Below:
Ballast Quay (below left), where Stewart Granger visits dentist Norman Bird at no. 21 (below right) in **The Secret Partner** (1961).

SE8: Deptford, St John's

The Crown and Sceptre, 92 Friendly Street on the corner of Albyn Road, is The Dog and Beggar in **Spider** (2002), where the young Spider looks for his father Gabriel Byrne. As an adult Ralph Fiennes returns and finds some rope outside no. 94, where the houses next to the pub are being renovated.

Ray Winstone's recording studio in **Five Seconds To Spare** (1999) is Apt Art on Creekside. Winstone comes to a sticky end in Deptford Creek at the rear, best seen from the DLR as it passes between Deptford Bridge and Greenwich.

SE13: Lewisham, Ladywell, Hither Green

Ray Winstone follows Lucita Morse's car from Cowhill Road onto Lewisham High Street in **Nil by Mouth** (1997) to confront wife Kathy Burke as she leaves hospital.

SE14: New Cross, New Cross Gate

In **Once a Jolly Swagman** (1948) Dirk Bogarde's speedway racing scenes are at New Cross Stadium, which used to stand between the old Millwall Den and the end of Hornshay Street. The site is now Bridge House Meadows.

The exterior of 'The Winchester' in **Shaun of the Dead** (2004) is The Duke Of Argyll, on the west side of Monson Road on the corner with Barlborough Street. From Ecklington Gardens, Simon Pegg, Nick Frost, Kate Ashfield, Penelope Wilton, Dylan Moran and Lucy Davis act zombified as they struggle through a crowd of zombies besieging the pub.

Mark Rylance lives at 2 Alpha Road, where he shares **Intimacy** (2000) with Kerry Fox. When Fox leaves, she passes an Alpha Road sign – the pause button is vital to see it – into Deptford Broadway and the end credits roll over the same street. The house now has security bars protecting its door.

SE6: Catford, Bell Green, Bellingham

Herman's Hermits drive along Ademore Road to train their greyhound at Catford Stadium in ***Mrs Brown, You've Got a Lovely Daughter*** (1967). Despite the obvious signs, this is supposed to be Manchester. Later, at the trials in the same stadium, Peter Noone first meets Sarah Caldwell. Alex King runs his greyhound, Bullitt, at the stadium alongside Doggett Road in ***Small Time Obsession*** (2000). While Kirsten Parker helplessly looks on, Giles Ward beats up King, and at the end Juliette Caton bids him an emotional goodbye. The stadium has since been demolished.

SE23: Forest Hill

The splendid view from the top of Westwood Park is seen briefly in the opening credits of ***Small Time Obsession*** (2000).

Colin Firth takes Mena Suvari to the Horniman Museum on London Road to look at insects in ***Trauma*** (2004).

SE7: Charlton

In ***Blow Up*** (1966) David Hemmings parks in Clevely Close off Woolwich Road to visit no. 33, an antique shop on the corner of Clevely and Lancey Close. This shop has now been rebuilt. Hemmings photographs the close and then notices the entrance to Maryon Park. In the park, after passing the tennis courts, which are still there, he follows Vanessa Redgrave leading a man up the hill in the middle of the park. He photographs the rendezvous, and what could be a murder, at the top clearing. Later Hemmings returns to the same location in the dark and discovers the body. At the end of the film, still with no clear answers, he watches a group of students driving their jeep to the courts and miming a game of tennis.

Matthew Rhys' brother's body is found washed up just west of the Thames Barrier in ***Sorted*** (2000).

Left:
Vanburgh House,
Maze Hill, seen in
Mona Lisa (1986).

SE18: Woolwich, Plumstead

There is a nice pan of this stretch of the river, before the Thames Barrier was built, in ***Made*** (1972) as Carol White and Roy Harper admire the view from the Wooolwich Ferry Approach, close to Woolwich Church Street.

The Market Street side of Woolwich Town Hall is dressed as Keighley's 'Victoria Hotel' in ***Blow Dry*** (2001), seen briefly as the hairdressing competitors arrive.

The Royal Woolwich Arsenal is a huge riverside site formerly owned by the Army and now being converted to flats. Glenda Jackson goes insane here in ***The Music Lovers*** (1971). Ian McKellen as ***Richard III*** (1995) meets killer Adrian Dunbar working at the barracks. The play rehearsal scenes are held here in ***The Leading Man*** (1995). Guinevere Turner's fetish club in ***Preaching to the Perverted*** (1997) is on the waterfront. Stellan Skarsgård and Sean Penn are ambushed here in ***Kiss Kiss (Bang Bang)*** (2000).

SE3: Kidbrooke, Blackheath Vale

Bob Hoskins drives Cathy Tyson to Vanburgh House, 121 Maze Hill on the corner with Westcombe Park Road in **Mona Lisa** (1986). While she handles business, Hoskins is forced to wait outside.

Hugh Burden and Stewart Granger drive up to Granger's house at 1 The Paragon in **The Secret Partner** (1961). Nicole Kidman and Martin Donovan return to his house at 11 The Paragon, which John Gielgud subsequently bequeaths to Shelley Winters in **The Portrait of a Lady** (1996).

Philip Davis drives his car through Gary Oldman's football game on Blackheath Park in **The Firm** (1988).

Left:

The Secret Partner (1961). Stewart Granger and Hugh Burden arrive at Granger's house, 1 The Paragon.

Ben Waters, drunk, is nearly run over at Telemann Square in the Ferrier estate south of Kidbrooke station in **Greenwich Mean Time** (1999).

SE28: Thamesmead

Gary Oldman and Lesley Manville live at 11 Mallard Path, close to Chamberlain Close, in **The Firm** (1988). At the time a new development, it is now overgrown with vegetation.

SE2: Abbey Wood, South Thamesmead

In **A Clockwork Orange** (1971) Malcolm McDowell decides that he needs to reassert his leadership over his fellow droogs, so pushes Warren Clarke into the artificial lake called Southmere and slices his hand when he tries to get out. This scene is on the west side of the lake parallel to Binsey Walk, with the skyscrapers on Yarnton Way in the background all making up a huge concrete estate east of Harrow Manor Way.

The same estate appears in **Beautiful Thing** (1996). Glen Berry and his friends go for a dip in the lake. His mother Linda Henry enjoys a drink at the Lakeside complex to the north. South of Binsey

Below:
Southmere Lake, seen in **A Clockwork Orange** (1971) and **Beautiful Thing** (1996).

Walk is the site of their flat, the balcony of which overlooks Tavy Bridge Piazza. The balcony is immediately above a row of shops. To the east of these shops is a staircase, and their flat is the second door to the left. In the film it is no. 269; in reality it is no. 19.

SE9: Eltham

Catherine McCormack tends graves in peoples' absence at Greenwich Cemetery, identifiable by its semi-circular World War 1 memorial, in **Born Romantic** (2000).

The interior of Eltham Palace off Court Road is the private cinema of **Richard III** (1995). It is also Michael Gambon's house in **High Heels and Low Lifes** (2001), and is seen briefly after the wedding in **I Capture the Castle** (2002).

Butler Harry Andrews escorts Robert Mitchum to the conservatory on what is now the Mansion Site of the University of Greenwich's Avery Hill Campus, near Bexley Road, to meet James Stewart in **The Big Sleep** (1978).

Left:
The Mansion Site conservatory, Avery Hill Campus, seen in *The Big Sleep* (1978).

east central london

This tiny district has the richest history of London, devastated by plagues, fires and bombing and frequently rebuilt. Now gleaming office blocks tower over tiny alleys, numerous churches and residential pockets to the north.

EC3: Monument, Bank, Leadenhall, Tower Hill

Monument

At the top of the Monument, Roger Moore betrays his firm's secrets in *The Man Who Haunted Himself* (1970).

In *The Sandwich Man* (1966) Ron Moody trades a carpet for cod at old Billingsgate Fish Market. In *You Must Be Joking* (1965) Michael Callan chases a cart down St-Mary-At-Hill, through the fish market, and watches the historic Lloyd's Lutine Bell roll out of the cart into the Thames. Jerry O'Connell takes Sophie Thompson to a fashion show at the market in *Fat Slags* (2004). Leo Gregory drinks himself into the night on a bench in *Green Street* (2005).

In *If Only* (2004) Paul Nicholls's favourite restaurant is 'Tantra' at 22 Eastcheap, out of which Jennifer Love Hewitt runs to her fateful taxi driven by Tom Wilkinson. The accident itself happens at the intersection of Eastcheap and Botolph Lane.

Bank

Bernard Miles asks for directions in front of Mansion House in *Chance of a Lifetime* (1950). In *The Lavender Hill Mob* (1951) Alec Guinness eludes the police at Bank tube.

George Segal recognizes Glenda Jackson heading up Cornhill sitting in a bus in front of the Royal Exchange in *A Touch of Class* (1973). Eric Portman purchases flowers in *Wanted for Murder* (1946). Paul Newman pops into the underground toilets in *The Mackintosh Man* (1973).

The Theory of Flight (1996) opens with Kenneth Branagh on the top of the Royal Exchange attempting to fly and falling onto a crash mat hastily inflated by the fire brigade. In *Piccadilly Jim* (2005) newlyweds Sam Rockwell and Frances O'Connor emerge onto the steps of the Royal Exchange. Elijah Wood exits the tube to meet sister Claire Forlani in *Green Street* (2005) while workmen clear the area of debris from a football fight.

On Threadneedle Street is a row of shops where Paul Bettany shelters in the rain in *The Heart of Me* (2002). He buys a bracelet at 'Roberts' jewellers, actually Tiggy Twilight, at number 30, but collapses outside number 33.

At Mont Blanc, 11 Royal Exchange on the corner with Cornhill, Colin Firth buys a new diary for Renée Zellweger in *Bridget Jones's Diary* (2001). Jimi Mistry enlists his brother's help at the same shop, this time cast as 'Le Beau Chapeau', in *East Is East* (1999), while it also appears as a flower shop which Vanessa Redgrave visits in *Mrs Dalloway* (1997).

Empire State (1987) opens with a car crash at 33 Lombard Street, actually in Clement's Lane, with Catherine Harrison staggering out of the wreckage.

Leadenhall

Michael Brandon and Leigh Zimmerman launch their book at Waterstone's, 1 Whittington Avenue, in *Are You Ready For Love?* (2006).

Joss Ackland and Tom Smothers meet Charles Gray at the London Metal Exchange, by Leadenhall Market, in *The Silver Bears* (1977). Police chase the diamond thieves' car through Leadenhall Market in *Pool of London* (1950), while Angelina Jolie as *Lara Croft: Tomb Raider* (2001) rides her bike through it, and the car chase in *Johnny English* (2003) passes through it into Lime Street. David Morrissey's favourite café in *Basic Instinct 2* (2005) is on Lime Street.

In *Harry Potter and the Philosopher's Stone* (2001) Daniel Radcliffe and Robbie Coltrane enter the door diagonally opposite 43 Leadenhall Market to take them to 'Diagon Alley'. In *High Hopes* (1988) dispatch rider Philip

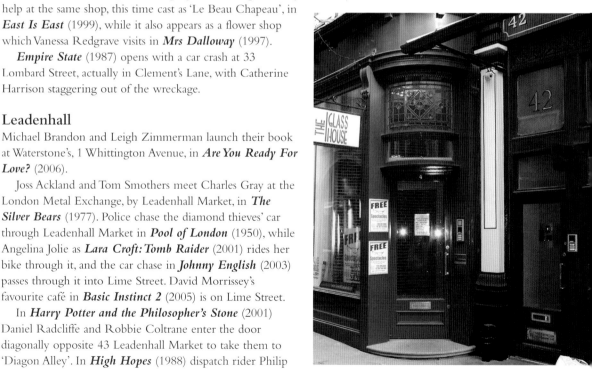

Below:
43 Leadenhall Market, seen in *Harry Potter and the Philosopher's Stone* (2001).

Davis descends in a lift in Lloyd's of London to his bike parked at the top of the steps at 120 Leadenhall Street. *The Avengers* (1998) features both the top of Lloyd's, where Uma Thurman fights her double dressed as a teddy bear, and the bottom, where Ralph Fiennes takes on Eddie Izzard and his henchmen. In *Proof of Life* (2000) Russell Crowe works for an insurance company in the building. The interior, notable for its ascending array of escalators, is seen in *Different for Girls* (1997), *Spy Game* (2001), *Code 46* (2003) and *Green Street* (2005). The police take Frankie Muniz to the Lime Street entrance in *Agent Cody Banks 2* (2004). Also from here, a 'Firm' member spots Elijah Wood and Henry Goodman entering *The Times* offices in *Green Street* (2005).

In *Proof of Life* (2000) Russell Crowe visits the Pizza Express under Luc's. The Pizza Express is a butcher's in *Brannigan* (1975), when John Wayne playing a Chicago cop meets Richard Attenborough buying a steak there. They enter The Lamb opposite to start a fight and gain Del Henney's trust.

Tom Selleck as *Lassiter* (1986) arrives on his Triumph at his fence's fish stall, and is later captured at the market. Colin Dale's grip onto a van containing the kidnapped Susannah York fails here in *Just Ask for Diamond* (1988). Damian Lewis and Ben Chaplin meet up in *Chromophobia* (2005), and Kate Isitt chats to Demi Moore on her mobile in *Half Light*

Left:
At Leadenhall Market Kate Isitt chats reassuringly to Demi Moore in *Half Light* (2006).

(2006). Elijah Wood and father Henry Goodman chat about his Harvard expulsion over coffee in **Green Street** (2005).

In **Children of Men** (2006) the Argentine embassy is based on Crosby Square. As Clive Owen passes by and walks down the steps to Undershaft he is bundled into a van by his kidnappers. In **Miranda** (2002) John Simms visits Kyle MacLachlan, who works in Aviva Tower at 1 Undershaft. In **Stormbreaker** (2006) the site is digitally changed to Mickey Rourke's huge offices. Here Alex Pettyfer and Sarah Bolger ride to the square in front of the tower to confront Rourke. The Swiss Re building (familiarly known as the 'Gherkin') at 30 St Mary Axe, on the bombed Baltic Exchange site, houses David Morrissey's psychiatric practice on level 16 in **Basic Instinct 2** (2005). Jonathan Rhys-Meyers starts his newly acquired job here in **Match Point** (2005).

Damian Lewis works at 16 St Helen's Place off Bishopsgate in **Chromophobia** (2005).

Tower Hill

The robbery in **The League of Gentlemen** (1960) targets the 'City And County Bank Limited' on the corner of Great Tower Street and Mincing Lane. Kieran Moore sets up a smoke barrel on the south side of Great Tower Street, as do Terence Alexander and Norman Bird on the north side. During the foggy chaos, Jack Hawkins and company raid the bank, since rebuilt.

Up on the east side of Mincing Lane is Minster Court, where Adrian Pasdar works in **Just Like a Woman** (1992). Minster Court is renamed 'House Of DeVil' for Glenn Close to sweep into in **101 Dalmatians** (1996).

In **Sliding Doors** (1998) Gwyneth Paltrow is fired from her job at the Corn Exchange building at 55 Mark Lane. In **The Long Arm** (1956) the trail on Peter Burton starts from his office on the corner of Byward Street and Mark Lane.

In **Children of the Damned** (1963) the children take refuge in the blitzed St Dunstan-in-the-East between St Dunstan's Hill and Idol Lane, and are besieged there by the army.

Stewart Granger's shipping company is by the river on Three Quays Walk in **The Secret Partner** (1961). Judy Garland and Gregory Phillips enjoy a river trip to Tower Pier in **I Could Go on Singing** (1963). Alan Whicker reports from the pier on the permanently berthed cruise ship **The Magic Christian** (1969).

In **Shooting Fish** (1997) as Dan Futterman, Stuart Townsend and Kate Beckinsale leave the bank by a side entrance of the vast Ten Trinity Square, their car is broken into at the corner of Muscovy Street and Seething Lane. In **Shiner** (2000) on Seething Lane Michael Caine's minders Andy Serkis and Frank Harper turn a car onto its side to clear the way for Caine's car.

In **Two Way Stretch** (1960) the military led by Thorley Walters and John Wood leave the Trinity Square exit in a jewel escort. In **A Warm December** (1973) Esther Anderson and Sidney Poitier enjoy the same building, now standing in as the 'Museum of Ethnography'. In **Sweeney!** (1976) Ian Bannen arrives to deliver a speech on oil. In **The Steal** (1994) Stephen Fry's office is in Trinity House, the British Lighthouse Authority masquerading as '27 Wall Street'. Helen Slater and Alfred Molina discuss ways of breaking into the firm's computer system by All Hallows Church.

Edward Woodward exits Tower Hill tube to join Eric Porter in a car in **Callan** (1974).

Nastassja Kinski wanders around the pathway north of the Tower of London in a trance in **To The Devil, a Daughter** (1976). Michael Crawford, Oliver Reed and Lotte Tarp visit the Tower of London to admire the Crown Jewels in **The Jokers** (1966). After Mark Dightam as **The Boy Who Turned Yellow** (1972) loses a mouse during a school trip, he returns to the Tower at night with Robert Eddison to retrieve it.

In **The Frightened City** (1961) Olive McFarland helps Sean Connery to escape, but is swiftly arrested in the tunnel under Tower Bridge. While Gary Cooper and Deborah Kerr visit the riverfront, Cooper suspiciously accosts Eric Portman in the tunnel in **The Naked Edge** (1961).

Donald Houston and Moira Lister chat on the riverfront after their visit to the tower in **A Run for Your Money** (1949).

Left:
A stunning shot of Tower Bridge shown in **The Frightened City** (1961).

Left:
Tower Bridge, near
the Tower of London
(top), where Gary
Cooper and
Deborah Kerr walk
along the riverfront
(bottom left and
right) in ***The Naked
Edge*** (1961).

Michael Caine as ***Alfie*** (1966) photographs Shelley Winters here. From Dead Man's Hole, the steps underneath Tower Bridge, Franco Nero and Michael Gambon supervise a hanging in ***The Innocent Sleep*** (1995), all witnessed by Rupert Graves.

David Hemmings requests a court-martial from John Gielgud in the Royal Mint on Mansell Street in ***Charge of the Light Brigade*** (1968).

EC4: Blackfriars, St Paul's

Blackfriars

Tim Curry and Matthew Rhys fight on the prow of HMS President, permanently moored along the Victoria Embankment, in *Sorted* (2000).

Anthony Hopkins, Jim Broadbent and Michael Byrne walk from Fleet Street through Middle Temple to Fountain Court to hire barrister Simon Callow in *The Good Father* (1985). Robin Phillips as *David Copperfield* (1970) and Nicholas Pennell walk up Middle Temple Lane to Hare Court, to discover Pennell's lodgings are next to Ralph Richardson's. Dirk Bogarde's chambers in *Victim* (1961) are in the Carpmael Buildings just south of Elm Court. In *The Medusa Touch* (1978) Lino Ventura interviews barrister Alan Badel at the west end of Temple Church, and they walk up Middle Temple Lane onto Fleet Street. Phil Collins as *Buster* (1988), Larry Lamb and Michael Attwell wait at the same spot by the church to accost 'bent brief' Rupert Vansittart as he exits 3 Dr Johnson's Building and walks up Inner Temple Lane.

In *The Da Vinci Code* (2006) Tom Hanks, Audrey Tautou and Ian McKellen investigate Temple Church. Hanks and Tautou flee from Paul Bettany along Fleet Street.

In *Brothers-in-Law* (1957) Ian Carmichael and parents pass under the 1730 gate on Crown Office Row, which leads to the Inner Temple gardens. Later Carmichael enters 6 King's Bench Walk, where he is taken on as Miles Malleson's pupil, pursuing him to the Royal Courts of Justice. Later he and Richard Attenborough receive a brief as they approach Middle Temple Hall on Fountain Court. Carmichael's chambers are further north, in the corner of King's Bench Walk, in *School for Scoundrels* (1960). Albert Finney, with Hugh Griffith's encouragement, woos Susannah York at her house in the same corner in *Tom Jones* (1963), and Allan Cuthbertson works here in *Performance* (1970).

In *Brothers-In-Law* (1957) Terry-Thomas chases Ian Carmichael from Cheshire Court, past Ye Olde Cheshire Cheese on Fleet Street, and into Bolton Court. At a coffee shop on the site of The King and Keys, 142 Fleet Street, between Prêt-à-Manger and Peterborough Court, Clive Owen survives a bomb blast in *Children of Men* (2006).

Fleet Street was for a long time home to Britain's national newspapers until they began to move out in the 1980s. None now remain, though many of their buildings do, including the Daily Telegraph's Peterborough Court with its eye-catching clock. This is seen when Richard Burton as *The Spy Who Came in from the Cold* (1965) crosses the street to buy cigarettes

while trying to lose a possible tail, and again in ***A Run for Your Money*** (1949), when Alec Guinness brings Donald Houston to his paper, *The Weekly Echo*.

The Daily Express building still survives at no. 121, near the east end of the street, and is the centre of the action in ***The Day the Earth Caught Fire*** (1961). Journalist Edward Judd drinks at 'Harry's' in St Bride's Avenue, where he discusses Earth's impending doom with Leo McKern and Reginald Beckwith. In ***Defence of the Realm*** (1985) Gabriel Byrne escorts plastered Denholm Elliott out of the Punch Tavern on the corner of Bride Lane.

At International Press, 76 Shoe Lane on the corner of Little New Street, the heliport on top is used in ***Entrapment*** (1999) when Sean Connery and Catherine Zeta-Jones leave

Above:
Fleet Street and Cheshire Court (above left), where Terry-Thomas emerges from Cheshire Court (top) in pursuit of Ian Carmichael (bottom) in ***Brothers-in-Law*** (1957).

London for Scotland, in **Dead Fish** (2004), when Billy Zane welcomes Karel Roden, and in **Stormbreaker** (2006) after Damian Lewis rescues Alex Pettyfer.

Colin Blakely lures Martin Sheen to what is now the Crowne Plaza Hotel, New Bridge Street, in **Loophole** (1980) to rob the bank next door, actually Unilever House. While Blakeley keeps watch from Bridge House, 181 Queen Victoria Street, the gang enter via the sewers and make their escape under Blackfriars station. The Unity Domestic Bureau seen in **23 Paces to Baker Street** (1956) is in the next block – now rebuilt – north of Blackfriars Passage. Robert Mitchum takes Sarah Miles to The Black Friar, at Blackfriars Court, in **The Big Sleep** (1978). Here Mark Tandy is arrested on a morality charge in **Maurice** (1987).

Stephen Fry as **Wilde** (1997) exits a shop with Jennifer Ehle on the west side of Addle Hill and notices rent boys ('Looking for something, sir?') opposite.

The Rising Sun, at 61 Carter Lane, is the pub outside which Colin Firth enjoys fisticuffs with Jack Dee, Stephen Marcus and Mike Binder in **Londinium** (2001).

St Paul's

Rex Harrison's wives arrive for his trial at the Central Criminal Court on the corner of Old Bailey and Newgate Street in **The Constant Husband** (1955). Ian Carmichael runs out of it in **Brothers-in-Law** (1957), pursued by Terry-Thomas. In **Gideon's Day** (1958) Jack

Below:
The Old Bailey (below left), seen in **The Constant Husband** (1955), **Gideon's Day** (1958), **The Naked Edge** (1961), **The Jokers** (1966), **The Strange Affair** (1969), **Night, After Night, After Night** (1969), **Sweeney 2** (1976) and **Brothers-in-Law** (1957), where Terry-Thomas pursues Ian Carmichael (below right).

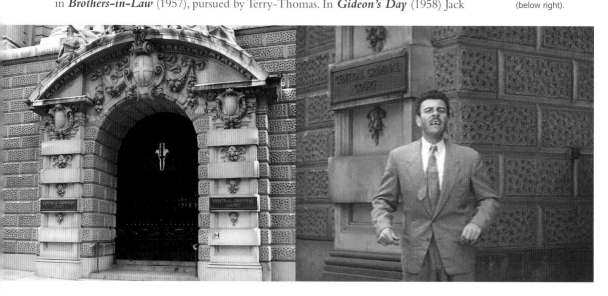

Hawkins, or a double, hurries out of a police car to give evidence in court. Gary Cooper and Deborah Kerr step out of the court in *The Naked Edge* (1961). The Crown Jewels are returned to the nation by *The Jokers* (1966) by resting them on top of the statue of Justice on the roof. Inside, Jack Watson is acquitted in *The Strange Affair* (1969) and Jack May serves as a judge in *Night, After Night, After Night* (1969). In *Sweeney 2* (1976) reluctant John Thaw is subpoenaed to give disgraced boss Denholm Elliott a character testimony.

Built after bombing in World War II, Paternoster Square, north of St Paul's Cathedral, houses the office of Laurence Harvey in *Darling* (1965), Karl Malden in *Hot Millions* (1968), and Roger Moore in *Crossplot* (1969). Peter Cook conducts an interview here in *The Rise And Rise Of Michael Rimmer* (1970). The whole area around St Paul's has since been rebuilt again.

Above:
St Paul's Cathedral, seen from this angle in *Great Expectations* (1948) and *Lost* (1955).

Jimi Mistry attempts a robbery at a 'Bloomsbury Bank' cash till on Ludgate Hill, the approach to the cathedral, in *Born Romantic* (2000) before taking refuge in a salsa club in SW9. Richard Widmark is chased across the west front of St Paul's in *Night and the City* (1950). Here too, in *The Madness of King George* (1994), Nigel Hawthorne, cured of porphyria, Helen Mirren and Rupert Everett ascend the steps. At the thanksgiving service for *Lawrence of Arabia* (1962) in the cathedral, reporter Jack Hedley asks various luminaries such as Harry Andrews for their opinion of Lawrence. The finale of *The Hands of the Ripper* (1971) seems to take place in the Whispering Gallery, though this may be a studio set.

The period shot of a carriage passing the south side of the cathedral in *Great Expectations* (1946) is matched in *Lost* (1955) when David Farrar drops off David Knight

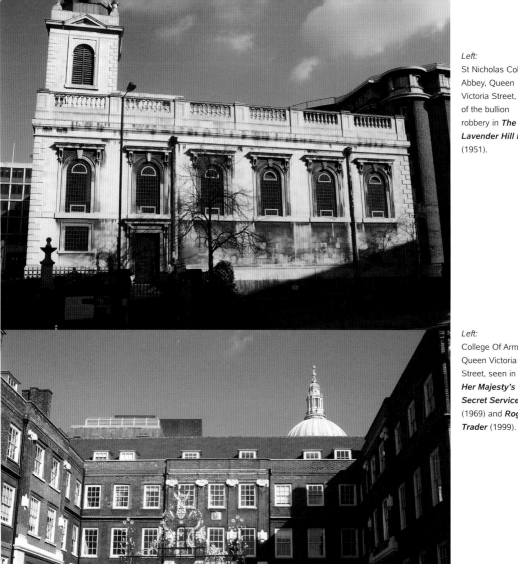

Left:
St Nicholas Cole Abbey, Queen Victoria Street, site of the bullion robbery in ***The Lavender Hill Mob*** (1951).

Left:
College Of Arms, Queen Victoria Street, seen in ***On Her Majesty's Secret Service*** (1969) and ***Rogue Trader*** (1999).

and Julia Arnall. Earl Cameron and Susan Shaw view the ***Pool of London*** (1950) from the Stone Gallery near the top of St Paul's. Shaw spots Max Adrian climbing over bomb rubble to get to a roof at the top of Peters Hill.

In ***The Lavender Hill Mob*** (1951) the bullion robbery takes place in front of Wren's St Nicholas Cole Abbey on Queen Victoria Street. Alfie Bass sits on the Abbey steps, Sidney James stands on Lambeth Hill, Stanley Holloway paces on Old Fish Street Hill. Bass steals the van driving up Friday Street, then he descends Lambeth Hill and turns into Booth Lane – impossible now – to hide in a warehouse. Alec Guinness ends up falling into the Thames roughly about where the Millennium Bridge is now.

In ***On Her Majesty's Secret Service*** (1969) George Lazenby drives to the College of Arms on Queen Victoria Street, on the west side of Peters Hill steps. In ***Rogue Trader*** (1999) chairman John Standing arrives here to address Barings Bank. Oliver Reed drives Michael Crawford to his solicitor on the other side of the steps in ***The Jokers*** (1966). Roger Moore chases Dudley Sutton down the steps in ***Crossplot*** (1969).

Below:
Dudley Sutton flees down Peters Hill steps after a failed assassination attempt in ***Crossplot*** (1969).

Michael Bentine as **The Sandwich Man** (1966) meets Norman Wisdom as a Catholic priest at the 'All Angels Boys Club' in Knightrider Court. In this same location, Damian Lewis confides too much to his friend Ben Chaplin in **Chromophobia** (2005). Rod Silvers parks his taxi underneath the Millennium Bridge – in a pedestrian space mocked up to look like a road – in order to spy on activities at the Tate Modern across the river in **Agent Cody Banks 2** (2004).

The interior of Mansion House, particularly the Egyptian Hall's white columns with gold rims, is seen in **The Golden Bowl** (2000).

Graham Stark drives Sophia Loren as **The Millionairess** (1960) to London Bridge (predecessor of the current one of that name), from where she jumps into the Thames. Later just east of Swan Lane Pier, unrecognizable were it not for the view of Southwark Cathedral across the river, Loren tips Dennis Price into the water while Peter Sellers offers assistance.

Russell Crowe and Michael Kitchen chat on a Greenwich to Westminster cruise between Southwark and Blackfriars bridges in **Proof of Life** (2000). On Southwark Bridge John Simms rehearses his job-quit speech for his pregnant wife in **Wonderland** (1999).

EC2: City, Barbican, Liverpool Street

City

From Old Broad Street Catherine Zeta-Jones spies on Sean Connery as he travels the escalator in Tower 42's atrium to visit 'Cryptonic' in **Entrapment** (1999). Further down Old Broad Street is the Stock Exchange, where Connery abandons his hire car to take Zeta-Jones off in a helicopter, supposedly from the roof but actually from that of a different building in EC4. Matthew Rhys collects his dead brother's things from Tower 42 in **Sorted** (2000). Clive Merrison's office in **Saving Grace** (2000) is also in the tower.

On Lothbury, fans spot an enigmatic figure under the credits of **Velvet Goldmine** (1998).

In **The Killing of Sister George** (1968) Beryl Reid drunkenly invades a taxi as it approaches Guildhall Yard from King Street, and assaults the nuns inside. The taxi crashes on the junction with Gresham Street.

In **The Human Factor** (1979) Nicol Williamson is picked up by a contact from a coffeehouse in the St Vedast building on Cheapside between Foster Lane and St Martin's Le Grand. He follows him across Small Change and then, going back on themselves, they cross to 16 St Martin's Le Grand. Tom Berenger crosses St Martin's Le Grand at its intersection with Gresham Street to arrange an arms deal in *The Dogs of War* (1980).

Barbican

The Hunger (1983) ends with Susan Sarandon admiring the view from Lauderdale Tower in the Barbican development. The flat that Paul Bettany inherits from David Thewlis in *Gangster No. 1* (1999) is in the Cromwell Tower at the Barbican. Malcolm McDowell jumps off the balcony. Jonathan Pryce and Charlie Dore visit an exhibition at the Barbican Arts and Conference Centre in *The Ploughman's Lunch* (1983).

At London Wall, overshadowed by 1960s tower blocks – some of which no longer survive – Laurence Harvey goes for an interview in *Life at the Top* (1965). In *Blow Up* (1966) David Hemmings drives west along it from his visit to SE7. In *The Italian Job* (1967) Michael Caine inspects a reel of film on the back of a milk cart heading east. Nicholas Parsons's office is established here in *Don't Raise the Bridge, Lower the River* (1967), and Susannah York and Dirk Bogarde crack codes in *Sebastian* (1968).

Post-war Wood Street, without recent redevelopment, is part of the policeman's beat in *Pool of London* (1950). In *Crossplot* (1969) Roger Moore chases Dudley Sutton from EC4

Below left and right:
Dudley Sutton is
pursued on the St
Alphege Highwalk,
London Wall in
Crossplot (1969).

to St Alphege Highwalk at Wood Street (since subsumed by an immense block over London Wall, but similar to the Bassishaw Highwalk further east). Here Francis Matthews shoots Sutton and tosses the gun to Moore to implicate him. Arthur Lowe attempts to assassinate Peter Cook and falls out of a high rise onto Richard Pearson in **The Rise and Rise of Michael Rimmer** (1970).

On the junction of Moor Lane and Fore Street, Des Brady's killing spree begins in **Day of the Sirens** (2002). Paul Nicholls works nearby at Citypoint off Ropemaker Street in **If Only** (2004).

The police station to which Spike Milligan is taken in **Postman's Knock** (1962) is Britannic House on Moorgate. Opposite is Moorgate tube, to where Barbara Shelley guides Milligan after his release.

Liverpool Street

James Garner's hotel is on the Finsbury Circus side of Britannic House in **The Americanization of Emily** (1964). Outside the hotel, he invites his driver Julie Andrews to a bridge party.

The 'Church And Universities Club' is Salisbury House on Circus Place in **The Missionary** (1982). Here Michael Palin first catches a glimpse of Maggie Smith. London Wall Buildings in Finsbury Circus on the corner with Broad Street Place stands in for Barings Bank in **Rogue Trader** (1999), and Tom Hollander's office in **Martha, Meet Frank, Daniel and Laurence** (1998).

As Heather Graham approaches from the colonnade adorning 1 Throgmorton Avenue, she meets Joseph Fiennes at the pedestrian crossing on London Wall opposite Blomfield Street in **Killing Me Softly** (2002). She works at 4 London Wall and watches Fiennes in 'Summit Books', actually Aus Travel, across Blomfield Street.

On Sun Street young Jamie Sweeney shoots Adrian Dunbar in his car parked by the UBS building, and escapes by cycling off into Finsbury Square in **Shooters** (2000). Between Sun Street and Liverpool Street used to stand Broad Street station, which Paul McCartney explores during the 'No More Lonely Nights' sequence in **Give My Regards to Broad Street** (1984), finally finding Ian Hastings and the missing master tape there. The station was replaced by Broadgate Circus, which stands in for Milan in the 'I'm The Leader of the Gang' segment of **Spice World** (1997). Rupert Graves and Nisha K Nayar ice-skate here in **Different for Girls** (1997).

In *I Was Monty's Double* (1957) John Mills arrives at Liverpool Street station, ascends the stairs past the old tearoom and tries to evade his shadow. In *The Informers* (1964) Margaret Whiting, seeing off her son, is threatened by Colin Blakely and Kenneth J. Warren. In *File of the Golden Goose* (1969), when Yul Brynner and Edward Woodward catch a taxi from the rank on the west side – then partially uncovered – a shot of the old lettering on the wall, since gone, cunningly hides 'Street', thus leaving it to read 'Liverpool Station' in an attempt to pass it off as Liverpool Lime Street. Later Brynner meets a contact in the tearoom. John Hurt as *The Elephant Man* (1980), returning from the continent, is chased by a crowd along the iron crosswalk and is cornered in the lavatories. Paul Freeman walks along the iron crosswalk in *The Dogs of War* (1980). In *Runners* (1983) the station stands in for St Pancras, as Fox meets runaway daughter Kate Hardie on the same iron crosswalk. Liam Neeson appears at the station in *A Prayer for the Dying* (1987). In the mid-1990s the station was extensively refurbished.

Philip Davis emerges from Liverpool Street tube to be picked up by the rest of the gang in *Face* (1997). Directly above this exit is the London hideout for Tom Cruise, Jean Reno, Ving Rhames and Emmanuelle Béart in *Mission Impossible* (1996). Cruise calls the FBI from the mainline station across the street – at a place under the escalators where there are now cash machines – and encounters Jon Voight there. Kristin Scott Thomas meets husband Damian Lewis at platform 7 braving the newshounds as their world falls apart in *Chromophobia* (2005). Alex Pettyfer and Alicia Silverstone follow Jimmy Carr to a photo booth, a secret entrance, next to the subway exit for Bishopsgate (East) in *Stormbreaker* (2006). Bill Murray as *The Man Who Knew Too Little* (1997) gets stuck on a third floor ledge of the Great Eastern Hotel, Liverpool Street.

David Morrissey hands over a suspicious capsule to David Thewlis in The Magpie, New Street, in *Basic Instinct 2* (2005)

Biker Rupert Graves picks up Steven Mackintosh in Cutler's Gardens off Devonshire Square in *Different for Girls* (1997).

Offices on the corner of Primrose Street and Appold Street become the hotel where Anjelica Lauren-Smith is hidden in *24 Hours in London* (1999). Under the titles of *Fierce Creatures* (1997) Jamie Lee Curtis meets Kevin Kline at Exchange House's glass atrium, standing in for an

Below:
Fierce Creatures
(1997) Jamie Lee
Curtis and Kevin
Kline at Exchange
House, Primrose
Street.

office in Atlanta, Georgia. Rupert Graves rushes down the steps from Exchange House to Primrose Street in *Different for Girls* (1997). Bob Hoskins and Cathy Tyson cruise this street of hookers, supposed to be behind Kings Cross, in *Mona Lisa* (1986). Primrose Street is now totally unrecognizable from that appearance, but there is similar iron girder work still over the parallel Worship Street.

Close to the corner of Tabernacle Street and Worship Street, Tom Cruise's shadow passes Nicom House while Cruise is in Hatton Garden (EC1) in *Eyes Wide Shut* (1999).

Louis Dempsey and Andrew Howard park in New Inn Yard on the corner of King John Court to visit 'Dazzlers' sauna in *Shooters* (2000).

EC1: Clerkenwell, Finsbury, St Luke's, Farringdon

Clerkenwell

Paul Newman as *The Mackintosh Man* (1973) steals a package of diamonds from postman Eric Mason at 45–49 Leather Lane as a way of engineering a prison sentence.

Above:
Exchange House, seen in *Fierce Creatures* (1997) and *Different for Girls* (1997).

Opposite:
The Metropolitan Water Board, Rosebery Avenue (top) seen in *The Innocent Sleep* (1995) as a police station (centre), which Rupert Graves enters to report a crime (bottom).

In *Mojo* (1997) the entrance to 'The Atlantic Club', run by Ricky Tomlinson, is 24–8 Hatton Wall, close to Black Bull Yard. This is where Ewan Bremner's bicycle lands when chucked off the roof by Aidan Gillen.

Alan Shearman as *Bullshot* (1983) escorts Diz White to her hotel just north of the church in Ely Place.

Mike Reid walks out of Ye Olde Mitre Tavern in Ely Court and enters 'Denovitz Diamonds' at 13 Hatton Garden in *Snatch* (2000). In *Robbery* (1967) diamond thieves in a stolen ambulance put a timer device in their victim's car while he is inside 21 Hatton Garden. In *A Fish Called Wanda* (1988) Jamie Lee Curtis leaves and photographs 36–38 Diamond House with a camera hidden in her handbag. In *Eyes Wide Shut* (1999) Tom Cruise, while being followed, walks past the same spot, but with the shops' facades changed to look like a New York street. 'Goldman's Safe Deposit Centre', at 66 Hatton Garden, is the bank being robbed by a gang in *High Heels and Low Lifes* (2001) when Minnie Driver and Mary McCormack walk by.

The Ziggurat building between Saffron Hill and Onslow Street is the exterior of Matthew Rhys's brother's flat in *Sorted* (2000).

In *Mona Lisa* (1986) Bob Hoskins follows Clarke Peters by car down Rosebery Avenue, left onto Clerkenwell Road and left onto Back Hill. Peters enters St Mark's Italian Church and meets Kate Hardie inside. The baptism and funeral in *Queen of Hearts* (1989) are also held in this church. At 173 Rosebery Avenue, on the corner of Hardwick Street, is the Metropolitan Water Board, which is the 'Thames South Police Station' in *The Innocent Sleep* (1995). Here Rupert Graves recognizes Inspector Michael Gambon as an assassin.

Left:
I Believe in You
(1952). Cecil Parker
reports for work at
his probation office
(far left), which is
The Old Sessions
House in
Clerkenwell Green
(left).

After the robbery, performed by Kevin Kline, Michael Palin and Thomas Georgeson, in *A Fish Called Wanda* (1988) the gang makes its getaway in Clerkenwell Green, where Jamie Lee Curtis keeps a car running, nearly knocking over Patricia Hayes and her three dogs. They park in Robert's Place, a dead end, rushing down the stairs into Clerkenwell Close to change cars. Palin throws a bag of evidence into a skip under the arch over St John's Lane from a motorbike. The Old Sessions House on Clerkenwell Green is Cecil Parker's probation office in *I Believe in You* (1952). Monica Potter arranges to meet Rufus Sewell, Tom Hollander and Joseph Fiennes in the middle of the green in *Martha, Meet Frank, Daniel and Laurence* (1998), and The Crown Tavern is Lee Gregory's favourite hangout in *Suzie Gold* (2004). Near the corner of Farringdon Lane, Ray Winstone offers Sadie Frost a ring in the doorway of 31a Clerkenwell Green in *Love, Honour and Obey* (2000).

In *About a Boy* (2002) Hugh Grant lives halfway up St James's Walk. The entrance to his flat, seen several times when Nicholas Hoult visits, juts out onto the pavement, a specially designed construction. Grant goes to SPAT meetings to meet single mums at the Woodbridge Chapel, Hayward's Place, just around the corner. The church he nearly visits to do some soup kitchen work is St James's on Clerkenwell Close. Later Hoult walks with his girlfriend towards the church. Followed by Hoult, Grant passes by Scotswood Street heading north, then hides much further south in Comptoir Gascon, 63 Charterhouse Street, on the north side of Smithfield Market.

Left:
St James's Walk,
home to Hugh Grant
in *About A Boy*
(2002).

Opposite St James's Church is The Three Kings, playing Hampstead's 'The Magdala Tavern'. Miranda Richardson waits at the foot of the church steps for Rupert Everett to cross the road before shooting him in **Dance with a Stranger** (1985). Jude Law walks past the St James's Church in **Love, Honour and Obey** (2000).

Andrew Lincoln's art gallery is 26–27 Great Sutton Street in **Love Actually** (2003). Round the corner is Ely Yard, running under The Priory Hotel, where Daniela Nardini overdoes the clubbing in **Elephant Juice** (2000). She staggers out to Daniel Lapaine's car parked in Albemarle Way.

Policewoman Georgia Mackenzie pursues Steven Mackintosh from Hat and Mitre Court, next to Cafe Lazeez at 88 St John Street, across the main road into Passing Alley in **The Criminal** (1999).

The Vic Naylor Restaurant, 40 St John Street, is J D's bar, run by Sting in *Lock, Stock and Two Smoking Barrels* (1999). Vinnie Jones leaves after giving Nick Moran a gun catalogue, getting into his new car alongside son Peter McNicholl. Under the credits of *The Mean Machine* (2001) drunk driver Jones parks on the pavement outside Vic's Bar before his arrest inside.

Finsbury

Leo Gregory takes Summer Phoenix to meet his mother at Peregrine House, Hall Street in *Suzie Gold* (2004).

Samuel Bould follows Julianne Moore to Jason Isaacs's house at '65 Cedar Road', actually 65 Myddleton Square, in *The End of the Affair* (1999). Bould falls asleep in the doorway of St Mark's Church and is awakened by Moore. At the same corner the chase to recover a stolen mascot – a stuffed gorilla – starts in *Doctor in the House* (1954). Dirk Bogarde and the gang commandeer an ambulance and drive down River Street in pursuit.

After her bus ride Julia Foster runs down Skinner Street and turns into Rosoman Place in *Alfie* (1966).

Howard Keel leaves the Moorfields Eye Hospital on City Road near Old Street tube in *The Day of the Triffids* (1962). At the Bunhill Fields Burial Ground, between Bunhill Row and City Road, Chiwetel Ejiofor tells Audrey Tautou that he is married in *Dirty Pretty Things* (2002).

St Luke's

Joe Brown and Marty Wilde walk up Whitecross Street across Banner Street to a music shop, now called Sliced and Squeezed, in *What a Crazy World* (1963).

David Morrissey phones around in his search for Jane Horrocks from Great Arthur House on the Golden Lane Estate overlooking the Barbican YMCA in *Born Romantic* (2000).

Farringdon

Mad Cows (1999) opens with Anna Friel in Cowcross Street. Jude Law chases after Natalie Portman from his flat, 21a Cowcross Street, in *Closer* (2004).

Left:
Cowcross Street, seen in *Closer* (2004).

During the chase in *Johnny English* (2003) the hearse swings from Long Lane into Lindsey Street – nearly knocking over nuns on the pedestrian crossing – and the Aston reverses off the trailer on West Smithfield. In *Last Orders* (2001) John-Joseph Feild shows his son the workings of the meat trade at Smithfield Market, and joins Anatol Yusef in a café. In a flashback the Spice Girls remember the good old days at Bryan Brown's Rendezvous at the south-west corner of Smithfield Market on Farringdon Road in *Spice World* (1997). Back in the present they all meet up at the closed-down site.

On Holborn Viaduct, which runs over Farringdon Road, Harry Fowler buys a Trump comic before jumping onto a no. 18 bus in *Hue And Cry* (1946). Just north-west of the viaduct on Farringdon Street is the office, since rebuilt, from where Jean-Pierre Léaud is fired in *I Hired a Contract Killer* (1990).

A taxi drops Renée Zellweger, dressed to the nines, at St Bartholomew's Hospital in West Smithfield near Giltspur Street, where she is soaked by passing lorries in *Bridget Jones: Edge of Reason* (2004). Jason Flemyng and friends, including Bill Nighy, leave the hospital by the exit further east after visiting Anthony Higgins in *Alive and Kicking* (1996).

Hugh Grant, John Hannah, Kristin Scott-Thomas, James Fleet, David Bower and Charlotte Coleman picnic on a bench in front of St Bartholomew the Great, on West Smithfield, before the doomed fourth wedding in *Four Weddings and a Funeral* (1994). Inside, Anna Chancellor punches out Grant when he admits to loving someone else. The interior of St Bartholomew's also stands in for Nottingham Cathedral in *Robin Hood: Prince of Thieves* (1991), in which Kevin Costner, disguised as a beggar, meets Mary Elizabeth Mastrantonio under Alan Rickman's nose. In *Shakespeare in Love* (1999) Joseph Fiennes prays next to the shrine-tomb of Prior Rahere after Marlowe's death. Ian Hart and son Samuel Bould, secreted in Rising Sun Court, spy on Julianne Moore approaching the church's north entrance and going inside to pray in *The End of the Affair* (1999).

Joseph Fiennes lives at '2 Fleet Court', actually Bartholomew Place, a tiny cul-de-sac off Bartholomew Close, in *Killing Me Softly* (2002). Heather Graham flees from the flat chased by Fiennes and runs west into Middlesex Passage, hiding outside a basement while Fiennes tramps the cross-latched walkway above.

Off King Edward Street, in Postman's Park, Jude Law and Natalie Portman walk after her release from A & E in *Closer* (2004). Near the end, Law returns and finds the plaque commemorating the bravery of Alice Ayres among the many embedded in the wall protected by a covered walkway. Damian Lewis sits here in *Chromophobia* (2005).

Opposite:
St Bartholomew the Great, seen in *Four Weddings and a Funeral* (1994).

east london

Covering a huge area east of the City and out towards Essex, the atmospheric docks have given way to high-rise Canary Wharf, while mean streets and housing estates provide dramatic social and gangster settings.

E1: Tower Bridge, Whitechapel, Spitalfields, Bethnal Green, Stepney, Shadwell, Wapping

Tower Bridge

Tower Bridge is one of London's most potent symbols, with frequent cinematic establishing shots. Bonar Colleano takes his ship's papers to the 'Amalgamated Steamship Company', which used to stand on the north-east side of the bridge in *Pool of London* (1950). Shipmate Earl Cameron chats with Susan Shaw on the bridge. Jerry Lewis drives over the bridge in *Don't Raise the Bridge, Lower the River* (1967). In *Bring Me the Head of Mavis Davis* (1998) Rik Mayall attempts to kill ex-wife Jacolyn Mendoza on the north side of the bridge. He is rudely interrupted by Danny Aiello's thugs and beaten up. Malcolm McLaren explains *The Great Rock'n'Roll Swindle* (1979) here, until Steve Jones spots him from a boat on the Thames. Joseph Long jumps from the bridge, and survives, in *Queen of Hearts* (1989). In *Blue Ice* (1992), spied-upon Todd Boyce photographs containers on their voyage to Tilbury. Sam Neill contemplates ending it all in *The Revengers' Comedies* (1998) but instead goes to the aid of fellow would-be suicide Helena Bonham Carter. Renée Zellweger crosses the bridge northbound from work in *Bridget Jones's Diary* (2001). In the sequel, *Bridget Jones: The Edge of Reason* (2004), she heads south. In *The Mummy Returns* (2001) a chase through London from the British Museum ends at the bridge, and Brendan Fraser jumps over it when it's half raised. In *Dead Fish* (2004) Gary Oldman's grip on the van roof eventually relaxes and he ends up on a barge passing underneath the bridge.

The 1970s Tower Hotel nestles in the shadow of the bridge. At the end of ***Brannigan*** (1975) Chicago cop John Wayne bids farewell to Judy Geeson before leaving in a taxi for Heathrow. At the climax of ***Sweeney!*** (1975) John Thaw confronts Barry Foster at the entrance. Making a break for it across the footbridge over the inlet to St Katharine's Dock, Foster is shot by assassins parked on the red bridge of St Katharine's Way. Roger Moore visits the hotel in ***The Wild Geese*** (1978) to kill the London capo's nephew David Ladd with the strychnine-laced heroin he's peddling. In ***Venom*** (1982), Sterling Hayden has an appointment in the hotel's bar, while Gary Oldman and Philip Davis have a hostile meeting there in ***The Firm*** (1988). In ***The Leading Man*** (1995), Lambert Wilson throws a prop gun into the Thames from the promontory just west of the dock entrance. Richard E Grant meets George Wendt to pitch film ideas in the open-air part of the hotel bar in ***Spice World*** (1999). Ashley Olsen and Brandon Tyler chat near the dock entrance in ***Winning London*** (2001). Jerry O'Connell tells Geri Halliwell she's too thin in ***Fat Slags*** (2004).

Before the hotel was built the area comprised warehouses with varying degrees of damage remaining from World War II. Dirk Bogarde and John Whiteley hide on a nearby barge in ***Hunted*** (1951). Herman's Hermits meet Lance Percival, who takes them to 'digs' in the B warehouses in ***Mrs Brown, You've Got a Lovely Daughter*** (1967). Ralph Richardson collects Alastair Mackenzie as the young ***David Copperfield*** (1970), who's working in the warehouses. Later St Katharine's Dock stands in as a 'Gravesend' emigration dock for Australia when Robin Phillips bids farewell to Richardson and Megs Jenkins. In ***Attack on the Iron Coast*** (1968), where the Dickens Inn now stands, Lloyd Bridges's troops train on an assault course for their World War II mission, while Andrew Keir and Maurice Denham observe his ruthless style disapprovingly. In ***Battle of Britain*** (1969) the A warehouses are once again set on fire as part of the Blitz on London. Just south-west of the Dickens Inn, Lorna Heilborn hides in a warehouse, from the top floor of which she pushes Kenneth J. Warren in ***The Creeping Flesh*** (1973).

Richard Widmark drives Nastassja Kinski to Ivory House where he has a flat in ***To the Devil, a Daughter*** (1976). When Kinski goes walkabout in her first trance, Widmark has to use the winch bridge between St Katharine's and East Docks to get to her. In her second trance, she first heads south over Tower Bridge, but then, contrary to the real geography, ends up on the pathway north of the Tower of London (EC3). In ***Who Dares Wins*** (1982), Lewis Collins picks up Judy Davis and she then takes him back to her first-floor suite in Ivory House.

Bob Hoskins's boat is moored further to the east, in front of Miller's House Wharf off St Katharine's Way, in **The Long Good Friday** (1980). Once his guests, including Bryan Marshall and Eddie Constantine, are safely aboard, the boat travels downstream. Oliver Tobias as **The Stud** (1978) reviews his life with Doug Fisher on a cold and desolate day on the same jetty.

Jude Law walks with Natalie Portman to his workplace at 9 St Thomas Square, off Mare Street, in **Closer** (2004).

Sidney Poitier catches a no. 15 bus heading for Poplar and East Ham from the corner of Tower Bridge Approach and East Smithfield in **To Sir, with Love** (1967).

Whitechapel

At the junction of Dock Street and Cable Street Clive Owen is released by his kidnappers in **Children of Men** (2006). Wilton's Music Hall on Grace's Alley (between Wellclose Square and Cable Street) is another survivor of the Blitz. Its interior is fairly distinctive: a small stall area, a gallery-like circle held up by unmistakable pillars. The interior is transformed into a nightclub run by the Kemp brothers as **The Krays** (1990). In **Chaplin** (1992) Geraldine Chaplin, as Charlie's mother, is booed and her 5-year-old son takes over to turn the audience around. It is a salsa club in **Janice Beard 45 wpm** (1998) where Eileen Walsh is romanced by Rhys Ifans, much to Patsy Kensit's dismay. It is a music hall in **The Importance Of Being Earnest** (2002), and the theatre where Charlie Hunnam as **Nicholas Nickleby** (2003) and

Jamie Bell prepare to stage *Romeo And Juliet*; the company bid farewell to the pair outside. In **Kiss Kiss (Bang Bang)** (2000) both exterior and interior are seen as Stellan Skarsgård takes on the job of looking after Chris Penn. In **A Prize of Gold** (1955) Richard Widmark chases Nigel Patrick from Mill Yard across Cable Street, turning into Ensign Street and then into Grace's Alley, and passing Wilton's – then painted a gleaming white – before emerging much further east at Shadwell Basin.

Left:
Richard Widmark runs past Wilton's Music Hall in **A Prize of Gold** (1955).

Across from Aldgate East tube in Drum Street, a cul-de-sac surrounded by the A11, a policeman turns back Michael Chomiak and Shivani Ghai from traffic jams in **Day of the Sirens** (2002). Stephen Rea lives at 50 Crispin Street, an old convent, in **The Crying Game** (1992). Opposite is White's Row car park, the open-air top level of which is seen after the robbery in **B. Monkey** (1996).

Biker Rupert Graves collides with a taxi at the junction of Middlesex Street and Catherine Wheel Alley in **Different for Girls** (1996). This is right outside old schoolfriend Steven Mackintosh's workplace, called Lamborne House but now East India House. On Gun Street Rosanno Brazzi hides out with his gang of monks in **The Final Conflict** (1981). He passes Artillery Passage as he sets off for W9.

Spitalfields

On the south side of Spitalfields market is Brushfield Street, seen briefly in **Martha, Meet Frank, Daniel and Laurence** (1998) when Joseph Fiennes and Monica Potter drive by Gumbi Records in his battered red Saab sandwiched between red buses. With Anjelica Huston for company, Kate Beckinsale buys **The Golden Bowl** (2000), first admired by Jeremy Northam and Uma Thurman at 42 Brushfield Street.

On the corner of Bishopsgate and Spital Square stood an empty lot that, for a while, housed Fatboy's Diner, the real thing imported from America. In **Sliding Doors** (1999) John Hannah takes the blonde version of Gwyneth Paltrow on a date there. The diner has now been moved inside Old Spitalfields market, where at the indoor football pitches, no longer there, Alec Newman practises his photography before his motorcycle crash in **Greenwich Mean Time** (1999). Penélope Cruz goes to 15 Spital Square on the corner of Folgate Street for a clandestine liaison with Ian Holm in **Chromophobia** (2005). A baby is left outside the door of 15 Elder Street with a caption reading 'Dublin: Birthplace of Oscar Wilde' near the beginning of **Velvet Goldmine** (1998). As Michael Chomiak drives pregnant wife Shivani Ghai to hospital he is bumped from behind at the junction of Folgate Street and Elder Street in **Day of the Sirens** (2002).

Ken Stott and Nick Moran walk with Dominic Monaghan from 45 Fashion Street to their van parked in front of Epra Fashions in **Spivs** (2004).

3 Fournier Street is 'Miller's', the hairdressers where Jaye Davidson works in **The Crying Game** (1992). Round the corner is the Clifton Restaurant, 138 Brick Lane on the corner of Woodseer Street, which Rea and Davidson leave when Miranda Richardson settles down. It is now City Spice. Opposite, on the corner of Brick Lane and Hanbury Street, is the old brewery, which provides the roof, supposedly York Hall's (E2), for 'Golden Boy's' musings and the shootout in **Shiner** (2000).

Jimi Mistry lives with his troubled father at 97 Sclater Street, seen when Catherine McCormack visits him in **Born Romantic** (2000).

East of Brick Lane and along Pedley Street, turning north onto the very seedy Fleet Street Hill, is a footbridge over the Liverpool Street line, which leads to Cheshire Street (E2). In **Naked** (1993), David Thewlis and Susan Vidler cross the bridge to meet up with Ewan Bremner in the grim arches between Wheeler Street and Brick Lane. In **Lock, Stock and Two Smoking Barrels** (1999) Jason Statham and Nick Moran are on the run from the law. On the footbridge's steps their suitcase of dodgy gear opens explosively. In **Face** (1997) Ray Winstone is confronted by his partners-in-crime on the bridge. He runs down the steps towards Fleet Street Hill and is given a beating under the tunnel. In **Gangster No. 1** (1999), Paul Bettany impresses David Thewlis by smashing up a cab and its owner under the tunnel. Clive Owen and Julianne Moore cross the bridge and join Chiwetel Ejiofor, who's waiting for them with a car in **Children of Men** (2006).

Bethnal Green

On the north side of Fieldgate Street is Tower House, seen as the 'Hotel Splendide' where Jean-Pierre Leaud and Margi Clarke hide from a hitman in *I Hired a Contract Killer* (1990). The building was restored in 2005.

At 21 Brady Street is the pet shop from where the deadly mamba is bought in *Venom* (1982). It stood on the corner of Brady Street and Winthrop Street, but the block has now been extensively rebuilt and Winthrop Street has all but disappeared.

In *Face* (1997) Robert Carlyle and Steven Waddington entrust their share of a robbery to an old couple living at 368 Bancroft Road. Later they return with Ray Winstone to find the couple dead and their loot missing.

Stepney

Philip Davis and Imelda Staunton live in flat 82 of the Cressy Buildings on the corner of Hannibal Road and Cressy Place in *Vera Drake* (2004). Eddie Marson and Alex Kelly walk in St Dunstan's Churchyard in front of Mercer's Cottages on the corner of Whitehorse Road and Stepney High Street.

Below:
Cressy Buildings (below left) seen in *Vera Drake* (2004) as abortionist Imelda Staunton makes her way home (below right).

In **Sparrows Can't Sing** (1963), Wickham House, the huge tower into which Barbara Windsor moves with George Sewell, used to stand between Jamaica Street and Stepney Green before its demolition in the 2000s. The buildings on the west side of Jamaica Street still survive. South, on the corner of East Arbour Street and Aylward Street, is the police station – now closed – outside which young Harry Eden throws a brick at David Wenham's head in **Pure** (2002).

Shadwell

In **Violent Playground** (1957) 'Scotland Road School, Liverpool' is St Mary and St Michael's School on the corner of Commercial Road and Sutton Street. David McCallum holds children

Above and left:
In **Violent Playground** (1957), Stanley Baker discusses a school siege with his superintendent Moultrie Kelsall in 'Liverpool' (bottom), actually the corner of Commercial Road and Sutton Street (top).

hostage while Stanley Baker, Anne Heywood and Peter Cushing attempt to talk him out of it. Not much of the corner has changed. The George is still going, as is the school, and the building on which a sign saying 'Liverpool Plastics' was mounted to add that north-west feel.

The back of the church of St Mary and St Michael is seen in ***Sparrows Can't Sing*** (1963) when James Booth visits Roy Kinnear at 43 Cowley Street. The street has been completely re-laid as Oyster Row, and the back view of the church hidden by new building. Booth's search for his wife Barbara Windsor takes him to the west to '93 Cable Street', which is actually on the east side of Cannon Street Road between Cable Street and The Highway.

Sidney Poitier teaches at 'North Quay Secondary School' in ***To Sir, With Love*** (1967). This was a real school just north of Glamis Road in Johnson Street, since redesigned as flats but nevertheless recognizable, as is the tunnel and railway line to the north. Back in 1967 Johnson Street continued up to Commercial Road, but a new estate and park has swallowed up that end of the road.

On his way to attend the funeral of the mother of one of his pupils, Poitier turns from Glamis Road into Juniper Street to find his whole class there, including Judy Geeson and Lulu smiling winningly. The street has been rebuilt and renamed Redcastle Close but there is a little bit of a cobbled street to the west still surviving as Juniper Street. Joanne Whalley appears to live in Gordon House, a high rise on the corner of Glamis Road and The Highway, in ***The Good Father*** (1985). In Shadwell Park, overlooking the Thames, Anthony Hopkins ends their relationship.

In ***A Prize of Gold*** (1955) Richard Widmark chases Nigel Patrick to the swing bridge at Shadwell Pierhead. The geography is much confused as both approach the bridge, first with St Paul's Church by Shadwell New Basin in the background, but then Widmark approaches Glamis Road from Shadwell Pierhead with St Mary's Church on Cable Street in the background. Patrick falls to his death from the raised bridge into London Docks, now Shadwell New Basin. The bridge is now cemented in and much has been rebuilt in the area, but The Prospect of Whitby on Wapping Wall is still there.

The pan at the beginning of ***Hue And Cry*** (1946) takes in Rotherhithe, the Thames, and Shadwell New Basin before zooming into St Paul's Church, though subsequent action takes place lower, alongside Shadwell New Basin, before suddenly cutting to Pier Head. Many changes have taken place since the film was made.

Left:
Sidney Poitier
approaches his new
school (top), located
on Johnson Street
(bottom) in **To Sir
With Love** (1967).

Wapping

In *Sammy and Rosie Get Laid* (1987) Ayub Khab Din drives Wendy Gazelle to her Wapping flat in St Hilda's Wharf on Wapping High Street. Sidney Poitier exits Wapping tube station on Wapping High Street to catch a bus under the credits of *To Sir, With Love* (1967). Michael Palin and Maggie Smith rescue flotsam in front of the King Henry Wharves next to Wapping Pier, off Wapping High Street, in *The Missionary* (1982).

Between Wapping High Street and the Thames, where Orient Wharf now stands, is the site of 'The Lion And Unicorn', Bob Hoskins's pub, which explodes – from 'a gas leak' – in *The Long Good Friday* (1980) as cars carrying Hoskins, Helen Mirren and Eddie Constantine approach on Scandrett Street. Just around the corner on Green Bank is St Patrick's Church, which provides the interior shots for Hoskins's mother's visit to a Good Friday service.

In *Hussy* (1980) John Shea takes Helen Mirren to his warehouse riverside flat at Oliver's Wharf, 64 Wapping High Street. Shea buys ice creams for himself and Mirren's son Daniel Chasin on Scandrett Street.

In *The World Is Not Enough* (1999) Pierce Brosnan continues his speedboat chase from E14 on – impossibly – the Ornamental Canal in Wapping. Speeding from the bridge between Mace Close and Waterman Way, he soaks two traffic wardens clamping a car parked by the canal and turns east towards Wapping Lane, where there is another dead end. He mounts a boathouse, slides through streets and joins the Thames back in E14.

In *To Sir, With Love* (1967) Sidney Poitier gets off a no. 23 bus at Tench Street and turns north into Reardon Street to attend a funeral.

Wapping Pier Head, the entrance to London Dock before it was filled in, still sports photogenic Regency houses. In *Hue and Cry* (1946), on the east side of Pier Head, the boys fight over a comic that turns out to have details of forthcoming robberies in one of the storylines. Here Stewart Granger visits Conrad Phillips, who lives at the basement of 6 Pier Head in *The Secret Partner* (1961).

In *Jack & Sarah* (1995) Samantha Mathis chats with Laurent Grévill in front of the garden between the two pier heads. Her friend lives around the corner at Oliver's Wharf. In *The Squeeze* (1977) Freddie Starr drives Stacy Keach to 1 Pier Head to meet Edward Fox. Fox is on his boat and Keach joins him there before they set off for a river trip.

E14: Limehouse, Canary Wharf, Millwall, Blackwall

Limehouse

In **Sparrows Can't Sing** (1963) Melvyn Hayes cycles up to Griffith Davies by the swing-bridge on Narrow Road at the entrance to Limehouse Basin. Later in the film, Barbara Windsor, pushing her pram, manages to get caught as the bridge rotates. Robert Carlyle and Lena Headey descend the steps from Commercial Road leading to Limehouse Basin in **Face** (1997).

Cillian Murphy escapes from the zombie priest in **28 Days Later** (2002) by running down the stairwell of St Anne's Limehouse to St Anne's Passage.

Canary Wharf

In **The Long Good Friday** (1980) Bob Hoskins's yacht moors at the western end of West India Dock North. The area is barely recognizable today except for the exterior of the North Quay Warehouses, now converted into flats and the Docklands Museum. The sheds on the north and south quays have since been demolished and the dock itself is narrower thanks to land reclamation.

Michael Gambon has Daniel Craig dangled from the roof of the Marriott hotel, then a building site, on Hertsmore Road next to West India Quay DLR station in **Layer Cake** (2004).

Cesar Pelli's tower at 1 Canada Square, once Britain's tallest building and now joined by further huge tower blocks, houses John Malkovich's office in **Johnny English** (2003), in which the entrance on South Colonnade is seen. An identical tower – a hospital – is digitally superimposed so Rowan Atkinson can raid the wrong building.

The west escalator of Canary Wharf tube is seen briefly in **28 Days Later** (2002) and the east escalator in **Agent Cody Banks 2** (2004) and more so in **Spivs** (2004), when Tamer Hassan gives chase to Ken Stott, Rita Ora and Christos Zenonos, who escape onto the tube. Ralph Fiennes meets Richard McCabe at the same tube in **The Constant Gardener** (2005). They take the west escalator and cross the walkway over West India Dock south towards South Quay.

At the beginning of **Basic Instinct 2** (2005) Sharon Stone drives Stan Collymore through the Limehouse Link into the Canary Wharf complex and ploughs into the docks from Heron Quays.

Sean Bean escapes when his prison van is ambushed on Churchill Place in **Patriot Games** (1992).

Katrin Cartlidge and Lynda Steadman view a penthouse of a smart dockside development in Chandlers Mews in **Career Girls** (1997). Called 'The Harbour' in the film, it's actually The Anchorage.

In **The Steal** (1994) Peter Bowles insists on stopping to buy a newspaper outside The North Pole, 74 Manilla Street, while Alfred Molina, his fake chauffeur, is trying to abduct him.

In **The Long Good Friday** (1980) Bob Hoskins's police contact is found nailed to the floor in an empty warehouse near Burrell's Wharf, 262 Westferry Road.

Millwall

The speedboat chase between Pierce Brosnan and Maria Grazia Cucinotta in **The World Is Not Enough** (1999) continues from SE1 to the narrow canal between Whiteadder Way and Falcon Way, a dead end. Brosnan emerges into Millwall Outer Dock, cuts to and from E16, passes under the Glengall Bridge into West India Dock North. Cucinotta steers through a police boat, under Trafalgar Way and into Blackwall Basin while Brosnan re-routes to E1. At the north end of Millwall Inner Dock the Spice Girls catch a speedboat for the My Boy Lollipop sequence in **Spice World** (1997). Karen Black is chauffered to the HQ of her TV station airing **Crimetime** (1996) on Harbour Exchange Square. Her office overlooks North Quay, and is the same view seen during the diamond robbery in **Love, Honour and Obey** (2000).

Off Manchester Road is the Samuda Estate. Robert Carlyle, Ray Winstone and Steven Waddington visit Philip Davis in Dagmar Court in **Face** (1997). Davis checks his stash of loot in the garages under Reef House. Chiwetel Ejiofor visits a tower block on the same estate overlooking the Greenwich peninsula to clean up the mess left by a kidney extraction from a Somali in **Dirty Pretty Things** (2002).

Below:
In **Face** (1997) Philip Davis, Steve Waddington, Ray Winstone and Robert Carlyle (top) gather on the Samuda Estate off Manchester Road (bottom).

On the jetty next to South Dock Entrance off Preston's Road Alison Garland walks in *All or Nothing* (2002), unaware that her brother James Corden is being rushed to hospital.

Blackwall

On the other side is '23 Coldharbour, Poplar' the address given by David Hemmings in *The Walking Stick* (1970). Samantha Eggar moves in with him to enjoy the views of the Greenwich peninsula across the Thames, at that time with no Millennium Dome, but two gasholders instead of one.

Anna Friel runs along the platform of East India DLR station to Trafalgar Way in *Mad Cows* (1999).

Alec Newman crashes his motorbike, suffering a paralysing accident, on the curve of Blackwall Way in *Greenwich Mean Time* (1999). Ian McKellen dispatches his chauffeur in *The Da Vinci Code* (2006) close to Blackwall Stairs.

Drug dealer Freddie Annobil-Dodoo lives on the 24th (top) floor of Ernö Goldfinger's Balfron Tower of the Brownfield Estate at the south end of St Leonard's Road in *Greenwich Mean Time* (1999). He enlists Ben Waters to push drugs around the estate. His Mercedes is parked in Tayburn Close. Cillian Murphy and Naomie Harris spot the lights of Brendon Gleeson's flat in the same tower in *28 Days Later* (2002) as they walk along the DLR track close to Canada Square on their way back from Deptford.

The fight between rival football 'firms' – led by Charlie Hunnam and Geoff Bell – at the climax of *Green Street* (2005) is at the cleared space of Orchard Wharf, off Orchard Place. In *The World Is Not Enough* (1999) Pierce Brosnan runs his boat through a restaurant built especially for the stunt on Trinity Buoy Wharf at the end of Orchard Place to rejoin his pursuit of Maria Grazia Cucinotta on the Thames opposite the Millennium Dome. Here too, Max Beesley admires the view of the dome in *Five Seconds To Spare* (1999). Paul Bettany axes Razaaq Adoti in front of the lighthouse on his way to becoming *Gangster No. 1* (1999).

The gasworks on Leven Road loom over Oban Street, the north-west corner of which is seen at the beginning of *Jubilee* (1977). Despite looking so run down in the mid-1970s, the terrace on the west side of Oban Street has now been restored, but the rest of the block between Oban Street and Portree Street has been completely rebuilt. During a police raid on the IRA safe house above a newsagent's on the corner of Oban Street and Leven Road, Mickey Rourke manages to escape in *A Prayer for the Dying* (1987). The Leven Street side of the corner has now been rebuilt, and the shop has gone.

E16: Canning Town, Silvertown

Canning Town

St Luke's Church, Jude Street provides Bob Hoskins's church in *A Prayer for the Dying* (1987). At the end of *The Leather Boys* (1963) Dudley Sutton tells Colin Campbell to wait for him in the Tidal Basin Tavern, now very derelict, at the north-west end of Royal Victoria Dock while he arranges a ship's passage. On his return he finds Campbell has changed his mind and he walks away west with the pub and Sutton behind him. In *Law And Disorder* (1958) Michael Redgrave hurries on Tidal Basin Road to a ship to meet son Jeremy Burnham.

Above and left:
The Leather Boys (1963). Dudley Sutton and Colin Campbell by the Tidal Basin Tavern (above) on Tidal Basin Road (left).

Silvertown

Much of the action in **Brazil** (1985) takes place at the grain mills, now mostly demolished, on the south side of Royal Victoria Dock. **The Sandwich Man** (1966) opens with a vista of the Royal Victoria Dock in action. Michael Bentine lives next to Dora Bryan in a terraced row on the north side of Evelyn Road just before it meets Boxley Street.

There has been much new development in the area since then, but some houses on the corner of West Road and Evelyn Road have survived from the 1960s. Jean-Pierre Leaud makes his way along Silvertown Road towards Margi Clarke's flat in one of the two tower blocks, since demolished, at the west end of Evelyn Road in **I Hired a Contract Killer** (1990).

In **The Long Good Friday** (1980) the remains of Bob Hoskins's Rolls Royce are examined on the south side of Royal Albert Dock, where the London City Airport is now. Hoskins orders bent copper Dave King to find out why his wheels are no longer going round as they walk along the eerily empty dockside with its redundant cranes. Prospective investor Martin Landau inspects the docks in **Empire State** (1987), while City Airport appears in **Shooters** (2000), when Gerard Butler arrives there. The climax of **The London Connection** (1979) takes place on a ship moored on the northern side of Royal Albert Dock. Jeffrey Byron and Larry Cedar rescue Mona Washbourne and David Kossof from Nigel Davenport's clutches, and enjoy a boat chase.

In **24 Hours In London** (1999) Lorelei King introduces John Sharian to Gary Olsen, Tony London and David Sonnethal on a square on the north side of Royal Albert Dock. The next scene takes place on a derelict piece of land immediately to the east of the Thames Flood Barrier. Here Sara Stockbridge and Luke Garrett, impersonating policemen, machine-gun a car full of Russians – and just for good measure toss in a couple of grenades, walking off eastwards as the car explodes.

The barrier itself is seen in aerial shots in **Split Second** (1992), which depicts a London suffering from constant flooding. Before Thames Barrier Park was planted, the empty space provides a large enough area for Rupert Graves to teach Steven Mackintosh motorcycling skills in **Different For Girls** (1997). The isolated structure in the background is grain elevator D, a rare survivor from the dock days. Ken Stott takes Rita Ora and Christos Zenonos to the finished park in **Spivs** (2004).

At the western end of Royal Victoria Dock Maria Grazia Cucinotta attacks Pierce Brosnan's boat with a grenade launcher in **The World Is Not Enough** (1999) before returning to E14. There are further scenes of the docks in **The Day of The Triffids** (1962), when Howard Keel tries to rejoin his ship, in **Sparrows Can't Sing** (1963), when James Booth arrives back from two years at sea, and in **Bedazzled** (1967) with Peter Cook and Dudley Moore. Antiques wrapped up in paper used in a counterfeiting money operation are delivered to the docks in **File of the Golden Goose** (1969). John Wayne pushes Tony Robinson into the docks in **Brannigan** (1975). Mickey Rourke turns up on the run from the IRA near the start of **A Prayer for the Dying** (1987). The docks stand in for Hamburg in **Voyage of the Damned** (1976) and for New York when Warren Beatty and Diane Keaton return from Russia in **Reds** (1981).

E6: Upton Park, Wallend, Beckton

Molly Parker and son Harry Eden live at 8 Rochford Close in view of the south stand of West Ham United's stadium in **Pure** (2002). The flat where first Marsha Thomson and then Keira Knightley live is immediately south of the stand at the rear of Barking Road. Just to the north is Priory Park, where Thomson rescues Eden from bullies by the large elaborate climbing frame in the play area. Later Knightley obtains her drugs here from David Wenham.

Before the stadium was developed into an all-seater, Stanley Baker and his gang discuss the use of guns during a match in **Robbery** (1967). Charlie Hunnam takes Elijah Wood to his first football match here in **Green Street** (2005).

Beckton Gas Works, whose days are numbered with the advent of superstores, remains pretty much inaccessible and is barely visible from Royal Docks Road. During the 1970s and 80s the abandoned works provided industrial buildings and settings for films, including **Brannigan** (1975), at the climax of which John Wayne finally catches up with John Vernon near Armada Way.

The works provide the setting for some fancy 007 helicopter stunts in **For Your Eyes Only** (1981), the school riot in **Pink Floyd The Wall** (1982), John Hurt's childhood scenes in **1984** (1984) and a Japanese detention centre in **Empire of the Sun** (1987). Incredibly, director Stanley Kubrick transforms the same area – with a few palm trees – into Vietnam for **Full Metal Jacket** (1987), the explosions in which subsequently rendered many of the structures unsafe.

E13: Plaistow, West Ham

In **Pure** (2002), the café where Keira Knightley works before she is fired is in the Queen's Market off Green Street, next to Upton Park tube. Harry Eden pleads for his mother's job back at Pike J, a butcher's, at 34 Queen's Market.

E15: Stratford Marsh, Mill Meads, Temple Mills, Stratford New Town

As a courier, Jonny Lee Miller strides along the south side of Buxton Road – dominated by the tower block Henniker Point – in **Love, Honour And Obey** (2000).

E7: Forest Gate, Upton

In **Bullet Boy** (2004) a bashed wing mirror on Winchelsea Road near Pevensey Street leads to the argument that regrettably eventually escalates into tragedy for friends Ashley Walters and Leon Black.

Below left and right: Ashley Walters and Leon Black face road rage in Winchelsea Road in **Bullet Boy** (2004).

In **Love, Honour and Obey** (2000) Jonny Lee Miller's gun jams, frustrating his attempt on Rhys Ifans's life on Capel Road at its junction with Chestnut Avenue. Geraldine McEwan and Karl Johnson live at Holmdene, 49 Capel Road, at the corner of Latimer Road in **Pure** (2002).

E3: Old Ford, Bromley-by-Bow

In **Face** (1997) Robert Carlyle, Ray Winstone, Steven Waddington and Philip Davis walk along the pedestrian bridge over the A12 (East Cross Route) to their car on Wendon Street, followed by 'the filth'.

Rhys Ifans returns to his car parked outside Tesco between Otis Street and Three Mill Lane in **Love, Honour and Obey** (2000). Jonny Lee Miller and Jude Law have daubed 'Mug' all over it. East over the bridge on Three Mill Lane, Ray Winstone visits a film set to jealously watch Sadie Frost in a kissing scene. The car park of the Three Mill Lane complex appears in **Spivs** (2004), when Dominic Monaghan, Ken Stott, Nick Moran and Kate Ashfield plan to drive off the lorry-load of illegal immigrants.

E2: Shoreditch, Bethnal Green

Shoreditch

Paul Bettany and David Thewlis park in Old Nichol Street, cross Boundary Street and enter the first door on the south side of Boundary Passage to visit James Foreman in *Gangster No. 1* (1999). A little later in the film Bettany spots Eddie Marlan ratting to Foreman.

Arnold Circus appears four times in *Day of the Sirens* (2002). First Des Brady attacks a church in 'Stoke Newington' (actually St Leonard's, Shoreditch), then enters Rochelle Street school, Arnold Circus, for some shooting. Thirdly he shoots Galit Herschkovitz on Navarre Street opposite Iffley House, and finally a building on the north side of Calvert Street stands in for the Old Bailey as the killer's van arrives.

Nuala O'Neill and Ciaran McMenamin shelter in the long disused pub, The Flying Scud, 137 Hackney Road at the corner with Cremer Street, after rioters attack their bus in *Titanic Town* (1999), set in Belfast. 'Images' is a real nightclub, 483 Hackney Road, seen in *Shooters* (2000) when Adrian Dunbar picks up Andrew Howard. Clive Owen passes by cages of 'illegals' as he walks down Ravenscroft Street from the Hackney Road end in *Children of Men* (2006). The block from which rubbish is being thrown into the street is James Hammett House.

Gary and Martin Kemp as *The Krays* (1990) storm into The Royal Oak, 73 Columbia Road, and liberally shoot it up with machine guns. In *Honest* (2000) Melanie Blatt, Nicole and Natalie Appleton pass the same pub. Later, Peter Farinelli asks about Nicole inside. Opposite, all are attacked after they enter 146 Columbia Road. This is the shop 'Glitterati', above Marcos & Trump, then D J L Spencer.

Ron Pember helps Herbert Norville to move out of 94 Quilter Street, thus starting *The Chain* (1984); later Leo McKern moves in from the top of the chain to the bottom, where he first started. Jamie Foreman drives his brother to 65 Quilter Street in *Empire State* (1987). Brenda Blethyn lives with daughter Claire Rushbrook at 76 Quilter Street in *Secrets & Lies* (1996), though her address is quoted as SE17. Marianne Jean-Baptiste drops off Blethyn at the corner of Quilter Street and Durant Street after their first meeting in Holborn (WC2).

In *The Firm* (1988) Gary Oldman and his gang walk along Wellington Row, pass The Queen Victoria at 72 Barnet Grove and enter The Prince Of Wales at 59 Barnet Grove to attack Philip Davis and his gang. Both pubs have now been converted into flats.

Bethnal Green

Off Queensbridge Road, Haggerston Park appears in **Trauma** (2004) twice, first when Colin Firth spots Mena Suvari through the columns in the south-west corner and again when, after their session together with clairvoyant Brenda Fricker, they walk close to the all-weather football pitch.

Phil Collins as **Buster** (1988) picks up a fellow gang member from his prefab on Pritchard's Road, overlooked by gasometers. The site near Marian Place has now been redeveloped, but the gasometers survive.

David Thewlis's club in **Gangster No. 1** (1999) burns by Regent's Canal at the corner of Corbridge Crescent and The Oval. The perpetrators shoot at and miss Paul Bettany as they drive off down The Oval.

On the corner of Old Bethnal Green Road and St Jude's Road is Apollo House, where Andy Serkis lives in **Shiner** (2000). When Michael Caine and Frank Harper visit, Serkis's flat appears to be on the east side overlooking Poyser Street. In **Snatch** (2000) Robbie Gee's pawnshop is at 88 Teesdale Street, off Old Bethnal Green Road, though when he is walking the dog it appears to be off Hatton Garden (EC1). In the same film, Ade drives a car with Robbie Gee and Lennie James into a petrol station on Bethnal Green Road between Wolverley Street and Jersey Street. Ade struggles to get his frame out of his seat while Gee shows off his massive gun to James.

On Patriot Square is Bethnal Green Town Hall, which is the police station Steven Mackintosh leaves in **The Criminal** (1999).

At York Hall on the corner of Cambridge Heath Road and Old Ford Road Michael Caine hosts his evening of boxing in **Shiner** (2000). On the steps Andy Serkis produces a gun to establish parking rights for Caine. In the same film, Serkis and Frank Harper pick up punters for another boxing match from The Panther on the west side of Turin Street. The pub has now been demolished.

In **Lock, Stock and Two Smoking Barrels** (1999) P H Moriarty and henchman Lenny McLean rule the roost at 46 Cheshire Street near the corner of Grimsby Street. Outside, Vinnie Jones smashes into Nick Moran's car and proceeds to beat up Frank Harper with a car door. Further to the east, just beyond the junction with Hereford Street is the Repton Boxing Club, which is the venue for the game of three-card brag. Nick Moran throws up outside when he loses to Moriarty and is threatened by McLean to repay his debt of 'half a mil' within a week. Harvey Keitel visits a mobster here in **The Young Americans** (1993). Also on Cheshire Street, Clive Owen and Julianne Moore get off the bus for Three Colts Corridor which leads to the footbridge to Pedley Street in **Children of Men** (2006).

On the south-east corner of Brick Lane and Bethnal Green Road is East End Kebashish, 120 Bethnal Green Road, dressed as 'Kismet Cars And Café' in **Born Romantic** (2000). Here Adrian Lester has to listen to Ian Hart's philosophy of women while waiting for his next driving job. Jane Horrocks recognizes an old photo of herself on a flyer stuck on a bus shelter as she walks along Bethnal Green Road.

E8: Dalston

Jean-Pierre Léaud visits The Village, a pub on the corner of Kingsland Road and Forest Road, where Joe Strummer is playing in **I Hired A Contract Killer** (1990). Then he walks south and witnesses a jewel robbery opposite The Prince Of Wales, at 474 Kingsland Road, in which perpetrators Nicky Tesco and Charles Cork accidentally shoot Peter Graves, and for which Léaud is blamed.

In **Dirty Pretty Things** (2002) Chiwetel Ejiofor and Audrey Tautou live above 98 Kingsland High Street. They go through the supermarket to get to the stairs at the rear, which one can see from Birkbeck Mews. In **The Low Down** (2001) Aidan Gillen lives at 8 Sandringham Road above the All Nations Hairdressing Salon opposite Argos. Gillen walks through the Ridley Street market just to the south and helps out a girl 'needing £15 to get home' by going to the NatWest cashpoint at 74 Kingsland High Street, opposite Dalston station. 33 St Mark's Rise is Lesley Sharp's flat and David Thewlis's destination in **Naked** (1993). There he meets Katrin Cartlidge, and they walk down Kingsland High Street, passing Abbot Street. At the end Thewlis stumbles into Downs Park Road to whatever awaits him.

Director Mike Leigh returned to this area of Hackney for **Secrets & Lies** (1996). Brenda Blethyn, newly confident, has her hair done at Edna's Hairdressing Salon, 105 Shacklewell Lane, and tells her road-sweeping daughter Claire Rushbrook that she's missed a bit.

After stealing a suit, Phil Collins as **Buster** (1988) hails a taxi on the east side of Broadway Market. He lives with Julie Walters off Mare Street, at 30 Beck Road.

Below:
Phil Collins arrives home to Beck Road by taxi in **Buster** (1988).

Underneath the Mare Street bridge – next to Regent's Canal off St Andrew's Road – Gabriel Byrne enjoys Miranda Richardson's amorous touches in **Spider** (2002). Ralph Fiennes sits on a bench contemplating the gasometers opposite later in the film.

E9: Homerton, Hackney Wick, South Hackney

Jane Horrocks, responding to a flyer, gets in touch with David Morrissey on his mobile as he walks past 'Midas Locksmiths' at 8 Well Street, close to Mare Street in **Born Romantic** (2000). Later they enjoy a walk in Victoria Park to discuss the ground rules for their renewed relationship. Mark Strong and Daniela Nardoni enjoy the park's boating lake in **Elephant Juice** (2000).

At the same park, dubbed 'Streatham Park' in **High Heels and Low Lifes** (2001), Minnie Driver and Mary McCormack discuss the drop from the villains they are blackmailing. The actual drop at night is on North Carriageway, where a tramp, accidentally in the way, gets shot. Kevin Eldron and Mark Williams, as cops on the scene next morning, try to pick up the pieces. Later Driver and McCormack discuss their next move on the climbing frame in the playground near Royal Gate West. To the east of Lauriston Road – which runs through the park – is the Victoria Fountain, where Ken Stott takes illegal immigrants Rita Ora and Christos Zenonos to await, in vain, Nadia Ward in **Spivs** (2004).

Below:
Victoria Fountain, Victoria Park (below left) provides the backdrop for a scene in *Spivs* (2004). Ken Stott and Rita Ora at a failed rendezvous (below right).

Further north is Hackney Marsh, famous for its numerous football pitches. Billy Zane and Karel Roden take a pedalled rickshaw here in **Dead Fish** (2004). Luke Fraser and Leon Black play on goal posts in **Bullet Boy** (2004).

E5: Clapton Park, Lower Clapton, Lea Bridge

In **Bullet Boy** (2004) Ashley Walters lives at Sudbury Court on the junction of Redwald Road and Daubeney Road (quoted as flat 1402, with views over Hackney Marshes) with mother Claire Perkins and little brother Luke Fraser. Fraser finds the dead dog floating in the Hackney Cut of the River Lea, and Perkins tells Walters to leave on Daubeney Road. The police station in the same film is at 2 Lower Clapton Road, close to St John's church.

E10: Lea Bridge

Off Lea Bridge Road is Lea Bridge Ice Centre, where Ashley Walters, Luke Fraser and Sharea-Mounira Samuels skate in **Bullet Boy** (2004). Fraser and friend Leon Black play with a real gun on Leyton Marshes. Ken Stott takes Rita Ora and Christos Zenonos for a skating treat at the Ice Centre in **Spivs** (2004).

Phil Collins as **Buster** (1988), Larry Lamb and Michael Attwell plan the finer details of the Great Train Robbery on the roundabout at the south end of Seymour Road. The playground has been redesigned, but the three gasometers to the west, Eton Lodge (the nearby cottage) and the houses along Clementina Road are the same.

David Hemmings lives with his parents at 13 Perth Road in **Live It Up** (1963).

E11: Leytonstone, Wanstead, Snaresbrook

It Was an Accident (2000) features the southern-most point of Epping Forest when the gang, driving away from Max Beesley – whose car can't cope with the mud – hit a cow. One can just make out the café on Whipps Cross Road as they enter. Chiwetel Ejiofor and Thandie Newton are reconciled by Hollow Pond.

E17: Higham Hill, Upper Walthamstow

Chiwetel Ejiofor stands outside Blackhorse Road tube after his release from prison at the beginning of *It Was an Accident* (2000).

When Ejiofor picks up his son he is confronted by Max Beesley – who's annoyed with his interference in a post office robbery – on the open area between the branch of NatWest at 204 High Street on one side and Choices at 241 High Street on the other.

E4: Chingford Green, Friday Hill, Chingford Heath, Highams Park

In *It Was an Accident* (2000) James Bolam pushes Norby West in a wheelchair over the North Circular, but is refused free admission to the dogs at Walthamstow Stadium on Chingford Road when the boast that he used to drive for the Krays attracts only derision. At the end Bolam and Chiwetel Ejiofor meet on the stadium's roof in front of the neon sign.

Further to the north in the same film, Max Beesley tries to impress his date in a brasserie on Old Church Road while outside Cavan Clerkin relieves himself into Beesley's open-topped car parked opposite the branch of Threshers at 84 Old Church Road.

north-west london

North-west London reaches from Regent's Park, through the markets of Camden Town, onto Parliament Hill and Hampstead Heath where splendid views of London stretch over rows of suburban housing towards Hertfordshire.

NW1: Marylebone, Regent's Park, Camden, Euston, St Pancras, King's Cross

Marylebone

Peter Finch, heading for exile, shares a carriage with Yvonne Mitchell into Marylebone Station in *The Trials of Oscar Wilde* (1960). Spike Milligan arrives there in *Postman's Knock* (1962). In *The Day of the Triffids* (1962) Howard Keel visits the ticket hall, now a Marks & Spencer food store, and then meets Janina Faye, who's on the train that – out of control – ploughs into the buffers. Tom Courtenay as *Billy Liar* (1963) opts not to join Julie Christie as she takes the train to London from, supposedly, 'Bradford Central'. The train journey in *A Hard Day's Night* (1964) begins and ends at the station, with fans screaming for and chasing the Beatles. In *The Ipcress File* (1965) scientist Aubrey Richards is driven to the station and then mysteriously abducted from his compartment as his train leaves. In *Rotten to the Core* (1965) Anton Rodgers steals a silver case from Charlotte Rampling – heading for a train with Peter Vaughan – before leaving through the main exit onto Melcombe Place. Ian Hendry picks up instructions from a locker at Marylebone station in *The Internecine Project* (1974). In *One of Our Dinosaurs Is Missing* (1976) a fake chauffeur collects Derek Nimmo and drives through the main exit. Robin Askwith uses the same exit in *Let's Get Laid* (1977).

In *The Thirty-Nine Steps* (1978) the station is supposed to be St Pancras, where in the old ticket hall Ronald Pickup stabs John Mills, leaving Robert Powell to be considered the culprit. Powell returns to finds Mills's diary. In *The Lady Vanishes* (1979) Ian Carmichael and Arthur Lowe walk through the ticket hall to find their longed-for cricket match rained

Opposite:
Clarence Gate Gardens, Glentworth Street (left), is home to Scarlett Johansson in *Match Point* (2005), starring Colin Salmon and Scarlett Johansson (top right) and Jonathan Rhys Meyers (bottom right).

off, followed by Elliott Gould and Cybill Shepherd. In *Eye of the Needle* (1981) Donald Sutherland asks his cabbie to pull into the forecourt of the station to elude his pursuers.

In *Sliding Doors* (1998) Gwyneth Paltrow's bag is snatched on Melcombe Place outside the Landmark Hotel. She hits her head on the second tree along from Harewood Avenue.

Miranda Richardson tries to enter St Cyprian on the corner of Clarence Gate and Glentworth Street in *Tom & Viv* (1994). Scarlett Johansson lives in 64–84 Clarence Gate Gardens on Glentworth Street in *Match Point* (2005).

William Sylvester drives to the Marylebone Road entrance to Baker Street tube in ***Ring of Spies*** (1963). In ***The Man Who Haunted Himself*** (1970) Roger Moore trades industrial secrets in the Planetarium on Marylebone Road. While Wilfrid Hyde-White shows visitors around Madame Tussaud's Chamber of Horrors, Eric Portman vandalizes an exhibit in ***Wanted for Murder*** (1946). Soon afterwards, Stanley Holloway quizzes a taxi driver outside on Marylebone Road while detective Roland Culver investigates the chamber.

In ***Gideon's Day*** (1958) Jack Hawkins drives from Outer Circle into York Gate, opposite Marylebone Church, to drop off his daughter Anna Massey at the Royal Academy of Music on Marylebone Road. Paul Massie meets Jocelyn Britton at the entrance in ***Sapphire*** (1959).

Jim Broadbent and Fiona Shaw arrest Uma Thurman outside Ralph Fiennes's house on York Terrace East in ***The Avengers*** (1998). In ***Spy Game*** (2001) Robert Redford passes York Terrace and Cornwall Terrace on Outer Circle on his way to 'Langley, Washington D.C.'

Regent's Park

Clive Revill trips into the boating lake of Regent's Park just by the bridge that leads to Regent's College while searching for nannies in ***One of Our Dinosaurs Is Missing*** (1976). In ***The Thirty-Nine Steps*** (1959) Kenneth More attempts conversation with Faith Brook just south of the band stand unaware that, disguised as a nanny, she is watching a spy sending a message attached to a toy boat across the lake. She walks over the bridge to Clarence Gate, but suddenly cutting to Inner Circle, is run down by a car witnessed by More. On the bank by the bridge Jesse Birdsall meets Jane Horrocks feeding ducks in ***Getting It Right*** (1989). Celia Johnson and Trevor Howard hire a boat from the mock Tudor boathouse, no longer there, on the lake in ***Brief Encounter*** (1945). Howard rows into the chains under Longbridge and ends up knee-deep in water to the amusement of both. Gene Barry rescues Joan Collins's son, stuck on the children's boating pond next to Hanover Gate, in ***Subterfuge*** (1969). Bette Davis as ***The Nanny*** (1965) crosses Longbridge towards Inner Circle.

Ioan Gruffudd and Alice Lewis go to a Punch and Judy show in Queen Mary's Gardens in ***102 Dalmatians*** (2000). Gruffudd climbs over the café's roof to rescue Oddball from being carried away by balloons. The area between the small lake in the gardens and New Lodge is the venue of the SPAT picnic in ***About a Boy*** (2002). Hugh Grant entertains Victoria Smurfit while Nicholas Hoult accidentally kills a duck with a loaf of his mother's homemade bread.

Left:
Queen Mary's
Gardens, Regent's
Park (top), seen
during the picnic in
About a Boy (2002)
(bottom).

Oscar Homolka meets his contact in *Sabotage* (1936) in London Zoo's aquarium. In *The Vicious Circle* (1947) John Mills meets Lionel Jeffries by the lion cages. Then, after the police arrest Jeffries at the entrance, Mills meets Wilfrid Hyde-White there. In *The Fallen Idol* (1948) Ralph Richardson and Michele Morgan take Bobby Henrey for an ice cream at the Mappin Terraces, and they visit the zoo's Reptile House. Anne Bancroft meets James Mason in the zoo to hear revelations about Peter Finch in *The Pumpkin Eater* (1964). In *Arabesque* (1966) Gregory Peck and Sophia Loren take refuge in the Monkey House. In *The Jokers* (1966) the second bomb is planted in the Lion House. In *Bedazzled* (1967) Dudley Moore intellectualizes about caged animals to Eleanor Bron, passing Peter Cook, who's collecting for charity. Gene Barry, Joan Collins and her son visit the zoo in *Subterfuge* (1969), while Peter Cook hosts a do at the Mappin Terraces in *The Rise and Rise of Michael Rimmer* (1970). In *Percy* (1971) Hywel Bennett admires the rhinoceroses and later visits the Monkey House. Helen Hayes meets fellow nanny Joan Sims at the zoo in *One of Our Dinosaurs Is Missing* (1976). Jack Douglas falls into a puddle during an unsuccessful sexual tryst in *Carry On Emmannuelle* (1978).

In *An American Werewolf in London* (1981) David Naughton wakes up in a wolf cage after a lycanthropic night of debauchery. Naked, he runs past a zoo bench in front of the Mappin Terraces and steals a rather effeminate looking coat to cover his modesty. Glenda Jackson bumps into Ben Kingsley outside the Aquarium, under the Mappin Terraces, in *Turtle Diary* (1985). With keeper Michael Gambon they hatch a plan to release the turtles. Mark Addy and Charlie Creed-Miles shoplift a toy panda next to Lubetkin's Penguin Pool in *The Last Yellow* (1999). In *Harry Potter and the Philosopher's Stone* (2001) Daniel Radcliffe converses with a snake in a cage constructed just to the left as one enters the Reptile House. In *About a Boy* (2002) Hugh Grant dangles Isabel Brook's 3-year-old by the ankles in front of the flamingos to show what a great guy he is with children. Later, next to the penguin pool and monkey cages, he manages to persuade Nicholas Hoult to pretend to be his son in an attempt to attract single-parent Rachel Weisz. Stellan Skarsgård and Chris Penn visit the giraffes and the Penguin Pool in *Kiss Kiss (Bang Bang)* (2000). Outside the entrance in the car park, Skarsgård introduces Penn to the delights of Barry White, whisky and tobacco. In *Withnail & I* (1986) Richard E Grant and Paul McGann discuss fresh air in front of the wolf cages, now replaced, on a bench outside the east side of the zoo. They return to this spot at the end of the film, when Grant spouts Hamlet's 'quintessence of dust' speech.

At Primrose Hill Books, 134 Regent's Park Road, Mike Binder and Mariel Hemingway spot a display of Irène Jacob's book, eponymously titled *Londinium* (2001). Binder lives just around the corner at 2 St George's Terrace.

In *The Music Lovers* (1971) suicidal Richard Chamberlain steps into Regent's Canal underneath the railway bridge between Gilbey's Yard and Gloucester Avenue, but finds that the water only goes up to his knees. Railings now deter any further attempts. Demi Moore and Henry Ian Cusick live at 34 Regent's Park Road right next to the canal, fatally for their son in *Half Light* (2006).

Camden

In *Jack & Sarah* (1995) Richard E Grant, Samantha Mathis and baby Sarah walk around Camden Lock market and rest on a bench next to the wheel pump under the footbridge on the south side of the lock. A half-printed £5 note is found here in *Without a Clue* (1988). Jesse Birdsall takes Jane Horrocks on a date at Camden Lock in *Getting It Right* (1989). Andy Garcia runs through the market and across the bridge, where he catches a canal cruiser in *American Roulette* (1988). On board he meets Rosalind Bennett as they cruise south towards Regent's Park. Just east of here Kathy Burke dumps Douglas Henshall in *This Year's Love* (1999). Later Dougray Scott chats to a friend on the bridge. Ian Hart chats up Jennifer Ehle on Chalk Farm Road, while in the market Scott picks up Catherine McCormack from her stall, as does Hart later.

Dursley McLinden and Colin Dale bid Susannah York goodbye at the junction of Castlehaven Road and Chalk Farm Road in *Just Ask for Diamond* (1988).

In Stables Market the second staircase to the left (now covered) as one enters the market from Chalk Farm Road leads to Steven Mackintosh's gang's hideout in *Lock, Stock and Two Smoking Barrels* (1999). After Steve Sweeney talks his way inside, Frank Harper's gang bursts in, steals all the money and drugs and, for good measure, kidnap a traffic warden outside unit 137. The Olsen twins shop at the market in *Winning London* (2001).

In *This Year's Love* (1999) Jennifer Ehle and Ian Hart get drunk at the market. From the high vantage point, now built on, overlooking Harmood Street and Hartland Road, Kathy Burke spots boyfriend Dougray Scott chatting up a girl on the balcony of Freshh, the restaurant on the other side of Chalk Farm Road.

The establishing shot in *It Always Rains on Sunday* (1947), set in Bethnal Green, is Clarence Way, and the Holy Trinity Church with half a spire is now gone. Escaped convict

John McCallum hides by the church door, runs north up Hartland Road to avoid a policeman and makes his way to Clarence Way, where old flame Googie Withers lives with Edward Chapman. Further south on Hartland Road Susan Shaw makes a phone call. Fence John Salew lives at 60 Hawley Road, and is visited by Jimmy Hamley, Alfie Bass, John Carol, and later Jack Warner. Here too live Earl Cameron and Ann Lynn in **Flame in the Streets** (1961). John Mills, Brenda de Banzie and Sylvia Syms live close by at 60 Clarence Way. Jeff Goldblum cycles under Hartland Road railway bridge and turns left to – once again – 60 Hawley Road, which he shares with Geraldine James in **The Tall Guy** (1984).

Above:
Clarence Way (above left), seen as John Mills arrives home (above right) in **Flame in the Streets** *(1961).*

In **Radio On** (1979) David Beames lives above the Camden Plaza, which until 2000 stood in Chalk Farm Road near Inverness Street, opposite Camden Town tube.

Jean Kent as **Trottie True** (1948) lives at 24 Gloucester Crescent. Alongside 46 Inverness Street is her father's photography studio. A visit to Camden High Street's Bedford Theatre, now demolished, inspires her stage career.

The student flat shared by Katrin Cartlidge and Lynda Steadman in **Career Girls** (1997) is at 40 Rousden Street, off Camden Road. On their nostalgic journey they meet old pal Mark Benton sitting on the steps of the Chinese takeaway, which is now a private house, on the corner.

Jack Warner lives opposite The Constitution on St Pancras Way in **Train of Events** (1949). Daughter Susan Shaw returns her engagement ring on Canal Terrace round the corner. The whole area has since been redeveloped as Reachview Close. Johnny Sekka and Sylvia Syms chat about Montego Bay at the west end of Canal Terrace in **Flame in the Streets** (1961).

Kate Ashfield works at Shogun Property, 21 Pratt Street, on the corner of Bayham Street in **The Low Down** (2001).

Jennifer Ehle feels faint after a tattooing session at Douglas Henshall's 'Pricks and Chicks', 93 Plender Street, from which Henshall is eventually evicted in **This Year's Love** (1999). In **The Man Who Knew Too Much** (1955) James Stewart takes a taxi to the corner of Plender Street and Royal College Street. He walks along Plender Street and crosses College Place to the taxidermist Ambrose Chappell. Redevelopment since then has been extensive, with only Royal College Street now recognizable.

Hazel O'Connor and her band **Breaking Glass** (1980) play on in a power cut at The Music Machine, 1a Camden High Street. The Music Machine became the Camden Palace, and is now Koko.

John May's creepy hideaway is on the corner of Mornington Crescent opposite Arlington Road in **Night, After Night, After Night** (1969).

The Working Men's College at 44 Crowdale Road, on the corner of Camden Street, is the 'Tauber Academy' in **The Rachel Papers** (1989), where Dexter Fletcher enrols to meet Ione Skye. They stroll down Oakley Gardens opposite.

Peter Finch's 'seaside resort' visited by John Fraser in **The Trials of Oscar Wilde** (1960) is Tower House, at 12 Park Village East.

The entrance to Regent's Park Barracks on Albany Street is seen briefly in **Date With a Dream** (1948).

In **The End of the Affair** (1955) Deborah Kerr and Peter Cushing live at 40 Chester Terrace (by the arch) while Van Johnson lives at 4 Chester Place. Johnson meets Cushing walking in Chester Terrace and later he bumps into private detective John Mills just north of the arch. Here too, in **Voices In The Dark** (1960) Nanette Newman hands luggage to the

Left:
The corner of Gloucester Crescent and Inverness Street (far left), seen in **Trottie True** (1948). Daphne Anderson crosses Gloucester Crescent to post a letter (left).

chauffeur as the household of 40 Chester Terrace prepares to leave for Cornwall. It is also Judi Dench's house in **Mrs Henderson Presents** (2005). The arch is an establishment shot in **The Naked Truth** (1957). The investigation into **The Wreck of the Mary Deare** (1960) is held in Chester Terrace in another establishment shot. The entrance of Peter Finch's club is 37 Chester Terrace, just south of the arch in **The Trials of Oscar Wilde** (1960). Also outside no. 37 Julie Andrews, living above her means, is issued with a writ in **Star!** (1968). Bette Davis walks through the arch to 30 Chester Terrace and her duties as **The Nanny** (1965), and Richard E Grant visits his agent Julian Wadham at 26 Chester Terrace in **Keep the Aspidistra Flying** (1997).

At the south end – by a corresponding arch – Lem Kitaj lives in Chester Gate in an establishment shot in **The Boy Who Turned Yellow** (1972). Behind Chester Terrace, through which Nazi troops march, children goosestep alongside Pauline Murray on Albany Street in **It Happened Here** (1964). Albany Street is divided in half by barbed wire to contain the 'Jewish quarter'.

Sidney Poitier and daughter collect Esther Anderson from the embassy of 'Torunda' at 3 Cambridge Terrace in **A Warm December** (1973).

William Sylvester lives in the Melia White House on Osnaburgh Street, near Great Portland Street, in **Ring of Spies** (1963).

Euston

In Euston Tower, on the corner of Euston Road and Hampstead Road, Dirk Bogarde tries to meet TV executives in **Accident** (1967). Malcolm McDowell receives a job offer here from Ralph Richardson, from whose high office window Graham Crowden throws himself in **O Lucky Man!** (1973). And here, Peter Celler leaves Arthur Lowe's offices, gets into a car and drives straight back to the door of Thames TV studios, pursued by the cast of **Man About the House** (1974), not realizing, apparently, that it is the same building. As **The Man Who Haunted Himself** (1970) Roger Moore visits offices diagonally opposite Euston Tower to deny to John Carson that they agreed on an underhand company merger.

In **Dog Eat Dog** (2000) Mark Tonderai, Nathan Constance, David Oyelowa and Cronski have their money bag snatched on Euston Street, near Melton Street.

The **Train of Events** (1949) sets off from Euston Station with a glimpse of the much-missed Euston Arch. Policeman John Stratton meets partner Jack Hawkins on one of the platforms in **The Long Arm** (1956). Peter Finch sees off Mary Peach in **No Love for**

Johnnie (1961). Pauline Murray arrives in ***It Happened Here*** (1964). At the rebuilt Euston, Helen Mirren sees off son Daniel Chasin in ***Hussy*** (1980), and Martin Clunes exits in ***Staggered*** (1994). Anne Reid and Peter Vaughan take the Euston tube escalator in ***The Mother*** (2003).

Dominic Anciano and Ray Burdis shop at Euston Bookshop, 36 Eversholt Street, to spice up Burdis's sex life in ***Love, Honour and Obey*** (2000).

At St Pancras Parish Church, across Euston Road on Upper Woburn Place, Kate Ashfield waits for Aidan Gillen in ***The Low Down*** (2001).

St Pancras

In ***Voyage of the Damned*** (1976) Helmut Griem enters St Pancras Chambers, from the station side, to receive his mission details from Leonard Rossiter and Denholm Elliott. In the tunnel under the station between Midland Road and Pancras Road Nazis beat up Paul Koslo while friend Jonathan Pryce looks on helplessly. St Pancras Chambers' staircase appears in ***The Secret Garden*** (1993) and again in ***Batman Begins*** (2005), when Christian Slater and Gary Oldman rescue Katie Holmes. In ***McVicar*** (1980) a car passes St Pancras to the impossible sound of Big Ben's chimes.

In St Pancras station Dirk Bogarde meets Sarah Miles on platform 4 in ***The Servant*** (1963). Rita Tushingham and Lynn Redgrave ask for directions to Carnaby Street in ***Smashing Time*** (1967), and Mel Ferrer swaps cars to elude the police in ***Brannigan*** (1975). In ***The Fourth Protocol*** (1987) Michael Caine leaps out of his car to catch a train pulling out of platform 2. Peter Eyre and Nicholas Grace leave their van at the side entrance, search a locker on platform 6 and depart after binning a traffic warden who has the audacity to ticket their van in ***Just Ask for Diamond*** (1988). Alison Steadman takes Pauline Collins as ***Shirley Valentine*** (1989) to a photo booth in front of platform 6 for her passport to Greece. Margi Clarke buys tickets for France in the ticket hall in ***I Hired a Contract Killer*** (1990). Robert Downey Jnr as ***Chaplin*** (1992) is welcomed home after success in Hollywood by adoring fans. His mother's asylum is established as St Pancras Chambers. Emma Thompson joins Vanessa Redgrave at the ticket hall to visit ***Howards End*** (1992), but the trip is aborted when they meet Anthony Hopkins at platform 5. John Goodman as ***King Ralph*** (1991), James Villiers, Peter O'Toole and Richard Griffith formally welcome the Finnish royal family (Julian Glover, Judy Parfitt and Joely Richardson) at platform 6. In ***Shining Through*** (1992) Michael Douglas and Melanie Griffiths meet John Gielgud and board a train at 'Zurich station'. Richard E Grant and Helena Bonham Carter walk through the ticket hall, enjoy cups of tea in front of platform 6 and embrace in the alley leading to Midland Road in **Keep the Aspidistra Flying** (1997). Both Ian McKellen and Robert Downey Jnr enter the Chambers as 'Edward's palace' in **Richard III** (1995). Later McKellen meets Prince of Wales Marco Williamson at platform 3 with cronies Jim Broadbent, Tim McInnerny and Adrian Dunbar in attendance. McInnerny was back, catching the Orient Express in **102 Dalmatians** (2000) along with Glenn Close and Gerard Depardieu, followed by Alice Lewis and Ioan Gruffudd. In **Spider** (2002) Ralph Fiennes arrives in London at platform 1. In **Five Seconds to Spare** (1999) Max Beesley arrives to pursue his music career, while later Anastasia Mille is met and taken to identify her brother. In **The Golden Bowl** (2000) Nick Nolte and Uma Thurman arrive, standing in for New York.

King's Cross

Susannah York lives on the Clarence Passage side of the Stanley Buildings (supposedly 'south of the river') in **Just Ask for Diamond** (1988). **The Ladykillers** (1955) – Alec Guinness, Herbert Lom, Danny Green and Cecil Parker – rob a security van on cobbled Cheney Road opposite Clarence Passage, alongside King's Cross Station (N1). Pauline Collins as **Shirley Valentine** (1989) walks in the rain with her shopping down Cheney Road. The road, with added house fronts, is transformed into south London in **Chaplin** (1992). Michael Palin as **The Missionary** (1982) walks from Weller's Court into Cheney Road in a search for fallen women. On the roof of the 'Mission for Fallen Women', actually the Culross Buildings on Battle Bridge Road, Denholm Elliott asks Palin to give up his position. From this rooftop Malcolm McDowell views Euston Tower with Helen Mirren in **O Lucky Man!** (1973). In **Nuns on the Run** (1990) Camille Coduri is dumped on Cheney Road and walks into a lamppost on Clarence Passage. Eric Idle and Robbie Coltrane later escape down a drainpipe from Coduri's flat in the Culross Buildings. Andrew Howard and Louis Dempsey drive to Howard's drug-making factory south of the Culross Buildings in **Shooters** (2000).

Charlie Hunnam and Elijah Wood park between Battle Bridge Road and Goodsway in **Green Street** (2005) before catching their train from King's Cross.

In **High Hopes** (1988) John Watkins wanders to Stanley Passage, where Philip Davis offers him shelter in his and Ruth Sheen's flat in Stanley Buildings. From their roof Davis and Sheen point out King's Cross, St Pancras and even St Paul's Cathedral to Edna Doré. Ian

McKellen, soon to be *Richard III* (1995), organizes Clarence's assassination with Adrian Dunbar on the roof of the Stanley Buildings. Ewan McGregor and Christian Bale meet here in *Velvet Goldmine* (1998).

In *Still Crazy* (2000) the reunited 70s band Strange Fruit rehearses its classic repertoire behind the door between Clarence Passage and Weller's Court. Billy Connolly arrives to pick up Stephen Rea, Juliet Aubrey, Jimmy Nail and Bill Nighy in a tour bus destined for Europe. Frances Barber, stalking Timothy Spall, chases him down Cheney Road.

In *This Year's Love* (1999) Kathy Burke, who lives on the first floor of the Stanley Buildings overlooking Stanley Passage, walks by this door and finds Ian Hart, whom she has previously dumped in Weller's Court, waiting for her. Stephen Dorff is beaten up while Ian Hart looks on helplessly in front of 'The Anchor', a Liverpool pub, in *Backbeat* (1993). This is also the club where two transvestites throw out the *Hard Men* (1996). Round the corner in Clarence Passage, Vincent Regan announces his early retirement.

Underneath disused coal shoots on Camley Street (formerly Cambridge Street, dominated by gasholders – five on the east side and a further two in the distance between Goodsway and Battle Bridge Road – before the St Pancras Eurorail development), Michael Caine as *Alfie* (1966) simultaneously entertains Millicent Martin and introduces himself to the audience. In *Robbery* (1967) Barry Foster hurls himself out of the car escaping from the police after it passes under Oblique Bridge, near where the London Wildlife Trust offices are now situated. Peter Noone searches in vain for his greyhound around here in *Mrs Brown, You've Got a Lovely Daughter* (1967).

As *Alfie* (1966) Michael Caine pours out his heart to Murray Melvin along the Regent's Canal towpath, behind the lock keeper's cottage parallel to Wharf Road. In *Nuns on the Run* (1990) Eric Idle and Robbie Coltrane discuss bank robbing as a future. Samantha Mathis kills time in *Jack & Sarah* (1995) on a bench on the same towpath. In *Janice Beard 45 wpm* (1998) Eileen Walsh and Rhys Ifans walk along the towpath under the bridge between Goodsway and Wharf Road. Michael York takes Rita Tushingham to his barge in *Smashing Time* (1967). In *This Year's Love* (1999) Jennifer Ehle and Douglas Henshall chat on a wall from Wharf Road, overlooking the barge where she lives with her son.

At St Pancras Gardens on St Pancras Road Katrin Cartlidge and Lynda Steadman discover Joe Tucker's lack of commitment in a flashback in *Career Girls* (1997). The wedding of Douglas Henshall and Catherine McCormack takes place at St Pancras Old Church in *This Year's Love* (1999).

NW5: Kentish Town, Maitland Park, Dartmouth Park

In **This Year's Love** (1999) Ian Hart carries Jennifer Ehle, who's rather the worse for wear, to the Hope Chapel (decorated with an arched neon sign saying 'Church of Christ') on Prince of Wales Road opposite Anglers Lane, and makes a call from the phone box alongside.

Sinead Cusack works at the Owl Bookshop, now expanded to 207–209 Kentish Town Road, in **Bad Behaviour** (1993). Philip Jackson and Phil Daniels inspect 40 Willes Road, for which Jackson makes a planning application.

Rhys Ifans persuades Daniel Craig to meet up at the 'playground', actually the plain grassy area of Willington Close off Leighton Road, in **Enduring Love** (2004). Craig himself lives across the road down Leighton Place, in the block to the south-east.

The interior of The Assembly, on the corner of Fortress Road and Leighton Road, is Richard Burton's local in **Villain** (1970).

In **Career Girls** (1997) Katrin Cartlidge drives Lynda Steadman to her flat at 72 Caversham Road, on the corner of Bartholomew Road, dominated by St Luke's Church. On the corner of Caversham Road and Oseney Crescent is 31 Oseney Crescent, home to Toni Collette and Nicholas Hoult in **About a Boy** (2002). Hugh Grant first meets Hoult at 65 Lady Margaret Road, Victoria Smurfit's house. 2 Dartmouth Park Avenue, on the corner of Laurier Road, is Jeremy Irons's house in **Betrayal** (1983), briefly seen when Ben Kingsley hesitates in his car before visiting.

Below:
Caversham Road and St. Luke's Church (below left), as seen in *Career Girls* (1997) when Lynda Steadman and Katrin Cartlidge approach Caversham Road from Bartholomew Road (below right).

NW3: Primrose Hill, Swiss Cottage, Hampstead, Belsize Park, Chalk Farm

Primrose Hill

At Primrose Hill's paved circular viewpoint, furnished with two benches and a plaque illustrating London's skyline, Ian Richardson interrupts Michael Caine's model plane flying with his son in *The Fourth Protocol* (1987). Susan Fleetwood advises Kathleen Wilhoite and Jemma Redgrave to photograph their ghostly cellar in *Dream Demon* (1988). Jeff Golblum as *The Tall Guy* (1989) walks with Emma Thompson and later shares his woes with Emil Wolk and Timothy Barlow on a bench. Richard E Grant pours his heart out to David Swift in a sleet storm in *Jack & Sarah* (1995) on the eastern bench. Grant is back again, composing poetry this time, in *Keep the Aspidistra Flying* (1997). Also here Helena Bonham-Carter later temporarily terminates their relationship. In *Career Girls* (1997) Katrin Cartlidge and Lynda Steadman walk up here, seeing an old college friend jog past. In *If Only* (1998) two mysterious Spaniards confront Lena Headey on one of the benches. Hugh Laurie and Joely Richardson try to conceive here at night in *Maybe Baby* (2000).

Colin Firth, Irène Jacob, Mike Binder and Mariel Hemingway picnic to the west of the benches in *Londinium* (2001). Stellan Skarsgård and Chris Penn find Peter Vaughan lying under a tree in *Kiss Kiss (Bang Bang)* (2000). Edward Furlong reflects on a murder witnessed on the internet in *Three Blind Mice* (2002), and Summer Phoenix as *Suzie Gold* (2004) walks to the benches with Leo Gregory. In *Bridget Jones: The Edge of Reason* (2004) Renée Zellweger and Colin Firth enjoy a *Sound of Music* pastiche just west of the plaque. Rupert Grint walks past in *Driving Lessons* (2006).

Lynn Redgrave holds dance classes at the top of 7 Harley Road, James Mason's grand house, in *Georgy Girl* (1966).

Swiss Cottage

Jemma Redgrave's father buys 53 Eton Avenue, on the corner with King's College Road, for her in *Dream Demon* (1988). Outside, Kathleen Wilhoite rescues her from intrusive pressmen Jimmy Nail and Timothy Spall.

Old college flame Joe Tucker shows Katrin Cartlidge and Lynda Steadman round a flat at 52 Fellows Road in *Career Girls* (1997). The eyesore across the road that Cartlidge comments upon is Dorney House.

Pauline Murray makes her way to the basement flat of 47 Belsize Square in **It Happened Here** (1964).

Jenny Agutter, exiting Finchley Road tube, buys flowers in **Sweet William** (1980). At the O2 shopping centre Nick Moran and Kate Ashfield discuss their future in **Spivs** (2004).

Carol Lynley's daughter disappears from South Hampstead High School Junior Department on Netherhall Gardens, which is the 'Little Peoples' Garden School' run by Anna Massey in **Bunny Lake Is Missing** (1965)

Hampstead

Sam Waterston as **Sweet William** (1980) crosses Heath Street with Jenny Agutter for coffee at Louis's Patisserie, 32 Heath Street; they then visit St John's Church on Church Row, where Waterston lies on an unmarked grave in front of the gates. Nigel Patrick and Michael Craig visit 15 Church Row, a doctor's surgery, in their investigation of the murder of **Sapphire** (1959).

Jeremy Irons first meets son Rupert Graves's fiancée Juliette Binoche in his house, The Old Mansion, at 94 Frognal, opposite Oak Hill Park, in **Damage** (1992).

Terence Stamp as **The Collector** (1965) waits in a van for Samantha Eggar to make her way along Holly Hill from the tube and up a path to Mount Vernon. There he abducts her as a special addition for his collection. Mount Vernon is also seen in the van chase in **The Steal** (1994) before an extraordinary cut to far-away SE16. In **The Killing of Sister George** (1968) Beryl Reid leaves the Hollybush, 22 Holly Mount, and follows a succession of passages, including Mount Vernon.

Derren Nesbitt spies on Margaret Whiting and son walking round the pond at the top of Heath Street in **The Informers** (1964).

23 West Heath Road, on the corner with Platts Lane, is Glenn Close's house in **102 Dalmatians** (2000).

Hugh Grant visits Kenwood House on Hampstead Heath, where Julia Roberts is filming in **Notting Hill** (1999). By the railings south of the house he overhears her telling fellow actor Sam West that he is unimportant, and leaves despondently. Kenwood also plays the art school attended by Keri Russell in **The Upside of Anger** (2004), and the bungee jump takes place on the heath.

Keir Dullea lives at '30 Frogmore End' (in fact Cannon Hall, 14 Cannon Place), in **Bunny Lake Is Missing** (1965).

At the viewpoint over London on Parliament Hill Anthony Edwards and Jenny Seagrove canoodle in **Don't Go Breaking My Heart** (1998). Lucy Punch films her dating video here in **Are You Ready for Love?** (2006). Later in the film Andy Nyman and his date walk through the heath near Giancarlo Neri's sculpture *The Writer*.

Billie Whitelaw moves out of 55 Christchurch Hill to make way for Nigel Hawthorne and Anna Massey in **The Chain** (1984).

Derek Farr takes Hampstead tube on the corner of Hampstead High Street and Heath Street after escorting Dulcie Gray to Hampstead Fair on the heath in **Wanted For Murder** (1946). Rupert Grint tips buskers outside the station in **Driving Lessons** (2006). In **Don't Go Breaking My Heart** (1998) Anthony Edwards dashes out of the station and makes a speedy change in Gardener's Gift Shop, 11 Flask Walk.

Mark Dightam, who has just become **The Boy Who Turned Yellow** (1972), runs out of the station past a Christchurch Hill sign to his house at 11 Willow Road.

In **The Lost Son** (1999), Daniel Auteuil forces a member of a child-smuggling gang to drive him up Heath Street, arriving at 42 New End Square where, after breaking in, he finds that the trail leads to Mexico.

In **Darling** (1965) Dirk Bogarde lives with and then leaves wife Pauline Yates at Jasper House, 105 South End Road near the corner of Downshire Hill. Julie Christie, from a nearby phone box, spies on Bogarde playing with his family in the front garden.

After posting a letter at the modern post office on Hampstead High Street, Sam Waterston and Jenny Agutter hail a taxi in **Sweet William** (1980). Waterston is recognized by one of his wives, Victoria Fairbrother. On the corner of Downshire Hill and Keats Grove, in front of St John's Church, Brian Hall is forced to stop the taxi to avoid an accident.

Bill Paterson and Jimmy Nail operate from the police station on the east side of Rosslyn Hill in **Just Ask for Diamond** (1988). Ioan Gruffudd escapes from the station to catch a cab in **102 Dalmatians** (2000). Here Gilbert Wayne orchestrates his murder investigation in **Night, After Night, After Night** (1969).

Sam Waterston and Jenny Agutter visit Geraldine James at the Royal Free Hospital on Pond Street in **Sweet William** (1980). Here Emma Thompson waits, after work, for her date with Jeff Goldblum in **The Tall Guy** (1989).

In **Make Mine Mink** (1960) Terry-Thomas runs down Pond Street, enters the men's lavatories on South End Green and emerges dressed as a long distance walker before heading off down Fleet Road to evade the police.

At the running track below Parliament Hill, Anthony Edwards trains Ben Reynolds in **Don't Go Breaking My Heart** (1998).

Belsize Park

In **Georgy Girl** (1966) Alan Bates exits Belsize Park tube and, hesitantly, crosses Haverstock Hill to meet bride Charlotte Rampling and Lynn Redgrave at Hampstead Town Hall. Lynne Frederick and John Leyton are also married at the registry office there in **Schizo** (1976). They are chauffered around the corner into Belsize Avenue, where Jack Watson menacingly lurks behind a tree. Lucy Punch and Denise van Outen exit Belsize Park tube in **Are You Ready for Love?** (2006).

In **Sliding Doors** (1998) both John Lynch and John Hannah visit, on separate occasions, Zara Turner, who lives at 25 Primrose Gardens, in an attempt to find Gwyneth Paltrow.

Chalk Farm

Mark Dightam becomes **The Boy Who Turned Yellow** (1972) at Chalk Farm tube after being sent home early from school. Phil Daniels drops off his twin self at the tube in **Bad Behaviour** (1993).

1a Adelaide Road leads to Dursley McLinden and Colin Dale's detective agency in **Just Ask for Diamond** (1988). Saaed Jaffrey runs 'Mr. Patel's Mini Market', now Quick Stop Food and Wine, on the corner of Haverstock Hill.

NW8: St John's Wood

Ian Ogilvy works at an antiques shop, 'The Glory Hole', at 95 Lisson Grove in **The Sorcerers** (1967). He fights with Victor Henry in the shop and it spills outside into Lisson Grove, while Elizabeth Ercy looks on. Ogilvy runs to his car parked on Broadley Street. Ivor Heath in a police car arrives on the scene, picking up Ercy and then Henry at Plympton Street, before chasing after Ogilvy down Broadley Street.

Above:
Hampstead Town Hall, Haverstock Hill (top), seen in **Georgy Girl** (1966) and **Schizo** (1976). Lynne Frederick and John Leyton are married (bottom) in **Schizo** (1976).

In the members' stand at Lord's Cricket Ground David Epps, as Whitehall mole Blake, warns a Soviet agent that the **Ring of Spies** (1963) is about to be uncovered.

Joely Richardson takes one of her twin daughters, Lindsay Lohan, to the Abbey Road pedestrian crossing (made famous by the Beatles) near Grove End Road in **The Parent Trap** (1999). The Olsen twins enjoy the crossing in **Winning London** (2001).

In **Man About the House** (1974) one side of Alma Square is under threat from redevelopment and it is up to the inhabitants of 'Myddleton Terrace' to save it. The house where Richard O'Sullivan, Paula Wilcox, Sally Thomsett, Brian Murphy and Yootha Joyce live is 'no. 6' which is actually 40 Alma Square.

Peter Cook and Dudley Moore enjoy ice creams outside 14 Blenheim Terrace in **Bedazzled** (1967).

In **Schizo** (1976) Lynne Frederick and John Leyton live on 'Tennyson Avenue'. It is in fact 1 Carlton Hill, at the corner of Carlton Hill and Loudoun Road.

Colin Firth visits Kananu Kirini on the sixth level of the block overlooking Rowley Way, in the Alexandria and Ainsworth Estate, in **Trauma** (2004).

Below:
Rowley Way (below left), seen in *Trauma* (2004) as Colin Firth confronts Kananu Kirini outside her flat (below right).

Camille Coduri works in a clothes shop, now Viva (next to Larizia), at 72 St John's Wood High Street in *King Ralph* (1991). Opposite is Roja, at no. 13, and Café Josephine, no. 15, where Summer Phoenix as *Suzie Gold* (2004) hangs out with her friends. *Half Moon Street* (1986) opens with Sigourney Weaver jogging up St John's Wood High Street. She is nearly knocked over by a taxi on the corner of Greenbury Street and Barrow Hill Road.

Michael Caine and Susannah York set up a love nest at 2 Avenue Road on the corner of Prime Albert Road in *X, Y and Zee* (1972).

NW6: Kensal Rise, Kilburn, southwest Hampstead

Kilburn Park tube on Cambridge Avenue is disguised as Westminster, where Norman Wisdom sells newspapers in *Press for Time* (1966).

In Paddington Cemetery off Willesden Lane, south of the range of two lodges, two chapels with *portes cochères* and belfry, is the burial in *Room to Rent* (2002).

Jeremy Irons and Patricia Hodge set up a love nest at 9 Streatley Road, opposite Burton Road, in *Betrayal* (1983).

In *The Smallest Show on Earth* (1957) Leslie Phillips introduces Bill Travers and Virginia McKenna to their inheritance, 'Sloughborough's Bijou Kinema', squeezed into the west side of Shoot Up Hill near Kilburn tube, between two railway tunnels.

In *Elephant Juice* (1999) Daniel Lapaine urges Sean Gallagher to wink at a girl as they sit on a bench in West End Green. She works at a coffee shop at 335 West End Lane, now a Good Earth Express, and Emmanuelle Béart encourages Gallagher to ask her out.

Below: Paddington Cemetery (below left), as seen in *Room to Rent* (2002). After a burial the mourners pass through between the two chapels (below right).

NW10: Neasden, Church End, Stonebridge, North Acton, Park Royal, Harlesden, College Park, Willesden Green, Kensal Green

At Kensal Green Cemetery, north of the Grand Union Canal, critics Ian Hendry, Arthur Lowe, Robert Morley, Jack Hawkins, Harry Andrews and Coral Browne, along with policemen Milo O'Shea and Eric Sykes, attend Michael Hordern's burial in front of All Souls Chapel in *Theatre of Blood* (1973). A runaway horse galloping up Centre Avenue dragging Dennis Price's body interrupts proceedings, while Hendry follows Diana Rigg to her father Vincent Price's monument, which is a real and enormously elaborate sculpture to the Stevier family buried in the south-west wall of All Souls. In *Steptoe and Son Ride Again* (1973) Harry H Corbett blunders into a burial in the same place. Meanwhile Wilfred Bramble emerges from his coffin – to the consternation of mourners, including Yootha Joyce, Bill Maynard and Sam Kydd – during his burial service next to the south wall. Susannah York's burial is in the same area in *The Awakening* (1980). In *Secrets & Lies* (1996)

Below: Ben Keyworth approaches his den in Kensal Green Cemetery, Centre Avenue, in **Afraid Of The Dark** *(1991).*

Marianne Jean-Baptiste reflects on mortality at her foster-mother's burial. In *The End of the Affair* (1999) Ralph Fiennes meets Ian Hart on the steps of All Souls. Fiennes discovers Hart's son has been miraculously cured at his healer's grave, in the same place as Hordern's. In *Three Steps To Heaven* (1995) Katrin Cartlidge walks past an eye-catching Corinthian Temple tomb, Mary Gibson's monument of 1870, decorated with four Baroque angels. Opposite, Robert Mitchum visits the Molyneux monument with Peggy Ashcroft and Pamela Brown, followed later by Mia Farrow in *Secret Ceremony* (1968). East of the angels is Ben Keyworth's den in the vandalized temple-tomb to Sir Patrick O'Brien in *Afraid of the Dark* (1991).

West of Kensal Green, Richard Burton escorts Edith Evans to her husband's grave, sited in the south-west corner of St Mary's Roman Catholic Cemetery close to Mitre Bridge in **Look Back in Anger** (1959). Later Burton returns to lay flowers on Evans's grave, next to her husband's. The depot of UK Tyres in the background is still open for business at the time of writing this book.

The Leather Boys (1963), including Dudley Sutton, Colin Campbell and Rita Tushingham meet at the Ace Café just off the North Circular near Stonebridge Park tube, from where the race to Scotland and back is launched.

Phil Daniels lives with parents Kate Williams and Michael Elphick at 115 Wells House Road in **Quadrophenia** (1979).

British soldiers serving in Northern Ireland, Denzel Washington, Dorian Healy and Sean Chapman stagger out of the The Fishermans Arms onto Old Oak Lane in **For Queen and Country** (1988).

Ralph Fiennes as **Spider** (2002) revisits his childhood at 29 Goodhall Street, renamed Kitchener Street and supposedly in E1, where his parents Gabriel Byrne and Miranda Richardson still live, approaching from the alleyway behind.

Jonathan Rhys Meyers eyes up a schoolboy on Stephenson Street in **Velvet Goldmine** (1998). In **The Last Yellow** (1999) Mark Addy and Charlie Creed-Miles, pushing James Hooton's wheelchair, turn the corner from Stephenson Street into Goodhall Street for a club at the north-west corner of the street, supposed to be in Leicester.

Near Harlesden tube off Acton Lane is McVitie's, Waxford Road, seen in the factory scenes in **The Borrowers** (1997).

NW2: Dollis Hill, Cricklewood

Andy Robinson and Clare Higgins move into eerily dilapidated but now gently suburbanized 187 Dollis Hill Lane in **Hellraiser** (1987).

NW4: Hendon

Villains try to break into Pierce Brosnan's BMW 750i parked in the multi-storey car park of Brent Cross Shopping Centre in **Tomorrow Never Dies** (1997). Brosnan guides it around the car park by remote control until it reaches the roof, which is Hamburg.

In **School for Scoundrels** (1960) Ian Carmichael's top-floor flat, from where he frustrates Terry-Thomas's plan to win Janette Scott by making him wait outside in his car, is in Thurlby Croft, one of the blocks on Mulberry Close off Parson Street.

NW11: Golders Green, Hampstead Garden Suburb

In **The Upside of Anger** (2004), set in Michigan, the rear and interiors of Joan Allen and Kevin Costner's houses, skilfully intercut with shots of the Detroit suburbs, are located in Ingram Avenue and Spaniards Close.

John Gregson and Kenneth Cope park in Ingram Avenue on the corner of Winnington Road to investigate a kidnapping in **Tomorrow at Ten** (1964).

NW7: Mill Hill

In **Shooting Fish** (1997) Dan Futterman and Stuart Townsend live in a disused gasholder accessible by a pathway between 12 and 13 Lee Road, where they allow Kate Beckinsale into their life of scams. By 2002 the gasholder had disappeared.

north london

Spreading out from King's Cross and embracing Highgate, Muswell Hill and Southgate towards Hertfordshire, it seems north London is not as popular with filmmakers as one might first imagine, despite its many attractions.

N1: King's Cross, Islington, Old Street

King's Cross

In *The Ladykillers* (1955) Alec Guinness spies on the money van from the iron cross bridge that runs inside King's Cross station and across platforms 1 to 8. The van is on the road inside the station next to the current platform 1 (the platforms were renumbered in 1972), parallel to York Way.

The station stands in for Manchester Piccadilly in *Mrs Brown You've Got a Lovely Daughter* (1967), seen as Herman's Hermits leave for London. Later Peter Noone sees off Sarah Caldwell, and loses his greyhound in the process. In *Hoffman* (1969) Sinead Cusack bids farewell to fiancé Jeremy Bulloch as she boards a train, only to leave it when he goes. Jason Hoganson arrives from Newcastle at platform 5 in *Empire State* (1987). Andy Garcia catches a train from platform 7 in *American Roulette* (1988). Michael Caine and Susannah York leave for Scotland in *X, Y and Zee* (1972). *High Hopes* (1988) opens with Jason Watkins emerging from King's Cross tube onto Euston Road. *Career Girls* (1997) begins and ends at King's Cross, as Katrin Cartlidge meets and sees off Lynda Steadman. Catherine McCormack finds Kenneth Cranham – Jimi Mistry's father – confused and bewildered, trying to get a train 'to the beach' in *Born Romantic* (2000).

In *Harry Potter and the Philosopher's Stone* (2001) Robbie Coltrane escorts Daniel Radcliffe along the cross bridge. Radcliffe catches the Hogwart Express with Julie Walters's help through the brick arch just beyond the cross bridge, between platforms 4 and 5. In *Harry Potter and the Chamber of Secrets* (2002), despite an exterior establishing shot of next-door St Pancras Station, Radcliffe and Rupert Grint return to the same arch, but have to resort to a flying car. In *Harry Potter and the Prisoner of Azkaban* (2004) there is a brief shot of the Express departing. The station's western extension is seen in *A Cry from the Streets* (1958) when Barbara Murray interviews an errant mother in the refreshment rooms next to platform 15.

Guy Doleman visits Michael Caine's first floor HP Detective Agency at 297 Pentonville Road, at the time Ray's Surgical in *Billion Dollar Brain* (1967). Phil Daniels takes Hazel O'Connor for a recording contract interview to 200 Pentonville Road, near Killick Street, in *Breaking Glass* (1980).

In *Naked* (1993), David Thewlis gets a kicking from billsticker Darren Tunstall at the corner of Twyford Street and Caledonian Road. Des Brady enters Daytona Motorcycles on Pentonville Road to shoot up the employees and steal a bike in *Day of the Sirens* (2002).

Islington

In *Percy* (1971) Hywel Bennett's antique shop is at 116 Islington High Street, now Angel's Arcade, right in the corner next to Camden Passage. Colin Firth and Ruth Gemmell stroll in Camden Passage in *Fever Pitch* (1997) when Firth has to admit that his thoughts are not on DH Lawrence but Arsenal.

Alfredo's café, which is on the east side of Essex Road close to Islington Green, features as the Mods' hangout in *Quadrophenia* (1979). Outside the café Phil Daniels headbutts Mark Wingett for stealing his girlfriend, Leslie Ash. The café, closed in 1999, also briefly appears at the start of *Mojo* (1997). Colin Dale and Dursley McLinden visit the Screen on the Green cinema, on Upper Street, in *Just Ask for Diamond* (1988). Close to Highbury Corner, on Compton Terrace, is the Union Chapel, where radical vicar Kenneth Griffith holds peace concerts in *Who Dares Wins* (1982).

Robin Phillips as *David Copperfield* (1970) alights from his carriage at 4 Canonbury Place, just off Alwyne Villas.

Above:
King's Cross Station, seen in *Harry Potter and the Chamber of Secrets* (2002), *X, Y And Zee* (1972) and *Empire State* (1987).

Old Street

Just off City Road, opposite Ebenezer Street, is 15 Westland Place, Kevin McKidd and Tom Hollander's flat in **Bedrooms and Hallways** (1998). Now it is the Fifteen Restaurant. Just south, Julia Roberts's studio in **Closer** (2004) is at 3 Westland Place. Natalie Portman meets Jude Law outside, and later Clive Owen visits. The 'Soho' club Steven Mackintosh visits in **The Criminal** (1999) is in the Shepherdess Walk Buildings, 39–43 Underwood Street.

The Metro Bar on the corner of cobbled Coronet Street and Boots Street is the exterior of the club where Jaye Davidson sings in **The Crying Game** (1992). Off Boots Street, next to the pub, there used to be an alleyway where Stephen Rea has a punch-up with Ralph Brown, but new building has narrowed the space.

9 Hoxton Square houses the third-floor flat where Davidson lives. From here Davidson throws out Brown's clothes and goldfish before seducing Rea, and there too Miranda Richardson later tries to kill them. Davidson gets drunk in the square, where in **High Heels and Low Lifes** (2001) Minnie Driver and Mary McCormack rehearse their blackmail plan. Opposite Curtain Road, the exterior of Mother, at 333 Old Street, is used as 'The Mixer Club'.

Outside Old Street Magistrates Court, Mike Sarne meets Rita Tushingham after his trial in *A Place to Go* (1963).

In *Trauma* (2004) Colin Firth meets friend Tommy Flanagan near Enfield Cloisters, and they go into 71 Fanshaw Street near the corner of Hoxton Street. At 177 Hoxton Street is The Bacchus, standing in for 'The Blind Beggar' in *The Krays* (1990). Gary Kemp gets out of his car parked in Wilks Place, crosses the road and enters the pub to shoot Steven Berkoff.

Mike Sarne and Rita Tushingham walk east along Wiltshire Row as he proposes to her at the end of *A Place to Go* (1963).

Mark Addy and Charlie Creed-Miles pause on the bridge between Bridport Place and Southgate Road on their way to the de Beauvoir Estate in *The Last Yellow* (1999). They cross the car park between Granville Court and Corbiere House to arrive at flat 46 St Aubins Court, where Addy is required to become a hitman.

N5: Highbury

In *Four Weddings and a Funeral* (1994) Hugh Grant and Charlotte Coleman share 22 Highbury Terrace, on the corner with Highbury Terrace Mews. At the climax Andie MacDowell and Grant profess true love as the camera pans away to take in 21 and 20 before tilting up to the rainy sky.

Above:
Wiltshire Row
(above left), seen in
A Place to Go
(1963) when Mike
Sarne and Rita
Tushingham enjoy a
walk by the canal
(above right).

Opposite:
Jude Law and
Natalie Portman
meet outside 3
Westland Place (top
and centre) in
Closer (2004).
Westland Place
(bottom) can also
be seen in
*Bedrooms and
Hallways* (1998).

The Arsenal Stadium Mystery (1939) uses Highbury stadium for a match between Arsenal and Brentwood Trojans, during which a player is murdered. Harvey Keitel pays a quick visit to the stadium in *The Young Americans* (1993). Arsenal FC is Colin Firth's obsession in *Fever Pitch* (1997). Neil Pearson takes Luke Aikman to his first match, exiting Arsenal tube and walking down Highbury Hill to the west gate. Firth encourages Ruth Gemmell to look at a flat for sale at 73a Avenell Road, though the entrance is just round the corner in Conewood Street. The street party of May 1989, when Arsenal triumphed in the league, is held outside the east stand and main entrance on Avenell Road. In 2006 Arsenal moved to the Emirates Stadium in Ashburton Grove just to the southwest.

Joseph Fiennes takes Heather Graham for a tryst to 59 Highbury New Park in *Killing Me Softly* (2002).

N7: Barnsbury, Lower Holloway, Tufnell Park

For *The Ladykillers* (1955) Katie Johnson's house was constructed at the end of Frederick Street, now known as Frederica Street and developed beyond recognition. Behind the house is Copenhagen Tunnel from which, one by one, gang members Cecil Parker, Peter Sellers, Danny Green, Herbert Lom and Alec Guinness drop into goods carriages travelling under Caledonian Junction. A stable is now on top of the tunnel, and the best viewing is from the end of Vale Royal, a cul-de-sac off York Way, on the west side.

To the north-west, on Parkhurst Road at its junction with Camden Road, is HM Prison for Women, Holloway, from where Yvonne Mitchell, Joan Collins and Kathleen Harrison are released at the start of *Turn the Key Softly* (1953). The prison was rebuilt in the 1970s.

Just north of Holloway Road station, at the corner of Holloway Road and Jackson Road, Rita Wolf drives off without Dennis Lawson in *The Chain* (1984).

N4: Finsbury Park, Harringay

Finsbury Park

Opposite Finsbury Park tube on Seven Sisters Road is the Spanish palace-style theatre called successively the Astoria (in the 1930s), the Odeon (1940s to 1960s) and the Rainbow

Theatre (1970s); it was seen as the latter in **Breaking Glass** (1980), when Phil Daniels first meets Hazel O'Connor outside. Breaking down in mid-performance, O'Connor runs out of the theatre to the station, dressed in her 'Eighth Day' garb. If one can get inside the building, the foyer is an Istanbul restaurant at the start of **Murder on the Orient Express** (1974). The theatre is currently used as a church. At 183 Seven Sisters Road Daniel Craig telephones a fellow witness to the balloon accident in **Enduring Love** (2004).

Harringay

The library at the corner of Stapleton Hall Road and Quernmore Road, near Harringay station, is seen as a police station from where Ron Pember collects Herbert Norville in **The Chain** (1984).

At the Castle Climbing Centre on Green Lanes, opposite Myddleton Avenue, Heather Graham meets Natascha McElhone for instruction in **Killing Me Softly** (2002).

In **Face** (1997) Robert Carlyle, Steven Waddington, Ray Winstone and Philip Davis check on Damon Albarn and his share of their ill-gotten gains. Finding him dead, they make a speedy exit as plainclothes police have tailed them. They flee up Harringay Passage, a lengthy footpath running north and south, and split up. Carlyle and Waddington cross Mattison Road to Pemberton Road, turning right at the school towards Green Lanes and making their escape while the other two have to shoot their way out of N8.

N8: Hornsey Vale, Crouch End

In **Driving Lessons** (2006), after unsuccessfully calling for Rupert Grint at home, Julie Walters meets him outside 27 Coolhurst Road.

In **Love, Honour and Obey** (2000) Jude Law introduces Jonny Lee Miller to Ray Winstone at the Queen's Hotel, on The Broadway, which is minded by Dominic Anciano and Ray Burdis. Here later Winstone forces Rhys Ifans and Trevor H Laird to back down at the point of a shotgun. Anciano and Burdis also help the stabbed Perry Benson out of the pub and leave him to suffer round the corner on Elder Avenue.

Stellan Skarsgård lives at the triangular-shaped 12 Middle Lane Mews, next to North 8 Motors, in **Kiss Kiss (Bang Bang)** (2000). He takes Chris Penn here for his first views of the outdoors.

The opening shot of **Shaun of the Dead** (2004) looks south up Nelson Road. Simon Pegg and Nick Frost live on the south-west corner of Nelson Road and Weston Park, at 83 Weston Park, though the entrance, now with altered gate and higher gateposts, is in Nelson Road. His local shop is the Londis at 96 Weston Park, just to the east.

In **Face** (1997) Ray Winstone and Philip Davis, on the run from the law, emerge from the narrow pedestrian-only Harringay Passage onto Allison Road, where they are caught up in a gunfire battle. Winstone takes cover at the front of 84 Allison Road, while Davis forces a van to stop, fires on a police car (which bursts into flames) and hits the van. Amid the mayhem they escape.

N15: West Green, South Tottenham

The interior of The Salisbury, on the south corner of Green Lanes and St Ann's Road, stands in as an Irish pub at the beginning of **The Long Good Friday** (1980). Here too Robert Downey Jnr as **Chaplin** (1992) finds himself unwelcome with his former Covent Garden buddies after missing the fighting of World War I. In **Spider** (2002) Miranda Richardson looks for Gabriel Byrne here.

The Football Factory (2003) opens with Frank Harper and his gang emerging from Seven Sisters tube. Harper walks down Birstall Road arranging a fight on his mobile phone; it actually takes place in SE1.

The Prince of Wales's Hospital on Tottenham Green East, just off the High Road, is the site being converted to flats by labourers including Robert Carlyle and Ricky Tomlinson in **Riff-Raff** (1990). It is now 6 Deaconess Court, but still proudly displays the fleur-de-lis (the Prince of Wales's tri-leafed device) above its entrance.

N16: Stamford Hill, Shacklewell

Just off Stoke Newington Church Street alongside Spensley Walk is 209 Church Street, temporary home to Emer McCourt in **Riff-Raff** (1990). Here Robert Carlyle turns from Clissold Road into the crescent to return her lost handbag.

N6: Highgate

Truly Madly Deeply (1991) opens with Juliet Stevenson making her way home from Highgate tube, crossing Archway Road on Hornsey Lane.

Jenny Seagrove lives at Fern Lodge, 5 Millfield Lane, in *Don't Go Breaking My Heart* (1998). Anthony Edwards teaches Ben Reynolds basketball in the driveway.

Karl Marx's grave in the eastern half of Highgate Cemetery off Swain's Lane is the focus of David Warner and Irene Handl's visit in *Morgan* (1966). Philip Davis and Ruth Sheen admire the same grave before being joined by Chinese tourists on a similar pilgrimage in *High Hopes* (1988).

Peter Jeffrey and Joseph Cotten investigate Vincent Price's mausoleum, supposedly in Highgate Cemetery and probably in the western half, in *The Abominable Dr Phibes* (1971).

On Hillcrest, a road off North Hill, is a housing estate that includes Cunningham House, where Simon Pegg and Nick Frost rescue Kate Ashfield, Dylan Moran and Lucy Davis from zombies in *Shaun of the Dead* (2004).

N2: East Finchley

Penelope Wilton and Bill Nighy live at 37 Abbot's Gardens in *Shaun of the Dead* (2004). When Simon Pegg and Nick Frost rescue them from zombies, Nighy is attacked in the front garden.

Robert Shaw kidnaps his victim from 91 Winnington Road in *Tomorrow at Ten* (1964).

N10: Muswell Hill, Cranley Gardens

Adrian Scarborough and Heather Craney live at 10 Wood Vale in *Vera Drake* (2004).

Fortismere School is the school where Colin Firth and Ruth Gemmell teach in *Fever Pitch* (1997). The entrance is on Tetherdown, but the best view of the field where Firth instructs his under-14 side can be seen from Twyford Avenue (N6).

James Garner visits Julie Andrews and Joyce Grenfell at 72 Duke's Avenue in *The Americanization of Emily* (1964). Alexandra Palace (N22) looms in the background.

N22: Noel Park

In front of Alexandra Palace in *Shooting Fish* (1997) Stuart Townsend and Dan Futterman search a skip for abandoned electrical goods while Kate Beckinsale looks on.

In *1984* (1984), filmed before Alexandra Palace was refurbished after the 1980 fire, the shell was Victory Square. Speeches are delivered to an adoring crowd including John Hurt, Suzanna Hamilton and Richard Burton.

N13: Palmers Green, Bowes Park

Glenda Jackson as *Stevie* (1978) passes by Stevie Smith's blue-plaqued house at 1 Avondale Road on her way to 17 Avondale Road. The front gate and fence, seen when Trevor Howard visits to give her a lift, have now gone.

N11: Brunswick Park, New Southgate

The hospital picketed by unions at the start of *Britannia Hospital* (1982) is Friern Hospital, now converted into apartments called Princes Park Manor. The buildings lie south off Friern Barnet Road, down Royal Drive.

New Southgate Cemetery and its chapel appear under the opening titles of *That's Your Funeral* (1973).

N12: North Finchley, Colney Hatch, Woodside Park

Simon Pegg works with Rafe Spall in Garland Electronics at 765 High Road, on the corner of Hall Street, in **Shaun of the Dead** (2004).

N20: Totteridge, Whetstone, Oakleigh Place

To the east of Barnet Lane on Totteridge Village is St Andrew's Church, seen near the start of **Taste the Blood of Dracula** (1970).

N21: Grange Park, Bush Hill, Winchmore Hill

Maurice Purley Photography, where Timothy Spall has his business in **Secrets & Lies** (1996), is on the north side of The Green near Winchmore Hill station. The Green across the road is seen when scarred car-crash victim Emma Amos leaves, passing a bench on which Ron Cook, the former owner of the business, is sitting.

In **Stevie** (1978) in frosty Grovelands Park by the north-east corner of the lake, Trevor Howard recites Stevie Smith's 'not waving but drowning'.

N14: Osidge, Oakwood

Timothy Spall and Phyllis Logan live at 87 Whitehouse Way in **Secrets & Lies** (1996). Spall invites sister Brenda Blethyn, niece Claire Rushbrook with boyfriend Lee Ross, and assistant Elizabeth Berrington for a barbecue in which various secrets are revealed. Rushbrook storms off to the bus stop on Hampden Way.

Under the credits of **Stevie** (1978) Glenda Jackson exits Southgate tube and wanders through Grovelands Park before leaving by the Inverforth Gate on The Bourne. Julia Ormond meets Tim Roth on his day releases from prison outside and inside the Metro Café opposite the station in **Captives** (1994). In the café she shoots Mark Strong.

film index

10 Rillington Place (1970) 61, 143
11 Harrowhouse (1974) 37, 71, *71*
23 Paces to Baker Street (1956) 26, 30, 57, 94, 116, 194
28 Days Later (2002) 11, 31, 42, 90, 94, 149, 220, 222
84 Charing Cross Road (1986) 17, 38, 151
101 Dalmatians (1996) 16, 18, 38, 43, 54, 86, 88, 90, 111, 156, 189
102 Dalmatians (2000) 57, 143, 149, 157, 236, 244, 248, 249
Abominable Dr. Phibes, The (1971) 63
About a Boy (2002) 32, 47, 64, 70, 153, 159, 204, *205*, 236, *237*, 238, 246
Accident (1967) 12, 112, 242
Accidental Tourist, The (1988) 27, 51, 82, 94
Afraid of the Dark (1991) 47, 64, 119, 123, 253, *253*
Against the Wind (1948) 116
Agent Cody Banks 2 (2004) 19, 26, 40, 43, 99, 151, 155, 188, 199, 220
Alfie (1966) 22, 27, 47, 54, 56, 67, 91, 100, 132, 135, 149, 153, 191, 207, 245
Ali G Indahouse (2000) 92
Alive and Kicking (1996) 57, 208
All or Nothing (2002) 13, 174, 177, 179, 222
All the Little Animals (1998) 134
Alphabet Murders (1965) 38, 53, 55
American Roulette (1988) 10, 12, 30, 60, 62, 68, 134, 150, 151, 239, 256
American Werewolf in London, An (1981) 16, 31, 41, 124, 156, 160, 238
Americanization of Emily (1964) 200, 264
Amsterdam Kill, The (1977) 142
And Now ... Ladies and Gentlemen (2002) 36, 150
Arabesque (1966) 16, 86, 153, 238
Are You Ready for Love? (2006) 38, 41 78, 145, 155, 162, 163, 187, 249, 250
Around the World in Eighty Days (1956) 82, *83*, 90, 104, *108*, 109, 113
    Arsenal Stadium Mystery (1937) 260
Assassination Bureau, The (1968) 22, *102*, 102, 117

Astonished Heart, The (1949) 34, 44, 153
Attack on the Iron Coast (1968) 211
Austin Powers in Goldmember (2002) 150
Avengers, The (1998) 16, 19, 88, 150, 177, 188, 236
Awakening, The (1980) 13, 146, 152, 253
B. Monkey (1996) 39, 49, 70, 88, 109, 112, 122, 128, 153, 213
Baby Love (1968) 33, 37, *37*
Backbeat (1994) 245
Bad Behaviour (1993) 13, 246, 250
Barry McKenzie Holds His Own (1975) 23, 100
Basic Instinct 2 (2005) 19, 22, 40, 116, 187, 189, 201, 220
Basil (1998) 22, 44
Batman Begins (2005) 12, 243
Battle of Britain (1969) 23, 211
Bean (1997) 97
Beat Girl (1960) 19, *19*
Beautiful People (1999) 96
Beautiful Thing (1996) 174, 178, 184, *184*
Bedazzled (1967) 31, 42, 225, 238, 251
Bedrooms and Hallways (1998) 57, 64, 68, 258, *258*
Being Julia (2004) 18, 88, 103
Bend It Like Beckham (2002) 38, 39, 42, 59
Betrayal (1983) 12, 67, 76, 246, 252
Big Money, The (1956) 106
Big Sleep, The (1978) 26, 44, 56, 57, 84, *85*, 86, 100, 115, 143, 185, *185*, 194
Billion Dollar Brain, The (1967) 46, 257
Billy Elliot (2000) 90
Billy Liar (1963) 234
Bitch, The (1979) 33, 44, 55
Black Beauty (1994) 25
Black Joy (1977) 131, 132, 139
Black Windmill, The (1974) 12, 23, *23*, 57, 70, 72, 115
Blackmail (1929) 11, 91
Blind Date (1958) 15, 96, 98, 105, *105*, 108
Blow Dry (2001) 182

Blow Up (1966) 38, 60, 84, 87, 111, 132, 169, *169*, 181, 199
Blue Ice (1992) 19, 30, 71, 84, 105, 144, 147, 149, 158, *158*, 160, 210
Blue Juice (1995) 39
Blue Lamp, The (1950) 42, 48, 49, 67, 69, 74, 92
Bond Street (1948) 36
Born Romantic (2000) 11, 14, 130, 185, 195, 207, 214, 230, 231, 256
Borrowers, The (1997) 81, 254
Bounty, The (1984) 88, 176
Boy Who Turned Yellow, The (1972) 190, 242, 249, 250
Boys, The (1962) 39, 42, 48
Brannigan (1975) 17, 18, 34, 39, 42, 49, 87, 90, 138, 139, 141, 149, 161, 188, 211, 225, 243
Brassed Off (1996) 95, 117
Brazil (1985) 58, 224
Breaking Glass (1980) 28, 68, 241, 257, 261
Bridget Jones's Diary (2001) 22, 42, 156, *158*, 159, 162, 187, 210
Bridget Jones: The Edge of Reason (2004) 42, 44, 54, *55*, *158*, 159, 160, 208, 210, 247
Brief Encounter (1945) 236
Bright Young Things (2003) 26, 27, 86, 177, 235
Brimstone and Treacle (1982) 159
Bring Me the Head of Mavis Davis (1997) 42, 210
Britannia Hospital (1982) 264
Brothers-in-Law (1957) 22, 192, *193*, 194, *194*
Bullet Boy (2004) 226, *226*, 232
Bullet to Beijing (1995) 26
Bullseye! (1990) 32, 34, 56, 73, 96, 107, 116
Bullshot (1983) 78, 118, 203
Bunny Lake is Missing (1965) 17, 70, 91, 248
Business, The (2004) 108, 128, 163
Business Affair, A (1994) 16, 39, 70, 87, 96, 117
Buster (1988) 98, 152, 192, 229, 230, *230*, 232
Calcium Kid, The (2004) 101, 103, 140, 166, *167*, 168
Calendar Girls (2003) 85

Callan (1974) 15, 161, 190
Captives (1994) 111, 139, 140, 265
Career Girls (1997) 221, 240, 245, 246, *246*, 247, 256
Carry On Constable (1960) 81
Carry On Emmannuelle (1978) 16, 58, 87
Carve Her Name With Pride (1958) 44, 132
Casino Royale (1967) 16, 86, 92
Castaway (1986) 23, 46, 58, 112, 122, 130
Cement Garden, The (1993) 179
Chain, The (1984) 58, 96, 97, 114, 228, 249, 260, 261
Chance of a Lifetime (1950) 153, 186
Chaplin (1992) 144, 212, 243, 244
Charge of the Light Brigade, The (1968) 89, *89*, 176, 191
Charlotte Gray (2001) 176
Children of Men (2006) 91, 98, 128, 140, 155, 189, 192, 212, 214, 228, 230
Children of the Damned (1963) 36, 48, 160, *160*, 189
Chromophobia (2005) 97, 188, 189, 198, 201, 208, 214
Class of Miss MacMichael (1978) 152
Clockwork Orange, A (1971) 109, 111, 141, 184, *184*
Closer (2004) 10, 17, 46, 150, 154, 207, *207*, 208, 212, 258, *258*
Code 46 (2003) 188
Collector, The (1965) 19, 248
Constant Gardener, The (2005) 71, 91, 153, 155, 220
Constant Husband, The (1955) 58, 72, 97, 194
Cool It Carol! (1970) 37
Core, The (2003) 17
Corruption (1967) 59, 103
Cosh Boy (1952) 75, 76, *77*
Creep (2004) 23
Creeping Flesh, The (1973) 211
Crimetime (1996) 61, 65, 128, 177, 221
Criminal, The (1960) 26, 40
Criminal, The (1999) 27, 158, *158*, 205, 229, 258
Crooks Anonymous (1962) 54, 115
Crooks in Cloisters (1963) 74

Crossplot (1969) 34, 35, 59, 95, 104, 122, 195, 197, *197*, 199, *199*
Croupier (1999) 42, 51
Crucible of Terror (1971) 76
Cry from the Streets, A (1958) 13, 257
Crying Game, The (1992) 14, 103, 114, 174, 213, 214, 258
Da Vinci Code, The (2006) 96, 192, 222
Damage (1992) 15, *15*, 34, 37, 47, 56, 115, 248
Dance With a Stranger (1985) 43, 102, 159, 205
Darling (1965) 29, 42, 43, 78, 114, 116, 135, 195, 249
Date With a Dream, A (1948) 131, 241
David Copperfield (1970) 18, 19, 20, 21, 35, 192, 211, 257
Day of the Jackal, The (1973) 11, 25, 86, 92, 94
Day of the Sirens (2002) 17, 42, 149, 150, 200, 213, 214, 228, 257
Day of the Triffids, The (1962) 21, 149, 207, 225, 234
Day the Earth Caught Fire, The (1961) 128, 136, 193
Dead Fish (2004) 40, 51, 130, 164, 194, 210, 232
Deadly Affair, The (1966) 24, 54, 86, 100, 107, 122, 144
Dealers (1989) 162
Death Line (1972) 10, 13
Death Wish 3 (1985) 168
Deep End (1970) 125
Defence of the Realm (1985) 14, 90, 94, 124, 193
Diamond Skulls (1989) 100, 104, 111
Diamonds (1975) 102
Die Another Day (2002) 86, 88, 149
Different for Girls (1996) 46, 49, 156, 158, 164, 169, 188, 200, 201, 202, *202*, 213, 224
Dirty Pretty Things (2002) 91, 158, 207, 221, 230
Divorce of Lady X, The (1938) 34
Do Not Disturb (1965) 103
Doctor At Large (1957) 12, 104
Doctor in Clover (1966) 12, 38, 73
Doctor in Distress (1963) 81
Doctor in Love (1960) 12
Doctor in the House (1954) 12, 29, 136, 256
Dog Eat Dog (2001) 242
Dogs of War, The (1981) 199, 201
Don't Go Breaking My Heart (1998) 36, 37, 145, 173, 249, 251, 263

Don't Raise the Bridge, Lower the River (1968) 199, 210
Doomwatch (1972) 134
Dracula AD 1972 (1972) 56, 84, 107
Dream Demon (1988) 247
Driving Lessons (2006) 247, 249, 261
Duet For One (1986) 117
East Is East (1999) 187
Easy Money (1948) 34
Elephant Juice (2000) 152, 154, 156, 205, 231, 252
Elephant Man, The (1980) 162, 201
Emergency Call (1952) 75
Empire of the Sun (1987) 225
Empire State (1987) 148, 187, 224, 228, 256, *257*
End of the Affair, The (1955) 48, 53, 241
End of the Affair, The (1999) 48, 70, 137, 206, 208, 253
Endless Night (1972) 46, 87, 150
Enduring Love (2005) 10, 98, 155, 246, 261
Enigma (2001) 17
Entertaining Mr Sloane (1970) 171
Entrapment (1999) 26, 157, 193, 198
Every Home Should Have One (1970) 56
Executioner, The (1970) 15, 34, 53, 101
Expresso Bongo (1959) 34, 39, 83
Eye of the Needle (1981) 126, 128, 235
Eyes Wide Shut (1999) 38, 105, 123, 202, 203
Face (1997) 201, 214, 215, 220, 221, *221*, 227, 261, 262
Fallen Idol, The (1948) 104, 105, 238
Fanny By Gaslight (1944) 104
Fat Slags (2004) 43, 149, 155, 163, 186, 211
Felicia's Journey (1999) 28, 142
Fever Pitch (1997) 257, 260, 264
Fierce Creatures (1997) 201, *201*, 202
Fifth Element, The (1997) 19
File of the Golden Goose, The (1969) 41, 42, 43, 64, 84, 86, 88, 136, 151, 153, 201, 225
Final Conflict, The (1981) 36, 44, 53, 54, 66, 70, 213
Final Test, The (1953) 166
Finding Neverland (2004) 22
Firm, The (1988) 183, 184, 211, 228
Fish Called Wanda, A (1988) 21, 22, 49, 71, 114, 138, *138*, 163, 164, 203, 204
Five Seconds to Spare (1999) 40, 123, 180, 222, 244

Flame in the Streets (1961) 240, *240*
Follow a Star (1959) 38
Football Factory, The (2004) 43, 74, 124, 125, 163, 165, *165*, 262
For Queen and Country (1988) 14, 68, 74, 167, 254
For Your Eyes Only (1981) 225
Forbidden Cargo (1954) 46, 106, 161
Foreign Correspondent (1940) 94, 100
Foreign Moon (1995) 40, 107
Four Feathers, The (2002) 95, 176, 177
Four Weddings and a Funeral (1994) 19, 114, 152, 177, 208, *209*, 259
Fourth Protocol, The (1987) 17, 50, 56, 103, 118, 243, 247
Fragment of Fear (1970) 19, 87
French Lieutenant's Woman, The (1981) 26, 60, 159, 162
Frenzy (1972) 17, 19, 32, 38, 46, 73, 84, 119, 150
Frightened City, The (1961) 94, 190, *190*
Full Metal Jacket (1987) 225
Funeral in Berlin (1966) 15
Funny Money (1983) 32, 106, 137
Game for Vultures, A (1979) 36, 97, 98
Games, The (1969) 74
Gangster No. 1 (2000) 34, 199, 214, 222, 228, 229
Genevieve (1953) 119, 148, 149
Gentle Sex, The (1943) 153
George and Mildred (1980) 147
Georgy Girl (1966) 36, 49, 57, 68, 71, 175, 247, 250, *250*
Getting It Right (1989) 163, 236, 239
Gideon's Day (1958) 23, 194, 236
Give My Regards to Broad Street (1984) 12, 18, 29, 71, 85, 117, 161, 164, 200
Goal! (2005) 90
Gold (1974) 91, 94
Golden Bowl, The (2000) 78, 88, 92, 198, 213, 244
Golden Lady, The (1978) 68, 102, 112
Golden Eye (1995) 26, 46, 123
Good Die Young, The (1954) 153
Good Father, The (1985) 74, 90, 130, 132, 133, 142, 192, 217
Goodbye Gemini (1970) 96, 108, 223, 256
Goodbye Mr Chips (1969) 77, 113
Gorgo (1961) 91, 136
Governess, The (1998) 25
Grass is Greener, The (1960) 34
Great Balls of Fire! (1989) 149

Great Expectations (1946) 195, *195*
Great Rock'n'Roll Swindle, The (1979) 14, 41, 210
Greek Tycoon, The (1978) 18
Green Man, The (1956) 10
Green Street (2005) 101, 186, 187, 188, 189, 222, 225, 244
Greenwich Mean Time (1999) 139, 174, 175, *175*, 178, 184, 214, 222
Greystoke (1984) 116
Gumshoe (1971) 10, *11*, 17
Hackers (1995) 62
Half Light (2006) 188, *188*, 239
Half Moon Street (1986) 12, 61, 78, 101, 134, 135, 252
Handful of Dust, A (1988) 88
Hands of the Ripper (1971) 153, 195
Hanover Street (1979) 86, 104
Hard Day's Night, A (1964) 31, 63, 67, 234
Hard Men (1996) 39
Hardcore (1977) 97
Harry Potter and the Chamber of Secrets (2002) 256, *257*
Harry Potter and the Philosopher's Stone (2001) 23, 187, *187*, 238, 256
Harry Potter and the Prisoner of Azkaban (2004) 157, 257
Heart of Me, The (2002) 30, 137, 187
Hellraiser (1987) 255
Help! (1965) 28, 36, 77
Hennessy (1975) 61, 66, 78, 84, 95, 97, 114, 118, 164
High Heels and Low Lifes (2001) 96, 97, 107, 185, 203, 231, 258
High Hopes (1988) 187, 244, 256, 263
Hoffman (1970) 112, 142, 143, 256
Holocaust 2000 (1977) 88, 103
Honest (2000) 17, 23, 228
Hopscotch (1980) 33, 155
Horror Hospital (1973) 153
Hot Enough for June (1964) 147, *147*
Hot Millions (1968) 50, 73, 175, 195
Hours of 13, The (1952) 116
How to Get Ahead in Advertising (1989) 147
Howards End (1992) 28, 43, 78, 82, 83, 91, 158, 243
Hue and Cry (1947) 79, 155, 208, 217, 219
Human Factor, The (1979) 17, 26, 36, 198
Hunger, The (1983) 12, 199
Hunted (1951) 94, 99, 100, 211
Hussy (1980) 133, 219, 243

I Believe in You (1952) 19, 23, 122, 139, 204, *204*
I Capture the Castle (2003) 73, 150, 185
I Could Go On Singing (1963) 26, 38, 134, 150, 189
I Don't Want to Be Born (1975) 36, 96, 105, 111
I Hired a Contract Killer (1990) 65, 208, 215, 224, 230, 243
I Was Monty's Double (1957) 201
I'll Never Forget What's'isname (1967) 37, 87, 122, 152
I'll Sleep When I'm Dead (2003) 14, 101, 131, 168, 172
I.D. (1994) 18, 163, 164
Ideal Husband, An (1999) 175
If Only (1998) 28, 42, 47, 49, 62, *62*, 71, 123, 128, 247
If Only (2004) 18, 51, 64, 70, 96, 117, 138, 151, 186, 200
Importance of Being Earnest, The (2002) 22, 26, 81, 87, 212
Incognito (1997) 22, 43, 107, 151, 155, 167
Indiana Jones and the Last Crusade (1989) 98
Indiscreet (1958) 27, 32
Informers, The (1964) 15, 19, 49, *50*, *51*, 94, 201, 248
Inn of the Sixth Happiness, The (1958) 16, 50, 83, 90
Innocent Bystanders (1973) 16 32 36 85 90 94 97 *97*
Innocent Sleep, The (1995) 134, 147, 152, 154, 155, 191, 203, *203*
Inside Out (1975) 46, 52
Inspector Clouseau (1968) 84
Intelligence Men, The (1966) 97, 146
Interlude (1968) 59, 71, 101, 111, 117, 151
International Velvet (1978) 58
Internecine Project, The (1973) 52, 146, 234
Intimacy (2001) 11, 51, 68, 126, 130, 148, 180
Ipcress File, The (1965) 15, 54, 72, 86, 91, 106, 116, 117, 234
Iris (2001) 99
Isadora (1968) 11
It Always Rains on Sunday (1948) 239
It Happened Here (1964) 60, 242, 243, 248
It Was an Accident (2000) 232, 233

Italian Job, The (1969) 29, 46, 65, 73, 146, 173, 199
Jack & Sarah (1995) 19, 60, *60*, 61, 64, 117, 123, 219, 239, 245, 247
Jackal, The (1997) 87
Janice Beard 45 wpm (1999) 130, 212, 245
Jigsaw Man, The (1983) 77, 146
Joanna (1968) 16, 44, 50, 53, 86, 112, 118, 146, 152
Johnny English (2003) 19, 22, 96, 119, 124, 150, 187, 208, 220
Jokers, The (1967) 85, 92, 100, 111, 112, 114, 116, 153, 190, 195, 197, 238
Jubilee (1977) 86, 99, 117, 162, 165, 222
Juggernaut (1974) 149
Just Ask for Diamond (1988) 29, 147, *147*, 188, 239, 243, 244, 249, 250, 257
Just Like a Woman (1992) 29, 113, *113*, 128, 145, 160, 189
Keep the Aspidistra Flying (1997) 13, *13*, 85, *85*, 147, 158, 242, 244, 247
Killing Me Softly (2002) 14, 27, 49, 81, 153, 200, 208, 260, 261
Killing of Sister George, The (1968) 75, 109, 119, 198, 248
King Ralph (1991) 25, 40, 42, 70, 86, 176, 243, 252
Kiss Kiss (Bang Bang) (2000) 146, 152, 182, 212, *213*, 238, 247, 261
Knack, The (1965) 37, 56, 59, 60, 70, 77, 85, 102, 107, 118, 148
Krays, The (1990) 23, 163, 167, 178, 212, 228, 259
L-Shaped Room, The (1962) 47, 62, 63, 102
Lady Vanishes, The (1938) 106
Lady Vanishes, The (1979) 234
Ladykillers, The (1955) 13, 14, 244, 256, 260
Lara Croft: Tomb Raider (2001) 177, 187
Lassiter (1984) 25, 43, 105, 109, 117, 126, 158, 162, 188
Last Minute, The (2001) 11
Last Orders (2001) 133, 149, 168, 208
Last Yellow, The (1999) 40, *40*, 238, 254, 259
Laughter in Paradise (1951) 42
Lavender Hill Mob, The (1951) 67, 186, *196*, 197
Law and Disorder (1958) 140, 223

Lawrence of Arabia (1962) 95
Layer Cake (2004) 98, 115, 174, 220
Leading Man, The (1997) 15, 16, 137, 149, 156, 162, 182, 211
League of Gentlemen, The (1960) 104, 189
Leather Boys, The (1963) 142, 223, *223*, 254
Left, Right and Centre (1959) 50
Legally Blonde (2001) 173
Leo the Last (1970) 61, 67
Leon the Pig Farmer (1992) 126
Leopard in the Snow (1978) 103, 117
Let It Be (1970) 38
Let's Get Laid (1977) 234
Life and Death of Colonel Blimp, The (1943) 33, 112
Life and Death of Peter Sellers, The (2004) 30, 91
Life at the Top (1965) 26, 75, 199
Lifeforce (1985) 10
Lighthouse Hill (2002) 35, *35*
Lion at World's End, The (1971) 123
Liquidator, The (1965) 55, 85, 97
List of Adrian Messenger, The (1963) 177
Little Drummer Girl, The (1984) 125
Little Voice (1998) 43
Live It Up (1963) 232
Loch Ness (1996) 116
Lock, Stock and Two Smoking Barrels (1998) 135, 156, 157, 206, *206*, 214, 229, 239
Londinium (2001) 11, 19, 32, 33, 34, 54, 103, 156, 157, 206, 214, 229, 239
London Belongs to Me (1948) 149
London Connection, The (1980) 50, 84, 224
London Kills Me (1991) 65, 69
London Voodoo (2004) 26, 165, 175
Long Arm, The (1956) 19, 25, 91, 94, 101, 151, 189, 242
Long Good Friday, The (1980) 26, 29, 50, 83, 131, 212, 219, 220, 221, 224, 262
Long Memory, The (1952) 10, 153, 161, *161*
Long Time Dead (2000) 163
Look Back in Anger (1959) 254, *254*
Looking for Richard (1996) 97, 155
Loop (1997) 162
Loophole (1980) 194
Lost (1955) 44, 52, *53*, 57, 107, 123, 195, *195*
Lost Son, The (1999) 17, 27, 43, 68, 87, 249

Love Actually (2003) 29, 33, 62, *62*, 69, 135, 144, 154, 160, 172, *172*, 205
Love and Death on Long Island (1997) 17, 98
Love is the Devil (1998) 11, 31
Love Story (1944) 117
Love, Honour and Obey (2000) 204, 205, 221, 226, 227, *227*, 243, 261
Low Down, The (2001) 14, 39, 86, 129, 134, 230, 240, 243
Lucky Break (2001) 35
Ma Femme est une Actrice (2001) 19, 36, 42, 101, 153, 155
Mackintosh Man, The (1973) 15, 86, 202
Mad Cows (1999) 16, 63, 98, 112, 117, 140, 164, 207, 222
Mad Dogs and Englishmen (1995) 109, 119, 162
Madame Sousatzka (1988) 29, 54, 65, 100, 117
Made (1972) 182
Madness of King George, The (1994) 177, 195
Magic Christian, The (1969) 36, 58, 85, 86, 94, 143, 152, 189
Make Mine Mink (1960) 57, 149
Man About the House (1974) 70, 242, 251
Man at the Top (1973) 32, 53
Man Who Haunted Himself, The (1970) 43, 54, 88, 100, 155, 186, 236, 242
Man Who Knew Too Little, The (1997) 62, *62*, 69, 108, 201
Man Who Knew Too Much, The (1934) 17
Man Who Knew Too Much, The (1956) 17, 241
Man Who Loved Redheads, The (1955) 104
Man Who Never Was, The (1956) 12, 43, 50, 75, 92
Martha, Meet Frank, Daniel and Laurence (1998) 47, 64, 65, 75, 81, 86, 98, 107, 137, 152, 200, 204, 213
Match Point (2005) 19, 35, 36, 37, 39, 59, 61, 64, 86, 101, 112, 147, 150, 154, 189, 235, *235*
Maurice (1987) 11, 12, 36, 194
Maybe Baby (2000) 35, 119, 128, 135, 137, 247
McVicar (1980) 243
Mean Machine, The (2001) 206, *206*
Meaning of Life, The (1983) 48
Medusa Touch, The (1978) 29, 92, 192

Melody (1971) 16, 37, 77, 119, 125, 129, 135, 148, *148*, 167
Midnight Lace (1960) 147
Mike Bassett: England Manager (2001) 46
Million Pound Note, The (1954) 54, 104, 116
Millionairess, The (1960) 198
Miranda (2002) 17, 189
Mission: Impossible (1996) 150, 156, 160, 201
Missionary, The (1983) 200, 219, 244
Modesty Blaise (1966) 87
Mojo (1997) 16, 156, 158, 203, 257
Mona Lisa (1986) 14, 27, 32, 40, 84, 87, 88, 134, 167, 170, *170, 171, 182*, 183, 202, 203
Moonlighting (1982) 57, 58, 72, 77
Morgan (1966) 33, 34, 56, 67, 73, 111, 122, 263
Morons from Outer Space (1985) 10, 58
Most Dangerous Man in the World, The (1968) 12
Mother, The (2003) 42, 76, 78, 151, 155, 243
Mr Denning Drives North (1952) 52
Mrs 'Arris Goes to Paris (1992) 75, 101
Mrs Brown (1997) 22
Mrs Brown, You've Got a Lovely Daughter (1968) 74, 149, 181, 211, 245, 256
Mrs Dalloway (1997) 12, 13, 28, 30, *30*, 43, *84*, 85, 90, 187
Mrs Henderson Presents (2004) 242
Mudlark, The (1951) 92
Mummy Returns, The (2001) 11, 13, 210
Murder By Decree (1979) 18, 86, 96, 159, 176
Murder on the Orient Express (1974) 261
Murder She Said (1961) 50
Music Lovers, The (1971) 46, 174, 175, 182, 239
My Beautiful Laundrette (1985) 100, 126, *127*, 129, 130
Naked (1993) 31, 41, 49, 156, 214, 230, 257
Naked Edge, The (1961) 190, *191*, 195
Naked Runner, The (1967) 12, 34, 88, 111, 146
Naked Truth, The (1957) 76, 122, 242
Nanny, The (1965) 236, 242
National Lampoon's European Vacation (1985) 59, 147
Never Let Go (1960) 48

Nicholas Nickleby (2002) 58, 88, 212, 213
Night, After Night, After Night (1969) 35, 42, 54, 135, 195, 241, 249
Night and the City (1950) 16, 18, 75, 150, 151, 195
Night Caller, The (1965) 146
Night of the Demon (1957) 11, 26, 134
Nighthawks (1981) 134
Nightingale Sang in Berkeley Square, A (1979) 22, 37, 73, 134
Nil By Mouth (1997) 148, 163, 168, 180
Nine Songs (2004) 132, 151
Nineteen Eighty-Four (1984) 12, 128, 225, 264
No Love for Johnnie (1961) 15, 28, 52, 54, 95, 174, 175, 242
Nobody Runs Forever (1968) 23, 76, 142
Nothing but the Best (1964) 36, 43, 50, 86, 89
Notting Hill (1999) 16, 18, 26, 46, 64, 65, 66, 69, 87, 248
Nuns on the Run (1990) 78, 125, 143, 244, 245
O Lucky Man! (1973) 18, 77, 90, 158, 242, 244
Object of Beauty, The (1991) 10, 55, 83
Obsession (1949) 36
October Man, The (1947) 50
Octopussy (1983) 36
Oh, Heavenly Dog! (1980) 95, 101, 150
Omen, The (1976) 36, 124, *124, 125*
On Her Majesty's Secret Service (1969) *196*, 197
Once a Jolly Swagman (1948) 109, 180
One of Our Dinosaurs Is Missing (1976) 115, 234, 236
Ooh, You Are Awful (1972) 48, 64, 83, 140, 153
Operation Amsterdam (1960) 99
Operation Crossbow (1965) 92
Optimists, The (1974) 18, 34, 41, 53, 109, 122, 124, 129, 134, *135*, 140, *141*
Otley (1968) 33, 61, 65, 66, 67, 68, 86, 88, 102, 109, 123
Our Mother's House (1967) 173
Pair of Briefs, A (1962) 21, 22, 147
Paradine Case, The (1947) 104
Parent Trap, The (1998) 35, 36, 112, 251
Parting Shots (1999) 28, 56, 68, 73, 87, 107, 138
Passenger, The (1975) 14, 67, 114

Passport to Pimlico (1949) 41, 166
Patriot Games (1992) 23, 43, 155, 176, 221
Peeping Tom (1960) 31, 58
Penny Gold (1974) 27
Percy (1971) 28, 31, 42, 51, 76, 77, 94, 257
Perfect Friday (1970) 32, 50, 94, 95, 104, 105, 106
Perfect Strangers (1946) 153
Perfect Strangers (2004) 19, 38, 40, 96, 149, 155, 162
Performance (1970) 35, 50, 58, 64, 115, 125, 140, 192
Permission to Kill (1975) 92
Personal Services (1986) 82, 123
Photographing Fairies (1997) 174
Piccadilly Jim (2004) 12, 28, 98, 136, 187
Pink Floyd the Wall (1982) 98, 225
Place to Go, A (1963) 259, *259*
Players (1979) 34, 142
Pleasure Girls, The (1965) 35
Plenty (1985) 59, 92, 100, 128, 178
Ploughman's Lunch, The (1983) 29, 88, 131, 135, 154, 199
Pool of London (1951) 156, 158, *158*, 159, 164, 168, 174, *175*, 187, 197, 199, 210
Poor Cow (1967) 125, 133, 140
Portrait of a Lady, The (1996) 25, 176, 183
Postman's Knock (1962) 23, 200, 234
Prayer for the Dying, A (1987) 201, 222, 223, 225
Preaching to the Perverted (1997) 22, 33, 84, 182
Press for Time (1966) 95, 252
Prick Up Your Ears (1987) 23
Private Life of Sherlock Holmes (1971) 24, 25, *25*
Prize of Gold, A (1955) 212, *212, 213*, 217
Proof of Life (2000) 188, 198
Pumpkin Eater, The (1964) 76, 112, 238
Pure (2002) 43, 216, 225, 226, 227
Quadrophenia (1979) 67, 72, 107, 254, 257
Queen of Hearts (1989) 107, 156, 157, *157*, 203, 210
Quest for Love (1971) 118
Quiller Memorandum, The (1966) 88
Quills (2000) 177
Rachel Papers, The (1989) 33, 57, 159, 241
Radio On (1980) 240

Raising the Wind (1961) 12, 59
Rancid Aluminium (2000) 65, 105
Red Shoes, The (1948) 19
Reds (1981) 84, 87, 225
Reign of Fire (2002) 17
Repulsion (1965) 74, 75, 114, 120
Revengers' Comedies, The (1998) 51, 210
Richard III (1995) 12, 21, 27, 98, 119, 128, 150, 155, 182, 185, 244, 245
Riff-Raff (1990) 262
Ring of Bright Water (1969) 101, 103, 106, 112
Ring of Spies (1963) 30, 44, 53, 57, 90, *90*, 154, 236, 242, 251
Rise and Rise of Michael Rimmer, The (1970) 92, 195, 200
Robbery (1967) 15, 54, 106, 137, 143, 144, 203, 225, 245
Robin Hood: Prince of Thieves (1991) 208
Rogue Trader (1999) *196*, 197, 200
Romantic Englishwoman, The (1975) 107
Room to Rent (2000) 40, 252, *252*
Room With a View, A (1985) 56
Rotten to the Core (1965) 73, 107, 234
Run for Your Money, A (1949) 50, 190, 193
Runners (1983) 17, 43, 47, 51, 64, 68, 70, 106, 201
Russia House, The (1990) 98, 147
Sabotage (1936) 16, 128, 238
Saint, The (1997) 59, 84, 98
Sammy and Rosie Get Laid (1987) 64, 69, 101, 108, 144, 219
Sandwich Man, The (1966) 14, 16, 32, 33, 90, 143, 173, 186, 198, 224
Sapphire (1959) 31, 123, 236, 248
Satanic Rites of Dracula, The (1973) 115, 118
Saturday Night and Sunday Morning (1960) 138
Saving Grace (2000) 49, 61, 69, 198
Scandal (1989) 46, 52, *52*, 99, 137, 149
Scandalous (1983) 89, 108, 115, 151
Schizo (1976) 14, 29, 250, *250*, 251
School for Scoundrels (1960) 149, 192, 255
Séance on a Wet Afternoon (1964) 18, 41, 142
Sebastian (1968) 31, 87, 102, 199
Secret Agent, The (1996) 25, 174, *175*, 176
Secret Ceremony (1968) 47, 48, 58, 253
Secret Garden, The (1993) 243

Secret Partner, The (1961) 150, 178, *178*, *179*, 183, *183*, 189, 219
Secrets & Lies (1996) 10, 18, 23, 228, 230, 253, 265
Sense and Sensibility (1995) 174
Servant, The (1963) 79, 102, 111, 243
Seven Days to Noon (1950) 47, 66, *66*, 92, 94, 95, 115
Sexy Beast (2000) 10, 35
Shadowlands (1993) 13
Shakespeare in Love (1998) 45, 208
Shanghai Knights (2003) 95, 176
Shaun of the Dead (2004) 180, 262, 263, *263*, 265
Shine (1996) 16, 118
Shiner (2000) 24, 43, 190, 214, 229
Shining Through (1992) 23, 176, 243
Shirley Valentine (1989) 11, 32, 243, 244
Shooters (2000) 200, 202, 224, 228, 244
Shooting Fish (1997) 98, 189, 255, 264
Sid and Nancy (1986) 39, 46, 58, 67, 72, 84, 92, 164
Silver Bears (1978) 187
Sink the Bismarck (1960) 91
Sitting Target (1972) 107, 129, 134, 138, 144
Slayground (1983) 70
Sleepy Hollow (1999) 26
Sliding Doors (1998) 15, 28, 31, 47, 62, 75, 109, 123, 189, 214, 235, 250
Slipper and the Rose, The (1976) 159
Small Back Room, The (1949) 111, 179
Small Time Obsession (2000) 114, 139, 181
Smallest Show on Earth, The (1957) 74, 252
Smashing Time (1967) 31, 38, 243, 245
Snatch (2000) 81, 147, 153, 166, 203, 229
Soft Top Hard Shoulder (1992) 162
Soldier of Orange (1977) 21
Some Voices (2000) 48, 70, 72, 139
Sorcerers, The (1967) 100, 102, 250
Sorted (2000) 19, 24, 34, 38, 39, 41, 43, 62, *62*, 146, 154, 181, 192, 198, 203
South West 9 (2001) 131, 139
Sparrows Can't Sing (1963) 216, 217, 220, 225
Spice World (1997) 64, 118, 123, 137, 158, 160, 200, 208, 211, 221
Spider (2002) 157, 166, 180, 231, 244, 254
Spivs (2004) 179, 214, 220, 224, 227, 231, *231*, 248
Split Second (1992) 95, 224

Spy Game (2001) 188, 236
Spy Who Came In from the Cold, The (1965) 15, 72, 114, 137, 192
S★P★Y★S (1974) 46
Squeeze, The (1977) 22, 32, 41, 55, 64, 67, 68, 69, 137, 219
Stage Beauty (2004) 177
Stage Fright (1950) 12, 33, 35, 96, 103
Staggered (1994) 16, 42, 243
Star! (1968) 22, 115, 124, 242
Stardust (1974) 32
Steal, The (1995) 75, 162, 165, 190, 221, 248
Steptoe and Son (1972) 22, 66, 68
Steptoe and Son Ride Again (1973) 68, 253
Stevie (1978) 74, 265
Still Crazy (2000) 245
Stormbreaker (2006) 38, 55, 98, 111, 116, 123, 126, 130, 135, 194, 201
Straight On Till Morning (1972) 120, *120*, *121*, 152
Strange Affair, The (1968) 84, 134, 148, 195
Stud, The (1978) 43, 103, 120, 212
Subterfuge (1969) 15, 16, 23, 36, 43, 44, 50, 54, 56, 96, 151, 236, 238
Success Is the Best Revenge (1984) 55, 57, 118, 119, 123
Sunday Bloody Sunday (1971) 55, 140, 174, 176
Suzie Gold (2004) 33, 65, 204, 206, 247, 252
Sweeney! (1976) 46, 56, 59, 77, 84, 95, 114, 115, 120, 126, 190, 211
Sweeney 2 (1978) 18, 73, 142, 144, 145, 195
Sweet William (1980) 107, 248, 249
Swimming Pool (2003) 98
Tailor of Panama, The (2001) 146
Tall Guy, The (1989) 19, 240, 247, 249
Tamarind Seed, The (1974) 92, *93*, 103
Taste the Blood of Dracula (1970) 265
Term of Trial (1962) 106
That Summer (1979) 74
That's Your Funeral (1973) 264
Theatre of Blood (1973) 54, 75, 68, 107, 112, 140, *141*, 144, 146, 253
Theory of Flight, The (1998) 33, 187
There's a Girl in My Soup (1970) 109
Thirty-Nine Steps, The (1959) 239
Thirty-Nine Steps, The (1978) 94, 95, 109, 118, 234
This Happy Breed (1944) 34, 53, 92, 132, *133*, 139

This Year's Love (1999) 42, 139, 141, 145, 146
Three Blind Mice (2003) 12, 31, 46, 63, *63*, 128, 146, 147, 153, 247
Three Steps to Heaven (1995) 253
Thunderbirds (2004) 12, 151, 152
Thunderpants (2002) 59, 77, 126
Till Death Us Do Part (1968) 144
Titanic Town (1999) 228
Titfield Thunderbolt, The (1953) 37, 116
To Catch a Spy (1971) 33, 99, *99*, 106, 112, 117
To Sir, With Love (1967) 212, 217, 218, 219
To the Devil, a Daughter (1976) 11, 43, 190, 211
Tom & Viv (1994) 13, 88, 235
Tom Brown's Schooldays (1950) 159
Tom Jones (1963) 21, 192
Tomorrow at Ten (1964) 255, 263
Tomorrow Never Dies (1997) 26, 255
Touch and Go (1955) 23, 44, 103, 108, 109, 116, 186
Touch of Class, A (1973) 16, 32, 38, 39, 55, 75, 106, 118, 146
Town Like Alice, A (1956) 15
Train of Events (1949) 16, 91, 240, 242
Trainspotting (1996) 52, 58
Trauma (2004) 154, 181, 229, 251, *251*, 259
Travels With My Aunt (1972) 18
Trials of Oscar Wilde, The (1960) 234, 241, 242
Trottie True (1949) 44, 58, 116, 240, *241*
True Blue (1996) 143
Truly Madly Deeply (1991) 152, 263
Turn the Key Slowly (1953) 17, 28, 260
Turtle Diary (1985) 14, 47, 151, 238
24 Hours in London (1999) 135, 165, 201, 224
Twenty-One (1991) 49
Twinky (1969) 101, 109, 115, 123
Two Way Stretch (1960) 190
Up the Junction (1967) 128, 129, 134
Upside of Anger, (2004) 105, 248, 255
V for Vendetta (2005) 17
Vault of Horror, The (1973) 97, 145
Velvet Goldmine (1998) 31, 79, 79, 80, *81*, 132, 147, 198, 214, 245, 254
Venom (1982) 211, 215
Vera Drake (2004) 30, 215, *215*, 264
Vicious Circle, The (1957) 27, 29, 94, 103, 119, 151, 238
Victim (1961) 17, 18, 19, 75, 78, 83, 102, 105, 123, 192

Villain (1971) 78, 79, 129, 138, 246
Violent Playground (1957) 216, *216*
Virtual Sexuality (1999) 63, 65, 68, 69, 119, 162, 164
Voices in the Dark (1960) 241
Voyage of the Damned (1976) 225, 243
Walking Stick, The (1970) 32, 33, 37, 152, 222
Wanted for Murder (1946) 53, 54, 94, 97, *110*, 111, 186, 236, 249
War Zone, The (1999) 167
Warm December, A (1973) 26, 112, 134, 137, 151, 190, 242
Waterloo Road (1945) 153
Wayne's World 2 (1993) 16, 42
Wedding Tackle, The (2000) 72, 137
What a Crazy World (1963) 27, 207
What a Girl Wants (2003) 87, 152, 155, 158, *158*, 159, 175, 177
Where the Spies Are (1965) 18
Whistle Blower, The (1986) 85, 92, 99, 154
Who Dares Wins (1982) 16, 56, 90, 91, 94, 115, 152, 211, 257
Wild Geese, The (1978) 104, 211
Wilde (1997) 21, *21*, 26, 33, 39, 44, 90, 194
Wimbledon (2004) 34, 44, 142, 151
Wings of the Dove, The (1997) 54, *55*, 88, 91, 123, 177
Winning London (2001) 29, 44, 86, 96, 155, 175, 211, 239, 251
Winslow Boy, The (1999) 132
Wisdom of Crocodiles, The (1998) 124, 153
Without a Clue (1988) 96, 239
Withnail & I (1986) 49, 61, 63, 67, 109, 238
Wonderland (1999) 39, 130, 198
World Is Not Enough, The (1999) 146, 162, 179, 219, 221, 222, 224
Wreck of the Mary Deare, The (1959) 153, 242
Wrong Arm of the Law, The (1963) 81, 136
X, Y and Zee (1972) 146, 252, 256, *257*
X-Files, The (1998) 18
Yellow Rolls Royce, The (1964) 87
Yield to the Night (1956) 44
You Must Be Joking! (1965) 33, 42, 100, 101, 186
Young Americans, The (1993) 10, 27, 116, 156, 158, 164, 229, 260
Young Sherlock Holmes (1985) 162

street index

Abbey Road 251
Abbey Street 163
Abbot Street 230
Abbot's Gardens 263
Abingdon Street 96
Achilles Way 32
Ackerman Road 130
Acklam Road 69
Adam Street 27
Addington Street 150
Addison Avenue 59, 60
Addison Road 58
Addle Hill 194
Adela Street 68
Adelaide Road 250
Adelphi Terrace 27
Ademore Road 181
Admiralty Arch 16, 91
Air Street 42
Albany Street 241, 242
Albemarle Street 36
Albemarle Way 205
Albert Embankment 146, 147
Albert Gate 102
Albert Mews 57
Albyn Road 180
Alderbrook Road 139
Aldford Street 34
Aldrington Road 139
Aldwych 23 24
Alexandra Avenue 137, 138
All Saints Road 62, 63
Allington Street 82, 83
Allison Road 262
Alma Square 251
Alpha Road 180
Alscot Way 163
Alwyne Villas 257
Anglers Lane 246
Ansleigh Drive 61
Appold Street 201
Apsley Way 32
Archway Road 263
Argyle Square 13, 14
Argyle Street 13
Argyll Street 38
Arlington Road 241
Arlington Street 87
Armada Way 225
Arnold Circus 228
Artesian Road 47
Artillery Passage 213

Artillery Row 99
Arundel Street 22
Arundel Terrace 144
Ascalon Street 129
Ashburton Grove 260
Ashley Place 99
Askew Road 72
Astoria Road 132
Atlantic Road 131, 132, 139
Aubrey Road 56
Audley Square 33
Avenell Road 260
Avenue Road 252
Avenue, The 81
Avondale Road 264
Aylward Street 216
Back Hill 203
Baker Street 29
Balckfriars Court 194
Ballast Quay 177, 178
Bancroft Road 215
Bank End 156
Bankside 97, 155
Banner Street 207
Barge House Street 154
Barking Road 225
Barlborough Street 180
Barlby Road 68
Barnet Grove 228
Barnet Lane 265
Barrett Street 29
Barrington Road 131, 132
Barrow Hill Road 252
Barter Street 10
Bartholomew Close 207
Bartholomew Place 207
Bartholomew Road 246
Bartle Close 61
Barton Street 96
Bassishaw Highwalk 200
Bathurst Mews 52
Battersea Church Road 135
Battersea High Street 134
Battle Bridge Lane 159
Battle Bridge Road 244
Bayham Street 240
Baylis Road 153
Bayswater Road 46
Beak Street 38
Beauchamp Place 112
Beaufort Street 123
Beck Road 230

Bedale Street 158, 159
Bedford Square 12
Beechmore Road 137, 138
Belgrave Mews West 104
Belgrave Place 103
Belgrave Road 107
Belgrave Square 101, 104
Belinda Road 131
Bellenden Road 169
Belsize Avenue 250
Belsize Square 248
Belvedere Road 150
Bennett Street 87
Berkeley Square 37
Berkeley Street 37
Bermondsey Square 163
Bermondsey Street 160
Bermondsey Wall East 164
Bermondsey Wall West 163, 164
Bernard Street 10, 14
Berwick Street 39, 41
Bethnal Green Road 229, 230
Bevington Road 69
Bexley Road 185
Binsey Walk 184
Birdcage Walk 85, 86
Birkbeck Mews 230
Birstall Road 262
Bishop's Bridge Road 49
Bishop's Terrace 168
Bishopsgate 189, 201, 214
Black Bull Yard 203
Black Prince Lane 77
Black Prince Road 147, 166
Blackfriars Passage 194
Blackheath Hill 174
Blacklands Terrace 111
Blackwall Way 222
Blackwell Lane 179
Blagrove Road 69
Blandford Street 28
Blantyre Street 123
Blenheim Crescent 65
Blenheim Terrace 251
Blomfield Road 48, 71
Blomfield Street 200
Bloomsbury Street 11
Bolingbroke Road 59
Bolton Court 192
Bolton Crescent 168
Booth Lane 197

Boots Street 258
Borough High Street 159
Boss Street 163
Bosworth Road 68
Botolph Lane 186
Boundary Passage 228
Boundary Street 228
Bourne, The 265
Bow Street 19
Boxley Street 224
Bradmead 129
Brady Street 215
Bramerton Street 109
Bramford Road 140
Bramham Gardens 120
Bramley Road 67, 68
Bravington Road 69
Bray Place 111
Brewer Street 40, 41
Brick Lane 214, 230
Bride Lane 193
Bridges Court 134
Bridport Place 259
Brixton Road 131, 132
Brixton Station Road 131, 132
Broad Court 20
Broad Street Place 200
Broadgate Circus 200
Broadley Street 250
Broadway (W13) 81
Broadway (SW1) 84
Broadway Market 230
Broadway, The (N8) 261
Broadwick Street 41
Brompton Road 112, 114
Brompton Road 102
Brunswick Gardens 57
Brushfield Street 213
Bruton Lane 37
Bruton Place 34
Bruton Street 34, 37
Brydges Place 17
Brynmaer Road 138
Buckingham Gate 83, 84
Buckingham Palace Road 106, 107
Bunhill Row 207
Burlington Arcade 43
Burlington Gardens 38, 43
Burnley Road 132
Burton Place 13

Burton Road 252
Burton's Court 111
Bury Place 10
Bury Street 87
Buxton Road 226
Byward Street 189
Cable Street 212, 217
Cadogan Pier 109
Cadogan Square 101
Caldwell Road 132
Caledonian Road 257
Calvert Street 228
Camberwell Green 169
Camberwell New Road 168
Cambridge Avenue 252
Cambridge Circus 39
Cambridge Heath Road 229
Cambridge Terrace 242
Camden High Street 240, 241
Camden Passage 257
Camden Road 260
Camden Road 240
Camden Street 241
Camilla Road 163
Camley Street 245
Campden Hill Road 56
Campden Hill Square 56
Canada Square 220, 222
Canning Passage 57
Canning Place 57
Cannon Place 248
Cannon Row 94
Cannon Street Road 217
Canonbury Place 257
Capel Road 227
Caradoc Street 178
Carey Street 22
Carlisle Place 100
Carlos Place 36
Carlton Gardens 86
Carlton Hill 251
Carlton House Terrace 88, 89
Carlton Mews 91
Carlton Terrace 90
Carnaby Street 38, 243
Carriage Drive North (SW11) 128
Carriage Drive South (SW11) 137
Carter Lane 194
Carter Place 168
Carting Lane 26

Cartwright Gardens 13
Castellain Road 70
Castelnau 144
Castle Lane 84
Castlebrook Close 168
Castlehaven Road 239
Cathcart Road 124
Cathedral Street 156, 159
Catherine Street 19, 20
Catherine Wheel Alley 213
Causeway, The 140
Caversham Road 246
Caxton Street 84
Cecil Court 17
Central Avenue (SW10) 124
Central Avenue (SW11) 137
Centre Avenue (NW10) 253
Chadwick Road 170
Chadwick Street 98
Chalk Farm Road 239
Chamberlain Close 184
Chancel Street 154
Chancery Lane 22
Chandlers Mews 221
Chapel Street 104
Charing Cross Road 12, 17, 19
Charles Street 34
Charlotte Street 31
Charterhouse Street 204
Cheapside 198
Chelsea Bridge Road 100
Chelsea Embankment 107, 109
Cheltenham Terrace 111
Cheney Road 244, 245
Chepstow Place 47
Chepstow Road 47
Chepstow Villas 64
Chesham Close 103
Chesham Street 103
Cheshire Court 192
Cheshire Street 214, 229, 230
Chester Gate 242
Chester Place 241
Chester Row 103
Chester Street 106
Chester Terrace 241, 242
Chesterfield Hill 34
Chestnut Avenue (E7) 227
Chestnut Avenue (SW14) 145
Cheyne Row 108, 109
Cheyne Walk 107, 108, 122, 123
Chichester Place 48

Chichester Street 100
Chiltern Street 28
Chingford Road 233
Chiswick Mall 78
Chitty Street 31
Christchurch Hill 249
Christchurch Street 108
Church Avenue 145
Church Road 145
Church Row 248
Church Street (N16) 262
Church Street (W4) 78
Churchill Place 221
Circle, The 162, 163
Circus Place 200
City Road 207, 258
Clabon Mews 101
Clapham Common South Side 132
Clapham Common West Side 132
Clarence Gate Gardens 235
Clarence Gate 235, 236
Clarence Passage 244, 245
Clarence Way 239, 240
Clarendon Gardens 71
Clarendon Road 67
Clarendon Street 48
Claverton Street 100
Clementina Road 232
Clement's Lane 187
Clerkenwell Close 204
Clerkenwell Green 204
Clerkenwell Road 203
Cleveland Row 87
Cleveland Street 31
Clevely Close 181
Clifford Street 38
Clifton Villas 70
Clink Street 156
Clissold Road 262
Clydesdale Road 62
Clyston Street 130
Cockpit Steps 85
Cockspur Street 91 94
Coldershaw Road 81
Coldharbour Lane 131
Coldharbour 222
College Place 241
Collingham Gardens 120
Cologne Road 133
Columbia Road 228
Colville Terrace 64
Commercial Road 216, 220
Commondale 143

Compton Terrace 257
Conewood Street 260
Connaught Square 52
Consort Road 169
Conway Street 31
Coolhurst Road 261
Copeland Road 169
Corbridge Crescent 229
Cork Street 43
Cornhill 186
Cornwall Gardens 114
Cornwall Road 154
Cornwall Terrace 236
Coronet Street 258
Cosser Street 148
Court Road 185
Courtney Square 166
Courtney Street 166
Covent Garden 18
Coventry Street 43
Cowcross Street 207
Cowhill Road 180
Cranbourn Street 18
Crane Street 177
Cranley Mews 114
Craven Hill Gardens 46
Craven Road 52
Creekside 180
Cremer Street 228
Crescent, The 144, 145
Cressy Place 215
Crestfield Street 14
Crispin Street 213
Cromwell Gardens 116
Cromwell Road (SW19) 142
Cromwell Road (SW7) 114, 115
Crosby Square 189
Crowdale Road 241
Crown Office Row 192
Crowthorne Road 68
Crystal Palace Road 170
Cubitt Terrace 133
Culvert Place 138
Culvert Road 138
Cumberland Gate 36
Cumberland Park 28
Cureton Street 98
Curtain Road 258
Curzon Gate 32
Curzon Square 33
Curzon Street 33, 35
Cutler's Gardens 201
Dalling Road 77
Danby Street 169

Danebury Avenue 144
Darfield Way 68
Darien Road 134
Darrell Road 170
Dartmouth Park Avenue 246
Dartmouth Street 85
Dartmouth Terrace 174
Daubeney Road 232
Davies Street 36
Dawes Road 125
Dawsey Place 39
Dean Street 39
Deanery Street 34
Dean's Yard 96
Delamere Terrace 48
Denbigh Close 65
Denmark Hill 169
Deptford Broadway 180
Derby Gate 92
DeVere Gardens 57
Devonshire Square 201
Devonshire Street 29
D'Eynsford Road 169
Dock Street 212
Dockley Road 163
Doggett Road 181
Dollis Hill Lane 255
Down Street 43
Downing Street 92
Downs Park Road 230
Downshire Hill 249
Draycott Avenue 112
Drayton Green Road 81
Druid Street 160
Drum Street 213
Drury Lane 20
Du Cane Road 72, 73
Duke Street 29, 43
Duke's Avenue 264
Duke's Road 13
Dulwich Common 173
Duncannon Street 17
Durant Street 228
Durnsford Road 142
Ealing Green 81
Earlham Street 19
Earl's Court Road 56, 120
Easley Mews 29
East Arbour Street 216
East Cross Route 227
East Smithfield 212
Eastbourne Mews 50
Eastcheap 186
Eaton Mews North 103
Eaton Place 103

Eaton Square 103
Eaton Terrace 103
Ebenezer Street 258
Ebury Bridge Road 100
Ebury Street 106
Eccleston Square Mews 107
Ecklington Gardens 180
Economist Plaza 87
Edgware Road 49
Edinburgh Gate 102
Eel Brook Common 125
Effra Road 139
Egerton Crescent 112
Egerton Place 112
Egerton Terrace 112
Elder Avenue 261
Elder Street 214
Eldon Road 57
Eleanor Close 164
Electric Avenue 132
Elephant And Castle 148
Elephant Lane 164
Elgar Street 165
Elgin Avenue 70
Elgin Crescent 65
Elgin Mews 61
Elizabeth Street 107
Elm Bank Gardens 145
Elm Court 192
Elm Park Gardens 124
Elvaston Mews 115
Elvaston Place 115
Elveston Street 98
Ely Court 203
Ely Place 203
Ely Yard 205
Elystan Street 112
Embankment (SW15) 143, 144
Embankment Place 15
Emerald Street 14
Emery Hill Street 99
Emperor's Gate 114
Endell Street 19
Endsleigh Place 13
Enfield Cloisters 259
Ennismore Gardens Mews 119
Ennismore Gardens 119
Ennismore Street 119
Ensign Street 212
Essex Road 257
Eton Avenue 247
Euston Road 13, 242, 243, 256

Euston Street 242
Evandale Road 130
Evelyn Road 179, 224
Eversholt Street 243
Ewer Street 154
Exhibition Road 116
Exmoor Street 68
Eyot Green 78
Fairfield Street 141
Falcon Road 134
Falcon Way 221
Fanshaw Street 259
Farm Lane 125
Farm Place 56
Farmers Road 168
Farringdon Lane 204
Farringdon Road 207
Farringdon Street 207
Fashion Street 214
Featley Road 132
Fellows Road 247
Felsham Road 144
Festing Road 143
Fieldgate Street 215
Finborough Road 124
Finchley Road 248
Finsbury Circus 200
Finsbury Square 200
Fitzalan Road 166
Fitzroy Court 30
Fitzroy Square 30
Flask Walk 249
Fleet Road 249
Fleet Street Hill 214
Fleet Street 192
Fletcher Road 79
Flora Gardens 77
Folgate Street 214
Fore Street 200
Forest Hill Road 171
Forest Road 230
Forfar Road 138
Formosa Street 70
Fortress Road 246
Foster Lane 198
Fountain Court 192
Fournier Street 214
Francis Street 99
Frederica Street 13, 260
Freston Road 67, 68
Friday Street 197
Friendly Street 180
Friern Barnet Road 264
Frith Street 39
Frognal 248

Fulham Broadway 125, 126
Fulham Palace Road 74
Fulham Road 112, 123, 124,
   123
Furnival Gardens 75
Gainsford Street 162
Garrick Street 18
Gaunt Street 154
Gelding Place 163
George Court 15
Gerrard Street 39, 40
Gilbert Place 10
Gilbey's Yard 239
Giltspur Street 207
Glamis Road 217
Glebe Place 109
Glentworth Street 235
Gliddon Road 59
Gloucester Avenue 239
Gloucester Crescent 240
Gloucester Mews 49
Gloucester Road 115
Gloucester Terrace 48, 49
Golborne Road 68, 69
Goldhawk Road 72
Goodhall Street 254
Goodrich Road 170
Goodsway 244
Goodwin Court 18
Gordon Grove 169
Gower Street 12
Grace's Alley 212
Grafton Square 133
Grafton Street 36
Grafton Way 30
Grant Road 134
Gray's Inn Road 14
Great College Street 96
Great George Street 87, 96
Great Portland Street 29, 30,
   242
Great Pulteney Street 38
Great Queen Street 20
Great Russell Street 11
Great Scotland Yard 91, 92
Great Smith Street 96
Great Suffolk Street 154
Great Sutton Street 205
Great Tower Street 189
Great West Way 74
Great Windmill Street 41
Greek Street 39
Green Dragon Court 159
Green Lanes 261 262
Green Street 226

Green, The 265
Greenbury Street 252
Green's Court 41
Grenfell Road 61
Gresham Street 198 199
Greycoat Street 98
Grimsby Street 229
Groom Place 106
Grosvenor Crescent 104 105
Grosvenor Gardens 106
Grosvenor Place 105
Grosvenor Road 100
Grosvenor Square 36
Grosvenor Street 36
Grove End Road 251
Guildford Street 14
Guildhall Yard 198
Gulliver Street 165
Gun Street 213
Gunnersbury Lane 79
Hackney Road 228
Half Moon Street 43
Halkin Street 105
Hall Street 206
Hamilton Place 32
Hammersmith Bridge Road
Hammersmith Road 58, 77
Hampden Way 265
Hampstead High Street 249
Hampstead Road 242
Hanbury Street 214
Hannibal Road 215
Hanover Gate 236
Hanway Place 31
Harbour Exchange Square
   221
Harbridge Avenue 144
Harbut Road 133
Hardwick Street 203
Hare Court 192
Harewood Avenue 235
Harley Road 247
Harley Street 29
Harmood Street 239
Harringay Passage 261
Harrington Gardens 114
Harrington Road 114
Harrow Manor Way 184
Harrow Road 49, 69
Hartland Road 239, 240
Hastings Street 13
Hat And Mitre Court 205
Hatton Garden 202, 203, 229
Hatton Wall 203
Havelock Terrace 129

Haven Green 81
Haverstock Hill 250
Hawley Road 240
Haydon's Road 142
Haymarket 90
Hay's Mews 34
Hayward's Place 204
Heath Street 248, 249
Heathfield Avenue 140
Heathfield Terrace 78
Heddon Street 38
Henrietta Street 20
Herbert Crescent 101
Hercules Road 148, 166
Hereford Street 229
Hermitage Street 49
Hertford Street 35
Hertsmore Road 220
High Holborn 19
High Road (N12) 265
High Road (N15) 262
High Street (E17) 233
Highbury Corner 257
Highbury Hill 260
Highbury New Park 260
Highbury Terrace Mews 259
Highbury Terrace 259
Highcliffe Drive 144
Highway, The (E1) 217
Hill Street 34
Hillcrest 263
Hillgate Place 56
Hillgate Street 57
Hillingdon Street 168
Hillsleigh Road 56
Hinton Road 172
Holborn Viaduct 207
Holland Park Avenue 59
Holland Park Mews 59
Holland Park Road 58
Holland Park 59
Holland Street 155
Holloway Road 260
Holly Hill 248
Holly Mount 248
Holyrood Street 160
Hornsey Lane 263
Hornshay Street 180
Horse Guards Parade 86, 95
Horse Guards Road 87
Horseferry Road 98
Hoskins Street 178
Howland Street 31
Hoxton Square 258
Hoxton Street 259

Hunter Street 14
Hunt's Court 17
Hyde Park Crescent 51
Hyde Park Garden Mews 52
Idol Lane 189
Ifield Road 124
Imperial College Road 116
Imperial Road 126
Ingram Avenue 255
Ingrave Street 134
Inner Circle 236
Inner Temple Lane 192
Inverness Street 240
Inverness Terrace 46
Isambard Place 164
Islington Green 257
Islington High Street 257
Ivybridge Lane 27
Jackson Road 260
Jamaica Road 164
Jamaica Street (E1) 216
Jermyn Street 88
Jersey Street 229
John Adam Street 15, 27
John Ruskin Street 168
Johnson Road 217
Jonathan Street 166
Judd Street 13
Jude Street 223
Juniper Street 217
Keats Grove 249
Kelso Place 57
Kennington Lane 166
Kennington Oval 166
Kennington Road 148, 168
Kensal Road 68
Kensington Church Street 57
Kensington Court Palace 57
Kensington Gore 117, 118
Kensington High Street 57,
   58
Kensington Park Road 64
Kensington Road 116
Kentish Town Road 246
Kilkie Street 126
Killick Street 257
King Charles Street 92
King Edward Street 207
King John Court 202
King Street (EC2) 198
King Street (W6) 77
King William Walk 174, 175
King's Bench Walk 192
King's College Road 247
King's Road 101, 107, 111

Kingsland High Street 230
Kingsland Road 230
Kingsway 10, 20, 23
Kingswood Road 78
Knatchbull Road 169
Knightrider Court 198
Knightsbridge 102, 103
Knox Street 28
Kohat Road 142
Kramer Mews 119
Kynance Mews 57, 115
Ladbroke Grove 61, 68
Lady Margaret Road 246
Lafone Street 162
Lagado Mews 164
Lambeth High Street 147
Lambeth Hill 197
Lambeth Palace Road 149
Lambeth Road 147, 166
Lambeth Walk 166
Lamb's Conduit Street 14
Lancaster Gate 46
Lancaster Place 24
Lancaster Road 61, 63
Lancey Close 181
Langham Place 29
Langham Road 29
Lansdowne Crescent 67
Lansdowne Road 66
Larkhall Lane 133
Lassell Street 177
Latchmere Road 139
Latimer Road (E7) 227
Launceston Place 115
Laurier Road 246
Lauriston Road 231
Lavender Hill 134
Lawn Lane 129
Lawrence Street 108
Lea Bridge Road 232
Leadenhall Market 187
Leadenhall Street 188
Leake Street 153
Leamore Street 77
Leather Lane 202
Ledbury Road 64
Lee Road 255
Leicester Square 17, 18
Leighton Road 246
Leinster Avenue 145
Leinster Gardens 46, 47
Leven Road 222
Lewisham High Street 180
Lewisham Street 85
Lexham Gardens 55

Lexham Walk 55
Leydon Close 164
Leyfield Road 72
Lillie Road 119, 124
Lime Street 187
Limehouse Link 220
Lincoln's Inn Fields 21
Lindsey Street 207
Lisson Grove 250
Little Crown Court 40
Little Dean's Yard 96
Little New Street 193
Liverpool Street 200, 201
Lombard Street 187
London Bridge 158
London Road 181
London Wall 199
Long Lane 207
Longfield Avenue 81
Longridge Road 120
Lord Hills Road 48
Lordship Place 109
Lothbury 198
Lots Road 122
Loudoun Road 251
Loughborough Park 131
Loughborough Road 130,
132
Lower Clapton Road 232
Lower Grosvenor Place 82
Lower Mall 75
Lower Marsh Street 153, 154
Lower Regent Street 42, 43,
90
Lower Richmond Road 144
Lower Sloane Street 101
Lowndes Place 104
Lowndes Street 102
Ludgate Hill 195
Lupus Street 100
Lyall Mews 103
Lynton Road 163
Lyons Walk 58
Macclesfield Street 39
Macduff Road 138
Mace Close 219
Maguire Street 162
Maida Avenue 49, 71
Maida Vale 70, 71
Malet Street 12
Mall Road 59
Mall, The 86, 87, 88, 90
Mallard Path 184
Manchester Road 221
Manchester Square 28, 87, 88

Manilla Street 221
Manor Road (W13) 81
Mansell Street 191
Mare Street 230, 231
Marian Place 229
Mark Lane 189
Market Street 182
Marlborough Gate 44
Marlborough Road 87
Marloes Road 55
Marmora Road 171
Marryat Road 142
Marylebone High Street 28
Marylebone Road 236
Mattison Road 261
Mattock Lane 81
Maze Hill 183
Meard Street 39
Medway Street 98
Melbourne Place 23
Melbury Road 58
Melcombe Place 234, 235
Melrose Gardens 77
Melrose Terrace 77
Melton Street 242
Mepham Street 153
Middle Lane Mews 261
Middle Temple Lane 192
Middlesex Passage 207
Middlesex Street 213
Midland Road 243
Milestone Green Corner 145
Mill Street 163
Mill Yard 212
Millbank 97
Millfield Lane 263
Milman's Street 123
Mincing Lane 189
Monmouth Road 47
Monmouth Street 19
Monson Road 180
Montague Close 158
Montague Place 12
Montrose Place 104
Moor Lane 200
Moor Street 39
Moorgate 200
Moorhouse Road 47
Moreton Place 100
Mornington Avenue 58
Mornington Crescent 241
Morpeth Terrace 100
Moscow Road 46
Mossop Street 112
Motcomb Street 102

Mount Street Gardens 35
Mount Street 35
Mount Vernon 165, 248
Mountford Place 166
Mozart Street 69
Mulbery Close 255
Muscovy Street 190
Museum Street 10
Musgrave Crescent 125
Myddleton Avenue 261
Myddleton Square 206
Narbonne Avenue 132
Narrow Road 220
Navarre Street 228
Nazareth Gardens 169
Neal's Yard 19
Needham Road 64
Nelson Road 262
Netherhall Gardens 248
Neville Gill Close 142
New Bond Street 36
New Bridge Street 194
New Broadway 81
New Burlington Mews 38
New Cavendish Street 29, 30
New End Square 249
New Inn Yard 202
New Palace Yard 95
New Row 18
New Square Passage 21
New Square 21, 22
New Street 201
Newgate Street 194
Newman Passage 31
Newport Street 40
Newton Street 20
Nine Elms Lane 100, 129
Norfolk Square 51
Norland Road 59
North Carriageway 231
North Circular (NW10)
253, 254
North Cross Road 170
North End Road 58, 125
North Hill 263
North Row 33
North Terrace 112
North Worple Way 145
Northumberland Avenue 15
Notting Hill Gate 67
Oak Hill Park 248
Oakley Gardens 241
Oakwood Court 58
Oban Street 222
Old Bailey 194

Old Barrack Yard 105
Old Bethnal Green Road
229
Old Bond Street 36
Old Broad Street 198
Old Brompton Road 119
Old Buildings 21, 22
Old Church Road 233
Old Compton Street 39
Old Fish Street Hill 197
Old Ford Road 229
Old Nichol Street 228
Old Oak Lane 254
Old Palace Yard 95
Old Park Lane 32
Old Square 22
Old Street 258
Old Woolwich Road 177
Old York Road 141
Oldfield Grove 165
Olympia Way 58
Onslow Gardens 114
Onslow Square 114
Onslow Street 203
Orchard Place 222
Ormonde Street 111
Orpheus Street 169
Oseney Crescent 246
Osnaburgh Street 242
Osten Mews 114
Otis Street 227
Outer Circle 236
Oval, The 229
Ovington Square 112
Oxford Circus 32
Oxford Street 29, 31, 32
Oyster Row 217
Paddington Green 49
Paddington Street 28
Page Street 97, 98
Palace Gate 57
Palace Street 83, 84
Pall Mall East 91
Pall Mall 87, 88, 90
Palliser Road 59
Pancras Road 243, 245
Paradise Street 164
Paragon, The 183
Park Close 102
Park Lane 32, 33, 34, 35
Park Row 176, 177
Park Street (SE1) 157, 158
Park Street (W1) 34
Park Village East 241
Park Walk 107, 123

Parkhurst Road 260
Parliament Square 92, 95, 96
Parliament Street 92
Parson Street 255
Passing Alley 205
Paternoster Square 195
Patriot Square 229
Pavilion Road 101
Pedley Street 214, 230
Pegasus Place 166
Pelham Crescent 113
Pelham Street 112, 114
Pelton Road 178
Pemberton Road 261
Pembridge Square 47
Pembroke Place 56
Pembroke Square 55
Pennard Road 72
Pensbury Place 130
Pentonville Road 257
Penzance Place 60
Percy Circus 14
Perth Road 232
Peterborough Road 126
Peters Hill 197
Pevensey Street 226
Philbeach Gardens 119
Phillimore Walk 56
Piccadilly Arcade 88
Piccadilly Circus 41, 42, 43
Piccadilly 42, 43, 87
Pier Head 217, 219
Platts Lane 248
Plender Street 241
Plough Lane 140
Plough Road 133
Plough Terrace 133
Plympton Street 250
Podmore Road 140
Poland Street 41
Pond Street 249
Pont Street 102
Ponton Road 129
Poplar Road 172
Porchester Road 48
Portland Place 29, 30
Portland Road 60, 61
Portobello Road 61, 65, 69
Portree Street 222
Pottery Lane 60
Powis Square 64, 70
Powis Terrace 64
Poyser Street 229
Praed Street 51
Pratt Street 240

Preston's Road 222
Primrose Gardens 250
Primrose Street 201, 202
Prince Albert Road 252
Prince Consort Road 117, 118
Prince Of Wales Drive 137
Prince Of Wales Road 246
Prince's Square 47
Priory Avenue 78
Priory Grove 133
Priory Park 225
Pritchard's Road 229
Pullman Gardens 144
Putney Bridge Approach 124
Putney High Street 144
Queen Anne's Gate 85
Queen Caroline Street 74, 75
Queen Elizabeth Street 162
Queen Victoria Street 194, 197
Queen's Circus 126
Queen's Gardens 46
Queen's Gate Mews 115
Queen's Gate 116
Queen's Market 226
Queen's Road (SW14) 145
Queensbridge Road 229
Queensdale Road 59
Queenstown Road 126, 128, 129
Queensway 46
Quernmore Road 261
Querrin Street 126
Quilter Street 228
Ram Street 142
Ramsay Road 79
Randolph Avenue 70
Rathbone Place 31
Rathbone Street 31
Ravenet Street 126
Ravenscroft Street 228
Reachview Close 240
Reardon Street 219
Redcastle Close 217
Redcliffe Gardens 124
Redcliffe Square 124
Redcross Way 158
Rede Place 47
Redwald Road 232
Regency Street 98
Regent Street 38
Regent's Park Road 238, 239

Remnant Street 20
Ridley Street 230
Ripley Gardens 145
Rising Sun Court 207
River Street 206
Rivercourt Road 75
Robert's Place 204
Rochelle Street 228
Rochester Row 99
Rochester Walk 156
Rochford Close 225
Rockwood Place 72
Roehampton Lane 144
Romilly Street 39
Ropemaker Street 200
Rose Street 18
Rosebery Avenue 203
Rosmead Gardens 66
Rosmead Road 66
Rosoman Place 207
Rosslyn Hill 249
Rotherhithe Old Road 165
Rotherhithe Street 164, 165
Rotherwood Road 143
Rotten Row 55
Rousden Street 240
Rowditch Lane 138
Rowington Close 48
Rowley Way 251
Royal Arcade 36
Royal Avenue 111
Royal College Street 241
Royal Crescent 59
Royal Docks Road 225
Royal Drive 264
Royal Exchange 187
Royal Gate West 231
Royal Hospital Road 111
Rugby Street 14
Rupert Street 40
Russell Road 58
Russell Square 10
Russell Street 20
Rutland Gate Mews 119
Rutland Gate 119
Rutland Mews South 119
Rutland Mews West 119
Saffron Hill 203
Sail Street 166
Salamanca Place 147
Salamanca Street 166
Salter Road 164
Saltoun Road 131, 139
Sandringham Road 230
Savile Row 38

Savoy Court 26
Savoy Place 26, 27
Scandrett Street 219
Sclater Street 214
Scotland Place 91
Scotswood Street 204
Seething Lane 190
Serle Street 21
Serpentine Road 53, 54
Seven Sisters Road 260
Seymour Road 232
Shacklewell Lane 230
Shad Thames 161, 162
Shadwell Pierhead 217
Shaftesbury Avenue 39, 42
Shafto Mews 101
Shakespeare Road 172
Sheen Lane 145
Sheepcote Lane 138
Shepherd Street 35
Shepherd's Bush Market 72
Shoe Lane 193
Shoot Up Hill 252
Shorts Gardens 19
Silchester Road 61
Silverton Road 224
Silwood Street 165
Sirdar Road 61
Sketchley Gardens 165
Skinner Street 207
Sloane Square 101
Sloane Street 101
Small Change 198
Smallbrook Mews 52
Smith Terrace 111
Smugglers Way 140
Soho Square 38
Somerset Road 142
South Audley Street 33
South Carriage Drive 102, 116
South Colonnade 220
South Eaton Place 103
South End Green 249
South End Road 249
South Worple Way 145
Southampton Place 10
Southcombe Street 58
Southern Row 68
Southgate Road 259
Southside Common 142
Southwark Park Road 163
Southwark Street 158
Southwick Street 51
Spaniards Close 255

Spencer Park 140
Spensley Walk 262
Spital Square 214
Spring Gardens 15, 91
Spring Street 51
Spur Road 83
St Agnes Place 168
St Alfege Passageway 174
St Alphege Highwalk 200
St Andrew's Road 231
St Anne's Passage 220
St Ann's Road 262
St Bride's Avenue 193
St Christopher's Place 29
St Dunstan's Hill 189
St George Street 37
St George's Square 100
St George's Terrace 239
St Giles' Circus 11
St Giles High Street 12
St Helen's Place 189
St James's Gardens 60
St James's Road 163
St James's Street 87
St James's Walk 204
St John Street 205, 296
St John's Gardens 66
St John's Lane 204
St John's Road 134
St John's Wood High Street 252
St Jude's Road 229
St Leonard's Road 222
St Leonard's Terrace 111
St Luke's Mews 62
St Luke's Road 62, 63
St Margaret Street 95
St Mark's Road 68
St Martin's Court 18
St Martin's Lane 18
St Martin's Le Grand 198, 199
St Martin's Place 17
St Martin's Road 132
St Mary Axe 189
St Mary's Walk 81
St Pancras Gardens 245
St Pancras Way 240
St Peter's Grove 77
St Peter's Road 77
St Peter's Square 76, 77
St Petersburgh Place 46
St Stephen's Crescent 47
St Stephen's Gardens 47

St Stephen's Mews 47
St Thomas Square 212
St Thomas Street 160
St James' Court 82
Stable Yard Road 87
Stafford Place 83
Stafford Terrace 56
Stanford Road 57
Stanford Street 99
Stanhope Gate 34
Stanhope Street 34
Stanlake Road 72
Stanlake Villas 72
Stanley Crescent 64
Stanley Gardens 64
Stanley Passage 244, 245
Stapleton Hall Road 261
Statham Road 68
Station Approach 153
Station Road 144
Stephenson Street 254
Stepney Green 216
Stepney High Street 215
Stewart's Road 129
Stillington Street 99
St-Mary-at-Hill 186
Stockwell Park Crescent 132
Stockwell Park Walk 131
Stockwell Road 131, 132
Stoke Newington Church Street 262
Stoney Street 156, 157, 158
Storey's Gate 85
Strand On The Green 77
Strand 22, 24, 26, 27
Stratford Road 55
Streatham High Road 139
Streatham Hill 139
Streatley Road 252
Suffolk Street 90
Sullivan Road 168
Sumner Street 155
Sun Street 200
Surrey Street 23
Sussex Mews 52
Sussex Place (W2) 52
Sussex Place (W6) 74
Sutherland Avenue 70
Sutton Street 216
Swain's Lane 263
Swan Walk 111
Sydney Street 111
Tabernacle Street 202
Talbot Road 47, 64, 65
Talgarth Road 58

Tarves Way 174
Tavistock Crescent 63
Tayburn Close 222
Teesdale Street 229
Telemann Square 184
Temple Place 23
Templeton Place 120
Tench Street 219
Terminus Place 106
Terrace, The 145
Tetherdown 264
Thames Place 143
Thames Road 77
Thanet Street 13
Thicket Road 173
Thorncroft Road 130
Thorney Street 97
Thornley Place 178
Thornton Road 145
Threadneedle Street 187
Three Colts Corridor 230
Three Mill Lane 227
Three Quay's Walk 189
Throgmorton Avenue 200
Thurloe Place 114
Thyleigh Road 132
Tidal Basin Road 223
Tinworth Street 146, 147
Tooley Street 159, 160, 163
Tooting Bec Road 139
Torquay Street 48
Tothill Street 96
Tottenham Court Road 31
Tottenham Green East 262
Tottenham Street 31
Totteridge Village 265
Tower Bridge Approach 212
Tower Bridge Road 161
Town Hall Avenue 78
Townmead Road 246
Trafalgar Square 15, 16, 17, 91, 92
Trafalgar Way 221, 222
Treadgold Street 61
Trebovir Road 119
Treveris Street 154
Trinity Church Square 159
Trinity Road 141
Trinity Square 189, 190
Turin Street 229
Twyford Avenue 264
Twyford Street 257
Tyers Street 166
Undershaft 189
Underwood Street 258

Upland Mews 170
Upper Belgrave Street 104, 106
Upper Cheyne Row 109
Upper Ground 154
Upper Mall 75, 76
Upper Richmond Road West 145
Upper Street 257
Upper Tachbrook Street 99
Upper Woburn Place 13, 243
Uverdale Road 122
Uxbridge Road 72
Vale Royal 260
Vandon Street 83
Vauxhall Bridge Road 98, 99
Vauxhall Street 166
Vauxhall Walk 166
Vernon Place 10
Vernon Square 14
Vicarage Crescent 134
Victoria Embankment 15, 24, 27, 91, 94, 96, 192
Victoria Gate 53
Victoria Place 57
Victoria Road 115
Victoria Square 82
Victoria Street 82, 84
Villa Road 131
Villiers Street 15
Vincent Square 99, 112
Walcot Square 168
Walham Grove 125
Walker's Court 40
Walker's Place 144
Walworth Road 168
Wandsworth High Street 141, 142
Wandsworth Road 130
Wapping High Street 219
Wapping Lane 219
Wapping Wall 217
Wardour Street 39
Warriner Gardens 138
Warrington Crescent 70
Warrington Gardens 70
Warwick Avenue Bridge 71
Warwick Avenue 49, 70
Warwick Crescent 48, 49
Warwick House Street 91
Warwick Road 119
Warwick Square 107
Warwick Way 100, 107

Wat Tyler Road 174
Waterloo Place 88, 89, 90
Waterloo Road 153, 154
Waterman Way 219
Waverton Street 34
Waxford Road 254
Webber Street 154
Welbeck Mews 29
Welbeck Street 29
Well Street 231
Wellclose Square 212
Weller's Court 244, 245
Wellfit Street 172
Wellington Row 228
Wellington Square 111
Wellington Street 20
Wells House Road 254
Wells Road 72
Wendon Street 227
West Carriage Drive 54
West Central Street 11
West Cromwell Road 58
West Eaton Place Mews 103
West Eaton Place 103
West End Green 252
West End Lane 252
West Heath Road 248
West Lane 164
West Road 224
West Smithfield 207
Westbourne Grove 47, 64, 65
Westbourne Park Passage 47
Westbourne Park Road 47, 48, 64, 65, 66
Westbourne Park Villas 47
Westbourne Terrace Road Bridge 48, 71
Westferry Road 221
Westgate Terrace 124
Westland Place 258
Weston Park 262
Weston Road 160
Westway 48, 49, 61, 62, 68, 69, 70, 74
Westwood Park 181
Wetherby Place 114
Weymouth Street 29, 30
Wharf Road 245
Wheeler Street 214
Whipps Cross Road 232
White Hart Lane 163
Whiteadder Way 221
Whitecross Street 207
Whitehall Court 91

Whitehall Place 91
Whitehall 91, 92, 95
Whitehorse Road 215
Whitehouse Way 265
White's Row 213
Whitfield Place 30
Whitfield Street 30
Whittington Avenue 187
Wigmore Street 29
Wilcox Road 130
Wild Street 20
Wilfred Street 84
Wilks Place 259
Willes Road 246
Willesden Lane 252
William IV Street 17
Willington Close 246
Willow Road 249
Willow Walk 163
Wilton Crescent 102, 104
Wilton Road 106
Wilton Row 105
Wiltshire Road 131
Wiltshire Row 259
Wimpole Street 29
Winchelsea Road 226
Winchester Square 156
Winchester Walk 156
Windmill Street 31
Winnett Street 40
Winnington Road 255, 263
Winstanley Road 134
Winthrop Street 215
Witlon Place 105
Woburn Walk 13
Wolverley Street 229
Wood Lane 74
Wood Street 199, 200
Wood Vale (SE22) 171
Wood Vale (N10) 264
Woodseer Street 214
Woodstock Road 78
Woolwich Church Street 182
Woolwich Road 181
Wornington Road 69
Worship Street 202
Worsopp Drive 132
Wyatt Park Road 139
Wyndham Place 28
Yarnton Way 184
York Gate 236
York Terrace East 236
York Terrace 236
York Way 256, 260